Postcommunist Transformation and the Social Sciences

Postcommunist Transformation and the Social Sciences

Cross-Disciplinary Approaches

EDITED BY FRANK BÖNKER, KLAUS MÜLLER,
AND ANDREAS PICKEL

ROWMAN & LITTLEFIELD PUBLISHERS, INC.
Lanham • Boulder • New York • Oxford

ROWMAN & LITTLEFIELD PUBLISHERS, INC.

Published in the United States of America
by Rowman & Littlefield Publishers, Inc.
An Imprint of the Rowman & Littlefield Publishing Group
4720 Boston Way, Lanham, Maryland 20706
www.rowmanlittlefield.com

12 Hid's Copse Road, Cumnor Hill, Oxford OX2 9JJ, England

British Library Cataloguing in Publication Information Available

Library of Congress Cataloging-in-Publication Data

Postcommunist transformation and the social sciences : cross-disciplinary approaches / edited by Frank Bönker, Klaus Müller, and Andreas Pickel.

p. cm.

Includes bibliographical references and index.

ISBN 0-7425-1838-8 (alk. paper)

1. Social change—Europe, Eastern. 2. Post-communism—Europe, Eastern. 3. Social sciences. 4. Europe, Eastern—Social conditions—1989–. 5. Europe, Eastern—Economic conditions—1989–. I. Title: Post communist transformation and the social sciences. II. Bönker, Frank. III. Müller, Klaus. IV. Pickel, Andreas.

HN380.7 .A8 P675 2002
303.4'0947—dc21

2001048919

Printed in the United States of America

™ The paper used in this publication meets the minimum requirements of American National Standard for Information Sciences—Permanence of Paper for Printed Library Materials, ANSI/NISO Z39.48-1992.

Contents

Acknowledgments

First drafts of most of the chapters in the present volume were presented at the conference "Postcommunist Transformation and the Social Sciences: Cross-Disciplinary Approaches," in Berlin in October 1998, organized by the editors with Kathrin Rahn and Dariusz Aleksandrowicz. The chapters were revised and updated by their authors in 2000–2001. We would like to thank the Deutsche Forschungsgemeinschaft for generously supporting the conference and this publication as part of its funding for the Frankfurt Institute for Transformation Studies (FIT), the center of transformation research at European University Viadrina in Frankfurt (Oder). Financial assistance from the Social Science and Humanities Research Council of Canada is also gratefully acknowledged. Thanks for editorial assistance go to Anne Hoover, Sarai Nunez-Ceron, Marcin Kowalewski, and Stephan Stein.

Béla Greskovits's chapter was first presented at our 1998 conference. It was previously published in Michel Dobry, *Democratic and Capitalist Transition in Eastern Europe: Lessons for the Social Sciences*. Boston/Dordrecht/London: Kluwer, 2000. A slightly revised version is reprinted here with kind permission from Kluwer Publishers.

Chapter 1

Cross-Disciplinary Approaches to Postcommunist Transformation: Context and Agenda

Frank Bönker, Klaus Müller, and Andreas Pickel

In the late 1980s the social sciences inherited a new research area that has as its object the reform processes of postcommunist societies. Economics, political science, sociology, and other disciplines have since invested considerable energy to explain the unexpected disintegration of Soviet-type societies and the often surprising course of reform policy in the 1990s. The level of academic interest in these countries today is higher than it ever was during the Communist period. Events in the reforming countries are not only observed from the outside. International organizations, Western governments, and policy advisors also are in various ways involved in the reform processes.

For some time now, the postcommunist states have been classified as a special category of "countries in transition" in the country groupings of the United Nations and the international financial institutions. The rationale for this categorization goes beyond statistical indicators and corresponds only in part with the usual logic of grouping according to regions or gross domestic product. "Transition countries" alludes to a set of structural characteristics that distinguish postcommunist countries from developing countries, on the one hand, and the advanced OECD countries, on the other (IMF 1999a: 124ff.; IMF 2000b: 153ff.). The former had passed through a stage of rapid modernization and possessed a developed industry, universal welfare institutions, high educational levels, and egalitarian norms of social integration. On the other hand, their temporary modernization achievements were based on an unsustainable extensive-growth model and were accompanied by a degree of repression that stifled political participation and suppressed civil society. Some aspects of this past continue to have a significant effect on the present in economic, sociostructural, political, and cultural respects. A bloated industrial sector, underdeveloped services, fragile financial institutions, and other institutional weaknesses are still common characteristics of these countries, as available statistics document (Gros and Suhrcke 2000). On account of these countries' specific "post-totalitarian" legacy, they also differ from other former authoritarian regimes in their political trajectory (Linz and Stepan 1996: 244–54).

The classification as countries in transition thus links their common past with the reform efforts of the last decade as well as optimistic hopes for the future. For "transition" in this context refers to the transition from a planned economy to a market economy and from authoritarianism to democracy. The closely related concept of "transformation" derives its specific meaning from this context. The countries in transition are not simply undergoing growth and catching-up processes, but are experiencing profound changes in their institutions, social structure, normative legitimation, and values, as well. Transition and transformation allude to different sets of assumptions about the time horizon of postcommunist change and the appropriate criteria of success.

In this sense, postcommunist transformation constitutes a clearly defined research area. Moreover, the radical and profound character of the changes that strongly affect all spheres of society requires a cross-disciplinary perspective that can take into account the interaction between economic reforms, political liberalization, social change, and cultural identity. In contrast to the consolidated societies of the West, where reforms are implemented by democratically legitimated political elites in a relatively stable institutional environment, postcommunist reform policy from the start has been beset by serious difficulties and dilemmas that had already plagued the experiments with market socialism in the late Soviet Union. These also help to account for the numerous surprises of the last decade. Democratization has equipped the population with instruments to oppose the perceived costs of economic liberalization. The pluralization of the party system has created an arena for nationalist, ethnic, and religious identity politics, which in many places has fatally undermined the political unity of state and society. The decentralization of the state, desirable from a democratic viewpoint, has paved the way for local forms of authoritarianism, especially in the former Soviet Union.

In other cases, it is true, the dilemmas of postcommunist politics have not generated the destructive force predicted by pessimists in the early 1990s. However, these cases also illustrate the complexity of postcommunist transformation. If fundamental reforms in one sphere of society necessarily have spillover effects in others, a disciplinary perspective is bound to be too narrow. Such "nonlinear effects" at the intersection of economy, politics, social structure, and culture, however, have shaped the dynamic of postcommunist reforms of the past decade—both in their successes and their failures. This probably also accounts for the fact that transformation research has frequently been overtaken by events, especially in its failure to anticipate the depth of the postcommunist crisis. With analytical attention fixed on the surface of macroeconomic data, political rhetoric, survey results, and elections, the deeper dimensions of social change have fallen between the roster of social science disciplines. Growth rates and election outcomes as such say very little about postcommunist societies' prospects for consolidation—i.e., about the dramatic form in which the fundamental problem of social order manifests itself.[1] How is it possible for societies undergoing radical economic change and searching for a new relationship between economy, state, and civil society to develop a coherent institutional system that provides stability? How is it possible in a situation of widespread social deprivation, increasing inequality, uncertain prospects for the future, and scarce resources to negotiate a consensus that could sustain the transition to a new social order? After ten years of debate, there is still no agreement on the appropriate criteria for answering these questions. There is no agreement on whether the transformation is over, as some have been claiming for several years. It is also controversial on what level of development postcommunist societies are likely to end up—that of the successful transition countries of southern Europe or that of the failed developing countries of the Third World.

Transformation research thus confronts the following central problem: while it does have a sufficiently clearly demarcated research area, it lacks the theoretical foundation to link the results produced by individual disciplines. The debate on economic reform, transition and elite research in political science, sociological studies of institution transfer, nation building, and the risks of partial modernization occur simultaneously without generating theoretical synergies. A cross-disciplinary perspective of course cannot do without disciplinary models and results. Rather, while remaining anchored in individual disciplines, it makes an explicit effort to link them to the knowledge produced in neighboring disciplines.

The reasons for the theoretically unsatisfactory state of transformation research take us back to the *first generation of theories* applied to the postcommunist region that dominated the field until the mid-1990s. These early approaches had particular methodological and normative characteristics that help to account for their success. They claimed to combine the most advanced theories and methods of social science with superior Western values in formulating clear and unambiguous policy recommendations. This vision of a "self-organizing" and universally applicable democratic market society proved irresistible for postcommunist reformers. "Today liberal democracy is the only 'rightful' game in town," as Giovanni Sartori (1991: 443) seconded neoliberal discourse from the perspective of democratic theory.

Admittedly, numerous objections to the simple application of mainstream economic theory and standard International Monetary Fund (IMF) recipes to the failed planned economies had already been brought forward in the early 1990s. Political scientists had cautioned that formal institutions alone would be an insufficient focus for reforming political systems, while sociologists had pointed to unintended consequences of narrow economic reforms and the social embeddedness of markets. However, such academic critics could not assert themselves against the hegemony of a neoliberal reform discourse that was secured in a variety of ways. The ten commandments of the "Washington consensus" were buttressed by combining the institutional power of the international financial institutions and the U.S. administration with the intellectual prestige of economic theory and a faith in the organizational capacity of markets that was not easily shaken by counterevidence. Thus the orthodox stream of transformation theory to this day remains committed to the trinity of rapid stabilization, liberalization, and privatization as the essence of reform policy that accounts for reform success or failure, the formation of reform coalitions, and the consolidation of democracy (Aslund et al. 1996; Fischer and Sahay 2000; Mussa and Savastano 1999).

Yet the weight of objections to and fundamental criticisms of neoliberal orthodoxy emerging from all social science disciplines, including economics, has steadily increased. It has reached a sufficiently critical mass to justify a paradigm shift in transformation studies. This volume is based on the conviction that such a paradigm shift significantly improves the prospects for cross-disciplinary theorizing, which, we argue, could provide a major impetus to the advance of knowledge. Before we turn to the emerging new paradigm, the next section offers some historical and methodological background to the debate by reconstructing the neoliberal discourse of reform that dominated the new field of transformation studies in the early 1990s.

The Politics of Marketization and the Neoliberal Discourse of Radical Reform

The research area of "transitology," organized around a set of well-defined problems, emerged in the space of only a few years in the early 1990s. In the wake of the collapse of Communism and the disintegration of the Soviet Union, a dominant paradigm for the transition to the market and democracy was quickly established. This approach centered on a by now well-known set of fundamental reforms designed to shift stagnating planned economies onto a fundamentally new path of development. The early reform programs called for structural adjustment policies—stabilization, liberalization, and privatization—that international financial institutions had prescribed to Third World countries since the early 1980s. Since postcommunist countries were pursuing a project of systemic change, these were not just conventional economic policies but represented a "politics of transformation" (Bruszt 1992) based on a strong belief in the market as a kind of metainstitution of social change. We refer to this conception as the *neoliberal discourse of radical reform* to underscore that we are not simply dealing with an application of neoclassical economic theory to the problem of transformation. Rather, neoliberal discourse contains general conceptions of institutional change and collective action as well as political and normative judgments that are quite independent of specific theoretical justifications. It is for this reason that neoliberal discourse can be justified with reference to such diverse theoretical perspectives as the evolutionary tradition of the Austrian school, German ordo-liberalism, neoclassical theory, monetarist doctrines, or simply common sense—and it may well be consistent with all of them. The Latin American debt crisis of the 1980s gave birth to an economic reform strategy that has become known as the Washington consensus[2] because of its strong backing from Western governments under the leadership of the United States and the international financial institutions. It refers to a set of supposedly uncontroversial theoretical and political assumptions about the composition and sequence of market-oriented reforms for economic growth. This discourse was powerful not so much on account of its specific content but because it structured the field of legitimate arguments, suggesting a direct and consistent link between scientific analysis and policy-making, and introducing the politically and morally potent distinction between radical reformers and conservatives (or populists).

In the international development debate, the concept of self-reliance was abandoned in favor of the primacy of international trade and capital, which in turn required far-reaching structural adjustments of policies and institutions to the rules of a globalized economy. In the theoretical debate, industrial and trade policies fell out of favor as the whole field of development economics was called into question.[3] The barriers to development in the different regions of the Third World were diagnosed as a disease caused by state ownership, price controls, tariff walls, established distributional coalitions, and rent-seeking behavior. The state lost its traditionally central role for modernization in what amounted to a "universal rediscovery of the market" (Tanzi 1997: 17). At the same time, the end of thirty years of state expansion was hailed as a "watershed in economic history" (De Vries 1986: 157).

It is therefore no accident that after 1989 the transition countries were incorporated into this consensus, even if they were not viewed as classical developing countries. The context for interpreting the failure of Communism had thus been prepared. Communism's collapse appeared as the final confirmation of the inevitable failure of state-centered modernization approaches based on public ownership, planning, and protectionism. It was also widely seen as the ultimate refutation of development economics that had recommended a centrally planned distribution of resources and import substitution as appropriate instruments for combating poverty and inequality.

Yet it cannot be said that the neoliberal discourse was forced on the postcommunist countries from the outside, even though the international financial institutions very soon assumed the mandate for overseeing the economic reform process in Eastern Europe. The "elective affinity" between East European reformers and Western advisors probably runs deeper than is often assumed. To understand the hegemonic position of this discourse, its theoretical implications, and especially its recent revisions, let us examine its major constitutive elements.

The Political Context for Neoliberal Discourse

The origins of fundamental market reforms in Eastern Europe date back to reform attempts in the late Soviet period and the reform program of the first post-communist government in Poland.[4] In the Soviet Union, radical reformers promoted by Mikhail Gorbachev were able to gain the upper hand in the Communist Party after 1987. They had drawn their own lessons from the long history of failed attempts to make the planned economy more dynamic by introducing market incentives. The economic disintegration in the course of *perestroika* appeared to them as the final proof that the old system could not be reformed. "The time for gradual transformation has been missed, and the ineffectiveness of partial reforms has been proved by the experiences of Hungary, Yugoslavia, and China" (Yavlinski quoted in Aslund 1995: 37).

The dismantling of the economics ministry, the paralysis of the party apparatus, and finally the establishment of a sovereign Russian state seemed to create the political preconditions for the implementation of a "shock therapy" designed to effect the transition to the market in 400 or 500 days. The plan called "Transition to the Market" presented by the Shatalin group did not even contain the word *socialism*. A return to the methods of a command economy was improbable since there was no longer a functioning executive, while the legislature was immobilized, ultimately dissolving the unity of the Soviet state. It is no accident that programs such as the Shatalin plan failed to mention the legal, administrative, and institutional prerequisites for a market economy or to acknowledge the relationship between economic and constitutional reform. The politics of marketization and privatization was an attempt to use the institutional disintegration of the state and the weakness of politics as a means to eliminate those interest groups that still occupied the institutions of the old regime.

In this respect, the Russian radical reformers were inspired by the strategies that had been developed in Poland since the summer of 1989. The Polish "big bang" was designed under the specific political conditions confronting the newly elected Solidarnosc government: how to translate electoral success into a decisive break with the past without having their own experienced personnel staffing the ministries. The new government turned to Western experts for help in designing a program of rapid and comprehensive market reform. In a short period of time, several plans for a shock therapy were drawn up, inspired by the now famous metaphor that an abyss can only be crossed in one leap. Jeffrey Sachs, one of the most prominent advisors of the Polish government and later the

Russian government, saw shock therapy less as an economic strategy than as a political strategy for the dismantling of old structures. The initiative for the transition to a new society was entrusted to the beneficial effects of self-organizing markets. As Sachs (1994: xiii) reassured reformers, "[m]any of the economic problems solve themselves: markets spring up as soon as central planning bureaucrats vacate the field."[5]

The strategy proposed by J. D. Sachs and D. Lipton and adopted by Poland's liberal finance minister, Leszek Balcerowicz, initiated the new transition economics that brought together neoliberal political advisors and East European reform politicians. From a Western perspective this might not have been surprising. However, for East European economists it marked the final departure not only from communist views, but also from the idea of market socialism. After the defeat of the Prague Spring, the political intelligentsia of central and Eastern Europe had abandoned reform socialist alternatives since "totalitarian communism" seemed unreformable (Kovacs 1994). It had been proven beyond doubt that this order was incompatible with the introduction of market mechanisms and the institutionalization of even limited pluralism.

Against this background, it is understandable that the freedoms gained in 1989 were not risked in a new experiment in pursuit of a "Third Way." "In the course of the anti-communist revolution in Eastern Europe public opinion turned against any form of socialism, market socialism included." (Brus and Laski 1991: ii).[6] In this light, the attractiveness of the works of Friedrich Hayek, Milton Friedman, and Ludwig Erhard[7] for Eastern European reformers is not difficult to understand. The enthusiasm once devoted to socialist ideals was transferred to the market, which promised to be not merely a mechanism for efficient distribution but also the model of a "constitution of liberty" (Hayek) in which economic freedom is the precondition for all other freedoms.

Why it was market liberalism that came to fulfill East European needs for orientation can perhaps be best explained by identifying the different levels on which the neoliberal reform discourse has worked. Even before any theory of transformation was available, neoliberal doctrines offered a political strategy for the radical separation of political power and economic decision making that would make the transition to the market irreversible. And even before this strategy could be implemented, it had a powerful normative message. "The moral attractiveness of the market as a foundation for freedom and prosperity [formed] a crucial part of its appeal in Eastern Europe" (Glasman 1994: 200).[8] In this sense, liberalism had conquered the normative and intellectual terrain in Eastern Europe before the international financial institutions brought to bear their institutional power in support of a specific reform strategy.

The new field of transformation studies emerging in the 1990s, however, took off only when IMF and World Bank stepped in and became involved in the liberalization and stabilization of the Polish and Russian economies. The model for the new research field was a comprehensive analysis of the Soviet planned economy commissioned by the Group of Seven in the summer of 1990. One year later, IMF, World Bank, OECD, and the newly created European Bank for Reconstruction and Development (EBRD) presented a final report on the Communist economic system that advocated a program of radical market transition (IMF et al. 1991). *A Study of the Soviet Economy* became the paradigm for the type of research that in the following years was applied to all societies intent on leaving behind their communist pasts. At the same time, the study formulated the standard package of rapid and comprehensive reforms whose implementation more or less determined access to international loans. Price liberalization was designed to make production more responsive to scarcity and actual demand. Elimination of subsidies, privatization of state enterprises, and the competitive pressure from a newly emerging private sector were expected to provide the impetus for the reorganization of enterprises. Liberalization of foreign trade was to undermine the position of domestic monopolists, while liberalization of capital flows was to attract foreign investors and know-how. The state's task was to consolidate budgets, to depoliticize monetary policy, and to establish a legal order for the protection of private property.

The political influence of this paradigm is powerfully illustrated by the fact that between January 1990 and April 1995, twenty-four transition countries followed a stabilization program along those lines. The attractiveness of the reform package was in part due to the promise that in principle all societies were capable of establishing the basic institutions of a modern market economy regardless of their specific histories, the state of their economies, or the structure of their political systems.

Neoliberal Discourse and the Break with Area Studies

What have been the implications of the dominance of neoliberal discourse for the theoretical debate about the dynamics of postcommunist transformation? Most noticeable was the break with area studies, which since the late 1940s had provided the bulk of professional analysis of the region. It marked the end of one of the most significant academic innovations after World War II. Area studies were conceived as the interdisciplinary study of linguistically, geographically, and culturally relatively coherent regions that had been all but ignored in university curricula. Their task was to inject foreign policy, and subsequently development policy, with politically relevant insights into non-Western countries and societies that were beyond the intuitive grasp of an Anglo-American or European observer. The research focus on cultural and historical particularities of a region was clearly at odds with the formal models of analytical social science and the abstract universalism of orthodox modernization theory. On the other hand, area studies provided the impetus for comparative modernization studies linking general developmental processes with the characteristics of a specific region. Soviet studies, comparative communist studies, as well as the comparative study of economic systems, emerged in this context in the 1950s.[9]

The fields of communist studies and Sovietology are too broad to pass any simple judgment on their achievements. In the early 1990s, however, their reputation suffered a serious blow that had far-reaching consequences for the emerging field of transformation studies. The "strange death of Soviet Communism"[10] was followed by the demise of the sciences devoted to its study. The surprising end of the Soviet Union was interpreted as evidence for the meager analytical capacity of communist studies. The most advanced analysis of the late Soviet economy had examined *perestroika* along the lines of earlier reform cycles, even if a breakthrough to "comprehensive reforms" appeared more probable in the late 1980s. The scope for successful reforms appeared to be defined by the institutional legacy of the old system, the balance between reformers and conservatives, and the informal bargaining between the most important interest groups. The influence of the West and of international organizations was considered to be low (Hewett 1988: 373–91).[11] In the political science literature as well, the dominant view was that the evolution of the Soviet system would be driven and constrained by the system's well-known contradictions (Smith 1988: 335). In hindsight, diagnoses of this sort rested on weak foundations. As a result of an excessive preoccupation with the internal logic of power preservation and leadership politics, the critics charged, global pressures for change bound to break up the so-called socialist world system had been overlooked. Misplaced faith in the reformability of socialism had made a radical systemic break inconceivable.

Whether or not one agrees with this view, area studies in any event proved unable to influence the general approach adopted by the mainstream of transformation theory. "The competition between theory and area studies has come to an end—with the virtual defeat of the latter" (Johnson and Keehn 1994: 18).[12] Since Eastern Europe was returning to a state of "normalcy," there was little reason why in this context other laws should apply than in the West. Thus, as Peter Rutland suggests in chapter 6, communist studies was replaced by a *theoretical conception of transition* that emphasized the universal logic of market economies. The point of departure for this conception was the logic of break and reconstitution, the simultaneous economic, political, and sociological dimensions, which Martin Malia has succinctly summarized as follows: "the Soviets' total system ended in total collapse, which meant that at the exit from communism society was confronted with a total problem. Nothing could be salvaged from the old order; everything had to be replaced and rebuilt; the economy, the polity, the society itself" (Malia 1992: 69).[13]

Neoliberal Discourse as an Interdisciplinary Framework

These themes were analyzed in an interdisciplinary framework in which the organizing potential of markets was assigned a central role. A revived theory of totalitarianism found in the ruins of Communism little more than disorganized masses, a moralistic civil society of dissidents incapable of serious political action, civilizational incompetence, and nationalist demagogues. Radical liberalization appeared as the only effective way of "detotalizing" the regime: "in the postcommunist situation it is the process of economic reform that governs the prospects for democracy" (Malia 1992: 70). For much the same reasons, the political sociology of systemic change initially focused on the strategic conditions under which market reformers would be able to outflank the conservatives of the old regime and macroeconomic populists. Under postcommunist conditions economic liberalism and political liberalism became two sides of the same coin.

In the political, theoretical, and empirical context sketched above, neoliberal discourse established itself "as a basic paradigm for successful transition" (Fischer and Sahay 2000: 18)—a kind of metatheory of transformation that, in addition to a general theory of the market, supplied basic concepts for a political sociology of transformation. It also provided a basis for the explanation of diverging transformation paths and reform outcomes with operationalizable criteria of success and a quasi-experimental research design.

Atomized postcommunist societies appeared like a clean slate on which the economy could be restructured according to the model of general equilibrium theory, whose abstract axiomatics were converted into an axiology of political action. According to the assumptions of this theory, the coherent coordination of the decentralized activities of rational actors is ensured. Given initial endowments, preferences, technologies, and prices, such a model economy results in an optimal allocation of resources at equilibrium prices in which supply and demand are balanced. In addition, such an equilibrium fulfills certain criteria of welfare economics: in particular, no individual or collective actor could further improve its own position without negatively affecting the position of others. The academic reputation of this approach is based on its universalism and its mathematical precision, which reinforces the popular view "that there is a 'scientific' theory which demonstrates the efficiency of market economies" (Hahn 1992: 101).

The political economy of postcommunist reforms could thus be seen to imply that political actors create the preconditions of a "private ownership economy" (Debreu 1959) by creating private owners and by decentralizing price formation to the level of actors whose interaction would create an optimal equilibrium in all markets. It is in this sense that one should interpret Jeffrey Sachs's statement that shock therapy is not so much an economic theory as a political concept for the establishment of self-organizing markets. To achieve an optimal allocation of resources corresponding to actual scarcities, it is necessary to establish incentives and sanctions anchored in individual interests. This political theory of the market required hard budget constraints for entrepreneurs and the determination of wages and employment regulated through labor markets. Perhaps even more important than this basic assumption was its correlate that required the elimination of all institutional, sociostructural, and normative barriers to the postulated individualism of social actors. To this extent, shock therapy was aimed not only at the devaluation of obsolete physical assets, but also at the devaluation of old "social capital" and collectivist expectations of subsidies and welfare state patronage.[14] Systems theorists in sociology have interpreted this process as a delayed functional differentiation of a self-regulated economy from political power. In this sense, we can speak of a strategy of disembedding the economy and of individualizing social actors.

A further important element of the neoliberal discourse was a particular way of interpreting the political process of economic reform. Institutions and the strategies of actors were interpreted in functional terms with respect to their conformity to a generalized market model, which once again plays the role of a metanorm. Politics was assigned the task of generating credibility and intertemporal consistency, thus providing the appropriate institutional framework for achieving a new equilibrium of expectations and routine behavior. The institutional configuration of transition countries appeared predetermined by a universal path of transition that implies the transfer of the basic institutions of Western capitalism. Not only economic institutions but also institutions of social integration are assessed according to their market conformity. Policy-making was viewed in terms of its contribution to liberalization and growth, requiring a technocratic policy style summed up in Margaret Thatcher's famous phrase, "There Is No Alternative" (TINA). The political process was seen not in terms of parliamentary procedure, consultations with stakeholders, and the art of compromise, but in terms of a technology of implementation. The ideal institutional setting for unpopular policies would thus be an executive largely insulated from parliamentary controls and interest group "pressures."[15] A low level of institutionalization of collective interests seemed to provide ideal conditions for rationally designing the structure of the new system. Diverging views on the proper speed of liberalization were turned into a sharp division between two political camps, i.e., progressive reformers versus the reactionary conservatives, which made it possible to present every political election as a choice between the new and the old systems.

Neoliberalism as a Quasi-experimental Research Design

The dominance of the orthodox approach was also due to the empirical evidence and the quasi-experimental research design that demonstrated the scientific character of its doctrines. Since the beginning of the transformation process, the international financial institutions had been involved in modernizing the statistical systems of postcommunist countries, especially their shift to international standards. Transparent national statistics are "Articles of Agreement" for membership in the IMF and the OECD. Not surprisingly, the institutions representing the Washington consensus used their privileged access to the relevant data and their reorganization to draw an authoritative empirical picture of transformation that by and large confirmed the fundamental assumptions of the orthodox approach.

To claim that the IMF manufactured a favorable empirical description would clearly be an exaggeration. The reconstruction of the Communist-era data by the IMF and other international financial institutions has revealed grave distortions of the net material product, especially the undervaluing of services in favor of material measures and an inflated productivity of investment. In addition to the already well-known informal economy, a sector of "value-subtracting production" was identified in which raw materials, energy, capital, and labor were used for the production of goods for which there was no demand. Finally, it must be granted that the introduction of international statistical standards has made it possible in the first place to make intra- and interregional comparisons of postcommunist reforms.

The theoretical claims of the neoliberal discourse, however, went well beyond a mere systematization of the data. Already in the studies of the early 1990s before consolidated time series were available, firm causal relations were postulated between the initial conditions, particular policy measures, and the outcomes of transformation.[16] Initially, studies were limited to more narrow monetary and fiscal variables that were analyzed using standard econometric methods. Subsequently, increasingly complex indices were constructed, including the degree of liberalization and other institutional variables. Finally, political and social indicators were incorporated into the quasi-experimental design, creating the impression of an empirically corroborated theory of transformation in which a relatively small group of structural and macroeconomic variables were assigned the status of explanatory variables (Fischer and Sahay 2000: 15). On this basis, transition countries were divided into groups whose varying degrees of success could be explained in terms of the dominant causal influence of political commitment to the neoliberal reform strategy.

Anomalies and Alternatives

In spite of the hegemony of neoliberal discourse, political and theoretical alternatives to "market-induced modernization" were formulated right from the beginning of the transformation. Arguments from a Keynesian perspective in the early 1990s emphasized the "error of spontaneity" and "uncreative destruction" as dangers for postcommunist countries that might reduce their output, employment, and standard of living (Kregel et al. 1992). The systematic preference given to monetary variables at the expense of other economic indicators was in later years blamed for an unnecessarily long and deep recession (Laski and Bhaduri 1997). Others criticized the fatal effect of "do-nothing microeconomic policies" on restructuring (Amsden et al. 1994). An abstract, ideologically motivated separation between market and state, it was argued, ignored the constructive role of public policy or simply assumed the existence of a strong executive.

Alternatively, gradualist approaches advocated an extended and sequenced reform model to minimize the destabilizing effects of unemployment, asset stripping, and revenue losses and to achieve a fairer distribution of reform costs. Different variants of evolutionism from the start considered constructivist reforms as misdirected for ignoring historically and culturally evolved institutions. Institutional change, according to these perspectives, depends on decentralized information and trial and error at the local level rooted in existing institutions. Rapid privatization was viewed skeptically for two reasons. First, the formal transfer of property rights might not penetrate to the much more complex informal structures and processes in the enterprise. Second, the initial task was to establish an adequate institutional framework, unambiguous property rights, rational price systems, and capital markets (Clague and Rausser 1992; Eatwell et al. 1995).

In light of these criticisms, political scientists suggested a different weighting for the central variables. The antistate bias of the neoliberal discourse as well as its exaggerated fear of rent-seeking coalitions and interest groups of any kind were identified as the reasons for the failure to recognize essential preconditions for successful reform policy. The consolidation of the state was emphasized as a necessary precondition for stabilizing the new democracies. The representativeness of democratic political institutions is determined by electoral laws, the party system, and their openness for the articulation of social interests. A political strategy that is presented as being without any alternatives alienates political elites from social movements, associations, and trade unions, which constitute the space for public debate (Przeworski et al. 1995; Linz and Stepan 1996).

Systems of interest representation and party systems, as well as general elite consensus and civil society activity, however, are closely connected with a country's history. A third area of transformation studies was thus devoted to the question of whether the considerable differences between transition countries can be reduced simply to different initial conditions on an otherwise universal transformation path, or whether they point to fundamentally different values, systems of authority, institutional legacies, and organizational cultures that can be understood only in their particular sociocultural context. The study of such sociocultural constellations would then require the methods and approaches of historical sociology.

Some of these debates may well be outdated in the second decade of post-communist transformation. However, major criticisms of the neoliberal discourse have been confirmed by the course of events. Moreover, it is important to note that even within the international financial institutions there has been a gradual shift toward an alternative position that calls into question the core of the neoliberal paradigm—a position more recently referred to as the "post-Washington consensus" (Stiglitz 1998a, 1999; Kolodko 1999). Three defining events prepared the ground for the emergence of the new paradigm since the mid-1990s: the extent and persistence of postcommunist economic and social crises; the Russian crisis of August 1998; and the outcomes of privatization.[17]

The Postcommunist Crisis

Following the start of reforms, almost all postcommunist countries experienced a drastic drop in output, production, and employment. Even "the transformation 'successes' suffered output declines as deep of those of the Great Depression and recovered more slowly than the U.S. in the 1930s" (Gregory 1999: 2). Ten years later, it is hardly possible to call the group of countries in transition a growth region. At the turn of the century, their average growth continues to lag significantly behind that of developing countries, and even more behind the newly industrialized countries, as well as behind the G7 states (IMF 2000a: 2, 26–30). Poland succeeded after seven years of reforms to surpass its 1989 gross domestic product (GDP), followed only recently by Slovenia and Slovakia. Even the more successful countries needed almost a decade to reemerge from a surprisingly deep "transformational recession." János Kornai, who introduced this phrase for characterizing the unavoidable losses of the initial years of reform, confesses his surprise at the duration and depth of these recessions (Kornai 2000: 21; 1994). It seems that a sustainable recovery actually may well take two decades.[18]

Interregional comparisons of per-capita GDP are similarly sobering. The Czech Republic and Hungary now rank alongside Gabun and Trinidad/Tobago; Bulgaria is at the level of Papua New Guinea; Russia ranks with Namibia; and Poland, first among radical reformers, with Botswana (World Bank 1997: 245ff.). This is why postcommunist Eastern Europe and central Asia are among those regions in the world that have experienced the sharpest increase in poverty. Between 1990 and 1998, the number of people living on less than one dollar per day increased from 7.1 million to 24 million (World Bank 2000: tab. 1.1).[19] If this is to be "the end of the transition," one might ask whether it was worth the trouble.

A number of specific country developments were also at odds with the neoliberal view. Until 1995, Albania was considered a star pupil of the international financial institutions, with annual growth rates between 8 and 10 percent, a private-sector share of 75 percent, and an apparently adequate degree of political stability.[20] After the collapse of speculative pyramid schemes, however, the country quickly descended into anarchy. With Boris Yeltsin's reelection in 1996, Russia seemed to have successfully completed its transition to democracy and market economy, and thanks to IMF-bestowed credentials was able to return to international financial markets: "The Russian economy appeared stronger than at any previous time during the transition period" (OECD 2000: 34). Shortly thereafter the August crisis of 1998 hit, marking a major setback in the recovery process. But not only the problem cases among transition countries saw their economic recoveries interrupted. The Czech Republic, for example, in the late 1990s had a stagnating economy and a simultaneously deteriorating political situation.

These episodes not only document the unjustified optimism of reform advisors, but also indicate how fragile the postcommunist economies and societies still are. Data on growth rates, balanced budgets, and the size of the private sector may be valuable indicators, but they are not sufficient to assess the state of the transformation process. The numerous surprises of the last several years illustrate that economic indicators are too short term to furnish a basis for theoretically tenable conjectures about the trajectory of Eastern European transformation. The hopes they inspire are ominously reminiscent of the one-dimensional focus on the growth rates of planned economies and the resulting overestimation of their stability.

The Russian Crisis and the Dangers of Globalization

Growing doubts about the feasibility of the neoliberal program were evoked by the new dimension of the Russian crisis of August 1998 that demonstrated the vulnerability of postcommunist transitions to the changing fortunes of a globalized economy. The postcommunist states have pursued a relatively uncharted road of modernization through radical external liberalization, ignoring the lessons of West European postwar reconstruction and the East Asian developmental state.[21] They adopted a development strategy that was first introduced in the Latin American debt crisis of the 1980s—though they did so evidently with the goal of catching up with the West rather than the South. The loss of confidence in Russia as well as in Eastern European financial markets sparked by the Asian crisis has raised the question of whether the hasty liberalization of capital and currency movements contributed to further deepening the postcommunist crises.

The general rationale for world market-oriented modernization was based on a reassessment of the role of foreign direct investment and capital flows. Rather than being viewed these in terms of dependence and unequal exchange, they were perceived as an opportunity to import technological and organizational know-how and to make up for insufficient domestic savings. The rapid growth of private direct and portfolio investments in developing countries and emerging markets in the early 1990s seemed to confirm this view. Thus the activities of international financial institutions were to be reduced to providing services and expertise to facilitate private capital flows. However, the positive relationship between inflowing capital and domestic growth goes hand in hand with the well-known risk of abrupt outflows. The investment behavior of short-term investors and creditors is not shaped by real economic trends but by diffuse general perceptions that are prone to wild fluctuations. The rapid outflow of capital may produce not only dramatic economic consequences but also enormous social costs and political instability. The Asian crisis was surprising and unsettling insofar as the countries affected, unlike Latin America in the 1980s, did not suffer from notorious balance-of-payment deficits, high inflation, and excessive public spending. The lesson of this crisis, which resulted from general imperfections of capital and currency markets, was that in the face of systemic contagion, sound fundamentals may be a positive, but they are hardly a sufficient condition to be spared the effects of external crises.[22] In liberalized financial markets, changed risk assessments can easily spread from one region to another.

If even comparatively stable economies can fall victim to such a crisis, how much greater are the risks for the countries in transition?[23] In the case of the latter, the general problems associated with free capital markets are compounded by the specific problems of fragile banking systems and the inadequate regulatory capacity of weak states. In this context, one needs to ask whether the international financial institutions did not contribute to this situation with their inconsistent and ill-sequenced policy recommendations (Stiglitz 1998b: 12–16). As Peter Rutland explains in his analysis of the Russian situation, the IMF advised the Russian government to establish a market for government bonds to achieve a noninflationary financing of the state budget and the depoliticization of monetary policy. This artificial construction could appear successful only as long as the high interest rates for Russian bonds attracted significant foreign capital. However, it was illusory to think that this was a way of closing the gap between public spending and tax revenues, "on the assumption that some mystical reform package would generate economic recovery before they fell due for repayment" (Rutland in this volume: 123). The cooperation of Russian banks with foreign investors created a speculative pyramid in the market for government bonds and a bubble on the Russian stock market that exploded as a result of the Asian crisis (OECD 2000: 35–45).[24]

The abstract liberalism of Western policy advice, even if unwittingly, thus contributed to the emergence of this situation. A view restricted to a handful of economic variables, false priorities, and narrow goals failed to recognize the deeper causes of the Russian crisis. Due to a lack of interest in regional specificities, insufficient attention was paid to clientelistic politics and the informalization of the economy. Since the institutional environment, particularly in the financial sector, and the peculiarities of policy formulation were ignored, it was impossible to assess the potential effects of the standard reform program in the Russian context (Gould-Davies and Woods 1999: 18f.; Thornhill 2000). Finally, the Yeltsin government's carefully nurtured image as the only true reformers and committed democrats was never seriously questioned.

Other countries in transition suffered somewhat less from the effects of this crisis. They too are forced, however, to adjust their reform policies to the portfolio strategies of international financial markets, even if those policies are not related to domestic needs. Unlike other countries with developed capital markets, transition countries do not possess the means to fend off speculative attacks. As a result, they may be forced to adopt the "perverse economic policy of raising interest rates, increasing taxes, and reducing government spending in the face of recession" (Krugman 1999: 65).[25]

The Unfulfilled Promise of Privatization

A range of unanticipated consequences have emerged in a key area of transformation, that of privatization (Havrylyshyn and Odling-Smee 2000; Nellis 1999; Rosenbaum et al. 2000). The postcommunist privatization process is no doubt of a highly complex nature and does not lend itself to simple conclusions. The appeal of privatization policy, however, was precisely its apparent simplicity. The rapid introduction of private property rights was intended to separate the economy from the state and thus eliminate opportunities for rent-seeking, as well as create an entrepreneurial class interested in advancing market reforms and enterprise restructuring.

It became evident very soon that privatizing a planned economy was not a simple technical problem but a process in which there were different approaches and competing goals generating controversial results. There are widely differing views on the effects of privatization on employment, income distribution, and state finances. In the light of early experiences with privatization, Western advisors were soon forced to admit that their original assumptions had been somewhat naïve.[26] Western privatization methods, such as the British one, proved to be unworkable given the scope of the task, the amount of information they required, and the bureaucratic processes involved. The speed of privatization had to be balanced with considerations of efficiency and justice. Above all, it became clear that "the state" did not actually own the means of production. Different actors made competing de facto ownership claims on "collectively owned assets." The influence of ministers, local administrators, managers, and employees turned out to be one of the major conditions determining to what extent governments were able to implement their goals.

The initial view of privatization as an act of redefining property rights has been superseded by a more differentiated conception that takes into account the institutional, political, and structural dimensions of privatization. This is significant in several respects. Privatization can obviously not be part of a shock therapy. None of the transition countries has successfully accomplished the rapid privatization of the state sector. A general survey of postcommunist privatization in the 1990s concludes that at best results have been mixed (EBRD 1999: 32–34,

119–21). There are very few tenable generalizations about the relationship between methods, speed, and sequencing of privatization policy, on the one hand, and the performance of privatized enterprises, on the other. The single most important factor determining the quality of governance in privatized enterprises was the regulative capacity of the state and its active role in restructuring and the creation of competitive markets.

The extended duration of the privatization process, which allowed for prior restructuring, is credited with the relatively successful outcomes in Poland and Hungary. In countries pursuing rapid destatization, on the other hand, the problems of an unreconstructed enterprise sector were concealed by fuzzy ownership structures in which inadequately supervised investment funds and state-owned banks were involved. Thus the Czech Republic had initially moved far ahead of its neighbors with the development of a formally privatized sector when in 1997 it was caught in a structural crisis that is seen largely as the result of a hasty privatization policy.[27]

In the worst case, privatization itself has become the major obstacle for the continuation of the reform process. The collapse of transformation in Russia and other Soviet successor states, it is now evident, has been brought about by the pathologies of reform policy. The redistribution of property created interest groups that supported Yeltsin's stabilization course. The new capitalist elites very much favored a tight monetary policy that ensured them large profits on high-interest government bonds. They also favored rapid privatization, which gave them access to the more profitable sectors of the post-Soviet economy. Contrary to general expectations, the new capitalists have not evolved into a strong pro-reform constituency (Hellman 1998a). Rather, they have used their political influence to expand their strong market positions into monopoly positions. Their highest priorities were receiving tax breaks and privileged access to new areas of business. They have little in common with romanticized views of the postcommunist entrepreneur. "Profits rather than competitive markets are what capitalists seek to maximize" (Havrylyshyn and Odling-Smee 2000: 5).[28]

All this has led to paradoxical results. Postcommunist privatization has become the potentially most corrupt area of transformation, especially where the state has retreated and left the field to the unregulated struggle of interest groups. In some reform countries, renationalization is considered as a way of dealing with the most obvious pathologies of privatization. Jeffrey Sachs, one of the early proponents of the primacy of privatization, now advocates partial renationalization in Russia. What is generally missing are not private interests, but a "public service with the public interest in mind" (Nellis 1999: 25).

Towards a New Paradigm

The realities of postcommunist crises, unanticipated anomalies, and diverging development paths have challenged conventional conceptions of transformation. Since the mid-1990s neoliberal discourse in particular could no longer avoid facing up to these realities,[29] without, however, accepting their theoretical implications. Attempts to account for the depth of postcommunist crises in the framework of neoliberal discourse remained ad hoc or descended into cynical apologies comparing shock therapy with chemotherapy administered to a terminally ill patient regardless of the risks involved. However, an international institution could not simply dismiss the anomalies produced by its universalistic policies by pointing out that all its members were entitled to "equality of treatment."[30]

The disappointment with neoliberalism in Eastern Europe coincided with similar experiences in other parts of the world. The results of almost two decades of "structural adjustment" in Latin America have been meager. The mishandling of the Asian crisis further undermined the IMF's reputation. These developments precipitated changes in terminology that hollowed out the Washington consensus from within. Demands for "good governance" and "second generation reforms" shifted the abstract opposition between state and market toward a more constructive view of the role of public policy in creating an adequate institutional environment for markets. This "more proactive approach [for] improving the management of public resources through reforms covering public sector institutions" was initially presented as the result of a pragmatic learning process—the lessons of which were to be implemented in cooperation with other UN organizations that had broader mandates than the IMF (IMF 1997: vi, 3).

This "pragmatic evolution" had of course more general implications. The concept of second-generation reforms amounted to a de facto admission that radical reform policies had largely failed. This sparked heated debates within and between the international organizations, creating in turn a discursive space for the reassessment of postcommunist transformation policies. These ongoing debates clearly also have implications for the field of transformation studies. Theoretical critiques and heterodox approaches that for a long time were confined to the margins of academic debate have moved to the center of broader, interdisciplinary theorizing transcending the narrow conceptual repertoire of neoliberal discourse. Both the policy and academic dimensions of the debate are discussed in more detail in the next section.

The Washington Dissensus

The debate about good governance and second-generation reforms emerging in the mid-1990s was not primarily a platform for cooperation between the international organizations but signaled a significant shift in discourse that brought to light unresolved disagreements between them. "Good governance" was the phrase employed by the World Bank since 1989 for adopting broader political conditionality in response to the disappointing results of structural adjustment. The call for "adjustment with transformation" and second-generation reforms emerged in the African and Latin American contexts, where conventional programs had produced widespread dissatisfaction (Gibbon 1993; Naim 2000).[31] This gave rise to concerns in the Eastern European context that the postcommunist crises might replicate the disappointing scenarios played out in other regions.

Indeed, an interregional comparison of the results of world-market oriented modernization seriously calls into question the wisdom of the "political economy of patience." How much time should the populations of postcommunist countries reserve for the "intertemporal trade-off of macroeconomic reforms," i.e., for a "short-term" loss of income for the promise of subsequent rewards? In Latin America, the region with the longest experience of world-market oriented reform policy, results have not been encouraging. In the 1980s income distribution became increasingly unequal, and by the end of the 1990s average real wages had fallen below their 1980 level. Reform policies neither provided a major boost to investment or domestic savings nor significantly reduced budget deficits and external debt. The costs of disinflation, austerity, and structural adjustment can still be felt and have provoked a backlash against reforms and democracy (UN/ECLAC 2000; Stallings and Peres 2000; Karl 2000). For postcommunist countries much the same questions arise: how to reconcile the market, democracy, and trust in institutions in increasingly unequal societies; and how to avoid having the experience of postcommunist crises lead to cynicism and alienation from the formally established, but still unconsolidated, institutions. These questions take on even more urgency in the postcommunist context since the Communist state had established a level of expectations with respect to social infrastructure, employment, and social integration that had become unsustainable.

The impetus for the emergence of a "New Development Paradigm" thus resulted from a whole series of negative experiences with structural adjustment policies: "the Washington consensus failed to deliver on its promise" (Rodrik 2000a: 2). None other than John Williamson, who is credited for having coined the phrase "Washington consensus," identified its crucial weakness: "Policy needs to shift back from cutting a state that had become bloated to strengthening a number of key state institutions whose efficient functioning is important for rapid and/or equitable growth."[32] The IMF's adoption of concepts developed by the World Bank and other regional organizations did not resolve their more fundamental disagreements. On the one hand, the IMF interpreted "good governance" in a rather narrow fashion and focused almost exclusively on its impact on the development of the private sector. On the other hand, there were legitimate reservations concerning the IMF's mandate and competence with respect to "modernizing the state" in transition countries. Other lines of conflict emerged with respect to the mandate of the EBRD. The neoliberal strategy favored by the U.S. Treasury Department aimed primarily at opening up the resource-rich regions of central Asia and Russia for private investors. By contrast, the European Commission sought to use the resources of the EBRD for a more ambitious strategy of institutional integration aimed at preparing the central European states for membership in the European Union (EU) (Robinson 1997).

The unresolved conflicts between IMF and the World Bank[33] about an adequate conceptualization of postcommunist transformations are illustrated by a revealing inconsistency in the World Bank's 1996 *World Development Report, From Plan to Market.* Whereas part 1 explains reform outcomes along the lines of an orthodox IMF study strictly in terms of economic stabilization and different initial conditions, subsequent sections problematize the abstract universalism of privatization policies, emphasize the "differing cultures and traditions" of transition countries, and stress the importance of "long-term institution building" as well as a "competent and strong state."[34] The report's introduction already stressed that the postcommunist reform process differed from standard programs in its larger societal scope and in its path dependency from Communist modernization achievements, however distorted they may have been. In explicit opposition to a tabula rasa approach, the transition to a market economy was to proceed "without throwing away the achievements of the old" (World Bank 1996: 123). Such a (re-)combination of new and old institutions also seemed to make alternative endpoints of transition conceivable. "As transition proceeds, policymakers increasingly confront tradeoffs between a somewhat more laissez-faire market economy (as in the United States) and a somewhat more 'social' market economy (as in Germany or Sweden)" (World Bank 1996: 111).

As is customary in both institutions, inconsistencies and ambiguities of this kind were not publicly discussed and also went unnoticed by their critics on the left. The breakthrough to a new paradigm and a more open political debate is indicated by more recent discussions about a "post-Washington consensus"—a phrase adopted by the World Bank's former chief economist, Joseph Stiglitz (Stiglitz 1998b; Burki and Perry 1998). This turning point is of central importance insofar as it elevates the theoretical reservations emanating from academic social science to the same institutional level from which neoliberal discourse has derived much of its power. The abstract universalism of economic reform programs in fact seems to have contributed to the postcommunist crises. As John Nellis, a coauthor of *From Plan to Market,* puts it: "The international financial institutions must bear some of the responsibility for the poor outcomes, since they often insisted on the primacy of economic policy" (Nellis 1999).

To break out of such a narrowly defined reform approach, the so-called second-generation reforms set different priorities, based on a less technocratic conception of policy and institution transfer than that underlying the "rigid and dogmatic" standard approach. This broader conception was introduced in the late 1990s as the new paradigm of a *comprehensive development framework*

(Wolfensohn 1999). This paradigm defines transformation as a problem of social change encompassing the administrative capacity of the state, processes of democratization, market reforms, and the evolution of new norms of social justice. In this view, the social, institutional, and organizational structures of postcommunist societies do not appear external to market processes but are endogenous variables that determine the institutionalization of functioning markets and a sufficient degree of social cohesion. To cope with the corresponding problems of interinstitutional integration, the role of local knowledge and actors becomes much more important than in the general application of a particular model of capitalism (Rodrik 2000b). The new paradigm is based on political conditionality, that is, a belief in democracy as the best framework for resolving social conflicts as well as for stimulating long-term equitable growth and the evolution of "good institutions." Civil society is elevated to the "largest single factor in development" (Wolfensohn 1999: 25f.).

The comprehensive development framework has some obvious practical drawbacks since it leaves behind the quasi-mechanical approach of economic conditionality in favor of the institutional search processes available to a country in a specific situation. This entails a more complex research approach to effective reforms than the above-sketched macroeconomic empiricism of time series and quantitative growth models. Thus, for example, the relationship between policy variables and outcomes, i.e., between political action and economic trends, is extremely difficult to reconstruct without adopting far-reaching ceteris paribus clauses. The same is true for the problem of constructing institutional indicators, which only rarely match the level of sophistication of the statistical methods applied to them. This is particularly relevant for unconsolidated systems with defective or informal institutions whose latent functions are not well understood. Analogies to nominally equivalent Western institutions are often misleading (as illustrated by the case of Russian banks). Finally, neither economic nor political conditionalities follow simple incentive-response patterns but are filtered through processes of negotiation, communication, and implementation. This also applies to those channels through which external influences affect the policies of reforming countries. The rhetoric of radical reformers as well as the negotiations between international financial institutions and reform governments are to a high degree infected by "cheap talk" and "babbling equilibria," i.e., nonbinding, nonverifiable, inconsistent, or uninformative messages.[35] If the considerable complexity of such a situation is acknowledged, a strict methodological distinction between independent variables and dependent variables is no longer possible. The call for participation, empowerment, and ownership implies the involvement of a large number of political and social actors who, while drawing on external expertise, will articulate their own goals and ambitions in the design, timing, and sequencing of reforms.

Neoliberal critics of the comprehensive development framework have argued that its long-term, holistic approach will achieve too little by aspiring to too much (Bhagwati 1999, 2000; Srinivasan 1999). Moreover, they dismiss democratic, equitable, sustainable, and comprehensive development as "buzzwords of ageing hippies." The critics' skepticism about more sophisticated reform strategies is illustrated by their use of "societal transformation" exclusively in quotation marks.[36] The political intention behind these polemics is evidently to defend the traditional intellectual agenda of the international financial institutions and to fend off calls for their cooperation in "UN-style forums." The charges were directed above all against Stiglitz's unusually open criticism of their failed policies in the postcommunist context. Thus, notwithstanding the claims of a "universal economics" and the premature expectation that global modernization imperatives would return the countries liberated from the shackles of communism to the "normal world," development economics and area studies are being rehabilitated.[37]

The conflict between institutional and market-induced reform strategies demonstrates that the conceptualization of postcommunist transformation has become the focal point and arena for a struggle over basic political priorities. The sharp tone of the debate is due to the fact that the opposing positions are not so much divided on the question of growth as such, but on the depth of reforms necessary to achieve it. Is it enough to create a general institutional framework for the market? Or is it necessary to place the institutional, social, and human prerequisites for "high quality growth" (Rodrik 2000b) in the context of larger societal transformations?

It appears that the debate so far has gone in favor of the second position. Not only representatives of the Inter-American Development Bank assert that "the old reforms clearly need to be reformed" (Iglesias 2000). OECD and the ODA as well have, at least on a rhetorical level, endorsed a comprehensive view that clearly suggests an interdisciplinary perspective: "to take more fully into account how markets, societies and governance interact and evolve" (OECD/ODA 2000: chap. 5).[38] It is therefore no mere coincidence that the Global Development Network, established in late 1999 as a worldwide organization of research and policy institutes, is focusing on postcommunist reforms and has devoted its second major conference to the transdisciplinary theme, "Beyond Economics: Multidisciplinary Approaches to Development" (Giszpenc and Squire 2000).

It is difficult to assess at this point to what extent the actual policies of the international financial institutions will be shaped by the new paradigm of the comprehensive development framework. The calls by conservative critics from the U.S. House of Representatives for the IMF's disengagement from Russia (Cox et al. 2000) at any rate have not been heeded. Indeed, the IMF's ten-year review contains some unusually self-critical statements: "in retrospect it is clear that policies pursued in transition have not always been ideal. In particular, although the need for an institutional infrastructure to support the nascent market economies was recognized from the beginning, in practice such institution building was not always given adequate attention" (IMF 2000b: 127).

Second-Generation Theories: Shifting to Cross-disciplinary Approaches

For obvious reasons, the reorientation in the field of development policy has far-reaching theoretical and methodological implications for the field of transformation studies. Alternative approaches, hitherto confined to academic discussions without posing any serious threat to the hegemonic discourse of neoliberal reform, command increasing attention. Cutting-edge research focuses on the interactions between political, economic, sociostructural, and cultural change. Earlier controversies, such as on shock therapy versus gradualism, have dissolved as transformation is conceived as societal evolution that takes place on many levels and includes processes occurring at different speeds (Kornai 2000). Thus fundamental social science concepts that are not exclusive to any particular discipline have been incorporated into the theoretical vocabulary of transformation studies. These *thematic shifts* broaden the scope of analysis and are creating greater opportunities for cross-disciplinary cooperation. Philosophers of science would speak of a "progressive problem shift" that reintegrates the anomalies and ad hoc stratagems of an outdated paradigm (Lakatos 1978: 31–34). The explanatory problems and concepts developed in this problem shift provide the setting for the contributions to the present volume. They demonstrate that the call for cross-disciplinarity is no longer an abstract postulate but has already become a reality shaping the most fruitful approaches in the field.

With the new perspective comes an increased awareness that there are no global modernization imperatives that automatically would return the countries liberated from the shackles of communism to the "normal world."[39] The postcommunist countries, forced to integrate into the world market from a state of backwardness, are ill prepared for the forces of globalization. "Normalization" in this context may well imply what Adam Przeworski predicted soon after the fall of the Iron Curtain, i.e., that East European societies "too will confront the all too normal problems of the economics, the politics, and the culture of poor capitalism" (Przeworski 1991: 191). This poses the traditional development problem of how to slow down the trends toward structural heterogeneity, social segmentation, and peripheralization.

As the available empirical evidence shows, postcommunist political transitions also do not follow a universal path to liberal democracy. The much-cited "third wave" of democratization that portrayed the revolutions of 1989 as part of a global trend spanning from South Africa to Southeast Asia, may well have turned into a reverse wave (Diamond 1996: 20–37). Accordingly, the typology of political orders has been extended to include imperfect, fragile, delegated, etc., democracies. The most fruitful approach employs a comparative perspective paying close attention to the specific prehistories of postcommunist transitions as determined by different degrees of totalitarian sclerosis, the position of the elites in the ancien régime, the mode of political regime change, and other variables. The sterile opposition between area studies and comparative method has been transcended by conceptualizing postcommunist changes as particular versions of the more general problems of development and democratization.[40]

A broader perspective on the functioning of markets has established that markets do not generate an autonomous development dynamic and cannot be reduced to the price mechanism, thus undermining a fundamental assumption of neoliberal discourse. The thesis of market-induced modernization, according to which liberalization and privatization initiate a virtuous circle of social and political self-organization, has been replaced by sociological insights into the noneconomic preconditions of markets. This means that a number of variables from which the universal model abstracts need to be introduced into a dynamic perspective. It is interesting to note that the theoretical reasons for this were presented, not by sociologists, but by eminent proponents of general equilibrium theory who recognized that the strict conditions of the model are even more unrealistic in times of rapidly changing, uncertain, and contradictory expectations. Imperfect markets, asymmetrical information between insiders and outsiders, privatizations under conditions of imperfect competition, and infrastructural problems are instances that typically give rise to pathologies. The most valuable insight that can be derived from general equilibrium theory is the negative point that under conditions of postcommunist transitions markets cannot properly fulfill their coordinating functions. Somewhat ironically, pure economic theory predicted "for purely prudential reasons" the transition to a mixed economy; "that the state will play an important role seems inevitable."[41]

This fundamental theoretical argument concerning the political and institutional embeddedness of transition economies is confirmed by empirical research. In the EBRD's retrospective of the first ten years of transition, two entire chapters are devoted to the positive functions of the postcommunist state. The conventional wisdom of the political economy of reforms is called into question in several respects, in particular by strongly emphasizing the need for the institutional and political embedding of markets. "The evidence now shows clearly that the central lesson of transitions is that markets will not function well without supporting institutions, a state that carries through its basic responsibilities and a healthy civil society" (EBRD 1999: 5).[42]

The rediscovery of markets as institutions converges with the conclusion in the political science literature that pure market economies are not compatible with the formation of sustainable democracies. All modern democratic societies are mixed economies insofar as they establish legal norms for competition and property rights, have a sizable public sector and institutionally regulated class conflicts, and use tax and social policy to modify the distributive outcomes generated by markets (Freeman 1989). Precisely because these are not mere "mechanisms," Linz and Stepan sum up this "set of socio-politically crafted and accepted norms, institutions and regulations" in the concept of "economic society," which they assign a central role in the process democratic consolidation. Successful democratization—in addition to civil society organizations, free elections, rule of law, and a rule-governed state apparatus—also depends on the degree to which such an economic society can be established (Linz and Stepan 1996: chaps. 1 and 11).

In fact, mixed systems have emerged in all postcommunist societies (EBRD 1999: 121–23). General government expenditure as a share of GDP ranged in 1998 from 46.4 percent in Hungary and 41.1 percent in the Czech Republic to 37 percent in Russia, 29.5 percent in Ukraine, and below 20 percent for most central Asian CIS members. Thus, a high level of state intervention in the economy does not indicate lack of reform commitment. Hungary is near the top of the state intervention index of the EBRD while at the same time being one of the most consolidated transition societies. We would argue that transformation in the central European countries has been relatively successful and occurred without fundamental policy reversals precisely because institutions for social integration were maintained and the state did not collapse. A high degree of social cohesion and a capacity for political compromise seem to be crucial preconditions for a sustained reform policy and the formation of coherent institutional systems.

We can summarize the problem shifts in transformation research discussed so far as follows. The Hayekian dilemma of simultaneously introducing the market and democracy was transformed into an opportunity: successful reform implementation and the avoidance of policy reversals is dependent on the inclusion of large sectors of the population and consultation with interest groups (Hellman 1998a; EBRD 1999: chap. 6). For this reason, the renewed attention focused on the role of the state does not auger a return to the old authoritarian developmental state—a state model that is in fact much closer to the neoliberal ideal of an insulated executive capable of implementing radical reforms without having to take into account organized social interests. Recent transformation research therefore has devoted particular attention to the combination of market requirements, state capacity, the democratic openness of the political process, and civil society activity. The interplay of these elements is the common point of reference for more complex explanations of diverging transition paths and for different variants of political capitalism. In this view, "state capture" is a special case, and the concept of "partial reforms" takes on a new meaning. In the absence of an adequate regulatory environment, with underdeveloped representation of political interests, and a nontransparent decision-making process, privatization and liberalization can be hijacked by old and new interest groups that come to dominate the political process and state institutions. The culture of corruption, clientelism, distrust, and political cynicism so widespread under Communism can therefore survive under new conditions.

Capturing the actual forms of interaction between economic, political, and social reforms requires an appropriate analytical framework. Concepts such as trust, networks, social capital, and civil society that emphasize the problem of social cohesion in the context of political polarization, ethnic divisions, and social exclusion are more suitable for the problem of institutional consolidation.

Analyzing the demonstration effects of Western countries on the reform states calls for complex models of institutional transfer as developed in organizational sociology that can show how external models interact with local conditions. Approaches from the area of cultural sociology can shed light on established value systems that provide a source of legitimacy for the development of a complex social order. This takes us to the approaches and individual contributions in this volume.

Chapter Overview

The subtitle of this volume announces cross-disciplinary approaches to the study of postcommunist transformation. We believe that what needs to be crossed are boundaries, and in some cases chasms, separating the work of scholars addressing problems of transformation. These may be boundaries between academic disciplines, research traditions, or approaches. We cannot claim to have sketched more than the outlines of such a transdisciplinary or general social science approach in the introductory chapter. Many boundaries need to be crossed, and the authors assembled in this volume make their specific contributions, depending on which region of the social science world they inhabit. They do not present a ready-made theory of transformation but rather reflect the state of the debate in the various branches of transformation research. They share the goal of introducing hitherto neglected approaches into the debate without dismissing the valuable results of transformation studies to date. Significantly, while many of the contributions are based on different and controversial approaches, they converge on a common set of fundamental concepts. Key concepts are those of institution, network, trust, and social and cultural capital—concepts that are themselves cross-disciplinary.

László Csaba and Kazimierz Poznanski, each in his own way and with different results, attempt to bridge the divide between mainstream economics and institutional, evolutionary approaches. Martin Raiser connects the concerns of mainstream economics with insights from economic sociology. Bruno Grancelli attempts to reconnect a structurally oriented economic sociology to one based on rational choice assumptions. Peter Rutland wants to reinsert area studies approaches into transformation studies, and Wade Jacoby introduces theories from organizational sociology. Andreas Pickel and Jacqui True identify and seek to bridge an unfruitful division of labor between comparativists and international relations theorists in political science and political economy. Melanie Tatur and Willfried Spohn reclaim the significance of political and historical sociology in a field dominated by the approaches of economists and political scientists. Methodologically speaking, these are the lines along which the contributors attempt their own boundary crossings. Theoretically and empirically, each chapter makes a substantive contribution to a number of basic problems in the transformation debate.

The cross-disciplinary approach to economic transformation advocated in this volume poses an explicit challenge to the more orthodox forms of economics practiced in the mainstream of that discipline. László Csaba, a Hungarian economist, reviews the past and potential future contributions of economic theory to the study of systemic change. He is skeptical of sweeping rejections of neoliberalism while at the same time critical of neoclassical economists' general lack of interest in problems of postcommunist change. Yet he cautions us not to overestimate the importance of the orthodox mainstream in a discipline in which he observes a "renaissance of heterodox approaches." Csaba himself defends an empirically oriented economics that provides a basic analytical framework and has policy relevance. Csaba's contribution to our debate is particularly significant for at least two reasons. First, while calling for a broadened conception of economics, he ultimately wants to defend the traditions and methods of the discipline against its more radical critics. Second, he interprets the empirical evidence as confirming the basic correctness of neoliberal stabilization, liberalization, and privatization policies.

Poznanski must be counted among those radical critics whose interpretation of the results of the first decade of postcommunist transformation is diametrically opposed to Csaba's. In his publications, Poznanski has consistently opposed shock therapy and advocated gradualism. Yet while Csaba and Poznanski may be far apart in their respective views on appropriate reform policies and actual transformation outcomes, they concur in seeing the future of economic theory in institutionalist and evolutionary approaches. In his contribution to the present volume, Poznanski argues that the sharp economic decline of the early transition period was not an inevitable consequence of communism but a "state-made production collapse." In contrast to the policy-fixated orthodox reform approach, he sees the state as key to transformation success. Postcommunist Eastern Europe's crisis-ridden and disintegrating states were by and large incapable of creating the conditions for successful systemic change, thus the emergence of a "dysfunctional capitalism." The unprecedented postcommunist recession, moreover, has led to a massive "foreign takeover of domestic capital assets at drastically discounted prices." Thus, he points out, Hungary's and Poland's shares of foreign ownership at 70 percent and Estonia's at 80 percent far surpass typical levels in West European economies. He also contrasts the Eastern European transitions with China's, where a "responsible state" has protected domestic capital and facilitated the emergence of a domestic capitalist class, as well as having achieved much more favorable transition outcomes.

A closely related and central question in the transformation debate has been whether capitalism and democracy can be built on the ruins of the old Communist order. For many of the early optimists, the complete collapse of the old system appeared as a most favorable condition, a kind of tabula rasa, for new construction. Early pessimists warned that beneath the ruins of Communism lurked the old system's pathologies that would infect and subvert the fledgling liberal institutions. A third view maintains that the pessimists are right in assuming that the past lives on, yet wrong in associating Communist legacies only with constraints for systemic reform—a view that the Chinese experience seems to support. This view, revolving around key concepts such as path dependency and social capital, maintains that the new order can be built only *with* the remnants of the past. Existing networks are seen as the decisive fields and agents of transformation. Bruno Grancelli offers a critique of the network approach and sketches an alternative to it. While clearly sympathetic to this approach and the theoretical advance a focus on social capital represents, he identifies some of its serious blind spots, especially a lack of conceptual space for what he calls transformational leadership. Grancelli calls for a shift in focus from networks to the action of key individual change agents. "After a decade of post-communist transformation," he writes, "it would be advisable to begin focusing on other groups of actors as well: on those who have linkages with Western organizations and institutions." Methodologically, he advocates a "thick version" of rational choice to accommodate this shift in conceptual focus. With this, Grancelli is not returning to simplistic, acultural, and sociologically questionable assumptions underlying conceptions of "designer capitalism," but rather aims at a synthesis of approaches at a higher level.

Not only economic sociologists and political scientists, but many economists as well have attempted to probe more deeply into underlying mechanisms of successful market reform, in particular the role of so-called informal institutions.[43] Martin Raiser's contribution focuses on the central role of trust in modern market society. In line with the pessimists' view, he argues that postcommunist economies suffer from heavy legacies of distrust in the state and closed social and business networks that reduce competitive pressures on existing enterprises. Like Grancelli, he is critical of network approaches that consider the survival and adaptation of existing business networks as an efficient response to the uncertainty and imperfection of markets in transition. He maintains that only "extended" or generalized trust can support the move to a modern market system. In addition to a detailed and sophisticated discussion of the concept of trust, Raiser draws out central conditions for and obstacles to the emergence of generalized trust in former Communist countries. Unlike many pessimists, he believes that political action can and should help to overcome Communism's legacy of general distrust. "Policy can make important contributions to building trust, first and foremost by increasing trust in public institutions, which will in turn provide contract enforcement and allow successful transactions to build mutual confidence over time." A political strategy for the building of extended trust should include moral leadership, constitutional safeguards for competition and accountability, progressive distributional policies, and certain forms of direct state intervention.

Peter Rutland is equally skeptical of optimists' and pessimists' views in the transformation debate. Both the preachers of the "good news bible" and the "merchants of doom," he notes, tend to have very little region-specific knowledge. This charge, also echoed in Greskovits's chapter, is substantiated in his analysis with specific reference to the case of Russia. Rutland observes that the centrally planned economy paradigm, cultivated by economists with training in and in-depth knowledge of the specificities of Communist economies since the 1950s, rapidly declined with the collapse of Communist regimes. It was replaced by what he calls the transition economy paradigm, practiced overwhelmingly by economists with scant area expertise. Rutland shows that the fundamental assumption on which the old paradigm rested, namely that Soviet-type economies functioned in ways that could not be adequately captured by mainstream economics, was abandoned in favor of a universalistic one-global-economy approach. Reinforced by the dominant role played by international financial institutions in the transition, the traditional area knowledge was radically devalued. As "the most sophisticated, rigorous and comprehensive analysis of the transition economies yet produced, and a fine exemplar of the new paradigm," Rutland critically examines the World Bank's 1996 *World Development Report From Plan to Market*. Its assumptions of Pareto optimality, the historical inevitability of the Western market model, and the almost exclusive reliance on financial indicators create a highly distorted picture of the real economy and its dynamics of change. Especially with respect to Russia, economists have failed to develop the conceptual tools to deal with diversity and regional fragmentation. The distinctive features of the Russian case—such as the fragile nature of the federal state, the distinctive fusion of political and economic power, and the simple geographical challenge of creating an integrated national market—require a theoretical return to the basic assumption of the old paradigm according to which special cases call for special categories of analysis.

Are the central and East European candidates for European Union membership special cases? Wade Jacoby's analysis investigates what for those postcommunist countries aspiring to EU membership has become a major determinant of transformation, i.e., the preaccession process revolving around the adoption of EU laws and institutions. To this extent, they clearly are special cases that pose a particular set of theoretical questions for transformation studies. An essential factor that has facilitated their institutional consolidation clearly is their cultural proximity to the "European social model" that provides the overarching legitimation for the political conditionalities of their EU accession. Indeed, the conditions contained in the *acquis communautaire* could be interpreted as a comprehensive development framework of a special kind.[44] From a sociological perspective, the program of transferring a European institutional system into the Eastern European reform countries is of much greater significance for them than the hoped-for economic benefits of an expanded market. The central and East European accession candidates have committed themselves to a historically unique process of external evaluation in the reconstruction of their institutional systems as they work to become compatible with the existing rules and practices of the EU. Beyond macroeconomic stability, structural reforms, and functioning market economies, this includes standards of consumer and environmental protection, regional cohesion, and competitiveness in the EU market. In addition to economic criteria, the European Commission screens candidates' reform records with reference to chapters on democracy and the rule of law, human rights, minority rights, as well as the administrative structures necessary to implement EU laws. This raises the central question about the mechanisms through which such a very ambitious integration strategy will interact with local conditions. This problem of institutional transfer is at the center of Jacoby's contribution. His major question is how a particular kind of Europeanization is being institutionalized. Providing a survey of relevant social science literature, he shows the particular relevance of theories of organizational isomorphism and organizational dualism for his analysis of political institutions and actors involved in this transnational project of Europeanization by design.

Andreas Pickel and Jacqui True argue that the long-standing division in political science into the subfields of comparative and international politics, and of political economy into comparative and global, have precluded the development of theories that analyze both exogenous and endogenous dynamics in systemic change. They note that the "great divide" separating the two scholarly traditions and communities poses a particular theoretical challenge at a time when this separation appears more anachronistic than ever. The authors argue that a proper understanding of the multilayered postcommunist transformations requires an explicit and systematic attempt to capture the specific interactions of global, transnational, and intranational change processes. Based on a systemic and mechanismic framework, the chapter develops the core concepts of global, transnational, and intranational linkages. Pickel and True assemble major instances of the three types of linkages that can be found in the specialized and often unconnected literatures on the transitions in Eastern Europe. They illustrate their argument with case studies of the Czech Republic, East Germany, and Cuba.

Based on sociologically grounded perspectives, the chapters by Tatur and Spohn call for a return to state and society in transformation studies. Both authors show in different ways why and how we should conceive of economic and political transformation ultimately as sociocultural processes of change. Melanie Tatur contends that transformation needs to be conceptualized in terms of social institutions rather than simply as a political strategy for establishing a market order. She attempts to model the institutional arrangements mediating the systemic change process with special attention to its political-cultural dimensions. It is the latter that in her view explain the major variations in transformation paths and outcomes, as she shows in her surveys of countries in central-eastern and southeastern Europe. Tatur develops ideal types for analyzing various forms of postcommunist capitalisms that are related to specific types of states and patterns of social integration—which she calls "criminal," political," and "democratic" capitalism. She is not so much interested in using these concepts to describe the "essence" of the new market systems as in capturing distinct modes of transformation over time. The analysis is explicitly situated in the larger debate on the political and cultural preconditions for successful democratic market societies, specifically the literature on path dependency and social capital (North, Putnam, et al.). Tatur's conceptual apparatus is therefore also of relevance to "developing" societies without a communist past.

Willfried Spohn's approach to transformation of states and societies is historical-sociological, following Eisenstadt's theory of "multiple modernities." He argues that the evolutionist and system-functionalist premises of modernization theory in general and political transitology in particular that informed the early transformation debate have become increasingly untenable in light of a range of unexpected and negative transformation outcomes, including the powerful reassertion of nationalism. He sees his own theoretical efforts as part of an emerging neomodernization paradigm that emphasizes the historical contextuality, agency, and reflexivity of social actors and thus the path dependence and contingency of postcommunist transformation processes. The study of political change as transition to democracy and consolidation of democratic political institutions, Spohn contends, misses the more fundamental processes of state formation, nation building, and collective identity construction, including the completely understudied role of religion. He shows the structural interdependence of democratization with these three processes in his case studies of East Germany, Poland, and Russia.

In a self-reflective mode, Béla Greskovits places the postcommunist transformation debate in the larger historical context of earlier debates surrounding the transition from feudalism to capitalism and the transition to socialism. Inspired by a *tableau ideologique* first proposed by Albert Hirschman (1992), Greskovits draws our attention to a number of surprisingly unchanging intellectual themes that make their appearance in each of the three major transition debates. Greskovits's subsequent critique of the achievements of postcommunist transformation studies is an indictment of the intellectual, ideological, and scientific failures of transition scholars. Greskovits's challenge is taken up by Claus Offe in an equally uncompromising rejoinder in defense of transformation studies. Valerie Bunce in her commentary on Greskovits, on the other hand, is much more sympathetic to his arguments and augments rather than rejects them.

Notes

1. The classical formulation of the problem of order dates back to Parsons (1937). On the general problem of order as a key category of sociological theory, see Alexander 1982: 90–112.

2. The phrase is credited to John Williamson (1990). It was an attempt at the end of the Cold War battle between capitalism and communism to define a number of rather

basic ideas of good economics, initially aimed at the specific conditions of Latin America. In hindsight, Williamson regrets that his concept mutated into a form of market fundamentalism in support of "radical reforms." "My qualifications about this being an agenda for a specific part of the world at a particular moment of history were quickly forgotten, as the search for a new ideology, to endorse or to hate, was perceived to have succeeded" (Williamson 1997: 5). Williamson, however, is not entirely without blame. In consideration of the political climate in Washington, he had failed to incorporate the social dimensions and distributional consequences into his "one world consensus" (Waelbroeck 1998), even though he recognized their significance. For more recent revisions of his view, see Williamson 1997 and 1999. On the background and the flexible contents of the Washington consensus, see Bresser Pereira 1993: 18–23, 30–36, 65, n. 4 and 5; and especially Naim 2000.

3. See Hirschman 1981, the polemical diagnosis by Krugman 1995: 15–29, 81–84, and Waterbury 1999.

4. On what follows, see Aslund 1995: 27ff., Hough 1997: 103–39, and Nuti 1990.

5. Sachs 1994: xiii; cf. Lipton and Sachs 1990. A similarly optimistic prognosis was issued by Aslund (1992: 90) at the start of the Russian reforms: "No doubt, a few million enterprises will be created in Russia alone during the first year of freedom of enterprise and free prices."

6. This statement is especially significant since in past decades Brus had rehearsed all the arguments in favor of the compatibility of a socialist economy, market elements, and political liberalization (cf. Brus 1992). Now, however, he had come to the conclusion that the old debate between Oskar Lange and Friedrich Hayek had been decided both in theoretical and practical terms in favor of the Austrian School (Brus and Laski 1991: chap. 5). On the dissolution of East European reform socialism during the 1980s, see Chavance 1994: 119–31.

7. Erhard is considered the architect of West Germany's post-World War II "economic miracle."

8. The different criteria of success for neoliberal doctrines at scientific, policy, and ideological levels are discussed in Pickel 1997a.

9. On the tensions between the institutionalization of area studies and modernization theory, see Wood 1968 and Wallerstein et al. 1996: 36. For the history of communist studies and its relationship to modernization approaches see Müller 1998.

10. Thus the title of the special issue of *The National Interest*, no. 31 (1993), which in addition to a post mortem of Communism exposed the "sins of the scholars." For self-criticism by Soviet and communist studies scholars, see Fleron and Hoffman 1993, Solomon 1993, and Bence and Lipset 1994.

11. See also Hewett 1988: "Is Soviet socialism reformable? Yes, it is reformable, and is already reformed at a pace far greater than the conventional wisdom would suggest."

12. As Johnson and Keehn (1994: 20) have put it with reference to the new theoretical approach, "if the rest of the world is evolving to look like the democratic capitalism of the United States, then there is no longer any transcendent strategic reason for Americans to know anything about 'the rest.' American scholars need only continue to perfect mathematical proofs and the inevitability of the American 'rules of the game.'"

13. Strictly speaking, the concept of transformation in this view would be inappropriate, since it presupposes some kind of coherence as a starting point. "Governments

were faced not so much with the task of transforming existing socialistic norms into new capitalist ones, but rather with a state of *anomie*" (Dabrowski et al. 2000: 13).

14. This was to be the central function of privatization (Sachs and Lipton 1990: 308).

15. For a survey of the burgeoning literature on the political preconditions for the initiation and consolidation of economic reforms, see Bönker 2001: chap. 2.

16. See, for example, Lipton and Sachs 1992. The quasi-experimental design of transition economics subsequently also became a model for political science analyses, which, however, employed different explanatory variables.

17. A more comprehensive reconstruction of the debate would have to pay more attention to the Chinese experience. The "Sino-Soviet divergence" (Brus) has represented a major challenge to the neoliberal discourse and has featured also prominently in Stiglitz's critique of the orthodox approach (Stiglitz 1999). For neoliberal interpretations of the Chinese case, which emphasize its peculiarities, see Sachs and Woo 1994; Dabrowski et al. 2000: 6f.

18. To note the universal character of the output decline and the common problems is not to deny national differences. While all countries of Eastern Europe and the former Soviet Union experienced a severe transformational recession, some have recovered earlier and have performed better than others. Neoliberals have reacted to this differentiation, which clearly contradicts earlier universalistic claims, by attributing differences in performance to differences in the implementation of neoliberal prescriptions (Aslund et al. 1996; Dabrowski et al. 2000; Fischer and Sahay 2000). However, the evidence is thin. Quite aside from the methodologically questionable causal explanatory claims made by Fischer and Sahay as well as many other authors of the IMF and World Bank, it should be noted that even they are not able to show a clear relationship between balanced budgets and economic growth (Fischer and Sahay 2000: 9f.). The same is true for the relationship between privatization and economic growth (Gregory 1999: 7f.). What is more important, however, is a general point: In their quest for demonstrating the beneficial effects of particular reform measures, neoliberals tend to ignore "deeper" factors such as differences in initial conditions, state capabilities, or the pull of the European Union. Yet such factors ultimately decide what reform measures can be implemented and how they operate.

19. On the methodological problems of measuring poverty in postcommunist countries and on the relationship between poverty and neoliberal policies, see Clarke and Holmes 2000.

20. See *Transition* (World Bank) 8, no. 4: 29. Cf. Fischer, Sahay, and Végh 1996: 64.

21. Eatwell (1996) refers to the liberalization of financial markets and the corresponding development strategies as "the most important systemic transformation of the world economy since the establishment of the new world order at the end of World War II." In this context, he emphasizes the new approach of the IMF.

22. "History suggests that a laissez-faire international regime may well hinder rather than help the process of transformation in Central and Eastern Europe," as Eatwell (1996: 53) had warned. The criterion for successful reforms defined by Fischer (1998: 321), in contrast, redefines the problem as the solution: "sustainability also entails ability to withstand shocks." See also Bhagwati 1998; Rodrik 1998, Eatwell and Taylor 1999. For an early careful assessment of the effects of the Asia crisis on the Eastern European countries, see Fries et al. 1999.

23. This is the crucial point that Slay (2000) ignores in his polemic against Stiglitz, where he follows the apologetic IMF on the Asian crisis. The IMF's usually belated policy revisions referred to by Slay were always a response to earlier faulty diagnoses that never were treated as such however in order not to weaken the institution's authority.

24. The opening of the financial sector on the advice of the IMF is now also criticized by Aslund (1999: 22f.) as a sequencing error. "Ironically, Russia was flooded with foreign financing—primarily private but also intergovernmental—after serious attempts at economic reform had faded."

25. A notable exception was China, which on account of still existing capital currency regulations, was able to resist the devaluation pressure coming from other countries in the region. Despite their high external indebtedness, Poland and Hungary were less vulnerable to speculative capital flows since both countries had preserved capital controls and financed their current account deficits more through FDI than portfolio investments (*The Economist* 1999: 84).

26. Thus the self-critical diagnosis of Blanchard et al. 1993: 4–7, 37–80.

27. Nellis 1999: 10–12. Sojika (2000: 243) argues that early radical experiments have delayed the Czech reform process for many years.

28. This represents an empirical confirmation of the theoretical objections to the primacy of privatization formulated by Stiglitz (1994: 180). As Desai and Goldberg (2000: 15) add, "[t]he system of enterprise property rights has preserved firms as, above all, a source of rents." On the transmogrification of Soviet elites into post-Soviet rent-seeking coalitions, see Kotz and Weir 1997: ch. 7.

The theory of rent-seeking that is usually presented in this context is inadequate since it is based on a sharp (static) distinction between functioning markets and a self-interested bureaucracy. In the transition economies, on the other hand, there is the genuine dilemma of simultaneous imperfections in both the market and politics. As Poznanski shows in his contribution to this volume, foreign strategic investors are no panacea for this dilemma.

29. "No one foresaw the scale and the collapse in output that occurred in these economies, or the extent of the erosion of fiscal revenues that stemmed partly from it," as Michel Camdessus admitted in 1994, without, however, acknowledging those authors who had predicted precisely that. Dabrowski et al. (2000, n.1) simply adjust in an ad hoc fashion the optimistic goals of the neoliberal program announced at the start of the transformation to actual outcomes. "We speak here of the transition from communism, not the transition to capitalism. It is clearly not the case that all the post-Communist countries have become, or will inevitably become, normal and successful capitalist market economies." Such a lowering of standards clearly contradicts earlier universalistic claims. See Naim 2000 for an excellent reconstruction of adhoc revisions of the Washington consensus in light of unanticipated outcomes—a classic example of what philosophers of science call immunization strategies.

30. IMF 1999b, 259; Mussa and Sevastano 1999, 27f. However, the treatment, it should be noted, was not determined by all members but by the "Wall Street-Treasury Complex" (Bhagwati), and the flexibility in its application, especially with respect to Russia, by the U.S. administration.

31. The emergence of the World Bank's good governance discourse was closely related to the fact that with the collapse of Communism the distinction between authori-

tarian (pro-Western) and totalitarian (Communist) regimes had lost the strategic rationale that Jeanne J. Kirkpatrick (1981) had given it for U.S. foreign policy. Political conditionality could now also be imposed on those authoritarian and corrupt regimes that had previously received loans in the context of the anticommunist strategy of containment.

32. Quoted in *The Economist* (1996: 26), who with reference to the headquarters of the Inter American Development Bank, speaks about the emergence of a "Santiago consensus."

33. Further on this, see *The Economist*, 18 September 1999, under the headline "Sick Patients, Warring Doctors."

34. World Bank 1996: 87, 93; on the trade-offs of different privatization policies and speeds, see World Bank 1996: chap. 3, 52.

35. These and other methodological problems are discussed in Stallings and Peres 2000: 4–11. The "reform rhetoric-realization relationship" is discussed by Murrell 1995a; cf. also Pickel 1997a.

36. Bhagwati and Srinivasan actually call for a return to the policy advice of forty years ago—a time when the Soviet Union was seen as a threat on account of its growth rates. On the political background to the resignations of Joseph Stiglitz and Ravi Kanbur, the author of the *World Development Report 2000/2001*, see Beattie 2000; Wade 2001.

37. It goes without saying that this controversy also bears strong implications for EU enlargement. In line with the comprehensive development framework, the EU's accession strategy rests on a multidimensional and institutional strategy of integration. In contrast, the orthodox alternative, which corresponds to the well-known polemic of Václav Klaus (1994) against a supposedly overregulated EU, boils down to a variant of a deregulated free trade zone, which the United States favors in its sphere of influence (Dornbusch 2000).

38. Significantly, the concepts of the comprehensive development framework have also been incorporated into the new Poverty Reduction and Growth Facility (PRGF) that the IMF plans to implement in close cooperation with the World Bank (IMF 1999c). This also applies to the recent debate on a revision of IMF conditionality (see the "Joint Note" by Wolfensohn and Fischer 2000, as well as IMF 2001). An initial example for the World Bank's implementation of the comprehensive development framework is the country assistance strategy for Ukraine, which includes a complex and extended process of negotiation with both nongovernmental organizations and the government (cf. *Transition* [World Bank] 11, no. 6, 2000/2001). These developments clearly contradict conservative proposals to abolish the IMF or to reduce it to its "core activities" (see Feldstein 1998).

39. From an orthodox modernization perspective, this is argued by Mouzelis 1993 and Fukuyama 1993; for a neomodernization perspective see Müller 1995 and Tiryakian 1995.

40. The most ambitious attempt in this respect has been undertaken by Linz and Stepan (1996), who combine an intraregional comparison of postcommunist transformations with an interregional comparison of transitions from authoritarianism to democracy in southern Europe and Latin America.

41. Hahn 1992; Arrow 1995: viii; Intriligator 1997. The limited relevance of general equilibrium theory discussed by Hahn is consistent with the theoretical objections underlying Stiglitz's (1994) critique of the Washington consensus.

42. "Liberalization and privatization will not, *per se*, automatically lead to a

demand for institutions to support well-functioning markets," as the report subsequently notes (EBRD 1999: 7).

43. See especially the work of Douglass North.

44. This is particularly evident in the *Final Report of the Reflection Group* appointed by the European Commission to explore the preconditions and implications of EU enlargement (Amato and Batt 1999); cf. European Union 1999.

Chapter 2

Transformation as a Subject of Economic Theory

László Csaba

After a decade of systemic changes in central and Eastern Europe there is a growing pessimism among specialists and the general public, both on the subject of transformation as such and on the ability of the theorists to deliver anything meaningful. This applies a fortiori to the economics profession, where a peculiar "impossibility theorem" postulates theoretical economics' inherent inability to say anything meaningful about reality. And not only the uninformed public is ready to adopt such a defeatist stance. After my presentation of an earlier version of this paper to a research seminar at a large European university, the dean of the economics department commented: In the end, there is not much to be discussed, since postcommunist transformation and economic theory are unrelated. On another occasion yet another distinguished professor noted: Economists nowadays are like philosophers, they do not care much about reality. They prefer their self-contained theoretical constructs, and the art is in discussing minor modifications within the high guild.

But there is a feeling of discontent also among area specialists. Here we find accounts of traditional Sovietology that praise its accomplishments yet simultaneously concede the field's inability to predict the collapse of the Soviet system (let alone the sequence of events) (Schroeder 1995). This is certainly an analytical flaw and reflects a tradition of putting more emphasis on the collection of facts and figures than on the analytical and theoretical frame in which these are integrated. The decisive academic issues clearly are not the size of Soviet GDP or the share of defense spending, but the reasons for the collapse of

Communism and the nature of the crisis that triggered the regime change.

Understandably, there has been much irritation from the very outset over the "intrusion"of outsiders into this area. They have been criticized for a large number of fallacies, most prominently for having imposed their academic culture and inherited preoccupations on the political consultancy and decision-making process (Murrell 1995b: 169; see also chap. 4). This feeling has evolved into bulky volumes and vitriolic pieces that speak of an all-embracing neoliberal party line (Lavigne 1995: 248f.), blame neoliberalism for being irrelevant on growth and modernization issues (van Brabant 1998: 462, 477–79), caution against a naïve minimalist approach to state interventionism (Przeworski 1997: 412–15, 427f.), or attribute the alleged regionwide recession to a "hands-off" approach (Poznanski 1999; see also his contribution to this volume). The list could be extended at will by contributions by authors from the region itself. Most recently, Joseph Stiglitz (1999), the former chief economist and senior vice president of the World Bank, accused international agencies and advisors of having imposed their noninstitutional and one-sided visions on policies of transition countries, thereby making already bad things worse.

This chapter tries to overcome this obviously unproductive confrontation. My basic thesis is that economics, when interpreted in sufficiently broad terms, can contribute meaningfully to the interpretation of facts and figures, can provide an analytical frame for arranging them, and can even suggest some lines of action for policy-making. This does not mean that economics—or any other discipline—can claim exclusivity. The subject of analysis is a multidimensional and, in many respects, open-ended socioeconomic process, so that the use of different approaches is justified. However, both methodological considerations and practical experience caution against too much eclecticism or the mixing of competing paradigms from various social science disciplines. As Jan Prybyla (1998: 359) aptly put it, "One should be sceptical about one-size-fits-all constructs but also shun deconstructivist academic woolliness for which everything depends on everything. Attempts trying to present a theory of everything and in the end, of not very much at all, are not a suitable substitute for even an inadequate economic theory." In other words, while sociological, economic, and political science or social anthropology perspectives may well never coincide, this frequently does not reflect more than different viewpoints—just as the same nude can be painted from the back, from the side, or face-to-face. Thus in what follows I adopt a consciously one-sided, narrow economic approach and try to figure out what this discipline has to contribute to our understanding of systemic change and, conversely, what economics can learn from the postcommunist experience.

Economics and/in Reality

It is an interesting subject of philosophy and methodology what is, or is not, a science, who does or does not qualify as an economist, or which scholar has contributed to an area. Both in general and even more *in concretu* this poses difficult questions. Just to take the best-known examples: Adam Smith, the founding father of the discipline, was a professor of ethics and was considered mostly a philosopher, and so was Friedrich August von Hayek. Gunnar Myrdal has been seen as a general social scientist and policy advisor, James Buchanan as a political scientist, Myron Scholes and John Harsányi as mathematicians, Arthur Lewis as a "developmentalist,"Amartya Sen as a moralist and nutritionist, Robert Fogel as a statistician, and Douglass North as an economic historian.

Nevertheless, as the statement by the dean of the economics department cited above highlights, there is a clear tendency to narrow the field. It would have seemed easy to disqualify this approach, had it not been for the entire post-war history of economic thought from which formalization and methodological preciseness emerged as the dominant trend. This is well reflected in what is usually seen as the current encyclopedia of knowledge, the four-volume *New Palgrave* (Eatwell et al. 1987). The latter does not include any reflection on systemic change. This is partly due to the time of publication. However, even a second edition is unlikely to contain a heading on transformation. It is the genre itself that has substantially different concerns.

Reviewing the opus magnum in the *Economic Journal*, R. E. Bailey (1994: 661) noted that "the late twentieth century 'student,' it seems, should have the benefit of at least one year's training in economic theory and econometrics beyond the bachelor's level, in order to be at ease with the full range of articles contained in these volumes. These are dictionaries aimed at academic professionals, not educated laymen seeking enlightenment on some obscure piece of professional jargon. Nor are they likely to satisfy undergraduates demanding instant gratification in the rush to complete a late assignment." Further: "for the general reader much of the economic analysis will remain a mystery . . . the sheer weight of technicality provides a distorted view of contemporary economics . . . or more probably, it is the great preponderance of theory relative to application which gives the impression that the entries are unduly technical" (665f.). But later on the same reviewer finds entries on analogy, induction, relativity, and even ideology, which "serve to remind one of the freedom of a pluralistic methodology enjoyed by economics. The evidence of these works is that it is a broad church indeed, and in spite of (or perhaps because of) its manifest failings as a science, it is unlikely to be forced into any oppressive methodological straight-jacket" (667).

A similarly ambivalent picture emerges if one looks at "leading" economic journals. Against the background of a narrow self-interpretation of what economic theory is and should be, it is truly surprising to see a hundred flowers flourish, both in doctrinal and methodological terms. While the tastes of the mainstream and the related promotional practices do have a strong impact, it is hard to ignore the large number of applied research and of nontechnical articles, as well as the presence of several schools of thought. In addition to the *Journal of Economic Literature*, which has a long tradition of publishing survey articles of an entire subject matter for outsiders in a fairly nontechnical fashion and earned a very high reputation for this, the American Economic Association established the *Journal of Economic Perspectives* with the expressed aim to build a bridge between academics and practitioners and to foster mutually beneficial interchanges. For anyone following the papers and proceedings published in the *American Economic Review* it would be easy to cite a large number of pieces on "real-world problems"—from economic growth and financial market problems to social security reform. Likewise such standard-setting European journals as *Economic Journal* in Britain, *Kyklos* in Switzerland, and *Weltwirtschaftliches Archiv* in Germany all exhibit a clear move toward empirically relevant and preferably accessible pieces. It is the expressed editorial policy to downplay technical submissions presenting minor refinements of previously established models. In sum, the omnipresent and almighty mainstream seems to be a strawman.

Aside from differences in subjects, differences in approaches must be taken into account. The strongest alternative to the mainstream is, of course, institutional economics. Institutional economics has two main lines: the old and the new, which differ basically in their perceptions of the mainstream. While the old institutionalism was basically hostile to formalization and the idea of methodological individualism, new institutionalist approaches attempt to use the analytical techniques that have been developed by the mainstream to address organizational and institutional issues that have fallen victim to the mainstream's level of abstraction. Contrary to the strong words normally heard in introductory courses, these two schools are strongly present in the first-rate economic journals and publishing houses. This is more surprising in the case of the old institutionalist school, but the finding is amply documented in the exhaustive reviews by W. Samuels (1995) and G. Hodgson (1998).

Institutionalism represents the renaissance of heterodox approaches in economics. These approaches emphasize the priority of organizational structure in allocating resources and the central role of cumulative causations in explaining processes. "The economy is understood as a system encompassing more than the market and undergoing systemic evolution, in part due to institutional and technological change, and, *inter alia*, the factors and forces actually operative in the economy" (Samuels 1995: 572). While formalization inevitably focuses the attention of analysts on discrete states and their characteristics, the old institutionalists see the economy fundamentally in terms of process. In addition, they are also interested in legal structures and their impact on economic processes.

Because of its broader, evolutionary approach, old institutionalism tends to downplay quantitative evidence and the entire focus on equilibrium solutions that dominates formalized thinking. While considering the state of equilibrium as a highly restricted case of the process they analyze, adherents of this school normally highlight the insurmountable difficulties in specifying comprehensive real-world situations in quantitative models and think that simplifying assumptions, made for the sake of computability, may be crippling (Hodgson 1998: 187). Old institutionalists also stress that the quest for quantitative evidence is somewhat anachronistic, as if we still lived in the nineteenth century, when mechanics was considered as the great science, or in the pre-1989 United States, when the military industry defined the best research and development options. By contrast, both money and attention have been refocused to biology, which is good news for the evolutionary approaches.

New institutionalists, as R. Coase (1998: 73) recently explained, are sharing the old institutionalism's unease about the excessively technical orientation of the mainstream. However, they do accept the rational actor model and the idea of maximizing behavior, but are interested also in different coordination mechanisms. Therefore, this line of inquiry has taken great interest in property rights and in the procedures of collective decision making. While old institutionalism is holistic and antiformalist, new institutionalists accept the relevance of formalization. However, they treat historical and structural explanations as complementary rather than opposed to mainstream economics. As two authoritative monographs on these attempts have documented, the marriage is quite fruitful (Rutherford 1994; Pejovich 1995). The cost of heterodoxy is a lower level of abstraction and less general conclusions, which actually turns out to be a benefit in applied areas.

Heterodoxy includes several complementary approaches. One is evolutionary economics, which some consider a branch of institutionalism. While the borderline is anything but clear, evolutionary approaches are much less concerned with the institutional framework than with the market process. Major characteristics of these approaches are the idea of natural selection, the focus on self-generating processes and the interest in the forces that determine the capability of adjusting to a basically hostile external environment (Nelson 1995). Given its emphasis on the natural selection process as opposed to man-made optimal design, evolutionary economics has a great deal in common with the older Austrian school.

Other heterodox approaches address the way decisions are taken and priorities set. Both processes tend to fall outside the focus of formalized analyses, which tend to take them as exogenously given. A. Dixit (1996) has brought together the transaction costs approach and policy analysis by focusing on policy formulation and policy implementation in a multiple principal–agent framework. In his analysis, the multiplicity of principals is the source of an inherently blurred system of incentives.

Economics also can, and indeed is, concerned with the ways preferences are formed. In Amartya Sen's social choice framework, rationality is not reduced to the postulates of *homo oeconomicus*, but includes prudence and even generosity (Sen 1995, 1999). Preferences are not necessarily formed in a utilitarian fashion by ordering gains. Instead states of mind, freedoms, and capabilities of living according to one's preferences must be considered. This aspect, which has also been highlighted by Bruno S. Frey (1997), helps us to better understand the formation of preferences. As Sen himself notes, the social choice approach may be particularly helpful in modeling decisions that supersede microeconomic rationality, e.g., those pertaining to the environment.

This far from exhaustive review of some of the more interesting trends in theoretical economics may suffice for the present purpose. It shows that the international agencies which are ritually targeted by critics of transformation are not the fountain of economic knowledge. Furthermore, the oversimplified world of an introductory microeconomics textbook does not represent the state of art currently available in the profession. Lamenting the neoliberal straitjacket, the imperialism of formalization or the one-dimensional economic man thus means fighting a strawman. Such claims, which feature quite prominently in part of the transition literature, reflect a lack of information at best, and manipulation at worst. Analyses by mainstream economists themselves forecast a revival of an institutional focus and a stronger empirical reasoning at the cost of the previously fashionable deductive-normative approaches (Colander 2000: 130–32). And no lesser authority than Robert Solow (2000: 152–54) cautions against too strong an emphasis on trying to formalize and optimize everything.

Transformation: Theory and Evidence

The above sketched patchy summary of economic theory has indicated an agenda quite different from the one cultivated in the transition countries. Many of the topics that have dominated policy debates in Eastern Europe over the last decade have been misperceived, have lacked relevance, or have been purely ideological in nature. In particular, they have born little or no relationship to the broadly defined subject of economics—i.e., improving well-being by managing scarce resources. From this perspective, the controversy over shock therapy versus gradualism, the idea that any country can opt for a freely chosen pattern of governance, the quest for optimal privatization technologies, the alleged benefits of protectionist policies, and many other subjects seem strangely insignificant.

With the benefit of hindsight, the controversy over the costs of stabilization or the calls for industrial policies have missed the point. I have not come across any modeling that would have offered a credible alternative path or development pattern against which the actual costs of transition could be measured. True, there is no shortage of claims that transition costs were excessive. However, these claims are mere reflections of subjective value judgments, that is, political rather than academic statements, since their originators are usually not able to specify what costs could be considered acceptable at the margin and how such cost reduction could be achieved. References to absolute magnitudes are obviously meaningless, while references to other countries beg the question of comparability. For instance, the idea of deliberate industrial policy or a thickly knit social safety net presupposes a strong state that has simply been nonexistent, since the crisis of the Soviet empire has been triggering the entire process. Had there been a strong Soviet state, most of the former socialist camp would have, willy-nilly, still continued to experiment by tinkering with various sorts of market socialism, instead of trying—and probably often erring in—various modes of transition to some brand of free market capitalism.

If transformation is the child of crisis, traditional sovietological comparisons of various goals and plans could hardly serve as the best measures to evaluate governmental success or failure, let alone the progress of the entire process—especially since many of the most relevant aspects of the market order emerged spontaneously, quite outside the framework of formal institutions and legislation. This is most striking in the case of the expansion of the private sector. In this area, stagnation of the grand—and most contested—privatization projects could neatly coincide with a blossoming of new start-ups, as well as with a creeping process of spontaneous privatization. The speed of actual—not purely formal, bookkeeping—change in ownership patterns and restructuring did not prove to be among the independent, freely calibrated variables, the magnitude of which might have been a matter of deliberation.

Likewise, the rate of growth, one of the most important macroindicators, could not be set at will, as in a modeling excercise. It proved to be the outcome of a series of intended and unintended processes triggered by governmental actions and spontaneous processes, external and internal factors. If this is so, the very idea of a growth-generating policy seems to be misplaced. Governments do not, even in theory, possess the means whereby they could be efficient and thus could be held accountable for mastering a task that is in any case not theirs alone. While many of those trained in observing the rituals of the planned economy would interpret the predominant spontaneity as a sign of crisis, or as chaotic, adherents of the evolutionary or Austrian schools would consider it as perfectly normal, since the market economy is the only order that is the outcome of spontaneous human action, not of human deliberation or human design (Hayek 1989).

There are, however, areas where public policy does shape the actual mold of the otherwise spontaneous order. One of these fields is inflation, especially when structural factors, liberalization, productivity gains, and overall uncertainty, coupled with low credibility of the government and the newly created financial institutions, all point toward sustaining inflation. Meanwhile economic theory does provide a host of arguments proving the vices of inflation and the virtues of price stability.

Transformation experience has added two important empirical findings to our common knowledge. First, the evidence for the twenty-seven countries in transition shows that there has not been a single case in which softer policies would have resulted in a smaller drop in output or a smaller decline in living standards over the longer run (Gelb and de Melo 1997; Fischer et al. 1997). Furthermore, no country could enter a path of sustained growth without having brought down inflation to at least moderate levels. Conversely, all countries that could sustain disinflation did enter a growth path. The later disinflation occurred, the longer the transformational recession lasted. Premature reflation or growth based on the expansion of domestic demand, by contrast, invariably triggered renewed austerity, from the Czech Republic to Romania, in each and every case (Csaba 2001).

There are two interesting related findings. First, the expansion of growth to, say, East Asian levels has nowhere materialized. The reasons for this are a subject of controversy. Some argue that inadequate savings and overextended welfare spending do not allow for a real takeoff and a growth rate of GDP of above 4–7 percent (Gomulka 1998: 36–40). Other, more theoretical writings indicate deeper causes and note, first, that steady-state growth cannot be meaningfully raised by governmental policies and, second, that the growth-promoting effects of disinflation are limited (Barro 1997).

From this perspective, countries such as Poland, the Czech Republic, and Hungary can no longer count on the effects of disinflation. Instead, new and more lasting sources of endogenous growth need to be created, like those related to human capital formation (an area rather neglected in the previous decade). The latter would be important not only for growth, but for more general welfare reasons as well. As A. Young (1998) has demonstrated in a formal model, research and development outlays may not necessarily translate into higher output, yet, can be welfare enhancing by improving the well-being of the average consumer.

A related issue is why inflation has not come down from the moderate levels, as had been expected by most of those working with formal models. While bringing inflation down from very high levels has been expansionary rather than contractionary (Easterly 1996), the evidence on the effects of reducing the inflation rate from moderate to single-digit levels has previously been mixed. While an authoritative compendium of papers, published by the IMF and the National Bank of Hungary, presents theoretical and empirical evidence supportive of further disinflation, contributions to the same volume indicate in detail how intricate the credibility and coordination problems that need to be overcome are (Cottarelli and Szapáry 1998).

Here we have arrived at an important point, where quantitative empirical evidence has helped to overcome previously hotly debated theoretical issues in development and transition economics. While historically and institutionally oriented pieces offer analytical insights into how certain processes come about, quantitative tests help to arrive at generalizable conclusions that integrate bits and pieces stemming from different episodes. One of the more reassuring elements of the ongoing controversy is that, despite all methodological differences and disputes, formalized methods have delivered comparable cross-country evidence that is useful to settle at least some of those disputes.

Another area of major controversy was liberalization. It has several dimensions, as prices, wages, trade and financial markets, and later asset markets have to be freed from various entry and price-setting barriers. Whether this has to be done remains a subject of political debate, but it is no longer a matter of economic controversy. What remain highly controversial though are the speed, the scope, and not least the sequencing of liberalizing steps. Those dissatisfied with the current state of affairs either consider the price of liberalization as too high or regard the sequencing as mistaken. However, this view does not take the lower level of development and the legacy of decades of isolation into account. The ensuing distortions, rigidities, and behavioral deformations have increased the costs of adjustment in the postcommunist countries.

In retrospect, it is also no longer legitimate to question whether export-oriented growth is feasible. Exports of central European countries have expanded at a staggering pace in the 1990s. This was achieved through a reorientation of trade from soft CMEA markets to OECD markets, so that the EU now accounts for a larger share of trade in Hungary, Poland, and the Czech Republic than in Portugal or Spain. Opening up the economies helped orient structural change in that it contributed to the supply response and the overcoming of bottlenecks and shortages. Quite in line with Latin American experience (surveyed in Nogues and Gulati 1994), sustainability of trade liberalization proved to be the key. While more gradual opening strategies reverted to protectionism, sustained liberalization helped unlock other factors of economic growth, provided it was part of comprehensive reforms and could thus induce mutually reinforcing adjustment processes.

These findings are supported by the experience of the transition countries: those that could sustain the large coherent macropolicies across the decade, such as Poland and the Czech Republic or Hungary, have benefited from the same improvements. Meanwhile, those countries where policies proved unsustainable (e.g., Romania, Bulgaria, Albania, and Russia) or where such policies have never been launched (e.g., Ukraine or Serbia) are lagging behind. This is of course the macro view, which is of little comfort to those who have been crowded out of business or laid off. From the point of view of theory, however, it is the macro level that really matters (Solow 2000: 151).

Finally, privatization, the third pillar of economic reform in transition countries, needs to be addressed. In the literature referred to in the introductory section we recurringly find the view that the problem of ownership change has been overemphasized vis-à-vis other issues. In retrospect, it is hard to share this view. The best proof is indirect: none of the countries that has experimented with various "third way" solutions or has opted for a higher rather than lower share of public ownership has achieved higher growth rates, higher capital accumulation (both human and physical capital included), or lower unemployment. The comparisons that underpin this interpretation are rather trivial: the Baltic states compared to Belarus, Poland compared to Ukraine, Hungary compared to Bulgaria send unambiguous messages. Thus the burden of proof must be reversed. Those advocating a slower pace of privatization and more state guidance have to come up with more convincing arguments.[1]

These observations do not justify the ideological posturing of the early transition period. Nor should ownership change be mistaken for progress in economic well-being, especially in the short run. I still adhere to my earlier position that there is a natural rate of privatization[2] that is hard to override through direct government intervention, since the process is an outcome of the interplay of a series of factors and agents, domestically and internationally (Csaba 1995). For example, those who wanted to conclude major deals at the low ebb of the emerging market crisis were disappointed or simply stripped of a lot of assets. But the proof that a relatively fast emergence of a system based on private property is feasible and represents a guarantee against a backslide to statist totalitarian practices has indeed been delivered. Comparing Russia with Belarus or Slovenia with Serbia-Montenegro clearly shows that even those countries where structural reforms were delayed have achieved demonstrable gains in systemic terms compared to those that are still tinkering with improving the socialist heritage, manipulating old institutions via traditional techniques.

Privatization in these terms ceases to be a primarily quantitative issue, a plan-target to be attained at a fixed point in time. Rather, and quite like in market economies, it develops into a qualitative issue, namely, of delineating the proper spheres of business and politics, business and state administration. From this perspective it is not the number of commodity exchanges or the number of private shareholders that defines the path of progress. Also, the share of nonstate property in total national assets ceases to be a relevant criterion of measurement. What really matters is whether we see Korean or Italian type of intertwinings, whether we see politically unbiased allocative decisions, whether we witness the emergence of a capital market and banking arrangements that put up institutional barriers so that politically leveraged decisions will not occur in the future. From this perspective, it is the scope rather than the size of the capital market that really matters. It is the presence of strategic investors in the financial sector and the extent of foreign ownership that are useful indicators. With a decreasing share of industry in GDP—27.5 percent in 1999 in Hungary—generalizations based on the progress of ownership change in the industrial sector or even only in manufacturing seem to be of historical value at best. Meanwhile, progress or regress in the financial sector, transparent or nontransparent ways of conducting business, availability or lack of prudential arrangements, and disclosure requirements according to international standards are the real criteria of evaluation, rather than any arbitrary set of quantitative plan-targets.

From this at least two conclusions can be inferred. First, the type of market economy that emerges in individual transforming countries depends on how the issues discussed above have been resolved. Second, privatization is going to have efficiency-enhancing effects on two levels. One is the immediate one—static efficiency. Overcoming flawed incentives can produce miracles in terms of profitability and productivity by resulting in a better use of available assets. In dynamic terms, however, investment has to be factored in. Depending on the way new investment is financed, the potential for catching up, inherent in the Solow model (1956), is going to materialize. It is important to underline that the neoclassical catch-up model presupposes the availability of precisely those institutions and incentives for appropriate resource allocation that are just emerging in the transition economies. Thus their progress in financial sector reform will likely determine the efficiency gains from privatization in the short and medium run, as well as the growth-generating effects of ownership change in the longer run.

Lessons from the East Asian and Russian crises and contagion of 1997–99 have underscored the importance of institution building as the core of sound and sustainable development. As a most insightful summary paper of Stanley Fischer (1999) explains in detail, the crises have not proved the overall line of financial liberalization wrong, but they have definitely called attention to the eminent need for better regulation and higher transparency. What deserves attention, however, is that none of the fundamental reform suggestions go in the direction of capital controls or undoing liberalization in the financial sector. Instead, they all aim at fairer burden sharing by inducing more transparency and by "bailing the private sector in." Our more general considerations of the need to incorporate institutional and qualitative elements in devising a policy framework are directly reflected in proposals to update and tighten the Basle core principles on capital adequacy (Caprio and Honohan 1999). One of the most intriguing lessons of the Asian contagion has been the risks associated with mechanical quantitative risk assessment models. In particular, cross-ownership may render capital adequacy numbers irrelevant. The wide-ranging proposals all point toward enhancing personal responsibilities of bank managers, increasing risk awareness, raising reserve requirements, and introducing old-fashioned solidity requirements and disclosure practices. Such precautionary measures are a more appropriate reaction to financial market volatility than rationing or state discretion. These findings apply to transition as well as to developing countries, that is, to both groups of emerging economies.

Thus, a strong state rather than a minimal state, a competent state administration rather than a cheap state administration, is required for a successful transformation. A strong state is not necessarily a strongly interventionist one since its indicator of success is output (effects brought about by its intervention) rather than input (the number and variety of measures instituted to ward off responsibility for outcomes). Moreover, those who can be confident in the efficacy of their actions may not feel the same need to intervene.

On the Political Economy of Second-Generation Tasks

What has been said in the two previous sections leads to issues of political economy. The available evidence clearly shows that no country can avoid the tasks and pains of economic reforms, provided wealth is to increase and development to be sustained. The ongoing differentiation of the group of transforming economies also implies a differentiation of research subjects. For those studying the laggards, a great deal of policy analysis remains to be done. They have to address the question of how to graduate from the present stage to a more mature one. Although this is interesting per se, it no longer raises open theoretical issues. For those studying the more advanced or front-runner cases, a new agenda emerges. The countries that have successfully mastered the first-generation tasks now have to create financially sustainable welfare systems, find new models for rural development in densely populated regions, and address the problem of environmental decay. What is at stake is the redefinition of the role of government in an increasingly complex and globalized world.

This implies that what John Williamson (1994: 26–28) has called the Washington consensus has indeed remained a shared vision of good policies for advanced and less advanced countries alike. This consensus has informed the deliberations leading to European Monetary Union (Lányi 1997) and has found its way into development economics. As J. Waelbroeck (1998: 341f.) rightly stresses, the original term is misleading insofar as it suggests an almighty global government located at the IMF headquarters, which is imposing its views on a large number of undisciplined agents. If nothing else, the failure of the IMF to manage the contagion effect of the East Asian crisis on emerging markets in 1997–98 has overwhelmingly demonstrated the lack of such a supranational coordination mechanism, operated consciously by a group of technocrats.[3] On the contrary, what we witness here is voluntary compliance of a growing number of countries with a set of shared principles. These countries are supporting democratic values not only for efficiency considerations, but also for their own sakes. Therefore, it seems legitimate to follow Waelbroeck's suggestion and speak of "one world consensus." The underlying convergence of rules and values has been related to global interdependence, the information revolution, and the globalization of financial markets, as well as the resultant flow of ideas. These shape the norms and expectations of a growing number of opinion leaders and citizens alike.

The commitment to the Washington consensus has two implications. First, at the level of theory, there is no longer the confidence instilled by Keynes that macroeconomic equilibrium can be restored by simple devices. Economists now understand that rational expectations make economies difficult to control and that phenomena such as lack of credibility can deprive policies of their effectiveness.

Second, policy advice should not be directed toward a group that is but one among many shaping outcomes. Many other actors—from households to foreign investment funds—need to be convinced of the virtues of reforms. In line with the public choice school, policy-makers should be seen as self-interested actors maximizing their own gains rather than as selfless heroes. Thus, the target audience is the educated public at large, and the job is to improve governance, i.e., to elaborate procedures and institutions that incorporate proper theoretical findings into the interaction of state, private agencies, and groups of individuals.

This state of affairs has further implications. There is a growing convergence and similarity of the agenda of policy reform in the various country groups under discussion. However, this does not make the lives of analysts and policy advisers easier. In the case of second-generation reforms, there is no "proven way." The goals to be attained need to be discussed and elaborated. Normative concepts, such as those proposed by János Kornai (1997), can help to specify the agenda. Yet, there is no such thing as a single optimal outcome set by technical desiderata or considerations. Owing to the differing nature of tasks, the lengthy democratic decision-making process cannot be avoided. This is a major difference from the early transformation period. In the case of pension reform, for instance, the speed at which legislation is adopted says nothing about the sustainability or the quality of the arrangement; nor does the size of the fully funded pillar serve as a point of orientation or a success indicator. Fully funded systems can crash and so can pay-as-you-go systems.

As a consequence, issues such as political feasibility or coalition building are gaining relevance vis-à-vis traditional considerations of coherence or analytical simplicity. Dynamic modeling may be one of the more important analytical tools in forecasting what kind of compromise is self-defeating and what might be self-sustaining. Quantitative modeling does play a crucial role in specifying financial preconditions as well as conditions under which these can be met. The longer the time horizon of a reform the greater is the relevance of these approaches and the need for integrating them into the decision-making process.

One of the fundamental questions in redefining the role of the state in a democratic society is whether it is going to be captive to or regulative of vested interests (Rodrik 1996: 22–24). The thinner the dividing line between interest representation of various sorts and public organs, as well as between business and administration, the lower is the probability of arriving at Pareto-optimal outcomes. Corruption and rule evasion, often seen as a smaller evil or even as a lubricant in backward societies, may become serious impediments to change for the better. This might prove a particular challenge to postcommunist societies, where the traditionally extended underground economy and a decade of most ineffective legislation have made norm-breaching behavior more accepted than in most advanced countries.

More common causes of government failure in the second-generation tasks include: (1) inability to make commitments; (2) coalition formation and bargaining that dilute the agenda; (3) destructive competition, inherent in party politics, that thwarts the implementation of generally approved measures; (4) uncertainty about the consequences of change; (5) the simplicity constraint (the best professional arguments do not always sell well); and (6) secrecy of bureaucratic decision making, leaving the door open for special interest legislation (Stiglitz 1998b: 8–16).

There is no trivial textbook solution to these challenges. Misalignment of incentives is a nearly inevitable by-product of the type of democratic decision-making processes that were shown above to be inevitable in an attempt to find the best and most feasible solutions for reconstructing entire macrosystems. Making use of sociology and organizational science in devising the appropriate task force might be a tremendous challenge. In Hungary, for instance, public finance reform tended to founder more than once on the composition of the task force, drawn basically from among vested interests. The failure to combine technical economic imperatives with the political requirements necessary to secure public acceptance of reform policies at a later stage of implementation often resulted in stalemate. Only crises and coups, deplored by many analysts, could move things out of such a state of low-level equilibrium.[4] At the same time, improvised solutions resulting from these exigencies have rarely been sustainable and have delivered only part of what is technically achievable at any given point in time.

Another problem of consensual decision making has to do with the tendency to dilute concepts through excessive use. The more universally accepted a concept is, the higher the likelihood of it being broadened to the point where it loses its meaning. This has happened to such core concepts as the social market economy. As the excellent survey by D. Cassel and S. Rauhut (1998: 17–24) has demonstrated, political compromises and unintended consequences in the pursuit of a social market economy in Germany, in particular the extensive redistributive practices, reflect not only unfavorable real-world conditions but also the limits of the very concept of a social market economy. Therefore, it seems that this concept should be used only for denoting an approach, an emphasis on *Ordnungspolitik* and the idea of a competitive order trying to strike a balance with social justice, rather than for deriving concrete policy prescriptions.

And here we have come to an important conclusion. As the example would be easy to replicate for a series of widely shared concepts, from subsidiarity to optimal regulatory areas, there is no quick fix. Subscribing to the interpretation of what economic theory has to say that is offered in this chapter does not impose a straitjacket on further research. While providing a framework for conducting productive discussions, it is unlikely to settle disputes over methodology or policy proposals. Quite in line with the original Hayekian idea, what is likely to emerge is competition among systems, not in the sense of capitalism versus communism, but in the sense of varieties of capitalism (Dimitrov et al. 1999; Bara and Szabó 2000). This competition is already very real. In the West, the Swedish and the American model exist. In China, Russia, or Africa, unintended but powerful processes of decentralization have increased the number of different trajectories. The more we focus on the study of real-world systems and are thus forced to take into account empirical evidence, the more inclined we might be to follow Hodgson's call to redefine economics as the study of systems (Hodgson 1998: 190). In so doing we will not be forced to give up the traditions and methods of the discipline. Rather, these traditions and methods can continue to serve as an analytical framework for incorporating perspectives and worldviews provided by other branches of social science. Following Marshall, we would see economics not as a body of concrete truths but as an engine of discovery. For this point of view the mastery of science involves the acquisition of analytical skills needed to formulate relevant questions to which answers can be sought. This implies that with cross-cultural transmissions economic ideas also mutate, as W. Barber (1995: 1947) correctly observes. The point in sticking to the rituals of each discipline is, among others, retaining consistency of the viewpoint as well as the ability to communicate cross-cultural realities. It is a common language that makes specific and individual experiences transmittable to others.

Respecting the limits of a paradigm is also a way of becoming more open to competing approaches. In any event, it will always be the task of the policy advisor and policymaker to decide on the most suitable policy mix to achieve specific goals under given circumstances. No amount of compromise on the part of scientists with competing perspectives can deliver such a policy solution. On the contrary, it might be a good idea if policymakers and laymen could be sure what kind of questions economists, as opposed to sociologists or historians, are more likely to answer in a satisfactory manner, and which they cannot even attempt to answer. Thus, issues pertaining to wealth creation and maximization may be more properly addressed to this guild than are moral issues, legitimating principles, justice, and many other facts of life that are taken for granted by economists. One of the more obvious ways of appreciating other approaches and disciplines is to expect them to deliver answers to questions on which economists claim ignorance, though their presence is already implicit in economic assumptions or propositions.[5]

This is not a call to return to the intuitive economics of the nineteenth century. On the contrary, as the insightful analysis of W. J. Baumol (2000) shows, the contribution of twentieth-century economics was precisely that enhanced rigor, more abundant data, and more sophisticated methods allowed for more powerful empirical studies. Similarly Solow (2000: 151) underlines that macroeconomics will always remain the heart of economic theory "for the best possible reason: the need to understand current events, especially unfortunate ones, and formulate policies—even benign neglect is a policy—to deal with them. For the same reason, the characteristically close connection between macrotheory and empirical work is unlikely to change."

Notes

Preliminary versions of this chapter were discussed at seminars at the University of Helsinki, Free University of Berlin, Budapest University of Economics and Public Administration and TU Bergakademie Freiberg. Critical comments by seminar participants and the editors of this volume are appreciated. I also benefited from suggestions by my colleague Kamilla Lányi.

1. The Chinese experience, which has not followed the overall trends described above, is often invoked as an objection to the mainstream theory of transition. For my view on this contentious issue, see Csaba 1996, where I argue that the two cases cannot be compared for various theoretical and methodological reasons.
2. Just like NAIRU, the natural rate of privatization is neither constant nor exogenously determined, but follows from the changing pattern within the system. See Phelps (2000) on NAIRU (nonaccelerating inflation rate of unemployment).
3. This is likely to become even more explicit, if only part of the propositions of the Meltzer Commission for reforming the IMF are adopted (Meltzer and Sachs 2000).
4. For instance, the Polish wrestling over stabilization in 1987–89 left no way out but the shock stabilization by Balcerowicz. Another case in point might be the March 1995 Bokros Package. It was elaborated secretly and surprised even some cabinet members.
5. The economic approach has challenged a variety of disciplines by pushing its adversaries to take stock of what their paradigms have to deliver (Lazear 2000). Likewise, though probably in a less explicit fashion, economists have drawn on new findings from biology, psychology, and mathematics. Our knowledge about actors is greatly influenced by these findings.

Chapter 3

The Crisis of Transition as a State Crisis

Kazimierz Z. Poznanski

At the center of this analysis of postcommunist transition are two of its most striking aspects—state failure and foreign ownership. The analysis begins with an attempt to explain the regionwide recession not as an inevitable legacy of Communism but as a state-made production collapse. It is not state errors of judgment but the interests of its movers—reformers and others—that are behind this negative turn. Next, the analysis turns to the question of ownership reform to show that the same private interests are responsible for the state's creation of a dysfunctional capitalism where capital is mostly foreign and labor is domestic. Both these problematic outcomes are presented as sufficient to consider the whole postcommunist transition in the region a failure. Given the critical role of the state in derailing reforms, the failure of transition has to be viewed as a state failure.

One should look at the transition from communism to capitalism not from the perspective of its end position, but from its beginnings. This is how evolutionary thinkers from the so-called Viennese school, such as F. A. Hayek (1988), K. Popper (1943), or J. A. Schumpeter (1992), advise us to examine social reality. All things have their beginnings, and what happens thereafter and what transpires at the end are somehow determined by these starting points (Poznanski 1993). For this very reason, if one is unable to explain the genesis of something, one is also unable to understand the phenomenon at stake. The common, if not routine, way of examining the transition today, however, is to look the other way around, from the end point backward. This is the case in large part because the transition is taken mostly as an objective and not as a process. So understood, the transition becomes an exercise in escapism from the disliked reality of broken communism built around the state. The hardships of the process of reaching the desired objective are thus largely ignored. The focus is on the final solution, a market-based order, which seems to be within easy reach.

If we start our analysis from the right point, the postcommunist transition has to be viewed as basically a state project and not a market project. Though the market is the ultimate objective of the transition, the process of getting there is mainly in the state's hands. From this perspective, whatever happens to the economic system has to be explained in terms of what happens to the state. And what occurs to the economy itself, therefore, has to be linked to the state as well, since, as an evolutionary (in fact, any institutional) economist knows, any economy works the way its system works. Following this general logic of analysis I argue below that, if one cuts through imponderables, the transition is a process in which markets are formed by a crisis-ridden state. Given the poor record of state agency in general, the transition has run the risk of failure from the very outset, but the fact that the state left communism in the midst of a serious crisis made such failure all the more predictable. Now, ten years down the road, there is sufficient evidence to claim that the transition has indeed become a real failure, and it can be demonstrated that the failure of the transition stems not from the fact that good markets did not emerge, but rather from the fact that bad states did not deliver them.

That reforms have really been terribly misguided is demonstrated by their two central problematic outcomes. Dysfunctional states have generated unusually defective—imperfect—markets that instantly caused an exceptionally massive regionwide recession. This recession damaged local economies enough to make firms ripe for easy takeovers by foreign investors. More important, driven by personal concerns, state officials have targeted foreign investors for sales of local firms. Thus, unprecedented recession has been followed by an equally unheard-of massive foreign takeover of domestic capital assets at drastically discounted prices.

Transition Fallacies

Ideas can help solve real—practical—problems as faced by individual actors and groups, but they also can obscure such real-life problems. Ideas can confuse reality in various ways. One is to create the appearance of major change where there actually is either none or only very little taking place. Upbeat ideas then replace reality and push society into compliance with downbeat reality. Reality may indeed get even worse, but such regress will not be widely realized. This is the worst consequence of taking some escapist ideas for social reality. This, as I would like to call it, escapist way of thinking is exactly what most postcommunist reformers, and their backers, have adopted as a concept of transition. It is a dichotomist vision, where choices in front of reformers entail a market and a plan, that is, the state. The market and state are substitutes, and the difference between communism and capitalism is that the first basically means states, while the second essentially means markets. The transition from communism to capitalism is thus about substituting states with markets, eliminating states and establishing markets.

Thinking about the transition exclusively in terms of a replacement of communism by capitalism immediately brings positive images of change because we tend to associate capitalism with efficiency and progress, whereas communism is associated with waste and regression. Thus, when as a result of reforms the state agency is withdrawing and/or deteriorating, this itself is taken as evidence of systemic progress. As understood in this conventional approach, in the place of the "old," inferior state, a "new," but also superior, market (as a substitute) is stepping in.

For the same reason, this perspective on the transition projects an image of reforms as something easy and almost given. Seen as an artificially created enemy of markets, states just have to be pushed out of their way. Markets are natural, coming on their own when human instincts are allowed to express themselves. Eliminating states as economic agents of any significance is conceived as automatically bringing in markets. Therefore, it is not that systemic replacement—capitalism—has to be built; it is rather a result of the destruction of what previously existed in the way of a system.

Everything about this dominant paradigm is wrong, including the view of markets and states as substitutes. They are not, unless we are talking about an excess of the market or an excess of the state. But as a general proposition as it is used in transition debates, such a view is an inexcusable oversimplification. Markets and states are not substitute "goods" but complementary "goods," so their "consumption" must be joint. When left alone, either market or plan (and state as its animator), these institutions become useless if not hazardous for a given national economy.

It is quite correct to think of capitalism as superior to communism, and this is how evolutionary economics views both systems. But it is incorrect to assume that moving from communism to capitalism always means progress. It should, but it is not a given since both systems come in many varieties, none of which resemble textbook descriptions. In other words, each system comes in different degrees of perfection/imperfection. Clearly, the worst type of capitalism is hardly superior to communism at its best. Consequently, the transition from communism to capitalism may also lead to a systemic decline. Besides, all social institutions, economic or political, are human-built devices, and this equally applies to markets and states. The market is no more "natural" to human beings than the state in the sense that markets reflect normal and states reflect perverse instincts. It is not the instincts that produce institutions but the requirements of survival. Institutions are natural only in the sense that they serve these needs of survival. And facilitating exchange through markets is seen as needed for survival and, thus, as natural as allowing for their regulation through states (Stiglitz 1998b).

When one takes this evolutionary—truly institutional—approach, then communism has to be understood not so much as a social system with an excess of state but as one burdened with a bad state (Poznanski 1996). Moreover, it is not so much that markets are completely lacking under communism but that they are bad markets. States are bad because, with their wrongheaded ideology, they are permissive, willing to bail out the wrongdoers, who care not for costs and/or quality. Markets are also bad since, given the hostility of the state, they were mostly informal and rent-oriented. Since the state under late communism was bad, or failing, the transition had more to do than just restrict the state's scope in order to make room for markets. What was necessary was the reform of both the state and the market, and not simply a substitution of one by the other. While a simultaneous transformation of both was needed, the major challenge was to make sure that the balance between the two institutions, market and state, was not upset too much. In this sense, the transition was mainly a balancing act for the state to play (Poznanski 2000).

In this act, the role of the state is not to get out of the market's way, but instead to engage in an institution-building process. But to do it in a "natural" way, the state would have to get into the time-consuming business of facilitating the evolution of more formal and profit-oriented markets. And to pursue it in a "natural" way, the state would have to permit the existing institutions to work as a basis for the new, or revised, system. Most important, for the state to be able to do this job, it would have to be ensured that the state itself is not undergoing too radical a change.

Grand Delusion

The mainstream academic crowd in the transition debate believes not only that the postcommunist transition is a substitution, but also that in reality this is what is happening. In their eyes, the evidence of a parallel state withdrawal from the economy and an incoming market are more than abundant. The rather sudden end to the communist practice of plan targets, including price fixing, is viewed as one such piece of overwhelming evidence. A less sudden, but quite determined, disposal of public assets (capital), or privatization, seems to provide such proof of systemic substitution as well.

But as evolutionary theory would suggest, no such substitution is necessary, and it is rarely even possible. The practice of transition in Eastern Europe illustrates both points. As envisioned by the mainstream school, substitution of states with markets is largely an illusion. As long as the transition has been taking place in any given economy, the only real change has been not so much in the extent of state involvement, but in its specific reach, or function. At the end of the day, when a new role for the state had emerged, the state remained almost as powerful as it used to be.

There is no denying that central plans were given up, and quickly, as the main tool for state managing of national production. In this sense, the state has definitely moved out of the sphere of production. In this role under communism, the state was a dynamic player, mobilizing resources for constant capital expansion. What was missed by the mainstream school is the fact that while recently moving out of this area of production the state invented a new role for itself. What transition reforms did was at the same time to add a static role for the state to divide, or distribute, the existing capital.

This fact of a substitution, not between market and state but within the state itself, has been overlooked for a simple reason. Disposal of assets, through sales or giveaways, is typically seen as evidence of the state moving out of the economy. Indeed, the state-owned sector is shrinking as assets are disposed. But when defining transition we have to look at the process of disposal only. And if we do this, it should be obvious that nobody else but the state conducts the disposal. Since this is a new role, there is no withdrawal of the state during the transition but instead there is expansion.

It is not difficult to demonstrate that by assuming this new role, the postcommunist state more than compensated for the elimination of its heavy involvement in production. We just have to keep in mind that in the communist days the state was basically able to decide about the allocation of the annual surplus. This was a percentage of the annual income left after covering the running costs. But with the turn to the disposal of assets, the state is in a position to allocate the accumulated stock of assets that generates of the whole national product.

It is obvious to any economist that production is a function of capital without which no production is possible. The value of capital is derivative of the value of production that is generated with this capital. The assets—capital—represent a multiple of a national product in any economy. It takes several units of capital to make one unit of national product. Thus, while, practically speaking, the planning of production under communism involved only a fraction of the national product, postcommunist asset disposal involves a considerably greater proportion of the national product.

Taken to its logical conclusion, the above fact suggests that postcommunism as a process of shifting from communism to capitalism does not essentially differ from communism in terms of the state's scope. Basically state run, the transition thus appears to be an extension of communism at least on this one, very critical account. But, in fact, there are many other aspects of the transition that are reminiscent of the basic logic of communism. There are indeed so many of them that one is tempted to make a general proposition that the transition is a process of building capitalism with the hands of communism.

This impression gets even stronger when one considers the fact that by assuming the role of a distributor of the entire public capital the state did not change another feature of communist economics—the lack of assigned property rights. Under communism, at least formally speaking, capital was in nobody's hands. It was used by the decision makers, members of the party/state apparatus, without the right to dispose of it for their own benefit. Now, with the advent of privatization, assets are for disposal but the apparatus that has the right to control does not have the right to the proceeds, at least not legally.

These elements of institutional continuity should be enough for any critical analyst of the communist system to become doubtful about the easy success of the transition to capitalism. The transition process is basically a planning process with respect to asset disposal, since left to their own devices, states plan and do not respond to a market. And this is a planning process that entails resources that are in the form of unclaimed assets. The combination of these two elements, plans and commons, cannot be expected to produce anything beneficial, certainly not without special precautions.

Surely, rather than follow the mainstream view of postcommunist transition as a linear progress to an all-market system of capitalism, it would be wiser to see the process as open-ended. In fact, as all evolutionary thinkers tell us, systemic change of any kind is an open-ended process. Schumpeter, for example, who greatly disliked socialism, did not preclude that it might defeat capitalism, and argued that socialism may appear in many forms, including Soviet-type communism. Applied to the transition, his theory would imply that a return of capitalism is not a given but may be defeated by communism, again, in more than one way.

"Healthy" Recession

To test which theoretical position, mainstream or evolutionary, is closer to reality, one may try to use each of them to explain the single most striking initial event—the regionwide recession. The most amazing aspect of the ongoing reforms in Eastern Europe is that whenever there has been an attempt to implement them, these reforms produced an economic recession of unheard of proportions. Thus, the best way of studying the postcommunist transition is to explain it through an economic analysis of what has caused what appears to be the most striking, unusual aspect of transition.

After the political surprise of the Communist collapse in the region, another surprise, this time economic, followed: the regionwide recession. From 1989 onward, Eastern Europe, including the European parts of the former Soviet Union, has been submerged in a recession that has cost about 40 percent of its collective product. The least affected regions saw production going down by about 20 percent (e.g., Hungary and Poland); in many countries the decline reached more than 30 percent (e.g., East Germany), even 50 percent (e.g., Russia) or more (Lithuania, with 60 percent).

This also happens to be a very long-lasting recession, with many countries not yet in a recovery (e.g., Russia and Ukraine) and some hitting their second recession (e.g., Bulgaria in 1997 and the Czechs in 1998). Most likely the region as a whole will not be out of the recession or restore its prerecession production level before late in the next decade, meaning that technically speaking the recession will last at least fifteen years. The postcommunist recession should be viewed as the worst downturn in modern history, deeper and more durable than the Great Depression of the 1930s.

However, it is not only the extent of the economic catastrophe—production decline, emerging unemployment, or escalating poverty—that is truly amazing, but also the fact that this event gets almost no attention among economists working on the transition. Those who take the view of transition as a move from communism to capitalism usually cannot reconcile their positive position on systemic change with the striking reality of recession. How come, at the time of what they perceive as a progressive systemic change, all of the economies of the region have gone into an unprecedented recession?

As a rule, the presence of this postcommunist recession is denied, including statements that what is seen is due to poor statistical reporting of macroeconomic developments. Decline in output is said to be overstated by imprecise Communist statistics, which suffered from manipulation by the planners and state managers trying to falsely claim strong output growth. At the same time, postcommunist statistics supposedly cannot keep up with the pace of change and underreport the actual extent of expansion, the buoyant private sector, which operates in the gray area, or the effect of qualitative changes brought by product differentiation.

When not altogether denied, the transition recession is typically presented as some sort of fatalistic event, though fortunately a costless one and for this reason not worth examining closely. Economic downturn is inevitable because of the kind of deficiencies left behind by the Communist-era system; and not so painful since the collapse mostly works to remove these deficiencies. These opinions come mostly from the postcommunist reformers themselves, largely from the outspoken group of Polish economists linked to the region's first radical shock-therapy type of reforms.

This argumentation, while never fully articulated, can be traced to a number of sources, including the interesting book on the synthesis of the transition by Balcerowicz (1995). It is a representative work, also in the sense that it almost ignores the issue of recession. More than three hundred pages long, this book devotes only one or two full pages to the recession. On one occasion, this is done to present a downward recalculation of the Polish recession from some obscure secondary source, while on another it is to remind the reader that the shock-therapy program of his own making allowed for the least damaging production decline.

But there are also many brief remarks that are consistent with the general view of recession as unavoidable and, in a way, a useful or necessary development. The key point is that the Communist system suffered from some major hidden imbalances, most notably repressed inflation, disguised unemployment and so-called unwanted production (or, to use the words of Balcerowicz, "pure socialist production"). All of these built-in imbalances are in place because of direct state interventions, so that, for instance, unwanted production is tolerated because of unconditional state subsidies.

When systemic transition begins, the substitution process begins, and the state naturally gives up its direct interventions, so that, keeping with the same example, subsidies are cut off and unwanted production is eliminated. This withdrawal of financial support leads to an obvious decline in production, which might be conceived of as a recession sign, but it is not. According to this argumentation, we cannot talk about a real recession since a loss of unwanted production for which there was no effective demand does not detract from general welfare.

Not only is this a cost-free recession, but it is a very helpful one, since with the release of resources, say, capital, from unwanted production, there are possibilities for wanted production to expand with no additional capital input. What is necessary is just to mobilize the hidden reserves of production factors left by communism. This presumes an automatic recovery, so that it makes sense for the reformers not to go for a wholesale elimination of state interventions. In other words, this type of reasoning leads to the policy conclusion that radical, in the sense of removing the state reforms are most desirable.

However, this is not a credible argument, since the collapse of production shows a pattern that is inconsistent with the claim of unwanted production. In Poland, as in other countries, output downturn was universal, including products that no one could seriously define as unwanted (e.g., cars in Poland, including some older models that later picked up once the recovery began). And the production declines in many cases have been so deep that for them to be attributed to the Communist legacy would require unwanted production to have been at some impossibly high initial levels (e.g., 50 percent for Russia, or 60 for Lithuania).

Fixated Reformers

While the argument about "healthy recession" might be of some use for Poland, where output decline was limited, it makes no sense for Russia or Ukraine, which ended up in real economic catastrophes. Still, that argument is continuously recycled a decade later in those countries, an example being Yegor Gaidar (2000). A Russian counterpart of Balcerowicz, he joined the Yeltsin government in 1992 to manage the Russian economy as a "young reformer" when Russia needed reform, and badly. The economy recently inherited from the USSR was already in decline, and prices were getting out of control as well (Sachs 2000).

Gaidar chose to follow the so-called shock therapy program that another group of "young reformers" from Poland, led by Balcerowicz, had already tried without much success. As a result of shock therapy the Poles had faced a sharp decline in production, so there was a risk that if Russia followed the same path, an even worse decline might result. And so it did. Russia went into a tailspin, and nine years later, the poor economy keeps getting poorer. It is now reduced to half of its Communist-era size, along with unstable, unreliable currencies, and a 20 percent rate of unemployment.

Thus, Gaidar has an obvious problem: How are people going to look at his legacy many years from now? Is he the reformer who tried but was prevented from implementing his "package," or was it his program that actually introduced and opened the long road to halving the economy? Gaidar himself feels that a large part of the blame lies with the Soviet Union having demanded so much unnecessary production—of products such as tractors and tanks—that had to be cut once the market took the place of the state. But it is hard to imagine that the Soviets would have allowed this much useless production.

Besides, if with all this waste Russia was able to maintain production at twice the current level, it is hard to argue that the current decline can be traced to unnecessary production in the past. One cannot likewise close an eye to the fact that, beyond tractors and tanks, both the agricultural and weapons markets got depressed. There are fewer such goods not so much because they are not needed, but because of the overall demise of the economy. There is nobody to purchase them; peasants are too poor to buy these goods, and the military runs without money to buy "hardware."

When one thinks of Russia and its fate today, another large country usually comes to mind—China, also "red" in the past, but like Russia changing its colors. Like Russia, China has been in transition to capitalism, but unlike Russia it has achieved incredible economic growth. The comparison is most revealing. In 1980 the Soviet Union had a national product worth more than U.S. $556 billion, while China had U.S. $307 billion. In 1999, Russia had only U.S. $239 billion, while China showed U.S. $978 billion in national income. So Russia is chasing China backward, and one wonders how the picture is going to look ten years from now.

This contrast should serve as a kind of intellectual shock therapy for those thinking and writing about transition in general, and Russia in particular. To Gaidar, Russia's relative decline is due to the fact that Russia is less rural than China, and it is easier to reform the rural countryside than urban industry. End of story; no other variables to consider. This is a slightly problematic argument, particularly to an economist like myself, for there is no piece of Western economic theory on which this kind of argument can be based, nor is it easy to figure out why this variable should play such a critical role.

Even if it really were easier to reform rural production, one would logically expect that a less-rural Russia would simply grow more slowly than a more-rural China. Nothing else could follow from the argument offered by the proponents of the "healthy recession" argument. But it is unreasonable to expect that this single structural factor would make Russia and China move in opposite directions, with the former sinking and the latter booming. There is no way this factor could account for the Russian economy declining rapidly while China's grew exponentially; there must be some other factor, or factors, at play.

One hypothesis is that in Russia the state spiraled into its own crisis, so the economy was mismanaged and the market had no chance to settle in. This is in contrast to China, where the state remained strong while committed to allowing markets to have a chance to overtake the economy. The lesson for "young reformers" might be that if you want markets, you have to at least appreciate the state. Otherwise, while steering toward capitalism you may end up in a sort of industrial feudalism, as R. Ericson (1999) describes today's Russian economy.

State Failures

We need a different explanation of the postcommunist recession, such as evolutionary economics, which views the role of institutions as central. This theory warns against any radical, "constructivist" efforts to remake an existing system regardless of what this system is. Even if reform takes the given economy from an inferior to a superior system, the process has to be measured and cannot be forced on the agents. Though inferior, the existing system is the only one the agents are familiar with, and if evicted from this system, they will be unable to operate effectively.

In my personal view, this is exactly what has happened in all of Eastern Europe when moving to superior capitalism, where at the outset of the transition the economic system was really the state. The state was the formal owner and principal coordinator, while markets were submerged and undefined. Neglecting this reality, the radical reformers instantly caused too much damage to the state, and thus to the system. The agents responded to this systemic crisis by cutting their production and raising prices, so that the systemic crisis translated itself into an economic crisis.

One can only speculate about the motives of the antistate reformers, but it does not seem that ideology has been the major reason for allowing states to prematurely abandon state controls. It surely looked this way to many critics of the radical transition, but after more than a decade of state neglect this is not a credible argument anymore. It is more realistic to assume that the poor state of the state reflects the fact that its agents—officials—are largely driven by private interests and not by the needs of the economy. Thus, they are not interested in ensuring that the state serves these economic needs, and thus the goal of maximizing overall wealth, best.

By too quickly withdrawing the state from the system, reformers caused dual obstacles to production, namely, insufficient liquidity and excessive risk. Credit supply fell dramatically, way beyond what was justified by the need to harden financial discipline, that is, the budget constraint. After their premature commercialization without proper financial insurance by the state, banks refused to provide credit even when it was legitimate to do so. This is definitely the case in the Polish and Czech economies, where initially real credit supply dropped by a third.

The financial situation also dramatically worsened because equally rapidly, states took themselves out of the practice of supplying subsidies to the state sector. Mainly for the same reason of budget-line hardening, but also due to stabilization (deflation), budgetary supplements to producers were largely phased out. In fact, subsidization changed its focus from producer oriented to consumer oriented, mainly due to the pressing needs of the newly unemployed and early retirements. With no time for real structural adjustment, producers reacted by cutting their output.

The other, second recession force, excessive risk, was also caused by a premature state weakening of production functions, that is, a drastic withdrawal from import controls in the absence of quantitative contingents. Tariff reductions were typically very sharp and uniform; moreover, they took rates down to levels unusually low for countries at this level of economic development. Often, borders became routinely violated by smugglers and law-breaking officials who imported goods illegally. This meant a dramatic change from Communist-era security over markets to risks of capitalist competition.

On top of import-related risks, another risk was added, namely, the sudden watering down of property rights, due to the announcement that public assets would be quickly given up by the state for privatization. In addition to being unsure about their sale prospects, producers suddenly became uncertain over the legal status of their factories/banks. With this came raised concerns over job prospects for managers and workers. Higher risk always makes producers contract as a form of insurance, so that potential losses are minimized, and, again, production cuts were a response.

If so, how to account for the fact that countries have suffered from recession at often vastly different degrees? To address this question it is useful to make a distinction between organized changes, such as in Poland, where the state retained cohesion, or unintended and chaotic changes, as, for instance in Russia, where the state lost control over the process. Then we have to recognize that reforms differed also in terms of the degree of their radicalism, meaning that in particular cases the state, its control over the economy, had been allowed to be weakened more deeply than in other cases.

If we combine the two dimensions, a typology can be created, where the more radical and more chaotic transitions—as in Russia—produce worse recessions. And conversely, less radical and more cohesive reforms, as in Poland and Hungary, produce less pronounced recessions. In this typology, East Germany falls somewhere in between, with its most radical but also very organized state withdrawal, complete erasing of the existing Eastern state, led by the Western

Table 3.1:
Typology of Transition Pathways: Reform Approaches and State Behavior

	State Behavior	
Reform Intensity	*Organized*	*Disorganized (Chaotic)*
Radical-implemented	East Germany	Russia Ukraine
Radical-abandoned	Hungary Poland	Bulgaria Romania
Gradual-genuine	China Vietnam	organic process (as defined by Hayek)

state. Bulgaria and Romania, with their less radical reforms chaotically executed by corrupt states, are other intermediate cases in point.

It should be obvious that depending on what happened initially to the state, certain countries should find it easier to recover than others. In each case state reconstruction with different state roles and instruments is a precondition. In the situation of Poland, and even more so of East Germany, this rebuilding came easier (in the East German case this meant that the Western state directed the state replacement process). But in Russia, for example, the state has to be reconstructed much more extensively so it will have to take longer, and in fact as we have already seen, it does.

To complete this part of my analysis, one has to recognize that not all postcommunist transitions have produced a recession, the case in point being China and Vietnam. Many explanations have been offered to address this striking contrast in economic performance between these two transition economies and the rest of the group. The best answer is that unlike Eastern Europe, both China and Vietnam have engaged in a gradual—limited—package of reforms and that in both of them the states remained cohesive. This, of course, proves that recession was not Eastern Europe's destiny but a matter of "choice."

There is one other gradual pathway to capitalism that has not been taken by any of the postcommunist economies, one where gradual change is pursued in a chaotic fashion. Here, markets expand with a greatly weakened state, as in the organic process that Hayek considers to be typical of the capitalist descent. This is historically how capitalism has emerged, i.e., out of its feudal bedrock in places where the state was greatly constrained. It is not surprising that such a pathway has been bypassed by the Communist countries, since their starting point has of course been different.

Regional Divide

The transition is defined not only by the economic recession but also by a most peculiar pattern of systemic changes, specifically the emerging ownership relations. The direction in which postcommunist countries are heading is best illustrated by the patterns already established among those countries that appear to be the most advanced in pro-market reforms. Among those economies are East Germany, Hungary, and Estonia. Here, the bulk of capital—industrial and commercial—has already been taken over by foreign (or in the East German case outside) investors.

Specifically, in East Germany about 95 percent of the industrial/banking assets left from the Communist era went to buyers other than East Germans themselves, almost exclusively West Germans. This sort of corporate takeover, where the ownership of assets moves to outsiders, is somewhat less advanced in Hungary, where 70 percent of banking and 70 percent of industry is foreign-controlled. The actual asset positions are less extensive, since on average, foreigners hold about 80 percent of equity in their firms. Importantly, what is left is in state hands.

But this kind of trend is actually present everywhere, with clear indications that most of the countries may end up in similar situations, with almost complete domination of foreign ownership. Poland is definitely on this track, with 70 percent of banking already under foreign control and 35–40 percent of its industry. Now, the most capital-intensive industries (including petrochemicals, telecommunications, steel making) are being put up for sale. At the pace the assets are being sold today, it will not take more than three years for Poland's ownership structure to become like that of Hungary.

Both the case of Hungary and of Poland suggest that after a few slower years, turning over of assets to foreigners suddenly accelerates and then in two to three years, foreigners gain a dominant position. In Hungary the turning point was 1995, under the Socialist (former Communist) leadership of Guyla Horn. In Poland, the turning point was 1998, under a coalition of former dissident forces under Jerzy Buzek, with Balcerowicz again in charge of the economy. If this experience is exemplary for the region, one would expect countries such as Bulgaria and Romania or Slovakia to shortly show rapid increases in foreign holdings as well. All three have been slow with formal privatization, though they have seen a major change in property rights. They have taken the road of a sort of "nomenclatura capitalism," where most of the assets are still owned by the state. What has happened is that the factories/banks have been left without much central state control so that they have become like domains of their immediate bosses, i.e., mostly the former nomenclatura. They are using the assets largely for their own financial benefit, often by redirecting proceeds abroad.

There are signs that in all these cases nomenclatura capitalism may not last, since there are indications that recent governments favor large-scale sell-offs to foreigners. This is in part because this hybrid form of capitalism has proved unworkable, as demonstrated by a second wave of recession in Bulgaria and Romania. Another reason is that parties with links to the communist past have been displaced by new political forces. The only two important exceptions are East Germany and Slovenia, though for very different reasons. In East Germany privatization entailed a transfer of East German state assets to West German investors. Of the total, 5 percent went to East Germans through buy-outs and another 5 percent was bought by foreigners, while the balance ended up with West Germans. In Slovenia, privatization assumed mostly the form of buy-outs by the local managers/workers, consistent with the preexisting system of labor management with some assets, as in banking, dispersed through public offerings, also mainly among domestic investors.

In terms of the overall share of foreign ownership, the levels found in the most extreme cases in Eastern Europe have already exceeded the most extreme cases in Western Europe. In Ireland this share is at 40 percent, and in Austria at 30, though there has been no change in these shares for more than a decade. They also greatly exceed the average levels of foreign penetration reported by Western European countries in their industry, which is below 15 percent (e.g., 10 percent in more advanced Germany, but not much higher in less developed Portugal or Spain).

While in Western Europe foreign ownership concentrates in manufacturing—engineering and chemicals—in Eastern Europe as a whole, dominant foreign positions can be found also in banking and utilities as well as in mass media and culture. Here the contrast between Eastern Europe and Western Europe is even more striking than in industry in general. Hungary and Poland's shares of foreign ownership (70 percent) or Estonia's (80 percent), can nowhere be found in Western Europe, where the average share is under 10 percent (with Germany at 6 percent and Austria at 4 percent).

Thus, with these recent developments there is a major division developing in Europe. Taking a general view, one could claim that Europe is being split into two economic regions, one without its own capital, that is, Eastern Europe, and the other, Western Europe, with its own capital (part of which consists of the former East European capital). This is critical since economic systems are basically defined by their ownership characteristics. With these two different ownership structures being established, two different types of capitalism are formed as well.

It follows that the collapse of Communism has not ended the division of

Europe. After World War II Europe was divided ideologically into opposite political blocs that were largely insulated. Now, the transition is removing the old ideological split, allowing Eastern Europe to build new bridges to Western Europe. But while the ideological schism is fading into the past, a new split is emerging—an economic one. It is new, since not even in the interwar period was foreign ownership of capital in the region this high.

In fact, communism itself did not create the postwar division of Europe, for the continent had been fractured for more than a century (Berend and Ranki 1977; Berend 1986). The advent of communism did not remove the richer–poorer division, if anything it allowed the distance to increase, most visibly in the postwar divided Germany. Communism only created an impression of a closing of the historic divide, and what the current transition has done is to bring this fact up front. Transition, in one of its dimensions, should be viewed as the articulation of a hidden, repressed division of Europe into East and West.

"Highest" Stage

It appears that the opening to massive foreign takeovers is perhaps the most particular feature of the postcommunist reforms. Since nothing else is institutionally as striking as this ownership pattern, it seems that to understand these reforms most of all one has to get a good grasp of the corporate takeovers by foreigners. Economic and political forces, which have led to unusual conditions for foreigners to acquire domestic capital, have to be addressed as much as the related question of the potential consequences of building the kind of economies that are for the most part foreign owned.

In trying to account for these massive takeovers, there is a temptation to see the emerging strong foreign participation mainly as a result of a conscious policy by postcommunist reformers to bring the best results for these economies. This is the case, even though when the reforms were first initiated very few, if any, of the policymakers envisioned that the transition was going to lead to a foreign-dominated property structure. Just the opposite, for initial pronouncements were that the purpose of reforms was to turn assets over mainly to domestic owners.

The original concept of ownership reforms was for the state to engage mainly in privatization, i.e., mass transfer of public assets, rather than to take the alternative way of building a dominant private sector through "new entries." Privatization was pictured as taking two potential pathways, i.e., free of charge distribution to all citizens (the so-called democratic capitalism) and sales of assets, directly or through public offerings. In the case of free distribution, foreigners were to be automatically excluded, while in the case of asset sales, with few exceptions (e.g., Hungary) preferences were to be given to local investors.

Justification for a major transfer of state assets to foreigners has come later, when it turned out that regardless of the privatization option chosen, the assets mainly go to foreign buyers. With time a well-articulated set of arguments has been established by stressing that the legacy of Communism was such that no other way allowing large-scale sales of capital to foreigners was available. This is an extension of the mainstream argument discussed earlier about the causes of another major event—the recession, which is also blamed on some adverse aspects of the Communist legacy.

While recession is seen as inevitable, it is also viewed as "healthy"; similarly, in explaining the foreign takeovers, the stress is also on both their inevitability and their beneficial or "healthy" effects. Communism is said to leave not only imbalances that are responsible for the recession but also very little capital with which to build capitalism. Due to communism's wasteful nature, in physical terms there is not much capital of value left. But another adverse fact is that under communism households did not have much in terms of savings either.

This retrospective argument claims that the situation was so desperate that, if recalculated at world prices, the majority of products should be counted as value subtracting, that is, not adding to but subtracting from the national product. Lacking technological skills of their competitors, domestic producers stand no chance of surviving on their own. To continue domestic production it must be turned over to those with the expertise—foreigners, particularly because, in the absence of sufficient domestic savings, few domestic investors have the money needed for turning firms around.

The argument on the desperate state of economic affairs is combined with a very powerful forward-looking argument. Turning most of the assets abroad is a necessity, but foreign exposure is a desirable development due to globalization. It is said that Eastern Europe is joining the capitalist world at a very special stage, when national borders—and the nation state—are being brought down. This is because, with economic liberalization, not only products but also capital is free to move worldwide. Consequently, in this stage of capitalist evolution it no longer makes sense to talk about national origins of ownership.

The statistical evidence is apparently abundant, such as the fact that most of the products traded worldwide are not made in one location anymore but are assembled from parts made in various countries. Furthermore, the capital presence of foreign firms in almost any economy in the world is increasing rapidly. One powerful vehicle for such penetration is the activity of mergers and takeovers, where assets of various national firms are combined. This activity is the fastest growing type of cross-border operation, faster than the traditional form of exchange, that is, trade in goods and services.

The nationality of capital owners is considered to be irrelevant, since wherever anchored, cross-border firms do not follow the agenda of any particular country. In other words, they have become stateless. Under the discipline of the world market such companies do not feel in any meaningful way obliged to some local interests in their home countries.. The primary motives are maximization of efficiency and maximization of profits, so that the host country is rewarded with more jobs and higher wages for allowing foreign ownership.

In this view, Eastern Europe, with its extremely high, actually unprecedented, shares of foreign ownership, is not only in line with the recent trends but also presumably is on the cutting edge of them. In a way, the region is leading the way to the "highest stage" of capitalism, where capital knows no borders. This way, the region switches from the "lowest stage" of communism to the "highest stage" of capitalism. The region presumably goes from a dead-end system, which has exhausted its capacity for growth, to the one that offers exceptional growth—in a new version of the theory of the advantages of backwardness (Gerschenkron 1962).

"Slack Economy"

But there is a different explanation for the forces behind the capital transfers, one that posits that this institutional development is an unintended product of specific policy choices by the state. Not only was the postcommunist recession an avoidable development but the emerging ownership structure is one such avoidable outcome as well. If true, this would only strengthen the impression that postcommunist transition is less the process of unique trials and more the result of ordinary errors. Of course, the fact that this systemic outcome is unintended does not itself mean that it is a failure, since errors may lead to gainful results.

While the state crisis has been responsible for the postcommunist recession, the same state crisis is the cause of the massive selling of assets to foreigners. Overtaken by private concerns, the postcommunist states not only have largely abandoned the needs of stimulating production, but they also, for the same general reason, have neglected the needs of the domestic emerging capitalist class to get empowered with most of the divested large-scale capital stock owned by the Communist state. Maintaining vibrant production has not been the primary concern of rent-seeking officials, nor has it been to turn this production over to insiders or nationals. Moreover, very much the same unfortunate measures that caused the regionwide recession have been responsible for these economies' assuming a pattern of asset sales that has largely benefited foreign buyers. But even more important have been specific choices and decisions made by officials regarding individual sales of public assets. It is in these sales that one finds the strongest evidence that it is again the state crisis that is responsible for derailing the transition. That sales benefited mostly foreigners stems from the fact that the best opportunities for undue personal advantages have been offered by foreign acquisitions and not by sales to domestic buyers (Poznanski 1999).

The massive transfer of assets to foreigners is best viewed as a result of a peculiar macroeconomic imbalance created by almost all state reformers in postcommunist Eastern Europe. I like to call it the "privatization disequilibrium," where supply of domestic state assets for sale systematically exceeds the domestic demand for those assets. Since the states have decided to unload the supplies of assets in quantities that domestic investors cannot absorb, foreigners gained an upper hand. Specifically, their natural advantages have been only strengthened by this policy, so that domestic buyers have had almost no chance to compete with them for state capital.

It is quite ironic that such an imbalance was created, since for most of the reformers, as in Poland, under reform-leader Balcerowicz, the primary objective of economic programs was the equilibration of local economies. The main enemy of this new breed of reformers was, as Kornai (1980) coined it, the so-called shortage economy, or excess demand for goods. As in Poland, most of the reformers were successful in eliminating shortages, mainly by drastically cutting real wages and jobs. My claim is that this "product disequilibrium" has simply been replaced with "asset disequilibrium."

The decision to start privatization right away was critical, particularly since the early years were those of a very deep recession that weakened domestic producers. But even more important was the choice of very fast privatization, which was initially, quite unrealistically, expected to be completed in two to three years as, for instance, in Poland. But notwithstanding the eventual slowdown, the pace assumed by most reformers was phenomenal, especially compared with similar programs in Western Europe. It took Great Britain fifteen years to sell 10 percent of its assets whereas Hungary sold 80 percent in seven years.

Importantly, with the extremely fast pace of sales, reform-minded states have decided to offer firms not in smaller pieces, or packets, but in their entireties. Another preference has been to seek majority owners, also called "strategic owners," to take over more than 50 percent of an equity position. Often, the buyers would be also expected to commit themselves to an expensive investment program, which is a common practice in Poland. In reality, most of the buyers have been allowed to take positions ranging from 80 to 100 percent of total equity, at least in the case of Hungary and Poland. These enormous large-scale packets of assets have turned out to be completely out of reach for domestic investors. At the time when assets were made available for purchase, the demand conditions, namely, the financial potential of insiders, was not expanded but reduced. That not only left communism with at best modest savings, but by and large the first measures taken by the reformers reduced the stocks at least by half.

Even more important is the fact that with the advent of economic reforms the banking system was reorganized in a way that caused a sudden collapse of credit. Left without state "insurance," and in the absence of its private substitute, banks uniformly refused to finance the private sector. Instead, they turned to the financing of more secure proposals, often earning very a high yield on state debt instruments, as was clearly the case in Poland and even more in Russia, where banks have drained the state budget through high-yield bonds, but also through the supervision of budgetary subsidies. Thus, the liquidity crisis not only has contributed to the postcommunist recession but also has adversely affected the ability of domestic investors to acquire state assets. Of course, recession, as in Poland, lasted only a few years, but this does not mean that the liquidity crisis has ended. The shortage of credit has only softened but has not gone away, even in countries such as Poland, where the financial system has survived without a major downturn (in contrast with the Czech Republic or Bulgaria, where the banking sectors recently almost collapsed).

In those circumstances it was critical for the ability of domestic investors to buy state assets that they receive some assistance from the state. More specifically, some form of industrial policy was needed that would tilt the scales in favor of insiders, if not on the supply side then at least on the demand side. On the supply side the most obvious policy consisted of setting limits to foreign holdings in individual firms, along the lines of Kornai's early advice (Kornai 1990). Convinced that such limits of foreign shares are imperative, Kornai also argued for special financial instruments to affect the demand side, that is, to assist domestic buyers (e.g., low-interest credits, payment plans).

Nowhere have such measures been undertaken; in fact, to the contrary, a type of "negative" industrial policy favoring outsiders has almost uniformly emerged. In their race for foreign investment, states have lifted all possible restrictions on ownership positions or at best have kept them alive only temporarily (e.g., in Polish banking). Furthermore, foreign investors have been provided with incentive packages typically not available to their domestic counterparts (e.g., elimination of duties on imported parts and/or equipment, long-term tax holidays, as in the case of Hungarian and Polish car making).

New Economics

It is not only that the foreign-dominated ownership structure is a largely unintentional result of policy choices, but it also is doubtful that what has transpired can be viewed as the "highest stage" of capitalism. Those who view this development in positive terms may well be right, but one should be careful with passing any final judgment on the system in question. This issue is problematic not only because we have too few facts to work with, but because economic theory is silent on the merits of such a foreign-dominated type of economy as well. Even the most theoretically oriented academics have not ventured to analyze a system where, so to speak, capital is largely foreign and labor is mainly domestic.

At first sight, even selling all assets of state-owned banking and industry may appear like a promising strategy, since this should allow a host economy to use the proceeds to almost double its capital stock. If only the state invested the revenues from asset sales into new asset formation, the result would really be the doubling of the capital in use. As a result, foreign-held assets would be about equal to domestic-held assets, thus leaving reasonable control over the host economy in local hands. For whatever economic sovereignty is worth, it would thus be retained.

However, the story is different when state assets are sold below their real value, which seems to be the case in Eastern Europe, at least in Hungary and Poland, for which some calculations are available. Given the fast-paced nature of privatization and the related oversupply of assets, price discounting should not come as a surprise. According to one estimate for Poland, due to the rush with sales, the state was unable to make even a small investment to get the highest prices, so that revenues are half of what they might have been. Specifically, through 1999, about U.S. $5–7 billion in potential revenues were lost.

My own calculations for Poland (Poznanski 2000) show an even larger, almost unbelievable discount. At this point, with half of banking/industry sold, prices average around 10 percent of the real value. Similar calculations for Hungary show similar discounts and thus similar losses of potential increase in national capital stock. These forgone gains in capital formation mean that both countries have been denied a proportional increase in their national products. More specifically, if not for these conditions of sale, at the end of the transfers, their national products could have been almost twice as large.

Of course, these losses could be compensated, or even overcompensated, for with appropriate efficiency gains from a better use of capital by foreign owners. Even if such gains were delivered, this does not justify the kinds of discounts that are implied by the studies in question. So far there is no compelling evidence that efficiency gains are strong enough to allow these countries to at least break even. Admittedly, both Hungary and Poland demonstrate better overall economic results than most of the other countries, but it is also true that Slovenia, which left its assets to the insiders, outperforms both of them.

In my analysis of Poland, it is clear that even under the most favorable growth scenario, assuming that a 5 percent growth rate continues through the end of privatization, say in 2004, the national product will be too low to make up for the loss on discounted sales. By this year, Poland will be short U.S. $70 billion in national product, which will represent more than one-third of the national product that the assumed growth rate of 5 percent of GDP will generate. But if huge trade deficits and mounting debts force Poland into a crisis before 2004, the outcome may be even more unfavorable.

Leaving the question of pricing aside, there are still serious concerns about the merits of the emerging property structure. This is the case because an economy with mostly foreign capital has to be prepared for another loss, this time on a permanent basis. Discounted sales of assets eventually lead to an outflow of value abroad, but under such a system income from capital is subject to transfer as well. It cannot be assumed that income from capital will be indefinitely reinvested. Unlike in the communist economy, the ultimate purpose of investing is not investing but consumption.

With this comes a challenge, since the outflow of income from capital—

profits and rents—has to be financed. Specifically, the host economy has to earn foreign currency equal to the amount of capital income that is to be converted. For an economy that has difficulties with closing its balance, such an outflow represents an additional hurdle. Hungary already experienced initial problems of this nature in 1998, when suddenly the transfers of profits by foreign firms reached about U.S. $1.5 billion. This was equal to the inflow of direct foreign investment, so that for the first time Hungary's investment balance was nil.

Conclusions

Eastern Europe was in trouble during the Communist era, with repressive politics and wasteful economics. But even though communism is over, the region is not out of trouble. Moving toward capitalism is an inevitability and a great turning point. When all economies in the region immediately fell into a deep recession this should have been a warning signal that something was deeply wrong. This should have been interpreted as a sign that adverse changes had taken place in their institutions, particularly in their states. It could not be otherwise, unless recession is viewed as having little to do with the condition of institutions.

The conduct of privatization, as the main vehicle for institutional change, seems to offer additional reasons for concern about the status of institutions in the postcommunist period. It may well be that the emerging pattern of ownership, with exceptionally high foreign holdings, is less a solution to the regional problems and more an extension of the problems from the past. If so, then one would have to take the position that the transition, at least in its economic realm, is problematic, or that indeed we can talk about an ongoing transition crisis. And given the central role of the state in transition, the crisis of transition would have to be seen as a state crisis as well.

It has been largely lost in the transition debates that the reforms started in very adverse circumstances, if not those of economic adversities such as structural imbalances and/or technical obsolescence. The most important adversity was that these economies entered into major reform movements under severe state crises marked in particular by a decline of public interest. Not only was indifference to a general good widespread, but corruption was already in full swing, both conditions reducing the state's capacity to do the right things. Reforms have been thus captured by private interests and therefore largely derailed.

By prematurely abandoning its role in guiding production, the state caused an unprecedented recession, and by turning privatization largely into a private affair the same state made most of the assets go under foreign ownership. Recessions are normal, but not of such proportions as Eastern Europe's during the last ten years. The selling of assets by a given economy to foreigners is a norm in the modern world economy as much as buying assets abroad, but what is happening in Eastern Europe is an abnormality. It is abnormal to have an entire economy—its banking and industry—sold to foreigners, particularly when no offsetting purchases are made abroad.

Taking this state-centered perspective on the transition helps explain both the failings of Eastern Europe and the contrasts between the road taken by this region and the approach adopted by China. Conducted in the midst of a state crisis, the transition in Eastern Europe has resulted in an economic catastrophe, but the crisis-free state of China has retained sufficient control of production to ensure continuous growth. Having relatively crisis-ridden states, Eastern Europe has ended up with anomalous capitalism without its own capital, and without its own capitalist class; in contrast, under the guidance of a responsible state, China is building a normal capitalist economy.

Chapter 4

Trust in Transition

Martin Raiser

After a decade of reform in the countries of central and Eastern Europe and the former Soviet Union, very different types of market economies are evolving across the region. While almost all countries in the region have made significant progress in the liberalization of markets and (more varied) the privatization of state assets, reform progress differs dramatically in the area of institution building and in particular in the effectiveness of the new market-oriented institutions. At the same time, the transition has been marked by large differences in economic performance, which seem to be related to the types of economic systems that have emerged. A key question raised by the experience of transition so far is, therefore, in what way have institutional legacies and institutional change influenced transition outcomes?

This paper contributes to the growing literature on the role of informal institutions in the transition (Johnson et al. 1998; McMillan and Woodruff 1998a, b; Raiser 1997). It focuses on trust as a key ingredient in the institutional infrastructure of a market economy. The focus on trust is inspired by its importance for business formation (Humphrey and Schmitz 1996; Bigsten and Collier et al. 1998), which in turn seems to be crucial for explaining the variation in economic performance in the transition economies (Johnson et al. 1997). Entrepreneurship cannot flourish in an environment of distrust, since many economic opportunities are closed off. As K. Arrow (1975: 25) notes:

> Almost every commercial transaction has within itself an element of trust, certainly any transaction conducted over a period of time. It can

> be plausibly argued that much of economic backwardness in the world can be explained by the lack of mutual confidence.

The analysis distinguishes between the role of trust in bilateral exchange and a more general notion of trust in a society, akin to R. D. Putnam's use of the term *social capital.* Trust in bilateral economic exchange allows efficient trade to take place in the face of uncertainty and constrains opportunistic behavior. Social capital more generally facilitates the exchange of information and supports collective action. Moreover, this paper uses Zucker's (1986) distinction between various forms of trust in arguing that only "extended" or generalized trust can support the transition to a modern market system. I further argue that many existing business networks in the transition economies, grown out of former bureaucratic bargaining relationships, are not sufficiently open and trust is not sufficiently generalized to fully realize economic opportunities. In this the paper takes issue with some of the existing literature on business networks, which views their survival and adaptation as an efficient response to the uncertainty and imperfection of markets in the transition (e.g., Stark 1996). A key policy focus of the paper is on possible determinants of extended trust, paying particular attention to the potential complementarities between trust and the quality of formal institutions.

The first section of the paper discusses the role of trust in bilateral exchange and in the provision of collective goods. It then introduces the distinction between various forms of trust and develops the argument for the central role of extended trust. The section ends with an analysis of the determinants of extended trust. The second section examines the role of trust in transition. It first sketches the socialist legacies that may influence both the nature and degree of trust during the transition. It then looks at the role of trust in private business networks, both old and new. Finally, I develop the argument that the lack of extended trust, including distrust in the state itself, is one key factor behind the disappointing economic performance observed in many countries across the region. The third section draws some highly speculative policy implications, and the fourth section concludes.

What Is Trust?

Trust has become a buzzword in recent writings on the role of institutions in economic development (Humphrey and Schmitz 1996). There are numerous definitions of the concept and this paper makes no attempt to clarify or even cover all of them. I focus on two uses of the term: (1) trust as mutual confidence among parties to an economic transaction, and (2) trust as social capital facilitating the provision of collective goods.

When two individuals exchange goods and services they need to trust one another. This is particularly the case for incomplete contracts, where one party is unable to fully monitor the other party's fulfillment of her obligations taken under the contract, a typical problem in transactions that take place over time (see Arrow's quote above). The risk of opportunistic behavior could be so great as to prevent the exchange from taking place altogether. A lack of trust may thus impose prohibitively high transaction costs on contracting parties, thereby limiting mutually beneficial transactions.

The role of trust in bilateral economic exchange can be best illustrated with the use of a sequential prisoners' dilemma. In this game, payoffs are distributed such that the second player maximizes her return by cheating on player 1, after the latter has decided to play cooperatively. Anticipating this move, player 1 will not rationally cooperate and mutual cooperation, yielding the highest joint payoff, is never achieved. In various extensions of this game, the introduction of an additional moral or emotional payoff facilitates cooperation (Platteau 1994a, b). In Bolle (1998), for instance, type 2 players feel compelled to reciprocate to a cooperative first move because of feelings of thankfulness or remorse. Feelings of thankfulness and remorse may be instilled through social norms and the wish to be accepted as a member of society. In repeated games, trust can also be built through successful cooperation (Axelrod 1988). The trust one puts in a business partner can be interpreted as a kind of relational collateral, in a way similar to the role of collateral in the resolution of moral hazard in the credit market (Hart 1993).

In the bilateral transactions discussed so far the benefits accrue to the contracting parties only if they enter into the transaction—both lose if they do not trade, while losses are one-sided in the case of opportunistic behavior. However, social and economic interaction includes a variety of situations where the benefits accrue to a collective and similarly the costs of noncompliance are socialized. Examples of such collective goods are voting, participation in voluntary organizations, abstaining from littering the streets, or refusing to accept and pay bribes. The exclusion of individuals from the benefits (a functioning democracy, a lively civil society and decentralized care for weak members, clean streets, and a culture of honesty among officials) is not possible, and the costs of noncompliance to the individual are small. Hence the problem of the free rider arises.

Trust has a role to play in the provision of collective goods, too. If unaffected third parties are willing to sanction cheaters, reputational enforcement mechanisms can be built and can constrain an individual's exit options from an existing collective. There are a number of examples of such collective reputational enforcement mechanisms in history (Greif 1994, 1996; Milgrom et al. 1990). In the absence of a collective reputational enforcement mechanism, the provision of collective goods requires some common ideological motivation (North 1981) or the existence of altruistic preferences (Kirchgässner 1994). However, even if individuals behave morally or altruistically and obtain benefits from both the collective good and from their own contributions, a typical person would still contribute only if the combined benefits outweighed her personal costs. This will usually be the case only if the collective good is actually provided, and hence confidence that one's commitment is widely shared will be required.[1] In other words, it requires trust.

Forms of Trust

There are three types of relationships among parties to an economic transaction, and these give rise to three different types of trust. The first type of relationship is among kinship groups and family members. These relationships dominate economic transactions in subsistence economies and still characterize reproduction and the household economy (but also many small-scale crafts and trades). Transactions between members of a kinship group are based on what I call "ascribed trust," following Zucker (1986). The second type of relationship is between individuals that have known each other for a long time, without sharing the loyalty to a specific group. Transactions in this case are repeated and trust is "process based." Most business networks are characterized by this type of repeated relationship and the prevalence of process-based trust. The third type of relationship is between individuals who enter into a transaction with only limited information about the counterpart's specific attributes. For economic exchange to take place between these types of individuals, generalized or "extended trust" is needed. The importance of this third type of relationships and the correspondent economic transactions between largely anonymous individuals are a key element of a modern economic system.

The typology presented here suggests that the building of extended trust is a key challenge in economic development. Nonetheless, it is important to bear in mind the relationships between the various forms of trust. In particular, extended trust could not exist without the experience of reciprocity made in repeated interactions among family and other members of a social or business community. This includes social interaction, which may not have a direct business-related purpose, as shown in Putnam's (1993) analysis of the role of an active civil society in generating social capital. Where process-based trust is absent, extended trust cannot develop. Moreover, it is unlikely that extended trust in economic exchange could be sustained without the availability of third-party enforcement by the state. Hence, trust among anonymous individuals may be as much a function of their moral predispositions and social experiences as of their trust in government institutions to provide impartial enforcement. The behavior of government has therefore an important role to play in the reproduction of extended trust.

Determinants of Extended Trust

Institutions in general change in response to new economic opportunities—although the pace of such change can be slow. When reductions in information and transportation costs open new opportunities for exchange and specialization across existing spatial and social boundaries, process-based trust can become inefficient since it partially relies on loyalty that would restrict outside options. This can but need not imply the breakup of existing business networks. While some networks will cease to be used, other business relationships may be recast to fit the new environment (Humphrey and Schmitz 1996). Extended trust may be created through an expansion of existing networks, whereby these become increasingly open and allow members to seek outside economic opportunities.

Extended trust may also be created through moral innovations. A. Greif (1994) contrasts the development of two trading cultures in the Renaissance period in this respect. In the case of the Maghribi traders operating until the fifteenth century in the Mediterranean, a collectivist culture supporting strong reputational enforcement prevented the expansion of the trading network and led to its disappearance in the face of competition from the Italian city-states. The latter by contrast were characterized by a far more individualistic society and, as argued by J.-P. Platteau (1994a, b), benefited from the rise of universalistic morality in western political philosophy in supporting the emergence of extended trust, and trust in state institutions in particular.[2]

The willingness to search for economic opportunities outside one's established social and business contacts will also depend on the distance between social groups or the homogeneity of society and the risk associated with being cheated. P. J. Zak and S. Knack (1999), for instance, present cross-country evidence that the extent of trust between anonymous individuals (derived from the World Values Survey) is positively related to measures of social distance (income and land inequality and ethnolinguistic fractionalization). C. Offe (1999) suggests that extended trust is higher in societies in which the risks of being cheated may be pooled through social security arrangements (formal and informal through extended families, etc.), reducing the size of the material threat should cheating occur.

Probably the most important determinant of the emergence and sustainability of extended trust is the availability of complementary contract enforcement from the state. Zak and Knack (1999) establish a close statistical relationship between their measure of (extended) trust and the quality of formal institutions (the protection of property rights, the enforceability of contracts, the extent of bribery, and an index of investors' rights). The availability of third-party enforcement may be crucial to kick off a process of further economic specialization, involving trade across previously closed social communities. This process will in turn increase the confidence of agents in members of different social groups, thereby facilitating the emergence and reproduction of extended trust.

On the other hand, extended trust is also needed to make third-party enforcement by the state function efficiently. First, the state faces huge information problems in trying to judge the behavior of economic agents, and the costs of uncovering this information through the judicial system are very high. As a result, the reliance on third-party enforcement alone to prevent opportunism would be very inefficient and would excessively bind scarce administrative resources.[3] Second, the ability of the state to provide third-party enforcement is a function both of its monopoly over coercive power and the legitimacy and credibility of public institutions. In the absence of trust, a ruler may not be able to commit not to abuse his coercive power and efficient third-party enforcement may never emerge (Greif and Kandel 1994; Diamond 1994). Trust in the behavior of government officials may determine citizens' rule obedience and hence the effectiveness of third-party enforcement (Clague 1993; Rose 1993).

Trust in Transition

Central planning has left a profound legacy for the nature of formal and informal institutions in central and Eastern Europe, but analysts of this legacy have differed greatly in their evaluations of its impact on the transition. For some, socialism has left a legacy of distrust, which continues to hamper the emergence of a market economy (Rose 1993; Rose et al. 1997). For others, the very imperfections of central planning led to the formation of a second economy, in which the basis for market behavior was laid and social networks formed that could efficiently adapt during the transition (Stark 1996).

This paper generally provides support for the first line of argument. While the second economy seems to have in many cases provided a fertile basis for the emergence of a private sector, its development still is in many ways dysfunctional to an open-market economy. Business networks based on ties formed in the socialist second economy often remain closed to outsiders and hence prevent the emergence of effective competition. Moreover, there is in many transition economies a legacy of distrust in public institutions. Widespread bribery corrupts the impartiality of public officials and contract enforcement is often delegated to private agencies, which challenge the state's monopoly over coercive power. While potentially efficient and justifiable from the point of view of an individual enterprise, the social costs are huge.

The centralized nature of resource allocation did not require decentralized contracting between parties to a transaction (Greif and Kandel 1994). Contracts were made between the planning agency and producers. Monitoring problems were acute and enterprises effectively suffered little sanction from contract underfulfilment—they operated under soft budgets and soft contracts. Because the reliability of supplies under the planning system was low, enterprises were effectively forced to seek necessary inputs informally. Hence, one legacy of central planning was the emergence of informal networks between enterprises—often using specific contact persons—based on repeated interaction. Bureaucratic coordination furthermore led to extensive bargaining, in which personal connections to government officials were a crucial asset. Central planning relied extensively on process-based trust, with enterprises and local and national government officials closely linked through informal networks.

Another characteristic of central planning was the pervasive political domination of the Communist Party, underwritten by the ideology of the dictatorship of the proletariat. While the ideology was formed during the years of revolutionary struggle against an oppressive tsarist regime, and may have carried some legitimacy in this context, it was itself turned into a totalitarian dogma and thereby lost any of its moral justification. As a result of this lack of moral legitimacy, distrust in public institutions was a characteristic of all Communist societies. Associational life was kept largely outside the public sphere—circle of friends mattered more than involvement in football clubs, which might be exposed to political infiltration.[4] The scope for social interaction, which would have allowed extended trust to emerge and to be reproduced, was limited.

Chart 4.1 provides some evidence for the severity of the loss of trust. It draws on the results of the World Values Survey (WVS) for 1990, which included eleven transition economies.[5] The WVS includes a question on the extent to

Chart 4.1:
The Legacy of Distrust
Would you agree that most people can be trusted or that you cannot be too careful about other people? Percentage of respondents saying people can be trusted.

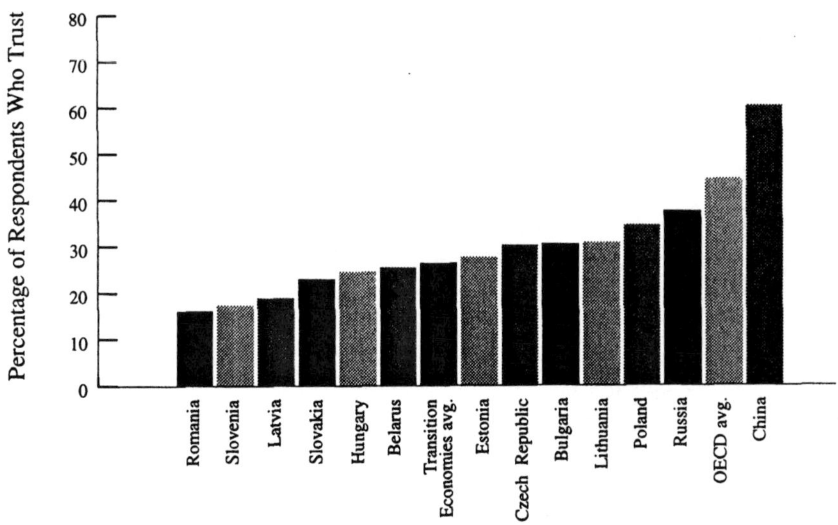

Note: OECD countries include Austria, Belgium, Britain, Canada, Denmark, Finland, France, Ireland, Italy, Japan, Netherlands, Norway, Portugal, Spain, Sweden, Switzerland, the United States, and West Germany

Source: World Values Survey, 1990. Data obtained from Christian Haerpfer, IHS Vienna.

which others, who were not personally acquainted who the respondent, could be trusted—a good measure of the extent of extended trust. Chart 4.1 shows that transition economies in 1990 had on average much lower values of extended trust than OECD countries. Interestingly, extended trust was higher in China, possibly one of the factors behind that country's more successful transition.[6] Note that there is no apparent pattern among the transition economies themselves, in the sense that within the group variation in trust does not correspond to subsequent success during the transition.

Chart 4.2, also from the WVS, shows the average degree of participation in various kinds of civic organizations. The organizations are split into organizations of civil society such as the church, sports clubs, arts clubs, environmental associations, and charities, and economic interest groups, including trade unions, political parties, and professional associations. The transition economies have much lower values for participation in organizations of civil society but higher levels of participation in political interest groups. Membership in the Communist Party and the trade union were often necessary for career development and probably do not reflect higher levels of political engagement in socialist countries. However, chart 4.2 reveals very clearly the underdevelopment of civil society and the relative density of networks that could be transformed into partisan interest groups during the transition. Following Putnam, the legacy of distrust and low civic engagement are arguably related and provided for a challenging starting point for institutional change during the transition.

Recombining Networks: Efficiency or Exclusion?

Given this legacy, how have economic transactions been shaped by existing social networks and new economic opportunities? There are three types of institutional links between enterprises in transition economies. First, there are business networks built on ascribed trust—usually confined to the local economy, with the potential to expand through selective interaction with outsiders. Second, there are networks based on existing ties between the previous members of the socialist *nomenclatura*—recombined during the transition to accommodate the reorganization of the enterprise sector through corporatization and privatization, but still built primarily on process-based trust. Third, there are links between modern corporations based largely on the allocation of property rights, formal contracts, and the integration into global production networks. For most transition economies, the second type of interaction is by far the most common. For all of them, moving beyond the first toward building effective linkages between all three of them remains a key challenge.

Chart 4.2:
The Legacy of Distrust
Active participation in social and political organizations

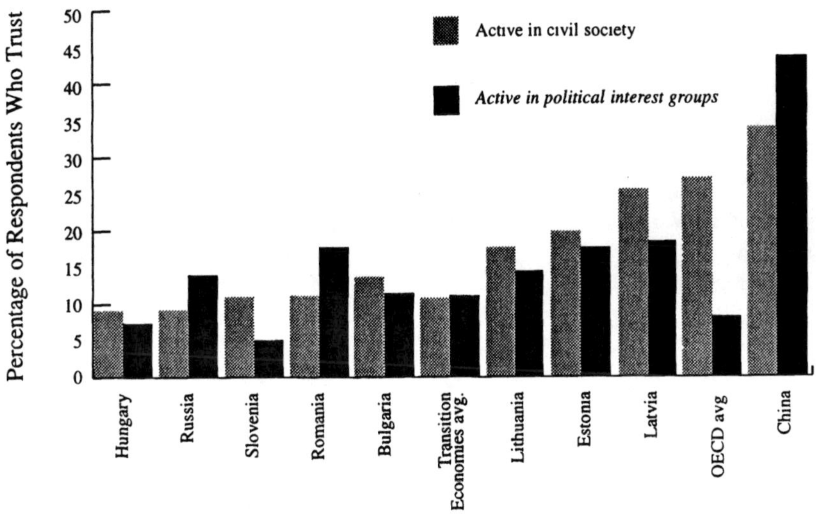

Note: OECD countries same as in chart 4.1. Civil society organizations include the church, sports clubs, arts clubs, environmental associations, and charities. Political interest groups include political parties, trade unions, and professional associations.
Source: World Values Survey, 1990. Data obtained from Christian Haerpfer, IHS Vienna.

Ascribed Trust

Kuczi and Makó (1997) provide a positive example of the beneficial role of ascribed trust in sustaining a network of joiners in a Hungarian village. In this example, villagers were bound together by family ties, ethnicity, but also social institutions such as a village foundation and Sunday club discussions. This facilitated a business organization built on oral contracts only, which allowed individual craftsmen to benefit from economies of scale and jointly contribute to a major development contract.[7] Integration with outsiders was provided by a national entrepreneur with remaining local ties, as well as by a local entrepreneur, whose relationship of trust with the individual craftsmen ensured contract compliance. T. Kuczi and C. Makó (1997) liken this arrangement to the organization of small-scale businesses in the famous industrial districts of northern Italy, a pattern that has found a number of successful parallels in developing countries (Humphrey and Schmitz 1996).

In a similar vein, McMillan and Woodruff (1998a, b) analyze the role of trust in Vietnam's emerging private sector, in a context where formal institutions for contract enforcement were almost entirely absent. They propose the willingness of suppliers to extend trade credit as a measure of trust toward a business partner and found that it is positively related to the costs of finding alternative customers. Trust was more easily sustained in local industrial clusters because search costs created a disincentive to exit.[8] By the same token, business networks were important sources of information among its members: "Gossip matters in this economy. Time spent in teahouses serves a purpose" (1998b: 18). But McMillan and Woodruff also point out the costs of business networks built on this type of ascribed trust. Thus, large and successful firms relied far less on family ties than small firms, suggesting that to be successful firms had to break out of clientelistic relationships. Moreover, only 29 percent of all enterprises surveyed by the authors said they would accept a lower price offer from a supplier with whom they had not done business with before. More than half would buy only parts of their inputs from the new supplier while continuing to trade with the old, more expensive partner, while 19 percent would reject the cheaper offer outright (1998b: 18).

Process-based Trust: Old versus New Networks

The "old boys networks" of managers of state-owned enterprises, party members, and other members of the socialist elite have in many instances provided the basis for the formation of new business organisations. Grabher and Stark (1997) provide a wealth of case studies of the nature and the origins of business networks during the transition. A number of salient characteristics of such networks can be distinguished.

Stark (1996) analyses the close linkages between old state-owned enterprises and private corporations in Hungary. According to Stark, the process of corporatization and spontaneous privatization in this country led to multiple remaining connections between state-owned enterprises, their privatized subsidiaries, banks and the state property agency—business networks that Stark calls "recombinets." Significant economic uncertainty during the transition and the specificity of physical and relational assets in such a network made it efficient to preserve it, even in the face of government policies aiming to break it up through privatization of individual units.[9] However, as Stark (1996: 997) admits, the resulting organizational structure blurs the boundaries between public and private and "creates acute problems of accountability." Indeed, recombinets may be an efficient short-run response of existing enterprises to the threat to survival. It is less clear whether they are similarly efficient at promoting deep restructuring in their constituent elements and at attracting outside investment—in many cases, including Hungary, a key element of effective business modernization.

J. B. Sedaitis (1997) distinguishes two types of business networks in postcommunist Russia. In a study of Russian commodity markets during the early

1990s, she found the simultaneous existence of "dense" networks based on previous bureaucratic ties (for instance resulting from the privatization of operational functions of industrial ministries) and "loose" networks, created with little reliance on relational capital. Dense networks had small and largely constant membership, and traded primarily subsidized standard goods acquired through bureaucratic channels and sold for barter. Enterprises would supply these markets because of the security of transactions even though prices were far below what would have been obtainable on competitive terms. Loose networks were larger and more variable in membership and oriented toward profit. Payment was largely in cash. Sedaitis highlights the advantages of dense networks in reducing transaction costs, but their inflexibility when it comes to innovation and exploitation of new profit opportunities.

During the transition, it would be expected that the importance of old relative to new business networks would decline, as more and more agents seek out new economic opportunities.[10] Competition between these alternative organizational forms provides a powerful means of efficient institutional adaptation. However, the initial dominance of old business networks has, in many transition economies, blocked off the emergence of such competition. Closed networks have been able to turn themselves into vehicles for rent-seeking, and new enterprises have been discouraged through persistent regulatory interference and corruption (Johnson et al. 1997). It is here that the greatest costs of the blurred boundaries between the public and private lie.

Global Networks: Linkages or Dualism?

East Germany is maybe the clearest case of an economy in which existing business networks have been largely destroyed from outside through corporate breakups and a top-down approach to privatization (Grabher 1997). Other economies such as Estonia's and Hungary's, have increasingly followed a similar strategy. As a result, a considerable number of firms in these countries are now integrated into global networks. Vertical integration through strategic investment from abroad or tight horizontal integration through outward processing trade has overcome weaknesses in the domestic formal institutional framework for contract enforcement. It remains as yet unclear whether these members in global business networks will become fully integrated into their host economies through backward linkages to domestic suppliers. EBRD project experience points to the possibility that one strategic foreign investment can lead to fundamental organizational changes in an entire network of domestic suppliers (Matouschek and Venables 1998). However, a dualistic economic structure where globally integrated enterprises rely largely on external suppliers, or indeed, a fractionalization and disintegration of domestic suppliers' networks is also a possibility, with considerably lesser benefits for the host economy.

Trust and the State in Transition

The legacy of low extended trust and reliance on closed business networks puts particular emphasis on the role of the state to provide the basis for more efficient economic specialization. As argued above, third-party contract enforcement through the state can make exchanges among anonymous parties possible, and the repeated experience of successful transactions can in turn generate extended trust.

To provide this function effectively, however, the state must transform itself. This requires the realignment of incentives of government officials and the building of public legitimacy. As long as officials remain members in old boys networks preserved for the purpose of rent-seeking they have few incentives to provide efficient third-party enforcement. Indeed, in many instances, the state has effectively been bought by narrow interest groups to legislate in their favor. Chart 4.3 reports the extent to which the state has been captured by special interest groups in the transition economies, drawing on the results of a large enterprise survey implemented by EBRD for the 1999 Transition Report. It shows very significant differences across the transition economies in the extent

Chart 4.3
The Extent of State Capture

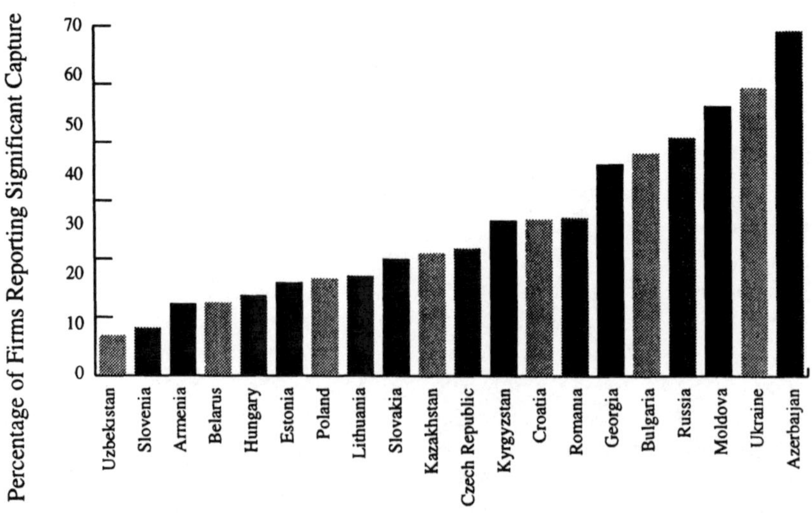

Note: Firms were asked whether the sale to private interests of parliamentary votes on laws or presidential decrees had had an impact on their business. Responses ranged across No Impact, Significant Impact, and Very Significant Impact. The firms reporting Significant Impact or more are included.

Source: World Business Environment and Enterprise Performance Survey, implemented by EBRD jointly with the World Bank. For details see Transition Report, 1999.

of state capture, with the most advanced and best performing countries in central Europe generally outperforming countries further east.

If government behavior is oriented at the preservation of rents for privileged interest groups, trust in state institutions is unlikely to emerge. This in turn reinforces the difficulties of relying on formal institutions to facilitate the emergence of extended trust in transition. Table 4.1 reports average scores for trust in a variety of state institutions for the years 1992, 1994, 1996, and 1998 (these institutions include the courts, the police, the government, the parliament, the army, and the civil servants). The data is drawn from the New Democracy Barometer, a survey of around 1,000 households in twelve transition economies. The table again reveals significant differences across countries in the extent of trust in state institutions. Trust in 1998 was highest in Romania, Hungary, and Poland and lowest in Serbia and Ukraine. With the exception of Romania (unex

Table 4.1:
Trust in State Institutions in Selected Transition Economies

	YEAR			
	1993	1994	1996	1998
Belarus		3.26	3.04	3.47
Bulgaria		3.02	3.39	3.50
Croatia		4.05	4.10	3.87
Czech Republic	3.97	3.98	3.78	3.46
Hungary	3.69	3.82	3.82	3.78
Poland	4.10	3.88	3.84	3.82
Romania		3.89	3.81	4.08
Serbia				3.10
Slovakia	3.97	3.77	3.72	3.68
Slovenia		3.85	4.09	3.60
Ukraine		2.94	3.22	2.60

Note: Trust scores range from 7 (high trust) to 0 (no trust). Data in the table are averages over the following institutions: the courts, the police, the army, the government, the civil service, and the parliament.

Source: New democracy Barometer. Data obtained from Christian Haerpfer, IHS, Vienna.

Chart 4.4: ***Trust and State Capture***

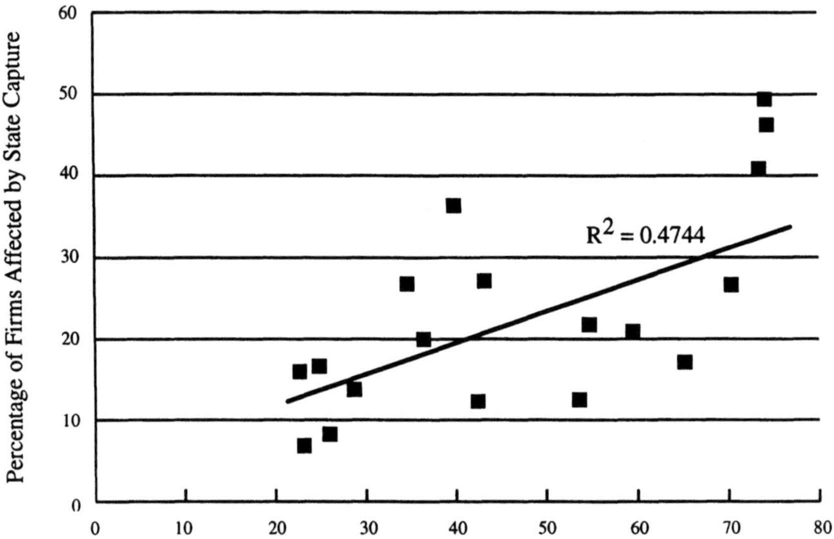

Note: State capture is measured as the share of firms, that report that the sale of parliamentary votes or presidential decrees "had an impact on their business." Trust in the legal system is defined as the share of firms that do not agree that "the legal system will uphold their contract or property rights in case of a legal dispute."

Source: World Business Environment and Enterprise Performance Survey. EBRD. Implemented jointly with the World Bank. For details see 1999 Transition Report.

pectedly high) and the Czech Republic (unexpectedly low), the average scores correspond roughly to progress in transition. Chart 4.4 returns to the enterprise survey and shows that the extent of capture and trust in state institutions (in this case in the legal system) are highly correlated across transition economies.

The relationship between trust in the state and state capture suggests that the differences across transition economies in this regard might be explained by the way in which Communism was dissolved and economic assets redistributed during the early transition years. What follows is the initial sketch of an explanation, recognizing the need for far more in-depth historical research.

In the former Soviet Union, the loss of authority of the Communist Party under Mikhail Gorbachev led to the disintegration of the state itself. In the face of large political uncertainty public officials began stealing state assets by the mid-1980s (Solnick 1998) and actively promoting the disintegration of the state's monopoly in coercive power. The almost complete privatization of the provision of public services allowed maximum short-term incomes to be derived from public office, at the cost of driving a considerable share of the economy underground and out of reach of the tax authority. Moreover, the assets stolen from state organizations often formed the basis of economic empires powerful enough to directly influence the course of policy-making. Bureaucratic networks transformed themselves into business organizations aiming to secure maximum rents. Corruption became endemic during the closing years of the Soviet Union, and this inheritance was carried over to the period of market-oriented reforms. In central and to a lesser extent Eastern Europe, political authority was never lost to the point of impairing the implementation of a national policy agenda. Melanie Tatur (this volume) argues with reference to Poland and Hungary that national elites in these countries were able to draw on historical traditions of nationhood and rally public opinion around the principles of free market economy and democracy, with the ultimate aim of regaining a place among the European nations (see also Smolar 1996). National elites appealed to different symbols in the process of reconstituting the state—continuity with the partial reforms in Hungary, and mass movement and conflict in Poland. These differences influenced the techniques of institution building and may yet have lasting effects. Yet in both cases, a national reform agenda provided a long-term prospect and potential gain that helped public officials to bind their own hands and achieve some policy credibility, against the background of public distrust.

The importance of the goal of membership in the European Union in binding policymakers' hands in central and Eastern Europe points more generally to the advantage of geographical proximity to the West. This significantly enhanced the set of economic opportunities and thus increased incentives for both public officials and private entrepreneurs to adapt their behavior. Exposure to Western trading partners offered access to modern technology and marketing but required a change in business practices. Gaining the trust of foreign investors was often crucial against a background of continuing legal and economic uncertainty.

The Role of Policy

A legacy of distrust is not easily amenable to policy changes. As J. Elster et al. (1998: 18) note:

> Cultural patterns, identities and legacies, associative practises that help or hinder the solution of collective goods problems, and the vigour with which entrepreneurial and other economic interests are pursued are among those determinants of change that cannot be easily legislated into—or out of—being.

Nonetheless, as the last section has shown, public policy can help to shape the evolution of trust. Given the central role of trust in the state itself in this regard, this section focuses on political strategies that might increase trust in the state. I suggest four main avenues for building trust in the state: moral leadership; political competition and accountability; justice in the distribution of resources; and direct interventions in the formation of business support and information services.

D. C. North (1981) has highlighted the role of the "ideological entrepreneur" and moral leader in catalyzing institutional change and garnering support for new rules of exchange. Clearly, moral leadership and example are key factors in the credibility of strategies to increase trust in the state. Moral and ideological leadership operates in different environments across the region. Elster et al. (1998) point out the different nature of existing political cleavages, which determine the appeal to either class or ideological or ethnic constituencies by political leaders. The authors argue that class conflicts, by allowing a "splitting of the difference," provide for a solution through a pluralistic and democratic political process, while ideological and ethnic cleavages often (although not inevitably) result in much less solvable conflicts over rules, procedures, and identities. Countries characterized by ethnic divisions or strong residual beliefs in the socialist ideology are disadvantaged during the process of political consolidation.

Moral leadership and the power of ideas alone cannot guarantee impartial enforcement by state institutions. Competition from within—through the voice

Chart 4.5:
Change in Inequality, 1989/1990–1995/1996/1997, Selected Transition Economies

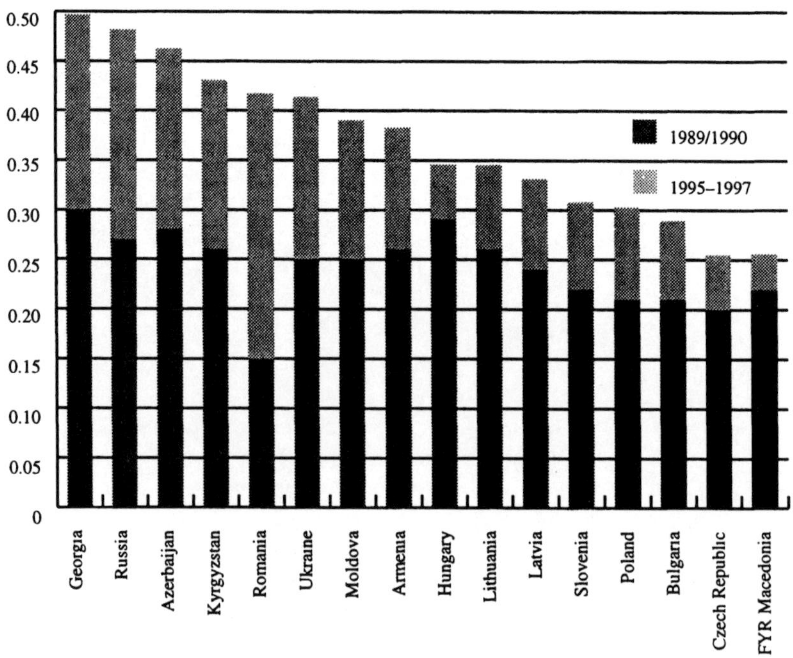

Note: Inequality is measured as the GINI-coefficient of earnings.
Source: UNICEF, TransMonee Database, 1999.

of democratic elections for public office—and from without—through the threat of exit of factors of production—is needed to discipline public officials. As Shleifer (1997) argues, the rapid turnover of local political elites in Poland following the collapse of Communism may have contributed to a lesser degree of discretionary intervention by local officials compared with Russia, where local elites remained more stable and government intervention was more acute. Economic crises across the region have forced governments to reconsider their policies to prevent further outflow of resources—into safe havens abroad and into the informal economies at home. Bulgaria, Croatia, and Slovakia are recent cases where economic difficulties have contributed both to a change in government and a dramatic reversal of policies to increase the attractiveness of the investment climate. Constitutional safeguards for open democratic government and policies that enhance a country's exposure to the discipline of foreign markets can thus be factors contributing to improvements in the quality of formal institutions and indirectly to the emergence of extended trust.

Government policies can also directly influence the social basis for extended trust. One key policy arena in this respect is redistribution. The perceived fairness of privatization policies may be an important source of legitimacy for formal institutions more generally, as many of them are geared toward the protection of the newly created property rights. Chart 4.5 shows that the most advanced transition economies in central Europe have had among the lowest increase in income inequality since the start of transition, which arguably has helped to legitimize their public institutions. Moreover, highly insider-skewed privatization policies have increased social distance and arguably undermined the basis for the development of extended trust in many transition economies, such as Russia's. Increased income inequality in the context of reduced incomes overall also increases economic risks for individuals on the lower end of the wealth scale. Higher risks will tend to fortify reliance on closed social networks at the cost of lower extended trust.[11]

Finally, as shown by examples from around the world, surveyed by J. Humphrey and H. Schmitz (1996), the state can directly promote the development of business networks built on mutual confidence. Government support for chambers of commerce, trade fairs, or other means for exchanging information and thereby overcoming barriers to the formation of trust are examples of such policies. As P. Milgrom et al. (1990) show, when impartial institutions exist that facilitate the exchange of information, prisoners' dilemmas between loosely connected traders may be overcome, even if the third party has no coercive power to enforce contracts.

Conclusions: Trust and Economic Performance

Trust is a central element in most economic and social exchange. Without trust, opportunities for mutually beneficial trade remain closed off, and cooperative outcomes are less likely. The result is lower economic welfare through less than optimal specialization and arguably lower social welfare more generally, as altruistic preferences remain unfulfilled.

This paper distinguishes between family- or kinship-based trust, trust based on reputational mechanisms as present in repeated interaction, and extended trust, understood as the ex ante willingness to cooperate with anonymous others. It argues that what matters in complex societies is the existence of extended trust. Extended trust and impartial third-party enforcement are to a large extent complements in modern societies, and are likely to have arisen simultaneously in response to new economic opportunities. But the emergence of extended trust during the process of economic development requires moral leadership by the ruling elites induced by competition from within and without, and a social structure that reproduces appropriate social norms in dense but open networks.

Trust matters for economic performance, as increasing evidence from market economies reveals. For instance, P. Keefer and S. Knack (1997) have recently found a positive association of trust to economic growth, where trust is measured by the degree of confidence individuals would have in an anonymous counterparty—the precise definition of extended trust as adopted in this paper. D. Narayan and L. Pritchett (1997) find that the density of associational life contributes significantly to average household incomes in a sample of Tanzanian villages. Importantly, it is not just the relational capital accumulated by an individual or a household that raises incomes; the effect also can be found at the village level. Trust itself is a collective good.

Although the transition is far from over, the institutional outcomes as well as the economic performance in the more advanced transition economies of central Europe and the Baltics and in the countries of the Commonwealth of Independent States (CIS) are nonetheless strikingly different. A general legacy of distrust in both regions has given way to relatively stable democratically legitimated government in one part of the region and the continuation of an opaque and oligarchic political structure in another. This paper hints at one possible historical root of this difference, namely, the varying way in which central planning and the Communist Party state were replaced. In particular, the root of political power in post-Soviet Russia and elsewhere in the CIS in the usurpation of state assets during the demise of Communist rule is argued to contrast with the shift in power in central Europe to an opposition movement, which albeit fragmented and weak, largely endorsed the tradition of Western liberal thought. These historical differences were compounded by differences in new economic opportunities, which increased the incentives for institutional adaptation.

Policy can make important contributions to building trust, first and foremost by increasing trust in public institutions, which will in turn provide contract enforcement and allow successful transactions to build mutual confidence over time. The paper highlights four elements of an appropriate political strategy: (1) moral leadership; (2) constitutional safeguards that allow for competition among government agencies and a democratically legitimized turnover of ruling elites; (3) distributional policies that influence the legitimacy of the new institutional structures through the perceived fairness of transition outcomes and that provide a basic safety for individuals, allowing them to break free of existing social networks; and (4) direct policy intervention to strengthen business networks through facilitating the exchange of information.

Notes

I would like to thank the participants in the Berlin conference for helpful comments on an earlier draft. Simon Commander, Joel Hellman, Thomas Nowotny, and Peter Sanfey—all from the Chief Economist's Office at EBRD—also provided very useful comments. The views expressed in this paper are my own and do not reflect the views of the EBRD.

1. Kirchgässner (1994) distinguishes between a typical moralist and three other types of individuals in this context. The "hero" will contribute to a collective good that requires a low participation rate, even when her personal costs of doing so are high relative to her benefits. The "idealist" will always contribute, even when the collective good is not provided, but her costs of doing so are small. The "fanatic" always contributes, but at high costs to herself. Generally, the presence of these three non-average types is too small to matter for the design of public institutions, although the existence of heroes in providing ideological leadership and setting an example for cooperation may be quite important.

2. This begs the question of whether this moral innovation was the result of the specific technological and social conditions prevailing in western Europe at the time. Only if universalist morality could be derived from first principles as suggested, for instance, by John Rawls (1974), it might count as a truly exogenous innovation, which might be successfully transferred to other social contexts. However, it is far from clear whether moral innovations would necessarily respond to economic opportunities, as moral norms may be manipulated by ruling elites. See, for instance, Harriss and de Renzio's (1997) critique of Putnam (1993). Recent work by Ernst Fehr and collaborators (Fehr and Gächter, 2000; Fehr and Schmidt, 1999) reciprocal fairness might be enough to stabilize cooperation, where the threat of retaliation by reciprocal types is enough to constrain opportunists. The motivation behind reciprocity is different from the moral types discussed by Kirchgässner. How people become embued with a sense of fairness is of course as much an open question as how they know to trust. In fact, the two may be different expressions of the same underlying moral disposition.

3. The costs of preventing free riding through formal institutions is prohibitive almost by definition.

4. The atomization of civil society in socialist countries is well documented. For an overview and references to the literature see Elster et al. (1998).

5. Data for twenty-one transition economies are now available from the WVS 1995. The results generally seem to confirm the persistence of lower levels of trust and civic engagement (Haerpfer et al., 2001).

6. An interesting piece of evidence confirming the legacy of distrust comes from an experimental study by Ockenfels and Weimann (1999). These authors find that East and West German students differ significantly in the extent of cooperative behavior. A key feature of their experiment is that it is anonymous, and hence existing social loyalties do not count.

7. Note that the characteristics of this network correspond to the requirements of density and openness outlined further above as conditions for the reproduction of extended trust. Also, technological assets were complementary, encouraging network openness.

8. Indeed, the authors find substantial evidence that enterprises are willing to sustain commercial relationship even following the default of a counterparty rather than sanction this behavior with the termination of cooperation. In the absence of enforceable collateral and high search costs, sustaining the relationship is the only hope of getting one's money back.

9. A similar phenomenon is described for the Czech Republic by Hayri and McDermott (1998); here however the state encouraged the preservation of "old-boys" networks.

10. The marginal benefits from forming a new business to exploit market niches would tend to decline as the new private sector develops, but the uncertainty of expected returns would also be reduced.

11. Constraints on the feasibility of privatization policies in the face of strong insider resistance have loomed large in the design of privatization policies in many transition economies. The argument here is not to negate these constraints, but rather to direct the attention toward the much less discussed aspects of fairness of the process. The recent partial reversal of reforms in Russia would provide an interesting test case for analysis.

Chapter 5

Networks, Social Capital, and Leadership: Methodological Remarks on Approaches to the Study of Postcommunist Transformation

Bruno Grancelli

Save for some economists, the term *transition* does not enjoy a great deal of popularity among social scientists. As Stephen Cohen (1999) writes, those who adopt the concept run the risk of producing "Russian studies without Russia." Cohen's harsh critique of the "follies of transitology" consistently hits the mark, for instance, when he points out that things in Russia have been given names that they do not fully warrant: the worst industrial depression of the twentieth century has been called *reform*; "a decreed market, featuring contract killings as the supreme form of litigation, has been called a *free market*"; the decimation of the highly educated and potentially entrepreneurial Soviet middle classes has been called the *creation of a middle class*; and, finally, the disguised form of Russian authoritarianism that has presided over all this is called *political reform* (42f.). This, and other forms of regression, prompt Cohen to conclude that the words *collapse*, *disintegration*, and *catastrophe* come more readily to the minds of most Russians than does *transition*. So great was the social catastrophe that began in 1991 that one may speak of "the literal demodernization of a twentieth-century country," and of "a tragic 'transition' to a premodern era" (46f.).

What is to be done in such a situation by Western scholars? After some polemics against U.S. "experts" who have allegedly usurped Russia studies, Cohen proposes a historical-comparative approach to reopen some fundamental questions about continuities and changes in Russian/Soviet history. As a starting point, he quotes the question posed by Robert Tucker in 1990: "What time is it in Russian history?" He replies that "Russia is in yet another Time of Troubles."

I believe that this historical reference can be accepted without subscribing to catastrophic pessimism. After all, even in a time of troubles not all social actors are troublemakers. It is certainly true that "transitologists" have been hostages to the idea that the formation of a "civil society" might bring about a change for the better in the system. It is also true that since 1991 a series of traumatic shocks have been inflicted on Russian society from above. What is questionable, however, is whether "aspects of the Soviet order . . . that could have been building blocks of a reformed Russia . . . were instead reduced to 'rubble'" (Cohen 1999: 45). It is here that the debate may begin.

The debate may start from the following question: to what extent is it possible to construct *with* or do we have to build *on* the ruins of the Soviet order? This is the central question asked by the proponents of the approach that views network capital as some sort of prime mover of postcommunist transformation (Grabher and Stark 1997; Stark and Bruszt 1998). This approach, which is critically analyzed in the first section of this chapter, has the merit of pointing research in the right direction inasmuch as it does not focus on civil society as understood, for example, by Robert Putnam in *Making Democracy Work* (1993), but instead focuses on relational structures among key actors of the postcommunist political economy. It is precisely the difficulties that arise in applying Putnam's research design in the study of regional governance in Russia that may furnish useful suggestions for the development of an approach that can shed light on the various kinds of actors that operate inside or outside, within or without the networks analyzed by Stark and his associates.

Social and economic networks certainly warrant consideration, but with the following caveats: Within networks (1) there are some actors more enterprising than others; (2) the social groups to which actors belong contribute differently to modernization and economic development; (3) those actors who belong to modernizing groups may possess more cultural capital rather than more social capital; (4) cultural capital (new skills and know-how) is formed largely through exposure to programs of training and technical assistance provided by Western institutions; (5) cultural capital is the precondition for a professional career in the more dynamic branches of the economy and for entry into new networks with outside actors; (6) actors with cultural capital can help establish the new standard-setting institutions that will undertake the requisite knowledge transfer to local organizations and institutions and, in general, help reduce the negative characteristics of the social capital bequeathed by real socialism.

The point, therefore, is that the differences *among* and *within* networks require reexamination with the help of the concepts of social capital and cultural capital. Moreover, decision-making processes of key actors in different local contexts need to be analyzed. Only in this way can a comparative assessment of the influence exerted by networks, institutions, and leaders on transformation processes be undertaken. This should also lead to a clearer understanding of the "developmental" or "predatory" roles of post-Soviet states, as well as of the contribution made by outside agencies that furnish technical assistance.

Including "transformational leadership" (Kozminski 1993) and structural differences among local and regional contexts in the analysis requires a theoretical framework that is substantially at variance with that of purely relational approaches such as network capital. First, the analysis should not focus exclusively on relations, but should also consider the actions of key players in the local political economy, which may consequently help supersede Soviet legacies. Second, that legacy should not be viewed solely in terms of improvisations on routines from the past Soviet management, but also in the light of premodern aspects of that management and from an international point of view. Third, the logic of risk spreading pursued by networks acting in an institutional setting more "predatory" than "developmental" should also be considered as an obstacle to moving beyond the current phase of protomarket and protodemocracy.

If the focus of research is on the leadership of key actors, a "thick" version of the rationalist perspective might prove of higher heuristic value. This alternative approach can be found in studies that use the concepts and methods of rational choice theory to conduct comparative analysis of institutional change and that seek to determine how the purposive action of key actors can alter the constraints on political and economic innovation (Grancelli 1996). The final section of the chapter briefly discusses this possible line of research.

Network Capital, Recombinant Property, and Postcommunist Transformation

Many features of postcommunist transformation seemingly reinvigorate those perspectives that have focused on "hybrid" forms of coordination, that is, those different from both market and hierarchy (Thompson et. al. 1991; Grahber 1993; Powell and Smith-Doer 1994; Grahber and Stark 1997; Stark and Bruszt 1998). Economies in transition are very interesting cases that yield a large amount of evidence on the ways in which Soviet legacies combine with the emergent forms of market. The social embeddedness of the economic sphere has been investigated by various case studies on enterprise management (Burawoy and Hendley 1992; Clarke 1996; Hendley 1998) and on financial—industrial groups (Gorbatova 1995; Huber and Wörgötter 1998).

One of the aims of studies that rely on the network capital approach is to highlight the double potential of Soviet legacies, which are regarded as both constraints and opportunities (Grabher and Stark 1997; Stark and Bruszt 1998). Rather than focusing on the adaptation of the post-Soviet political economy to Western models, these scholars are interested in the integration of the Soviet institutional legacies with those realities emerging during the transformation process. They focus on the long-run evolutionary potential of different forms that coexist in a given context rather than on the efficiency of the single organization or institution. The unit of analysis in this relational approach is not individuals, or corporate actors, but the capital that accumulates within social networks (Grabher and Stark 1997: 3)

One of the key concepts of this approach is "path dependency," which defines organizational innovation as adaptation to new environmental uncertainties through improvisations on past inventories and routines. Another basic concept is that of "recombinant property," a term that denotes complex forms of interlocking property that key private and public actors use to insure themselves against economic risk through the continuous redefinition and recombination of existing resources. This does not refer solely to goods previously hidden or underutilized; it also comprises a legal redefinition of resources in a framework of organizational reflexivity related to the ambiguity of the governance principles in the present stage of economic transformation.

The proponents of the network capital approach refuse to take efficiency and profitability as the sole guiding principles in the study of transformation processes. In their view, regarding the market as the only possible coordination mechanism would amount to repeating the Communist attempt to impose one legitimizing principle and one mechanism of coordination. In short, according to the network capital approach the main problem of the transformation process is not that of finding the optimal mix between public and private property; rather, it is that of defining the right organization of diversity able to achieve adaptability.

What comes to the fore here is the role of entrepreneurship, an issue on which there are two schools of thought. On the one hand, there are those who see real entrepreneurship only among the founders of new enterprises (Murrell 1992a; Boisot and Child 1988; Boisot 1994; Codagnone 1995); on the other hand, there are those who see the adaptive capacities of postcommunist managers as the main avenue for the introduction of at least partial innovations (Solinger 1991; Baglione and Clark 1997; Stoner-Weiss 1997; Hendley 1998). Those authors who subscribe to the network capital approach do not accept this distinction. They are loath to focus on individuals because they think that this implies (1) not seeing the social features of the processes that lead to the creation of new enterprises, and (2) proposing a misleading distinction between public and private actors, given that all of them began their careers as state actors (Sedaitis 1997).

This position has two important theoretical implications. The first is the rejection of the Schumpeterian notion of "creative destruction" because networks appear to be mechanisms better able to respond rapidly to the changing demands of the market and to exploit new opportunities. The second is a definition of social capital as a property of networks and not of individuals (Grabher and Stark 1997).

However, my impression is that this approach leaves too much out of the picture for reasons to be sought in the authors' assumptions. Indeed, one should ask: What are the macro-level results of all those combinations and recombinations of property? What is the result of the intermingling between public and private domains? As Grabher and Stark acknowledge, the outcome of all this fuzziness is a decentralized reorganization of assets and a centralized management of liabilities—a nice déjà vu for those familiar with, for instance, the pathological interweaving of public and private spheres in recent Italian history.

While network capital might provide the capacity to react to short-term problems, it is also creating problems of accountability. Grabher and Stark see two solutions to this problem: first, the embedding of decision-making centers in networks of autonomous political institutions able to limit the arbitrariness of incumbents; second, the extension of accountability to economic actors through "beneficial constraints" (Streeck 1997) on decisions concerning, for instance, the mobility of capital or the firing of employees. These constraints may result in the decision to upgrade workforce skills, which in turn creates incentives for firms to compete in market segments where quality matters. Some of these constraints should be applied in the postcommunist transformation as well. But here, the first step should be that of forming a critical mass of entrepreneurs through the privatization of small to medium-size firms and their isolation from the conditioning influence of the big ones (Grabher and Stark 1997).

Indeed, the assertion that rigidity may be a source of flexibility should be submitted to further empirical tests insofar as a more realistic hypothesis might be that rigidity breeds further rigidity, especially in the wide domain of public institutions and organizations. It is doubtful that "flexible rigidities" can form the basis for long-term adaptability, just as it is doubtful that this aim can be obstructed by short-term adaptation to world markets.

To sum up, the network capital approach can be of help in describing the ways in which networks of banks, firms, local authorities, and branches of state bureaucracy are going to single out firms to save, prepare restructuring strategies, negotiate over the allocation of resources, and settle disputes. But there are two evident shortcomings. First, although the focus is on strategic actors, the individual capacity to exert transformational leadership is omitted from consideration. Second, this is an approach in which exogenous variables are poorly investigated because what lies outside seems to be merely an "hyperrational capitalism" ready to impose its designs.

Network Capital and Other Relational Approaches: Ill-founded Concreteness?

By drawing attention to the fact that the collapse of the Soviet regime did not leave a tabula rasa in terms of human and social capital, the network capital approach may be of some service as a sociological antidote to the early recipes of "shock therapists." The time has come, however, to ask whether it is really true that all key actors do pursue only strategies of adaptation and risk sharing. Are we to think that their only concern is with "recombinant property"? Is it really possible that none of the actors wants to take economic risk? That none of them is interested in connections with outside actors? That the only thing that counts is the capital of networks and not the difference among actors in terms of human or cultural capital? In the end, what the proponents of this approach seem to miss is that firms are driven not so much by mixed property patterns as by the need to find new domestic and international markets (Fligstein 1996).

The analytical framework summarized above stems from studies that were carried out mainly in Hungary and other countries of central Eastern Europe. But here a paradox arises: when applied to the former Soviet Union, the network capital approach shows more shortcomings than related approaches that were developed with no reference to postcommunist countries. A good example is the comparative framework proposed by Michael Woolcock (1998), whose aim is to propose a theoretical synthesis and a policy framework for the study of social capital and economic development. Woolcock, too, refers to recent trends in comparative institutional studies of the role of the state in economic development (Evans and Stephens 1988; Evans et al. 1985; Evans 1995). But his model also refers to studies of ethnic entrepreneurship that demonstrate that social capital has both "benefits" and "costs" (Portes 1998; Light and Karageorgis 1994; Portes and Landolt 1996).

The theoretical synthesis proposed by Woolcock is based on the integration—at the macro and micro levels—of the concepts of "embeddedness" and "autonomy." The first step in his model is the reminder that embeddedness may take different forms: social links, cultural practices, political contexts. Each of these forms provides actors with specific sets of opportunities and constraints. A clear example of constraints is apparent when a high degree of closure, density, and informality of social relations hampers attempts by the more enterprising members of the community to join more complex networks of exchange under the rule of law. Thus, "autonomy" needs to be incorporated into the analysis (Woolcock 1998: 163f.).

The second step of this model concerns the criteria for evaluating the costs and benefits of embeddedness: at the micro level, one should ascertain the presence of autonomous social links—that is, connections with actors outside the community under investigation—while at the macro and meso levels it should be investigated not just who is linked with whom but also the orientations of the actors in the networks. Two other concepts are then proposed: "integration," which denotes links within the community, and "linkage," which is defined as connections with outside actors (Woolcock 1998: 168).

If the aim is to account for the weak signs of organizational and institutional innovation in the former Soviet Union, Woolcock's model seems to have greater heuristic value than the one centered on network capital. Woolcock's framework allows for a systematic investigation of the main issues in the current debate on social capital: first, how to create positive forms of social capital while containing the dark sides that may stem from the closedness of networks; second, how to establish mutually advantageous relations between a given community and external organizations and institutions; third, how to evaluate the action of different social groups in terms of its developmental outcomes; and, finally, how to create a positive synergy between politics and society and to promote the modernization of the state apparatus.

The virtue of this analytical framework is that it provides a typology of sources of the four types of social capital, labeled "integration," "linkage," "synergy," and "organizational integrity." This supports the view that a single concept does not suffice to explain the range of empirical situations, and invites examination of (1) the different types, levels, and dimensions of social capital; (2) the different performance outcomes associated with different combinations of these dimensions; and (3) different sets of conditions that support or weaken favorable combinations (Woolcock 1998: 159). The fact remains, however, that the actors remain faceless within Woolcock's framework. Thus, we may conclude that this comparative approach is indeed useful, even if it is less dynamic than Woolcock claims it to be. The reasons reside in a double imbalance. The first concerns the surveyed literature on small business, and the second the theoretical background.

In his analysis of the literature on small business, Woolcock overlooks two distinctions that can avert the risk of logical circularity when social capital is conceived as a property of networks. The first distinction is that between resources and the ability to obtain them by virtue of membership in different kinds of social groups. This is simply to say that networks are not always able to give their members guaranteed access to desired resources. The second distinction is that between those who require resources and those who are able to provide them—that is, between the owners of social capital and those agreeing to the owners' requests.

Not always can the resources needed be obtained within the network. Moreover, it may be that not all members of the network require precisely the same kind of resources. But if certain actors look for resources outside the network, it is most likely that access to these resources depends on other forms of capital—forms of cultural capital (know-how rather than know-who). What therefore needs to be emphasized is that network members differ because they have differing endowments of both social capital and cultural capital. The network capital approach focuses only on social capital, that is, on those who are currently in power. But these are not the only actors on stage. After a decade of postcommunist transformation it would be advisable to begin focusing on other groups of actors as well: on those who have linkages with Western organizations and institutions. Here an adaptation of Coleman's analysis (1988, 1990) of this particular kind of social change could be very fruitful. First of all, to achieve their interests, actors engage in exchanges and unilateral transfers of control, which usually take the form of authority or trust relations and the consensual allocation of rights that may be seen as forms of social capital. But the point is that these exchanges "need not only be seen as components of social structures . . . they may also be seen as resources for the individuals" (Coleman 1990: 300). But if this is so, one should study the nodes and not just the relations among them, and one should examine the reciprocal influence between the two forms of capital, seeking to answer questions such as: What is the role of external actors in the formation of cultural capital? Who are the actors that look for this form of capital? Can cultural capital help reduce the downside of social capital that is so strikingly apparent today?

In fact, the role of external actors is mentioned in Woolcock's essay when he asks whether one can facilitate the emergence of top-down relations that bring about development and innovation. As regards the issue of technical and financial assistance to developing countries, Woolcock makes an interesting point: if at first the beneficiaries must receive education and training, at a later stage they must begin to acquire growing responsibilities. On the other hand, the donors must possess credibility, which is the precondition for establishing a "synergy" between their work and that of the receivers. Thus, the synergy to consider is not just that between state and society: it also is that between external actors and the local ones who have established "linkages" with them.

The point is an important one, but one should move a step forward and rephrase the question: Who should provide the impetus (and how) for the modernization and development of this kind of postsocialist society? In the context examined here, the formation of a new leadership is a slow and contradictory process. Those who have acquired new cultural capital may sometimes lapse back into the old habits of a "predatory" local environment. Moreover, they are not so numerous and rarely rise to top positions. A critical mass of new cultural capital has not yet formed. However, the programs of training and technical assistance managed by Western institutions, despite their shortcomings, have led to the creation of local standard-setting institutions that have achieved self-sustainability and provide training and consultancy for enterprises and local governments (Grancelli 1999).

Transformational leadership in its various forms should be subjected to comparative investigation, possibly starting from one of the basic effects of the new cultural capital introduced from the outside: the enlargement of the temporal horizon of actors. This is of great importance in a context where risk sharing largely prevails over risk taking. The starting point should be to consider the entrepreneur—not the network—as the prime mover of change in the postcommunist political economy.

Shifting the Focus

Let us refer again to the question of building on or with the ruins of Communism. Generally speaking, one might think that the orientation to build on should prevail among people endowed with new forms of cultural capital and linkages with outside actors. By contrast, the propensity to build with certain legacies of the Soviet model might prevail among the great majority of managers and entrepreneurs who used to be members of the Soviet *nomenclatura*.

This distinction calls into question the path-dependent character of social capital as depicted in studies such as those by Francis Fukuyama (1995) and Putnam (1993). These culturalist approaches emphasize enduring cultural features, but they are unable to explain why variations nevertheless occur. To do so, the picture should include the character of a given set of social relations, the choices of social actors, politics, and policies and the processes of economic transformation (Bagnasco 1999). Indeed, as the application of Putnam's research design to the post-Soviet context has demonstrated, the crucial factor is not so much "civicness." Instead, the structural characteristics of regional economies or the choices of key actors in the local political economy seem to be much more important for economic development (Stoner-Weiss 1997; Baglione and Clark 1997).

What is needed, then, is a concept that helps explain economic development and modernization in that it refers not so much to a readiness to cooperate in a trustful community as to networks of relations among key actors open to different outcomes (Trigilia 1999: 430). Moreover, the approach should focus on actors who are outsiders with regard to these networks but have linkages with other kinds of networks in which cultural capital is the strategic resource for individuals.

The question then is this: are local actors—those with social capital and those with cultural capital—able to play a transformational leadership role more attuned to a modern market economy? This may be addressed by referring to the problem posed by James Coleman (1990: 652): how to replace the "primordial" forms of social capital that were typical of traditional societies and vanished with modernization. In Russia and the other states of the former Soviet Union the problem is that of modernization, but the shift is not the one depicted by Coleman: social capital has acquired many forms, including those that are genuinely primordial insofar as they have also fostered the development of a criminal economy (Germani 2000). This should be borne in mind when discussing whether to build on or with the ruins of Communism.

The reference to the downside of social capital in the post-Soviet context calls for a comparative approach capable of identifying the cultural and institutional constraints on the still prevailing particularistic appropriation of resources distributed through political–administrative channels: obstacles that only a modern polity and a "developmental state" (Evans 1995) can overcome. But what if local actors are unable or unwilling to create new forms of social capital able to foster development and societal modernization? To deal with cases like this, two possible policy solutions have been put forward. The first is the development of new networks more closely based than previous ones on cooperation among collective actors. The second is an extended engagement of institutions external to the local reality aimed at improving the capacity of local actors to plan patterns of development (Trigilia 1999: 436).

These two policy suggestions are useful reference points for a discussion of possible ways to refine the comparative model of social capital, economic development, and societal modernization. Such refining is based on a political economy approach that may be located in the area where the institutional approach meets the ideas-oriented approach; an area in which fruitful exchange between structural and cultural perspectives takes place in the search for a third pillar in the coordination of economic relations (Hall 1997). Some authors who refer to this approach criticize Putnam's view of social capital in terms of "civicness" by recalling Coleman and his focus on network (not culture) as a way to take into account strategic actors (Bagnasco 1999). What is important is that the situational and dynamic aspects should be taken into account by also including exogenous factors in the analytical framework (Piselli 1999).

From this perspective, the focus should be on the networks of associational links that breed trust and norms of reciprocity (such as those studied by Coleman and Putnam), on coordinating structures similar to neocorporatist relations (Schmitter 1990), and on social networks as cultural products that assist in the building of a "politics of trust" as a precondition for economic development (Ostrom 1990; Sabel 1992; Locke 1995; Mutti 1998).

An attempt to apply these approaches based on the primary role of politics in the study of social capital to postcommunist transformation may certainly yield useful information. However, it may also show that is not enough to insert some of Coleman's insights into a political economy perspective. Two points are worth recalling here by way of example: first, social capital as a means to enhance tacit knowledge; second, the overcoming of a particularistic use of social capital through the development of new networks based more closely on cooperation among collective actors.

As regards the first point, it is true that social capital may enhance tacit knowledge (Trigilia 1999: 432). However, one should bear the context in mind. In this regard, the "Third Italy" of small businesses and industrial districts is certainly different from the post-Soviet societies. In the latter, tacit knowledge may be of service, at best, within the continuous process of "recombining" property, but will increasingly turn into an obstacle to economic progress and modernization. This is where the European institutions come in and why they should be included. Through programs such as Tacis and Phare, the European Union is seeking to form new human or cultural capital, which is supposed to largely replace the tacit management knowledge of Soviet times. Instead of tacit knowledge, it is the transformation of post-Soviet societies that is required. What is needed is the purposive action and learning of political and economic entrepreneurs that, according to D. C. North (1990b), is one of the main sources of organizational and institutional change. There should be a shift in focus, therefore, from networks to the action of key individual change agents.

As to the second point on collective actors, in the former Soviet Union the conditions for the working of neocorporatist arrangements are still lacking, if only because of the weakness of labor and the practical impossibility of using the state administration for whatever policy may be devised by the political leadership. In this situation, the claim that Western institutions providing technical assistance should also act as "political entrepreneurs" (Stoner-Weiss 1997: 201) seems a good idea even if somewhat ahead of its time. The point, in fact, is that while in all postcommunist societies the transformation process has rapidly produced the constitutional and legal forms of interests representation, those very interests are at best in the making (Elster et al. 1998: 273). But if this is so, the corollary is that there is a precondition for the formation of interest representation: a management of economic organization quite different from the one still prevailing within the "economic dinosaurs" of post-Soviet economies. And this, again, is a problem of "transformational leadership" (Kozminski 1993) and not of relations among collective actors who exist only in embryonic forms.

Toward a Thick Rationalist Perspective

The analysis of Soviet legacies in terms of (primordial) social capital, then, requires us to address Coleman's problem without ignoring the basic lesson of rationalist approaches: individual interests do not necessarily turn into collective action, and collective action does not always yield collective goods (Olson 1965; Levi 1997). Indeed, one cannot build a really dynamic comparative model if the perspective remains sociocentric and merely relational. This implies that the heuristic value of the rationalist perspective should be assessed more carefully.

The debate on rational choice theory has been very lively in sociology and political science (Friedland and Robertson 1990; Coleman and Fararo 1992; Friedman 1996). Here it is worth quoting Woolcock's statement that rational choice theorists regard social capital as an informational resource that emerges from the interaction between rational agents needing to coordinate for reciprocal benefit. Consequently, they run the risk of trying to explain too much with to little (Woolcock 1998: 155f.).

Admittedly, some criticism seems justified: the rationalist perspective may, sometimes, overlook both the self and the context (Lichbach and Zuckerman 1997; Zey 1998). An evolution has occurred, however, in that rationalist approaches are becoming less parsimonious but more suitable for integration with other approaches to social change. Important attempts have been made to reconsider behavioral assumptions (Elster 1978) and to explore the domain of ethics and cultural patterns (North 1990b). Closer attention is paid to institutions, norms, context, power, and conflict; and there is no longer a preconceived hostility toward state intervention in the economy (Levi 1997). Finally, within the methodological domain, comparative statics has evolved toward forms of institutional analysis known as analytical narratives (Kiser 1996). In short, this perspective has become thicker. As this also has happened to structuralist and culturalist approaches, the shortcomings of one school can now be addressed by the other two.

The dialogue between rational choice and the other analytical perspectives may indeed provide the analytical framework within which to address an issue already mentioned in passing: is an ethic of *samostoiatelnost* (self-reliance) encroaching on a terrain saturated with rent-seeking? Is there an individual action oriented to the future despite the burdens of path dependency? If so, who are the rational actors? On these issues some concluding remarks follow.

Area specialists largely agree that the basic problem of postcommunist transformation is the adaptation of social capital. However, area studies often focus exclusively on legacies, networks, and institutions. What remains out of sight are the decisions of key actors. The comparative research on institutional redesign in postcommunist societies carried out by Elster et al. (1998) indeed shows how the actor is to be brought back in.

Everywhere, there are three key variables: Soviet legacies, institutions, and decisions. The outcomes of change are different, however. How can these differences be explained? In drawing theoretical conclusions from their fieldwork, Elster et al. (1998: 293) distinguish two levels: the *temporal structure of determination* and the *degree of intentionality*. Hence, legacies in terms of resources, mind-sets, and traditions bring about outcomes that have little to do with intentional causation because the constraints they impose are relatively immune from purposive action. Institutions are instead amenable, at least to some extent, to the redefinition of rules and objectives. Finally, decisions constitute the variable that has the closest bearing on the outcomes desired by individual actors in a given process of change. The implication of these distinctions is that durability will diminish in the shift from legacies through decisions while the degree of intentionality will to grow concomitantly (294).

How, then, can a synthetic approach be developed with which to compare the relative weights of legacies, institutions, and the decision making of key actors in different contexts? Within the analytical framework proposed by these authors, this question can be addressed by elaborating on two basic concepts: "forward linkages" and "backward linkages." The former concept applies when structures select institutions and agents and these, in turn, select decisions to be taken; the latter applies when a given range of choices set agents and institutions in motion, thereby creating new arrangements that modify structural legacies

(Elster et al. 1998: 296). It is evident here that the impetus for change may derive from both structures and agents, and the prime mover may also be a specific actor, a leader.

The next step is to shift the focus to new actors and new networks: as a first indication, one needs to know more about at least two kinds of actors. The first are those managers and entrepreneurs who have achieved a certain degree of emancipation from the traditional Soviet corporate ethic in favor of the ethic of self-reliance. These people, it has been surmised, sometimes undergo some sort of conversion from collectivism to individualism, which implies "a strong moral injunction against corruption and redistribution which they identify with the abandoned system" (Kharkhordin 1994: 423). It may well be true that strong structural continuities in the post-Soviet polity economy render the stated self-reliance of some business people more an ideology than an actual practice (Brym 1996: 414). It may also be true that the culture of these business people is inadequate for the capitalistic transformation of the former USSR, even if many of them (especially young and male) identify themselves with *homo oeconomicus* and display pro-Western attitudes (Dinello-Evdokina 1998: 299). These people nevertheless deserve more attention insofar as they display the ability to implement strategies of "sustainable adjustment" (Kuznetzov 1994: 485) in relation to changes in internal and international markets. In these cases, even if less numerous, there are technological and organizational changes, along with new links with foreign partners, brought about by a director with outstanding qualities as an organizer, decision maker, and creator of a new management team (Grancelli 1995). This kind of "new technocrat" is able to exert a transformational leadership insofar as s/he is implementing cultural change strategies attributed by Schein to the "organizational mid-life" growth stage: planned change and organization development, technological seduction, and incrementalism (Kozminski 1993: 184). In many cases these manager-entrepreneurs, with the help of foreign consultants (often expatriates), have been able to implement restructuring programs calling for drastic changes in the organization culture, such as: high work discipline and quality regimes, decentralization and the spinning off of new firms, and compensation systems linking pay and productivity and allowing for greater differentiation of pay scales. In short, they are leaders because they have been able to tackle the most sensitive issue in postsocialist firms: the elimination of the workers' council, that is, "the pillar of the populist industrial democracy" (Kozminski 1993: 185).

The second category of actors that warrants attention is those who have passed through the many programs of training and technical assistance of the European Community and various Western institutions. Despite their shortcomings, these programs have produced at least one important precondition for economic development and societal modernization: the existence of a good deal of self-sustainable standard-setting institutions able to create human capital and to transfer knowledge to local organizations and institutions. And what is worth noting here is that the one condition that led to the creation of a good training institution was the presence of a program manager who acted as a leader capable of creating an effective team and a corporate culture.

In conclusion, a lucky combination of competent administrators, charismatic governors, and well-trained and/or reasonable managers is perhaps as important as networks and civicness for transforming the political economy in post-Soviet societies.

Chapter 6

Comparative Economics and the Study of the Russian Transition

Peter Rutland

The study of socialist economic systems took root in American and British universities in the 1950s and 1960s, when a whole generation of esteemed scholars analyzed the structural features of the centrally planned economy (CPE).[1] The CPE was recognized as a sui generis form of economic organization, with laws of operation distinct from those of a market economy. Although inferior from the point of view of economic efficiency, the CPE was seen as a viable alternative and indeed rival to the capitalist system. Most university economics departments had a professor who specialized in comparative economic systems, and the Soviet system was the main focus of their courses. In the 1950s, study of the CPE overlapped with the lively field of growth theory, as economists such as Poland's Michal Kalecki built models for optimal growth paths in developing countries.

In the 1960s and 1970s attention shifted from the internal dynamics of the CPE to the ways in which the CPE could introduce market reforms. Most economists seemed to believe that it would be possible to introduce "market socialism": marketlike relations in an economy where enterprises were state or worker owned. A lot of intellectual effort went into modeling the dynamics of the Yugoslav-style self-managed economy. Interest in growth theory faded in the economics discipline as a whole, partly because of the poor performance of Nehru's development planning in India. The paradigm of studying CPEs as a special type of economy persisted up until the end of the 1980s—just when the first generation of trailblazing scholars was heading for retirement. With the collapse of the Soviet system, the study of CPEs also collapsed, and with it, perhaps, the whole notion of comparative economic systems.

The Shift to a New Paradigm

Since 1989-91, the CPE paradigm has been replaced by the transition economy paradigm. This paradigm is shaped by a teleological assumption: that there is only one set of laws about how a market economy functions. Although national economies start from different points of departure, and encounter various obstacles along the way, they are all ultimately converging toward a model of a developed market economy (read: Anglo-American).

The collapse of the CPEs had a devastating effect on the discipline of comparative economics in American universities. This is very paradoxical, since the opportunities for business and scholarship in the former socialist countries dramatically increased after the collapse of the CPEs. Suddenly, there were twenty-seven new countries in need of advice and assistance in building a market economy. There were twenty-seven new markets where Western firms could find customers and resources. New sources of data and research opportunities blossomed in comparison with the restrictive policies of the socialist era. Students flocked to courses on the transition economies, because it was exciting and because it could mean jobs for them.

But this new potential did not translate into university teaching of comparative economics. Although central data is not collected, it appears that not a single new assistant professor with a specialization in Russian/East European area studies has been awarded tenure at an American university economics department since 1993. As the old guard from the 1950s retired from the Ivy League schools, either they were not replaced by area specialists, or their replacements did not serve through to tenure. Very few economics departments have hired specialists in the postcommunist economies since 1991, although there is still some interest in applied economics with an international dimension in business schools.

The general discipline of economics has changed radically over the past thirty years. Mathematical modeling is now valued more highly than an understanding of the institutional structures of a given economy (Barber 1997). Some credit, but not much, is given to the ability to gather data about specific economies. Even the study of economic history—the institutional development of the U.S. economy itself—has largely disappeared from economics departments, and tries to eke out an existence in exile in departments of history and political science. Political science has seen a lively interest in the "new institutionalism": studying the origins of political and economic institutions. For a young economist, however, years spent learning a foreign language or trying to do fieldwork in another country is time spent away from honing one's mathematical skills. Such economists found it hard to compete with their colleagues who never left their university desks.

Why did this mathematization of the economics discipline occur? Partly it was a bid to emulate the perceived success of the natural sciences. Partly it was a rationing device: an apparently objective skill test that could enable departments to pick the best candidates, and journal editors to pick the best articles, by assessing their degree of mathematical sophistication.

At the same time that the flow of area specialists was being cut off at the roots, there was a determined effort to colonize the field of transitology from outside. This colonization came from several directions: from non-area studies economists and from international financial institutions. The term *colonization* is used here in a neutral sense, and is not meant to imply that this influx of talent and resources was inherently bad. On the contrary, it produced some of the best work on the transition economies (e.g., Blasi et al. 1996). However, it was significant that the study of specific national economies passed out of the hands of people who were trained in area studies and typically spent their entire careers perfecting their understandings of those economies.

Given the assumption of the universality of the laws of the market, economists who had no special knowledge of a given country or the CPE heritage had no hesitation about starting research on any particular transition economy. Thus, for example, specialists in international trade, labor economics, bank regulation, or utility regulation started research projects in the former socialist countries. To the extent that they needed local knowledge, they could hire local graduate students, or take data from government and international agencies.

At the same time, international institutions such as the European Union, IMF, World Bank, United Nations Development Organization, and International Labor Organization started channeling some of their massive resources into the study of the postcommunist countries, which hitherto had been closed to them. Not only did they want to bring these countries into the global economy, some of these institutions also saw the collapse of socialism as an opportunity to restore their battered international images. The World Bank was suffering from the abject failure of much of its lending for infrastructure projects in developing countries. The IMF had been created to manage a fixed exchange rate system that no longer existed, and repeated international financial crises raised doubts about their roles in the new economic order. The budgets—even the very existence—of these organizations was under attack in the U.S. Congress. The collapse of Communism provided a golden opportunity for those international agencies to put their expertise in market economics to work. The countries of the region accepted their advice—and their loans—with enthusiasm. Within a couple of years the IMF and World Bank were devoting up to one-third of their staffs and resources to work on the transition economies. The Europeans, feeling left out, created the European Bank for Reconstruction and Development to join in the game.

One positive and countervailing trend that should be mentioned is the influx into the field of comparative economics of new scholars from the region. People who were raised and educated in those countries have the language skills and an intuitive grasp of how the system works. If they go on to complete graduate school in the United States, then they can combine mathematical skills with area expertise.[2] Even so, in terms of professional careers they will be judged by their colleagues primarily for their mathematical expertise and not for their area knowledge. One can hazard a guess that in twenty years the only economists in university departments with area studies expertise will be persons who were born in the countries they are studying.

The Assumptions of Transition Economics

So, by the early 1990s the bulk of American research on the transition economies was being financed by international financial institutions, and carried out by economists who had not previously studied the CPEs. What were the implications of this for the way those economies were studied and the type of analysis that was offered?

Facts and Values

First, one should note that this unique situation led to an unhealthy blurring of the line between positive and normative analysis. Economists often found themselves in the role of giving advice to governments, and then having to justify or disown their advice in the light of consequent developments. The thrust of the analysis was heavily clouded by the conclusions that the author wished to draw. Much of the work had a triumphalist quality, starting from the assumption that Russia was well on the way to becoming a functioning market economy (Aslund 1995; Layard and Parker 1996). Most of the business press and newspapers presented a simplistic model of developments in Russia as a struggle between good reformers and bad Communists. There was a tendency to prominently report the good news while ignoring the bad news. Negative developments were attributed to the lingering influences of the communist past and were not seen as possibly the product of the transition process itself. This may be called the "Good News Bible" school of Russia analysis. (In Britain in the 1970s there was an abortive effort to launch a new edition of the Bible that kept the miracles but deleted the slaying and pillaging.)

The difference between facts and values is something that is taught in primary schools in the United States, yet the distinction has often been forgotten, even by senior economists. Prescription got mixed up with description. Economists typically wrote about what *should* or *must* happen in the Russian economy, and not what was actually happening. Analysis of the causes and consequences of economic problems was given short shrift: what counted was proposing a solution to those problems. The tone of analysis often switched around from optimistic to pessimistic and back again, depending on whether market reformers such as Yegor Gaidar and Anatolii Chubais were in or out of power, and on which group of Western advisors was welcome in the Kremlin. One should not necessarily blame the economists for this situation: it was a logical product of the environment within which such knowledge was generated. Host governments needed advice, and the international agencies were eager to provide it. Nobody wanted to hear that a problem had no solution; nobody was even very interested in looking at the costs of tackling a certain problem.[3]

Shifts in analytical conclusions (back and forth between optimism and pessimism) often correlated closely with the personal situations of the economists concerned: were they in or out as government advisors, were they on or off the international consultancy payroll? This does not mean that the advisors were doing anything illegal or immoral, simply that it is a recognized phenomenon that "Where you stand depends on where you sit." The world really looks different if you are riding around Moscow in a government limousine on a six-figure tax-free salary, or if you are a freelance journalist interviewing coal miners half a mile underground in Vorkuta. There are also some grounds for arguing that moral lapses did occur in some cases, since some advisors seemed to allow their personal financial interests to get too closely entwined with the international aid projects on which they were working (Wedel 1997, 1999).

Every action produces an equal and opposite reaction. The Good News Bible school more than met its match in the "Merchants of Doom" brigade, in whose writings rosy optimism was replaced by gloomy predictions of destruction. Russia was portrayed as a society characterized by chaos and suffering, and one that was therefore a source of dire threats to the West: ecological catastrophe, nuclear terrorism, organized crime. The possibility of a communist/fascist takeover was also hovering in the background, although in general the Mafia had replaced the Communists as the face of Russian evil. This depressing genre of journalistic reporting on Russia has a fine pedigree, going back at least to the writings of the Marquis de Custine in the 1830s. Despite the skewed premises, it has also produced some of the most interesting books on the Russian transition (Handleman 1995; Kotz and Weir 1997).

The dichotomy between these two schools of analysis, the Good News Bible and the Merchants of Doom, is artificial and unhelpful. What is lacking in these two literatures is an awareness of the diversity of experience in Russia since 1991: diversity both by social class and by region. In their rush to heap praise or blame on the Russian economic transition authors prefer to make broad and striking generalizations about macro-level trends: analysis of the regional dimension has been poorly represented.

Implications for Economic Analysis

What were the implications of this blurring of the fact/value distinction for economic analysis? In the following discussion I take as my model the World Bank's 1996 *World Development Report* (World Bank 1996), which is the most sophisticated, rigorous, and comprehensive analysis of the transition economies yet produced, and a fine exemplar of the new paradigm. However, the report's analysis is flawed by reliance on three assumptions: Pareto Optimality, the lack of alternatives, and financial indicators as a window on the real economy.

First, the old principle of Pareto Optimality was still shaping the analysis: the assumption that the shift to a market economy would be Pareto Optimal, generating a welfare gain that in principle (assuming adequate redistribution) could leave everybody better off than they were before. Economists treated the market as a modern alchemists' stone: a Golden Rule that would benefit everyone in the long term. (The idea that economics is about choices seems to have been forgotten.) The introduction of a market economy would lead to stability, growth, and prosperity for all inside the country in question, and would benefit both that country and their trading partners in the developed market economies. Pareto Optimality was taken for granted: one would have to be an economic ignoramus not to accept the validity of this principle. The gains from reform would leave everyone better off, or at least would create additional resources such that the winners could compensate the losers. If the costs and benefits were unevenly distributed across society, it was assumed that this would be a temporary phenomenon, a matter of a few years of belt tightening. The World Bank and IMF laid great rhetorical emphasis on the importance of a social safety net to protect groups who lost jobs and income in the transition to a market economy, although in practice they were less successful in bringing such social provisions into existence.

This new social safety net was to be provided by the state, acting of course in the public interest. How can we be sure that the postcommunist state would act to defend the public interest? Either because (1) economists assume that the state always acts in the public interest; or (2) the state will be acting on the advice of Western agencies, and they have the public interest at heart; or (3) these states are now democracies, so if people have a choice at election time the resulting government must be acting in the public interest. None of these assumptions would pass Political Science 101.

The second operating assumption was the TINA principle (There Is No Alternative). If economists started to feel uncomfortable with Pareto Optimality, they had a foolproof fall-back assumption: the notion that other policy options were bound to fail. The centrally planned economy had crashed in flames, and it was politically and economically impossible to go back to state planning. Not only were alternative models of economic organization not available, even delay was not a viable option. A lot of effort in the 1996 World Bank report is devoted to demonstrating that countries that tried to slow the pace of economic reform did worse than countries that bit the bullet early on. Countries that failed to liberalize prices and foreign trade (such as Ukraine and Romania) experienced a deeper recession and a later, slower recovery than countries that reformed as quickly as possible (such as Poland and the Czech Republic).

The World Bank's correlation exercise looks impressive and convincing. Indeed, nobody in their right mind would want to defend the economic policies pursued by Romania or Ukraine. However, even the World Bank report admits that China belongs in a special category, and is largely excluded from the analysis. The maintenance in China of capital controls, the nonconvertibility of the yuan, the lack of privatization of heavy industry, and the fuzziness of property rights all violate the holy trinity of liberalization, stabilization, and privatization that were being pressed on the East Europeans. The World Bank has also made some oblique references to Uzbekistan's state-controlled economy as possibly representing an alternative path, but overall reaffirms the orthodoxy that one set of economic policies is good for all twenty-seven postcommunist economies of east-central Europe and the former Soviet Union.

However, looking more closely at the TINA model one starts to have doubts about the One Size Fits All school of policy advocacy. There is no one path to privatization in the transition economies, for example. Some of the World Bank's successful countries did it quickly, through voucher schemes (Czech Republic, Russia); but others did it slowly through piecemeal sales (Hungary), or a combination of the two (Poland), or not really at all (Slovenia). Financial stabilization and the conquering of inflation—the acid test of the IMF model—also turn out to have rather heterodox roots. In Poland and the Czech Republic the reduction in inflation was largely due to the imposition of a tough excess wages tax. In Russia the "good" monetary figures were achieved through shifting large parts of the economy into noncash transactions, such as barter and arrears.

This leads to the third key assumption of transition economics: the primacy of financial indicators. One of the first steps in economic reform was price liberalization, designed to stop the shortages that were characteristic of the CPE, and that increased in severity in many CPEs in the last years of the 1980s. Price liberalization triggered an inflationary surge, and getting this under control became a key test of a government's commitment to reform. Currency convertibility and the stability of the exchange rate became the acid test of a country's success, while the importance of other numbers was downplayed. The exchange rate became the "nominal anchor" of monetary policy and the key symbol of a country's adherence to reform. Data on GDP and living standards were considered to be unreliable because they were based on CPE output structure and reporting conventions. Hence data purporting to show a massive, 50 percent fall in GDP in Russia since 1991 were explained away as the result of out-of-date price indices; the loss of negative-value-added production; a surge in under-reporting; a boom in the black economy, etc. In contrast to GDP data the exchange rate was seen as transparent, simple to measure, and easily understood. The reliability of inflation indices was not considered to be a serious problem by international economists—although it sparked fierce debate in many countries where pensions and minimum wages were tied to the consumer price index.

Partly this emphasis on prices and exchange rates reflected the expertise of the IMF economists who were redeployed to monitor the ex-socialist economies. Partly also it was the result of a conviction that economic institutions are malleable: prices create incentives which create institutions. Get the prices right, and you will generate the incentives for economically efficient behavior. Such profit-seeking behavior will naturally lead to the creation of the requisite structure of economic institutions. Domestic and foreign entrepreneurs will establish new firms, consumers, will buy their products, workers will be attracted by their higher wages, and so the virtuous circle will continue. These firms, consumers, and workers in turn will put pressure on the political system to create the network of laws and regulatory agencies necessary for a modern market economy to function. There was also the advantage that prices could be liberalized quickly and easily, since it involved the government doing less of something (price regulation). Managing the exchange rate could also be done fairly easily, through the creation of a central money market, and it was something that the IMF and international bankers knew how to do. Creating new capitalist firms, writing new laws, and devising mechanisms to enforce them were all tasks that would take much longer and were much more difficult to accomplish. The reformers assumed that those tasks could be postponed until later.

Alternatives

What were the alternatives to Pareto Optimality and TINA? Marxists would offer a class analysis, under which some social groups benefit from the changes while others are exploited. But one does not have to be a Marxist to believe that economics is not always a positive-sum game for all involved. Conservatives and liberals alike are also interested in analyzing how the political system works to see cui bono (who benefits).

Apart from winners and losers within a given country, there is also a differential outcome among countries. It is possible that whole countries may fail to make the transition to a viable market economy. The transition from plan to market may have dual equilibria: one successful point at which positive trends reinforce each other, creating a virtuous circle of growth and prosperity; and a second failure point at which negative trends become a vicious circle of exploitation and decline.

A patriotic economist will be interested in figuring out which countries (East and West) will gain most from the transition, and which will lose, and in which category his country will belong. International advisors may prefer to pass quickly over this question. Economic theory tells us that all countries stand to gain from participation in the international division of labor. However, economic practice tells us that there are parts of the globe where the writ of comparative advantage does not run. It is important to know whether your country will turn out to be Belgium or Benin.

The possibility of a negative equilibrium for a transition economy was not really considered by the World Bank report, nor by the Good News Bible school of commentators. It means asking questions such as: Which countries are likely to fall into the vicious circle? What are the alternative policies that could prevent this from happening, or dig them out of the hole into which they have gotten themselves? Such second-best policy solutions may look very different from the orthodox prescription of liberalization, stabilization, and privatization. We have not heard much serious debate along these lines. Apart from a handful of Russian economists (such as Sergei Glaziev), the Russian opposition has not come up with much in the way of plausible alternatives to the Gaidar/Chubais program. Their political statements tend to be incoherent in economic terms, and their economic programs smack of old-fashioned, central-planning notions.

Implications for Russian Regional Studies

The first section of this paper argues that since 1991 there has been a strong trend in comparative economics away from empirical and institutional investigation in the area studies tradition. Instead the emphasis has been on the introduction of a uniform policy package at the national level that focuses on a narrow range of policy variables and the accompanying indicators. This section explores the implications of this argument for the study of Russia's regions.

The Soviet economy was a highly centralized animal: not as highly centralized as the planners would have liked, but very centralized by the standards of Western economies. This fact was clear to everyone: from the managers who took their orders from Moscow to the consumers who traveled to the capital to buy their sausages and sewing machines.

Since 1991 the introduction of a market economy has meant a decentralization of political and economic power. However, the growing geographic complexity of the Russian economy has not really been acknowledged in the work of economists studying the transition. The great debate has been over the success or failure of the nationally adopted policy of shock therapy. Political scientists have been doing better: there has been a steady stream of books and articles exploring political life in the regions. The same could not be said of economic analysis. Just as there is one set of economic laws, it seems that there is one economy: the global economy. It is assumed that the process of economic integration that is bringing Russia into the global economy will be accompanied by the integration of Russia's regions into the Russian national economy.

Again, the contrast with the study of China is instructive. China scholars have developed a simple but plausible three-sector model, under which firms are categorized into those producing for the international market; those selling on the Chinese national market; and those confined to the local market within their region. Firms concentrated in each sector have a different set of preferences for national and regional economic policy, and correspondingly a different set of political alliances. To my knowledge no such studies have been done in Russia; the problem has not even been conceptualized in those terms.

Current Approaches to Russia's Regions

Despite the general downplaying of the subject in the dominant paradigm of transition economics, there is a growing body of work on the economics of Russia's regions. Much of this work has focused on the challenge of regional diversity. Regions have been categorized in terms of their performance as measured by available economic indicators (real wages, cost of living, wage arrears, unemployment, investment, industrial production, rate of privatization, net transfers to federal center, etc.) (Hanson 1997a; Smiryagin 1997). Various typologies are constructed of winners and losers, vanguards and laggards.

With 89 regions, unreliable or hard to get data, and multiple economic and political conditions, this is a daunting exercise. Analysts look for patterns in the data, or some unifying logic to frame the discourse. Have regional inequalities increased or decreased since 1991? Which regions are doing best in the market transition? Usually the typology offers four or five groupings. Economic success awaits the gateway regions with access to the international economy (Moscow or St. Petersburg); resource rich regions (Tyumen, Sakha) or regions who are leaders in market reform (Nizhnii Novgorod). However, when one looks closely at these typologies some puzzles emerge. Why are wage arrears and company debts high even in such a "leading" region as Tyumen? Why is such an obvious "gateway" region as Primorskii Krai mired in crisis?

What are the assumptions lying behind the construction of these typologies? Typically, the concern seems to be with political stability, which is seen as threatened by the growing regional diversity. It is noted that regional inequalities are strong, and were growing rapidly at least until 1995 (since then they seem to have leveled off). Only 10 of 89 regions are net contributors to the federal budget, and just seven regions provide more than half of all federal taxes.[4]

Various political models lie behind these analyses. One approach is to assume that the federal government sees its role as maximizing social welfare, seeking to ensure basic equality of provision of public goods and a minimum level of welfare in each region. It will therefore seek to redistribute resources from rich regions to poor ones and take steps to ensure the most efficient and equitable distribution of public spending. This public policy approach treats regional policy in Russia much like in any other developed industrial democracy (McAuley 1997).

A second approach is to assume that the federal government's main concern is not economic welfare but the preservation of national unity and political order. Here the relevant comparison is between Russia and other fragile federal systems, such as the former Yugoslavia or India. In this case, regional policy will be used to buy the loyalty of rebellious regions—those with protesting workers or ethnically driven autonomy movements. In this second approach, center-periphery relations are conceived as a bargaining game in which the currency of the interactions is federal dollars and electoral votes (Treisman 1999). This work has generated many interesting insights into the dynamics of regionalism, but it also leaves some questions unanswered. Do political leaders really think and act in these terms (consciously or unconsciously)? Or are the rational patterns that one sees in the data merely in the eye of the beholder?

One can also advance a third paradigm: to argue that, as in the days of the CPE, Russia is still a special case that demands its own categories of analysis. It can be argued that the texture of political and economic power in contemporary Russia is qualitatively distinctive in ways that are not being fully captured by the public policy and federal bargaining game models. This paper concludes by outlining three special features of the Russian case: the fragile nature of the Russian federal state; the distinctive fusion of political and economic power in Russia; and the simple geographical challenge of creating an integrated national market in Russia. These factors give a qualitatively unique dimension to the question of federalism and regionalism. (In all three respects, Russia's "uniqueness" is to a large extent shared with many of the other post-Soviet states, especially Ukraine, Belarus, and Kazakhstan.)

The Shrinkage of the Federal Government

First, when discussing regional policy one should note the federal government's incredible vanishing act. The federal authorities have simply lost their ability to regulate much of the country's economic activity and hence to raise taxes at the level expected and required of a modern state. Political scientists and historians have for some time been debating the challenge of building a nation-state in Russia, given the lack of congruence between ethnic and political identity and the absence of a unified national political elite. It is time for economists to join this debate, rather than assuming that the character of the Russian state can be taken for granted.

The federal state's ability to raise taxes has shrunk from about 25–30 percent of GDP in 1990 to 11 percent in 1997 (*Russian Economic Trends*, April 1998). In the latter year federal spending ran at 17.8 percent of GDP, leaving a deficit of 6.8 percent (including interest payments on the national debt). On top of that regional and municipal authorities raised and spent about 15 percent of GDP, and off-budget funds for pensions, social security, and unemployment raised and spent another 7 percent. For comparison: the U.S. federal government raises about 21 percent of GDP, and the Indian federal government about 33 percent.

The Russian federal government has walked away from providing a whole range of services that one normally considers a responsibility of the national state. Education and health care have been virtually entirely dumped in the lap of regional governments. More bizarrely, even the Federal Border Guards Service has to rely on "user fees" (legal and not-so-legal) and help from local governments along the borders. (Forty-five of Russia's regions now have foreign borders, twenty-nine for the first time after 1991, and most of them are paying for the construction and upkeep of border posts.[5]) Siberian regional governments, for example, have taken it upon themselves to guard the Russian border with Mongolia at their own expense.[6] There are frequent reports that military units have to provide work for local authorities in return for food, or survive by selling off their allocations of fuel and even equipment stocks. Regions with an above-average concentration of indigent military units on their territory, such as Primorskii Krai, can be dragged under by the burden of carrying their consumption of energy resources.

The gap between spending requirements and taxation capacity opened up already in 1992. For the next two years, the deficit was covered by the printing of money and the circulation of a bewildering variety of money substitutes. Then in 1995 at the behest of the IMF the government decided to get a grip on the money supply and securitized the deficit by issuing treasury bills (GKOs). This enabled a noninflationary financing of the deficit, and for a while everything looked fine. However, the debt mountain started to rise alarmingly. The total stock of GKOs rose from 2.4 percent of GDP in 1995 to 15 percent at the end of 1997. Another problem was that the market for these bonds was artificially created. It is not clear where the Russian commercial banks were getting the money to buy these bonds. They were not as a rule getting it by attracting domestic savings. In 1997 they only paid an average of 7 percent on savings deposits, less than the rate of inflation, and most savings were converted into dollars because of fears about the stability of the ruble and of Russian banks themselves. It seems as if a lot of the money to buy GKOs was coming from the Russian state budget itself, with the main buyers being the Central Bank and the state-owned Sberbank (which held more than two-thirds of personal deposits).

On top of these domestic machinations, by 1997 one-third of the loans for GKOs were coming from foreigners. International commercial banks kept buying GKOs so long as they were confident that Western governments would act as a lender of last resort for Russia. The market for Russian debt was very sensitive to political developments. Events that seemed to show that reform currents were ascendant kept the market afloat through 1996 (President Yeltsin's election victory in June) and 1997 (the "spring offensive" by the new young reformers who joined the government in March). Through 1997 this strategy seemed to be working in terms of bringing down the cost of borrowing. GKO yields, which peaked at 180 percent during the June 1996 presidential election, fell to 39 percent by December 1996 and 18 percent in July 1997. However, yields started to climb after the Asian crisis hit the Russian market in October. By March 1998 Yeltsin had to resort to another political coup—firing Viktor Chernomyrdin as prime minister and replacing him with Sergei Kirienko. However, the debt pyramid continued its inexorable rise, and GKO yields hit 100 percent at the start of July 1998, triggering the August collapse. Meanwhile, the promised reforms and improvements in revenue generation failed to materialize.

Critics charge that the Kremlin's dependence on GKOs resembled a giant political pyramid scheme with potentially devastating implications for Russia's political and economic stability. Indeed, one can argue that the Russian government was reckless in relying on GKOs to bridge the budget deficit, on the assumption that some mystical reform package would generate economic recovery before they fell due for repayment. This innovation—which had been urged on Russia by the IMF—served to buy the government a couple more years at the helm, but did not address the underlying stalemate in the development of the Russian economy.

The Rise of the Barter Economy

The second aspect of Russia's uniqueness with important implications for the transition paradigm and regional trends is the reemergence since 1991 of a dual economy. On one side is the monetized economy, the one you read about in *The Economist* and *Russian Economic Trends*. The firms in the monetized economy pay federal taxes to some degree, file accounts, issue stocks, float bonds, etc. This economy is largely driven by the revenues from oil, gas, and metals exports (that account for about 20 percent of Russia's GDP). It is largely based in Moscow, where all the trading firms are headquartered, and where 80 percent of bank capital is based.

On the other side is the "natural" economy, where barter is the norm. There, firms go to great lengths to hide their cash revenues, they never report profits, they often hide or don't pay their debts (to suppliers and to workers), and they rarely pay federal taxes (except with other forms of scrip). Some of this economy takes place through physical exchange of goods. A lot revolves around an elaborate and confusing chain of arrears. At the end of 1997 total enterprise debts to suppliers amounted to 12.5 percent of GDP, to tax authorities 6.6 percent, to off-budget funds 4.9 percent, and to workers in the form of unpaid wages 1.8 percent. This came to a grand total of 700 trillion rubles (U.S. $120 billion); or 26 percent of GDP (up from 22 percent at the start of the year).

Based on World Bank surveys, Barry Ickes estimated 40 percent of industrial transactions take place in the form of barter, and notes that the proportion seems to have actually been rising since 1993—that is, precisely as macroeconomic stabilization was supposedly taking hold (in the monetized economy) (Gaddy and Ickes 1998: 53). It is widely acknowledged that the utilities (railways, Gazprom, Unified Energy System) get significantly less than 40 percent of their domestic deliveries paid for in cash, probably less than 10 percent.

The captains of the natural economy often work in collaboration with the political leaders of their regions. For them to operate they need a physical space in which to reside. Unlike the monetized economy, which can exist in virtual space (in the computer hard drives of bankers or the imagination of financial journalists), the natural economy actually needs physical objects such as oil wells and steel mills, and these tend to be located in awkward and outlandish places, far from Moscow.

It is easy for local directors to draw the political elite into the natural economy: that is how the Soviet economy worked, after all, and the political elite, like the economic managers, is more comfortable dealing through personal networks than dealing in cash. Trust is what keeps the natural economy going, Goods are supplied and services rendered in full knowledge that they will not be paid for, and hence not taxed—but secure in the knowledge that the favor will be returned at some point in the future. It goes without saying that this "moral economy" is riddled with corruption and immorality. This is trust Soviet-style, and a long way from what Francis Fukuyama (1995) has in mind when he invokes trust as a vital prerequisite for the development of capitalism.

The allocation of what few federal funds there are is a painful process for all concerned. "The rhythm of the arrival of federal budgetary allocations resembles most of all the last beats of the heart before a man dies. So, the majority of governors do not even take the trouble to think for what purposes the money is earmarked. They spent it on what they think is of greatest importance at a particular moment" (Shpak 1997). According to Oksana Dmitrieva, chairman of the State Duma Budget Subcommittee: "Pumping federal money into the regions, given that they are not under the control of the center, is like trying to fill a barrel riddled with holes" (Dmitrieva 1997). The government is annoyed that once federal funds are sent to the regions they have no control over how they are spent, with funds often diverted to causes that the government does not approve (such as subsidizing energy prices). But the Kremlin lacks the political capacity to enforce its economic policies, even when it comes to spending federal program funds.

The sparks really fly when Moscow tried to extend the monetized economy to colonize some of the natural economy. The main vehicle for this was the privatization drive: selling state assets to new owners for cash will tend to move the firms in question closer to the money economy. Privatization through cash sales usually boiled down to transferring ownership from local elites to Moscow-based banks, possibly in cahoots with foreigners. (Sometimes the local elite joins forces with the foreigners and together they try to fend off the Moscow whiz kids.) Major scandals have erupted around the privatization of such crown jewels of the economy as Norilsk Nickel, Belgorod iron works, and Tyumenneftgaz —and in each case these disputes had a very strong Moscow versus The Provincials component. In some of these cases it boiled down to which faction the local police would physically support in their efforts to get into the administration building of the plant.

A second way the reform drive showed up was in efforts to make tax deadbeats pay up and to close down bankrupt firms. In late 1996 President Yeltsin formed the Temporary Extraordinary Commission for Tax Collection (whose initials mimicked those of Lenin's Cheka secret police), with Chubais at its head. This was clearly an effort to overcome the administrative degradation of the federal authorities by creating a new politico-bureaucratic institution. The new Cheka proved to be less effective than its Leninist predecessor: most of the firms on its hit list continued to accumulate tax arrears in 1997. Tax receipts for the year amounted to about 75 percent of the target level. One hundred major enterprises owed around 40 percent of all tax arrears, and two-thirds of these arrears were generated by the energy sector. In March 1997 a presidential decree called on firms to hand over to the government shares equal to their tax debts: the government would then sell the shares, in effect reprivatizing the firms. Another scheme was to broker individual deals to restructure old tax debts. In October 1997 the auto giant AvtoVAZ signed a deal to pay back 8 trillion rubles in tax arrears over ten years.

For all the talk of transparency and rule setting, all these maneuverings were highly politicized and were tied up with intraelite power struggles. Hence, for example, in December 1997 Chubais's Cheka announced that it had decided to declare two tax laggards bankrupt—the Omsk and Angarsk oil refineries, which owed federal taxes of 766 billion rubles (U.S. $128 million) and 526 billion rubles, respectively. The Angarsk refinery belonged to Sidanko, part of Vladimir Potanin's Oneksimbank empire, while Omsk belonged to Sibneft, owned by Boris Berezovskii's group. However, Chubais's effort to seize the firms' assets was blocked by Premier Chernomyrdin. Chubais also tried to put the squeeze on regions that were withholding taxes, especially the republics of Tatarstan, Bashkortostan, and Sakha (Yakutiya). He had little luck with those republics, although he easily quashed an attempted tax revolt by Irkutsk oblast in March 1997. To clear the 1997 budget Chubais, gritting his teeth, agreed to what he described as "disgusting" tax offsets (where a firm's tax arrears are set against debts to them from state organizations) worth 60 trillion rubles (Bekker 1997). After a year of effort, the federal government's attempts to close the gap between the monetary and barter economy seemed to be running in circles.

The Challenge of Geography

The one-size-fits all approach to economic transition assumes that prices will work their magic whatever the size and shape of the economy in question. That geography may have to be taken into account as an independent factor was implicitly and explicitly rejected by market reform advocates in 1991-92, when there was an open debate about whether Polish style "shock therapy" would work in Russia.

Seven years later, it seems clear that the geographers were right. Even Jeffrey Sachs, an advocate of rapid liberalization for the Russian economy, has rediscovered the power of geography (Sachs and Warner 1997). Sachs underlines one of the home truths in Adam Smith's *The Wealth of Nations*: that transporting goods by sea is much cheaper than transporting them by land. Sachs argued that the costs of sea freight are still radically lower than land freight, and through a correlation exercise found that proximity to the ocean is a decisive factor in explaining long-term rates of GDP growth.

Russia's economy has unique geographical characteristics of size, terrain, and climate that arguably set it apart from smaller economies. Added to that is the legacy of seventy-five years of Soviet rule, under which investment was directed in accordance with calculations of national strategy, creating a highly militarized economy far removed from the push and pull of market laws of supply and demand (Gaddy 1998). A vast economy that was built by nonmarket methods will probably have to be dismantled by nonmarket methods, at least in part.

Conclusion

If the above analysis is correct, then the prospects for the future of the Russian economy—and for the utility of Western assistance—look rather bleak. The economics discipline appears to have turned its back on area studies and thrown its weight behind an ambitious program for a rapid transformation of the former Soviet Union into a market economy. This program did not take root in Russian conditions. It now seems clear that the formulaic approach failed to take account of certain distinctive features of the Russian economy, such as its geographical size and distorted, militarized structure; the obstinate reliance of many economic agents on nonmonetary transactions; and the collapse of authority of the federal government.

These failings show up most radically at regional level, with the implication that policy solutions to tackle them must have a regional dimension if they are to succeed. However, one may doubt whether the economics profession has the expertise and personnel required to craft such a regionally aware strategy for reviving the Russian economy.

Notes

An earlier version of this paper was delivered to the Summer Symposium at the Slavic Research Center, University of Hokkaido, Japan, 23 July 1998.

1. Abram Bergson, Gregory Grossman, Herbert Levine, Alec Nove, Michael Kaser, and others, followed later by János Kornai, James Millar, and Paul Gregory. For a detailed analysis of the history of and challenges to the subdiscipline, see Millar 1995.

2. One example of a pre-1989 émigré is Harvard University's Andrei Shleifer (Boycko et al. 1995; Shleifer and Treisman 2000).

3. In 1995, one director of an international agency who was interested in commissioning a report from the present author complained: "You are telling me reasons why we shouldn't be doing this; I want to hear an explanation of how we can do it."

4. RIA Novosti, 30 October 1997. The seven are Moscow, St. Petersburg, the Khanty-Mansi, and Yamalo-Nenetsk autonomous districts, the regions of Moscow, Samara, and Nizhnii Novgorod.

5. Interfax, 2 July 1997. The Border Guards only got 38 percent of its planned budget funds in the first half of 1997.

6. *Izvestiya*, 18 April 1997.

Chapter 7

Talking the Talk and Walking the Walk: The Cultural and Institutional Effects of Western Models

Wade Jacoby

An important part of the postcommunist transformation process has involved the approximation by elites in central and Eastern Europe (CEE) of prevailing Western organizational models. The more general issue of the possibility of such an "institutional transfer" has long intrigued social scientists. Scholars have studied the use of foreign models during the forced-draft modernization of previously isolated societies such as Meiji, Japan, the efforts of colonial powers to "leave behind" certain formal institutional arrangements during decolonization, and the efforts of elites embedded in "epistemic communities" to promote "policy transfer" (Hamilton 1964; Rose 1993). Other scholars, such as Reinhard Bendix and Samuel Huntington, have commented briefly on the "demonstration effect" of foreign models, while a large literature tracks the "diffusion" of policy instruments from one U.S. state to the next (Walker 1969; Savage 1985). Drawing on Malcolm Rutherford's useful distinction between "design" and "invisible hand" roots of institutions, these approaches all tend toward the former and emphasize the conscious efforts of policy elites to respond creatively to political dilemmas (Rutherford 1994). One such political dilemma has been the desire of CEE elites to replace many apparently outmoded Communist-era institutions and to rejoin West European institutional trajectories. In so doing, and often aided by material support and expertise from Western Europe, elites have sometimes looked to existing West European models for templates of institutional reform.

Such transfer processes are exceedingly complex and may require far more than the simple "imitation" of best practices. Three difficulties stand out immediately: the *perception* (and possible misperception) of foreign models, political disagreements about their *desirability*, and difficulty in *implementing* foreign-inspired practices and designs. Unfortunately, the major macrosociological and political science tradition—that of diffusion—has a markedly difficult time with all three difficulties, preferring as it does to blend out uncertainty and disagreement in favor of tracking the spread of highly stylized models and generally ignoring the implementation phase altogether. Other disciplines can better augment a political science approach to transfer. Anthropology can be useful in exploring cultural receptivity. Economics contributes notions of transaction costs (pointing to the need to find indigenous sponsors) and search costs (to explain satisficing in organizational design). My own previous interdisciplinary approach combined the concepts of political science (to tease out the coalitions that attempted transfer) and the methods of historians (to find out how those transferred structures actually performed in a new setting) (Jacoby 2000). In that work I traced the fortunes over time of several institutional domains after the redesign by transfer during the Allied powers' postwar occupation of West Germany, found that elite efforts to imitate and transfer institutions—here defined to include both organizational structures and the formal and legal rules that they promulgate—can have profound influences on domestic structures and practices *even if the efforts are misinformed, halting, or incomplete.*

But for cases in CEE, it seems best to draw on a theory that provides an even richer vocabulary for describing the results of attempted imitation: the sociological theory of organizational isomorphism. Isomorphism is the congruence between a specific organization—in this chapter, usually national ministries or their subordinate agencies—and its broader "institutional environment" constituted by other organizational actors and the rules of their interaction (DiMaggio and Powell 1991). Complete isomorphism between individual organizations and their larger institutional environment is not necessarily a normative ideal; rather, isomorphism is a concept to measure the variable ways that actual organizations are embedded in a broader environment.

This paper proceeds in four steps. First, I define and ground the concept of institutional transfer with reference to other complementary theories, noting especially the fragmentation of the process and the unpredictability of its results. Second, I introduce the sociological concept of a functional dualism in organizations. The central idea, as articulated by John Meyer and Brian Rowan (1991), is that since many organizations depend on external support for their existence and prosperity, they often develop formal structures that are favored by others in their broader institutional environment. The theory suggests it can be highly profitable to an organization to develop a dual nature in which an exterior "ceremonial" structure "buffers" the "actual work activities" of the organization (41). I use evidence from the EU Commission's "screening" of aspirant member states and from the national bodies that coordinate harmonization with EU law to demonstrate the importance of this organizational dualism in CEE states, especially those poised for EU membership.

Third, I explore the power to set agendas and to change them in midstream. To do so, I point out the Commission's dual role in this process in both promoting transfer of West European institutions and monitoring their functioning. This focus on agendas raises, in turn, the thorny status of ideas as explanatory variables in political science. While the cases here are too messy and complex to show the independent power of ideas, common sense tells us that one idea has served as an enormously important focal point for citizens of central and Eastern Europe—the idea that "our country now needs to take its place in European institutions." My aim here is to show how a particular kind of "Europeanization" is occurring and to show how it is being institutionalized. In so doing, I address questions of power mainly through issues of agenda setting and gatekeeping.[1]

Finally, I introduce two axes of variation and indicate some brief empirical evidence to judge their plausibility. The three elements of an argument introduced so far—transfer as a fragmented and unpredictable process, the dual nature of organizations in an institutional environment, and the Commission's mixed role—are treated here as common factors influencing all transformations in the region. My choice to downplay these three potential sources of variation and treat them as more or less constant stems from my interest in two other sources of variation—policy domain and national administrative competence. Drawing from examples from the domains of the welfare state (health policy), production (regional policy), and consumption (consumer protection), I explore how transfer differs by domain. I also show that cross-national differences in the abilities of public administration to implement laws and structures modeled on EU or member state institutions affect the outcomes of those transfer efforts.

In a nutshell, I describe the recent rise of a new kind of institutional transfer in central and Eastern Europe. To simplify, I focus on two sets of actors in this transfer. For the EU side, I focus on the Commission, which runs both the screening process described below and a set of preaccession programs designed to bring CEE institutions and practices up to EU standards. On the CEE side, I focus on "national elites," that is, the politically powerful ministers and deputy ministers, who may or may not pay close attention to the demands of enlargement in their particular ministries but who, if they do, must always consider them in the context of a larger set of domestic concerns. My main point is that these national elites, responding to notions created and nurtured by the EU, have embarked on many reforms that challenge and even overwhelm the ability of the public administrations to implement. For their part, lower-level ministerial officials can choose to support enlargement mainly through enthusiasm and creative problem solving (but without much real power) or oppose it through indifference or obfuscation. In either case, however, there is an effort to avoid EU oversight, which, in turn, plagues other efforts at institution building. And taken as a whole, the process allows organizational complexity to grow without much "demand" for it inside the society.

Institutional Transfer and the Juncture of Internal and External Sources of Institutions

More than ten years after the collapse of Communist regimes, the time is ripe for a reappraisal of the sources of institutional design in CEE.[2] An enormous amount of basic descriptive work has been published, and conceptual typologies sketched quickly in the first years of the transformation have been thoroughly reworked in light of results from second and even third rounds of elections. The early almost exclusive focus on forces internal to the region has been augmented by a steadily growing interest in the "external influences" on the various political and economic transformations of the region (Carothers 1999; Dawisha 1997; Pridham et al. 1997; Grey 1997). While the writing on external influences chronicles well a range of Western actions to promote change, we still need a vocabulary for understanding outcomes as well as efforts. One promising route seems to me a focus on institutional transfer, especially one that avoids the false choice of internal voluntaristic imitation versus external imposition.[3] Indeed, the term *transfer* seems to me fortuitous precisely because, unlike *imitation* or *imposition*, it is neutral as to the agent of transfer and thus open to the possibility that mimesis and pressure are sometimes two faces of one process.

No account of transfer can elide at least four analytical challenges. Though these problems are, by no means, solved in the current chapter, sketching them underscores the conceptual ambiguity endemic to studying transfer. First is the problem of institutional antecedents. When examining the impact of Western models, how can we disentangle their effects from those of indigenous models or of the Soviet institutional legacies and Austro-German designs that have also left their marks in the region? Second is the issue of diffuse contributions. With multiple actors at the scene of institutional creation—both under "Roundtables" and postcommunist pluralism—how can the relative importance of Western models be described in a way that acknowledges the importance of other factors? Third, we must distinguish between paper changes and real effects. To emphasize only formal structural similarities could lead to an exaggeration of the importance of Western models. By the converse logic, in other cases, it may be that processes of modeling occur down in the inner workings of an organization so that surface differences in organizational appearance—"national diversity"—mask a deeper homogenization of organizational processes. Fourth, it will be a great challenge to measure the outcomes of institutions shaped through processes of transfer and mimesis. Since it is hard enough to measure institutional production of indigenous models, so it may be well nigh impossible to get the "share" linked to the use of Western models.

CEE elites' selective transfer and adaptation of foreign institutional models is best studied in a broader political context and not in isolation as a self-contained "independent variable." But which context? Most accounts of the use of Western institutional models have been highly descriptive (see, e.g., Pfaff 1993; Cox 1993). The current literature on CEE does, however, provide two good starting points. The first is that external influence is a multistranded process and not a discrete variable. For example, some authors who begin by setting up "external pressures" and "international imperatives" as alternative explanations of economic and political change in CEE—in the case of B. Crawford and A. Lijphart, alternative to "Leninist legacies"—eventually abandon the claim that these are "alternatives" (Crawford and Lijphart 1995: 194–96; Stark and Bruszt 1998: 5–8). For example, Crawford and Lijphart seem to suggest that ideological, sociological, and institutional legacies of the past are actually filtered by contemporary external pressures. This chapter explores the linkage they suggest between environmental pressures and national choices but abandons at the outset the conceit that external pressures are best conceptualized as a freestanding alternative explanation to "domestic reform processes."[4]

A second useful contribution—that of Frank Bönker (1994)—disaggregates the concept of "external determinants" into the interrelated phenomena of institutional modeling, trade relations, capital flows, and aid flows. Focusing on the first, Bönker lists five reasons why Western models might be attractive to CEE elites. Summarizing, transfer could: (1) motivate populations to accept temporary hardships in the name of reform, (2) minimize the search costs of harried elites, (3) provide focal points to facilitate agreement when "multiple equilibria" exist, (4) overcome legitimacy deficits faced by all newly created institutions, or (5) maximize chances of harmonization with EU structures.

I want to build on this political logic to flesh out the interaction between these external models and the internal politics of the region—a theme raised briefly in Bönker's conclusion. Thus, rather than viewing the transfer of institutional models as an "alternative explanation" to internal processes or as a subset of "external influences," the effort here is to view them as complementary to domestic politics (Jacoby 2001). I take it as nearly axiomatic that all transfer that succeeds will do so, in part, because some domestic actors—whether voluntaristically imitating or under pressure from the outside—want it to succeed. For this reason, when institutional creation processes are viewed in retrospect or at a distance, many cases of successful transfer may be hard to distinguish from "indigenous" developments.

Formal Structure as Myth: EU "Screening" as Religious Ceremony

I focus the inquiry on the screening process and subsequent negotiations because this has clearly formed the centerpiece of EU efforts to influence the national institutions of CEE states. Given the high stakes, an interesting paradox resulted. Just as the EU began, starting about 1997, a significant new effort to help with institutional reforms in CEE—often encouraging institutional transfer—some aspirant members grew reluctant to reveal precisely where they most needed the help. The paradox was the result of a dilemma for CEE elites—especially ministerial personnel—in which the detailed revelation of weakness was both a prerequisite for crucial external help and a potential risk. The risk has been that detailed evidence of institutional dysfunction later might be used against aspirant members by political opponents of EU enlargement. The stakes, of course, are extraordinarily high, and with each call from West Europeans to put off accession, the dilemma is sharpened. Even the 2004 date that emerged from the Nice Summit, while it calmed some jangled nerves, is not a guarantee for any particular country. In softer form now, the dilemma still exists. To understand this paradox, we must see that what was intended by the EU as a process of pragmatic institution building has led to a process that sometimes looks more like a religious ceremony—namely, the confession of (institutional) sins and shortcomings.[5]

The formal applications of ten CEE countries for EU membership has been coterminous with a change in the policies of the EU Commission, and in the nature of institutional transfer in the region. While Western models for organizational design and legal structures and procedures have been used in many ways throughout the region since 1989, the "transposition" of the EU's 80,000-page *acquis communautaire* now has become the formal target for aspirant member states.[6] Commission policies have slowly changed to reflect this shift. Most important here, the Commission's Phare program, which coordinates EU aid to the region, no longer refers to its institution-building programs as "demand driven" (Jacoby 2001). While demand-driven programming had meant that Phare was to respond to the priorities set by the governing elites in CEE states, the current arena is one in which Phare officials set the agenda for institutional changes in the run-up to accession. The policy shift is nicely captured in a statement one hears frequently from Commission officials in the region, "The CEE states are joining us; we are not joining them."[7]

A key part of the EU strategy of readying CEE states for membership is a detailed check on their existing structures and laws. Some of this was accomplished in national applications and associated Commission "opinions" on those applications. But much work was left for the so-called screening process involving ten countries designated by the EU at the London Council meeting in March 1998. Of those ten, five—the Czech Republic, Poland, Hungary, Estonia, and Slovenia—were initially tabbed as the "ins" to constitute the first wave of potential enlargement.[8] "Task forces" were assigned to each country with the job of exploring both existing legislation and the implementation capacity in all areas covered by the primary and secondary legislation of the EU. The task forces have been headed by non-nationals—for example, the task force for Poland by a French citizen and the task force for the Czech Republic by a British citizen. But the task force staff is joined by sectoral experts from each nation for meetings on the sector in question. The Commission has designated thirty-one discrete "chapters" for screening in a process that began in April 1998 and that has run into 2000. By April 2000, both screening and preliminary negotiations on eleven of the chapters had been temporarily closed, indicating an initial consensus in those areas between the EU and the candidate countries. No additional chapters were closed during the French presidency that concluded at the end of 2000.

Screening was intended to force national ministries to articulate and confront the gap between current structures and practices and EU-compatible ones. In many areas, the gap remains sizable. But does screening encourage national elites to acknowledge and address such gaps? Drawing a perhaps impertinent analogy between institutional deficiency and moral shortcoming, we can see that the gap is narrowing only partially and unevenly. Three features underpin this "confession" analogy, in which the Commission plays the priest and the national elites the penitent. First, self-revelation about inadequacies and shortcomings is the initial foundation of the exchange. Even though sectoral experts from the relevant directorates general can attend screening meetings, the Commission and its task forces have been highly dependent on national ministries to divulge the nature and magnitude of sins of omission and Commission. To be sure, the task forces conduct their own independent investigations of each domain, but they clearly rely very heavily on the relevant national ministries for key data about institutional form and organizational effectiveness.[9] And while many months of preaccession meetings have given the Commission far more sources of independent judgment on legislative transposition, the self-revelation feature seems likely to be repeated with the implementation phase, where once again the EU will be at a disadvantage in terms of access to information.

Second, the priestly authority has the right, indeed the obligation, to impose responsibilities upon the penitent to remedy the weakness, lest forgivable lapses give way to a pattern of recidivism. The Commission's approach articulates to prospective members the low tolerance for noncompliance with the *acquis* ("hate the sin"), which must be fully and completely implemented from the start of accession. But the Commission also emphasized that all ten CEE states are, unlike, say, Russia, already members of the community of European nations, notwithstanding their current weaknesses and shortcomings ("love the sinner"). While the notion that they were ever "outside" Europe causes many in CEE to grit their teeth, this is a case where it's better to be judged a reforming heretic than an infidel beyond the pale.

Third, the process often has been characterized by secrecy, which ostensibly protects East European states from prejudicial information being leaked to opponents of enlargement. On the other hand, complete secrecy would hamper the Commission's aid programs for institution building. The discovery of deficiencies through screening probably promotes the transfer of West European structures and practices even if such deficiencies are kept largely hidden from the EU. While a full confession might maximize the chances of securing EU aid for a troubled institutional domain and thus accelerate processes of institutional transfer, there is little to prevent ministerial elites from claiming more or less full compliance with the *acquis* and then quietly copying EU structures on their own, without formal aid programs. Thus, screening's process of uncovering deficiencies probably promotes more transfer of structures and practices *even* if those deficiencies are largely kept hidden.

The Commission constantly warns that the day of judgment will come. Up to now, however, a fourth potential area of similarity between screening and confession—the ultimate threat of excommunication—has *not* appeared. The Commission has taken great pains to reassure elites inside national ministries that their intentions are strictly to promote better institutional functioning. On the other hand, national elites understandably fear that disclosure runs the risk of compromising later negotiating positions with the Council of Ministers. The EU has tried to circumvent this dilemma by building two separate tracks for the disclosure–assistance and negotiation processes. Essentially, the preparations for membership, including Phare activities and the so-called Accession Partnerships, are run by the Commission's DG1A (external relations). Screening, on the other hand, is part of the Commission's contribution to the formal opening of negotiations—a process run by the member states through the EU Council of Ministers. As such, the task of the screening process is to explore any potential areas of difficulty prior to negotiations and to suggest solutions. While problems are "signaled" to colleagues in DG1A, the intent is that only "serious" problems would be reported to the council.[10]

In principle, screening could generate either promises from or problems for CEE ministerial officials. That is, wherever existing structures were inadequate, elites could promise to approximate Western legal structures, or they could acknowledge that, at least in the short run, they would have problems with that area. In the vast majority of cases, the latter route—"derogations"—was avoided. As a result, promises greatly outnumbered acknowledged problems. Since most comparative studies continue to emphasize large divergences between CEE structures and practices and those in the EU member states, this apparently smooth screening process seems paradoxical, implying as it does that the prospective members will be able to fully implement the *acquis* in each screened area by the time of their admission. In some areas, no doubt they will.

A closer look reveals at least one other process at work besides the ministries' sheer determination to catch up to EU practices, but it is one for which a social science concept is more useful than a religious metaphor. Recalling that

Figure 7.1: ***Determinants of Organizational Survival***

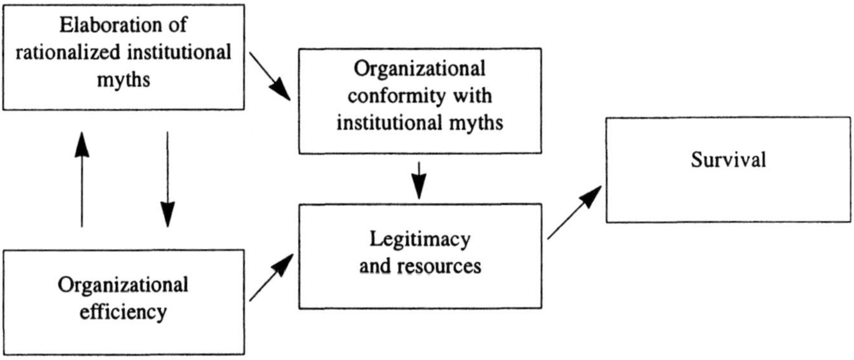

Source: Meyer and Rowan 1991: 53.

isomorphism is the congruence between an organization and its institutional environment, Meyer and Rowan (1991) argue that "loose coupling" between the organization's structure and its practical tasks is often due to a need to respond to myths whose affirmation helps perpetuate the organization.[11] Environments where "rational myths" have been widely propagated thus promote the diffusion of favored practices and structures "even if no evidence of their effectiveness exists" (61). In such cases, formal organizational structure is often "ceremonial" and is, to that end, "buffered" from the "actual work activities" of the organization. I argue that pressures from the EU constitute a significant institutional environment that promotes certain organizational structures. Specifically, the screening process functions as conduit for the EU's rational myths about organizational structure and function.

As Meyer and Rowan (1991: 45) note, when an organization adopts rational myths, it "displays responsibility" to other actors sharing its environment. Organizations that fail to take appropriate symbolic steps risk facing "turbulence" for inadequate isomorphism with their environment. To be sure, it is possible for some organizations—especially firms that produce for markets where customers can measure organizational efficiency by using prices—to avoid ceremonial obligations and still prosper. But as societies grow more complex, organizational goals often become more ambiguous and difficult to evaluate. When this condition holds—and I believe that it does for virtually every government ministry in the region—conformity with the larger institutional environment grows in importance.[12] Put differently, because CEE organizational outputs are extraordinarily difficult to measure, organizational shapes and routines gain popularity as indirect evidence of adequate design and performance. In this context, screening is setting the stage for the transfer of EU structures to CEE settings.

As a result of the revelations of screening, national ministries in CEE may

Figure 7.2: ***The Effects of Institutional Isomorphism on Organizations***

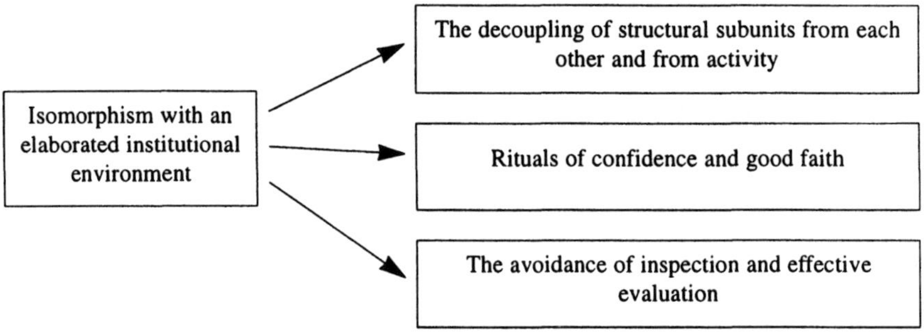

Source: Meyer and Rowan 1991: 60.

pursue externally sanctioned structural or policy models, even if the net contribution to the organization's efficiency is modest (or even negative). The expectation of remedial action—penance—is built into the structure of screening. The key tool of the screening process is the "harmonogram," a complicated grid listing for each area to be screened by the relevant EU directives and the applicant country's existing legislation pertaining to each directive. Depending on the gap that results, the harmonogram goes on to list a set of legislative and institutional tasks needed to meet the directive fully, and a description of the appropriate ministry personnel tasked with completing this action by a specified date.

Yet, while national ministries seek organizational forms and rules that carry the EU seal of approval, they also seek to avoid monitoring by outsiders, unless such monitoring can be "ceremonialized" and rendered harmless. As Meyer and Rowan point out, real evaluation can uncover problems that damage organizational legitimacy because "higher" political units often use evaluation to substitute for direct jurisdiction. And because "evaluation and inspection are public assertions of societal control which violate the assumption that everyone is acting with competence and good faith" (Meyer and Rowan 1991: 59), the screening process can be quite uncomfortable for the national ministries. Given long-standing fears in the region that the EU may use accession criteria to delay or suspend the process of enlargement, particular features of the ongoing negotiations may make revealing incompetence costly to the entire government (not just the ministry) (Inotai 1995: 7, 22–25). Potentially crucial in this regard is the principle that "nothing is decided until all is decided," which is a frank EU reminder that enlargement is a political decision, successful screening notwithstanding. This feature may help explain why the screening process has sometimes revealed few officially acknowledged problems in some deeply troubled policy domains. Understanding the valid concerns of national ministers also helps make comprehensible the apparent paradox of significant institutional deficiencies yet reluctance to pinpoint locations for institutional reforms. Betting that the complexity of monitoring compliance with the *acquis* may yet overwhelm the Commission, some ministries are steadfastly avoiding self-incrimination while seeking to ceremonialize what little independent inspection does occur.

Alongside this strategic behavior, to be sure, some ministries just feel overwhelmed by the size of the task. But the process of transposing the 80,000 pages of the *acquis* confirms Meyer and Rowan's claim that an increasingly institutionalized environment tends to increase the complexity of individual organizations. As examples of organizational responses to the environment created by the EU, the Czech Republic has established institutions at at least three different levels: the Government Council for Integration (an advisory body that includes ten ministers and the prime minister), a subordinate Working Committee of the Council (which is staffed at the level of deputy ministerial chiefs), and twenty-two separate working groups (which have responsibility for functional areas such as transportation or health care). Note that while some of these structures (such as the council) appear self-contained, the working groups add to the complexity of existing organizations.

Complexity also grows between existing organizations as well as inside them. As predicted by the theory of organizational dualism, the need to comply or appear to comply with EU law has thickened the connections between organizations, in part as a way of controlling external monitoring.[13] Given the time pressures to bring screened chapters up to EU standards, ministries often find that simply passing the new legislation is an overwhelming task. And as the national ministries adopt more legislation via a "cookie cutter" method of transfer, they make it easier for the EU to monitor them because the Commission can compare them both to member states and to other candidate countries by using the same categories. Thus, while organizational complexity within a nation makes EU monitoring more difficult, organizational homogeneity across the region makes it less difficult.

In sum, Meyer and Rowan's suggestion that organizational managers who focus heavily on abstract and ritualistic efforts inside the organization do this to the neglect of more pragmatic problems bears careful consideration as the transposition process reaches a crescendo. On the other hand, the existence of so many new interministerial coordination bodies casts some doubt on their claim that "the more highly institutionalized the environment, the more time and energy organizational elites devote to managing their organization's public image and status and the less they devote to coordination and to managing particular boundary-spanning relationships" (Meyer and Rowan 1991: 59). The ministerial imperative to look good in the eyes of the task force has not obviously impeded their efforts to make connections with other ministries, at least not in the Czech case just noted.

What does screening mean for the issues of transfer and power? To summarize, it appears that accessions' proximity has given a significant impetus to a new kind of institutional transfer in CEE. But only some of these transfers are likely to improve institutional functioning. In others cases, national elites are responding to ceremonial myths as a substitute for the kind of real implementation that their weak public administrations cannot deliver. Responding to environmentally sanctioned myths may help ministerial elites avoid oversight but may also undercut other serious efforts at institution building. Finally, organizational complexity is growing without much "demand" for it inside the society. Taken together, the dual nature of organizations is a factor that helps transferred rules and structures to "stick" even when they are meaningless to local actors. To the extent this is true, "loose coupling" may lead to cynicism and come to be seen as much less functional than Meyer and Rowan imply. While they see loose coupling as a coping strategy that allows mature organizations to serve multiple constituencies, perhaps in the newer organizations of CEE the imperative of securing external support undercuts the organization's daily work.

More generally, since EU structures presume the existence of party and interest group actors in the social-liberal to Christian democratic part of the political spectrum, they give power advantages to groups located there.[14] The transfer that results from screening comes against the profound, but diffuse, influence of liberal ideas about the organization of capitalist democracy (Pickel 1997b). Yet, to remark on the widespread appeal of liberal ideas and to insist on their relevance for individual organizations should not lead us to deny that other ideological forces and historical traditions will continue to generate and nurture other myths. Indeed, a core part of the theory of loose coupling recognizes that organizations not only must maneuver between symbolic demands and the demands of efficiency, but that they also must navigate the plurality of competing myths in any given institutional environment. This plurality certainly obtains in CEE, where, as Jon Elster et al. (1998: 15; italics in original) summarize the matter, CEE polities "are deeply contested among the poorly organized proponents of three divergent orientations. These three orientations or ideas focus, respectively, on the *distant past*, the *"modern" West*, and what is still deemed, increasingly, the accomplishments of the *immediate past* of the state socialist system."

Agenda Setting and Agenda Shifting as Indicators of Power

Up to this point, questions of power have been raised only indirectly. The focus on myth as a source of organizational legitimacy addresses power only as refracted through an institutional environment that generates changes in organizations and rules. That approach is better at explaining the importance of myths than in asking how certain models arise in the first place and whose interests they serve. To help raise this issue, questions about power can be posed in two ways: The first is the power to set the agenda, in this case, the national legislative agenda, in ways that "channel" the behavior of other actors (Birkland 1997). The second is the power to intervene at critical moments, and, as Walter Powell and

Paul DiMaggio have argued, to define "appropriate models of organizational structure which then go unquestioned for years to come" (DiMaggio and Powell 1991: 79). In this section, I show that the EU has demonstrated real power in the first sense (normal legislative politics) but not, as of yet, in the second (extraordinary intervention).

To argue that the EU has become an agenda setter in CEE is to run counter to the received wisdom that locates decisions about institutional design squarely in the domestic politics of each nation (Goetz 2000). While this domestic emphasis surely has been appropriate, it has always cried out for a complementary focus on external influences—influences that I believe are growing stronger rather than fading with time. The comprehensiveness of EU legislation is making it a very significant force for legislative change in the region, far out of proportion to other multilateral organizations in the region. This fact is somewhat obscured in some of the more comprehensive surveys that give more or less equal coverage to organizations such as the OECD and even the Council of Europe.[15]

As the kind of transfer promoted by the immediate accession objectives is fairly new—dating back, at most, to the Essen white paper in 1995—it is not yet possible to answer systematically some of the larger issues about how transferred structures and rules provide opportunities for the exercise of particular kinds of power. Yet, enough time has passed that one potential answer can be seriously doubted: institutional architecture designed through transfer is not simply the outcome of the design preferences of key domestic elites. Although consideration of domestic elites' preferences and expectations is necessary for persuasive accounts of institutional genesis, it is not likely to be sufficient.

Investigations of power in CEE, as of institutional transfer itself, require both external and domestic dimensions. This is so because processes of complexity that go beyond what any group of actors can manage have often resulted in structures that are not obviously purpose-built to the interests of any one key group. Institutional construction is an open struggle and one that is far from complete. Domestic confusion and dissension opens the door for external influence, so that EU pressure can be brought to bear with more force during screening and negotiations than at any time in the previous ten years. Clearly, the prospect of EU membership does change the legislative agendas of individual national ministries.

Returning to the Czech example, two factors are of immediate relevance for the agenda-setting power of the EU. These can be summarized under the headings "leverage" and "channels." Only recently has the Commission become an important agenda setter in the domestic politics of aspirant members. The Commission, using agents such as Phare and private consultants, has only been able to strongly influence the Czech legislative agenda when the Czech government has permitted it to do so. As Milada Vachudová (2001) has shown, the successive governments headed by Václav Klaus used glittering aggregate economic statistics to keep the Commission monitors at bay while professing their commitment to EU practices.

Only with the warnings in the Commission's report on the formal application for membership (coinciding with a sharp economic downturn) was the magnitude of the remaining work on transposition widely understood. All the while, as Klaus himself openly questioned whether EU institutions were appropriate for the liberal Czech Republic, national ministries felt comparatively little pressure to rapidly bring their structures and practices into line with EU rules. This skeptical distance changed only with the Josef Tošovský government, which portrayed an image of the Czech Republic as an apprentice eager to fulfill the requirements of membership. With this change in perspective, which has been continued by the minority social democratic government of Milos Zeman, national ministries have become much more responsive to the Commission's agenda.

Wider openings for Commission influence have gone hand in hand with Commission efforts to maximize its own leverage, especially with states that hope to join in the first wave. The Commission began writing "conditionality" clauses into its official documents with aspirant members as insurance against shifting political coalitions. For example, the Accession Partnerships speak of working together with the applicant "on the basis of a clearly defined programme to prepare for membership, involving commitments by the applicants to particular priorities and to a calendar for carrying them out. In addition, the subsequent allocation of financial assistance will be closely tied to the respect by the government of the commitments made in the National Program for the Adoption of the Acquis."[16] While this form of conditionality does not match that in multilateral lending documents, neither is it trivial. Certainly, the Polish experience in losing over $30 million in 1998 Phare monies focused the attention of national elites on the importance of paying homage to Commission priorities and justifying their work in approved Brussels vernacular.

So much for leverage; how about channels? Here, the story is less modest. The screening process already discussed contributed significantly to the Commission's new influence over the legislative agenda. For each chapter to be screened, a Commission organization called TAIEX prepared a checklist of the relevant EU directives. The responsible ministry then filled in this so-called A-list with the relevant existing and pending legislation, while noting any deficiencies yet to be addressed, along with a timetable for doing so. The resulting harmonogram, which functioned initially as an agenda for discussion during the screening of the relevant chapter, subsequently has become a key tool for ministerial actors to coordinate their legislative initiatives and, as it were, "announce" them as answers to legislative deficits. Commission experts from the relevant directorates general gain access to the domestic deliberation process insofar as they are allowed to critique the ministries' self-grading process, sometimes disputing judgments that existing structures represent "full compliance" or "partial compliance."

Another channel, created in spring 2000, is the Commission's "twinning" program. Here, the basic idea moves beyond the somewhat misleading image of an "EU model" to the more textured reality of different national applications of EU directives. Phare pays for personnel transfers between national ministries in member states and counterpart ministries in aspirant members. Of course, a certain amount of this has already taken place in the context of ad hoc bilateral aid programs and through Western academics who have done sabbatical projects in the public administrations of CEE states. The twinning program's role is clearly to reinforce the Commission message that laws must be implemented as well as passed.[17]

The Commission has not yet demonstrated the second kind of power, namely to intervene at critical moments. Indeed, there have been a number of cases where EU efforts at intervention in domestic decisions have been openly rebuffed, most notably the appeal to the parties in the Czechoslovakian dispute not to dissolve the state. Under what conditions might the EU develop the power of critical intervention? The most important precondition would seem to be the principle—emphasized since 1998—that successful screening of individual chapters notwithstanding, "nothing is decided until all is decided." This formulation means that while the initial monitoring of the readiness of the aspirant members must be done on a disaggregated basis, the negotiations for membership (which, again, are being conducted by the council) will proceed such that membership can go only to those who can fulfill *all* of its obligations. In sum, there is ample evidence that the accelerated accession process has given the Commission increased power to help set the legislative agendas in individual national parliaments given the fragmentation of government attention and the need for quick action. But it remains to be seen whether this tool might translate into a lever for the Commission to reach deeply into national-level legislative deliberations in situations where well-informed actors have strong preferences that run counter to EU requirements. Should this situation arise, it seems likely that it would require a Commission presence much stronger than the individual task forces and certainly stronger than Phare.

This section has advanced the claim that a particular kind of "Europeanization" is occurring through institutional transfer in CEE. That process, to be sure, includes a good deal of ceremonial activity as a way of satisfying the demands of an institutional environment suddenly dominated by the EU, but it is also a process in which power is quite evident. As we see in the next section, however, the Commission is far from blind to the possibility that national elites will talk the European talk while continuing to walk in a national walk. The Commission emphasizes that there should be little gap between what organizations say they do and what they actually do. This emphasis clearly stems from the fear of allowing in members that are organizationally unprepared for membership.

Variation: Policy Domains and National Public Administrations

To show the EU's dual role as promoter of transfer and monitor of its own work (and the resulting dilemma for ministerial-level actors), this paper has proceeded as if "transfer" happened in only one fashion (through screening) and as if "CEE" appears as an undifferentiated region. But there are, in fact, at least two axes of variation that are quite important: techniques of institutional transfer that vary by policy domain and the abilities of national public administrations to implement and animate rules and structures thus transferred.

The prospective responsibilities of membership have accelerated processes of institution building in the region, especially with the promulgation of The EU's Accession Partnerships and National Programs for the Adoption of the Acquis. Much of that institution building has been very hasty and done in response to inadequacies revealed during the screening process. In the wake of the screening, much more of this kind of transfer can be expected. Such "slavish" imitation contrasts with other cases where transfer has been a much longer process of imitation, experimentation, feedback, and adjustment. In these latter cases, Western models have been crucial not so much as templates, but as touchstones in a process of continuously negotiated inspiration. To explore this difference, consider first the policy domains of regional development policy and consumer protection. Neither domain figured prominently in the deliberations of political elites during the early years of the transformation toward a capitalist economy. Yet, robust institutions in both domains are required of EU members.

Because they were written around projections of future reforms, the initial Commission opinions on both the Czech and Hungarian applications were generally positive about the prospects for meeting the terms of membership in the medium term. Yet, the basic optimism of both documents could not mask the EU's great concern that there were virtually no functioning regional policy instruments in either state. From the perspective of the last wave of entrants, CEE reluctance to develop instruments of regional policy is striking. One of the primary motives for countries such as Finland to join the EU was the promise of access to structural funds that might help in the development of their economically weaker regions. It is, of course, hard to overestimate the importance of regional policy to EU activities. Spending from the structural fund is the second largest component of the EU budget, trailing only the CAP.[18] But access to funds is predicated on administrative mastery of complex procedures, that is, certain administrative competencies are a prerequisite for receiving structural funds. But because almost all legislation is directly applicable, there is very little need here to "approximate" laws. Rather, the task is to create competent regional actors.

In the Czech case, Klaus's preference for centralized control long prevented even the formal establishment of the agents who would conduct a regional policy.[19] While the EU paid a Czech regional planning group for three separate studies of foreign systems of regional policy formation, these domestic political considerations continued to block the space for such a transfer until Klaus's government fell.[20] That such agents long did not exist in a policy domain undeniably crucial to EU member states speaks strongly to the incompleteness of institution building in the region and of the growing incentives for a rapid transfer.[21] Despite worries expressed in the initial Commission opinion, the situation is somewhat better in Hungary. Building on pilot projects in the northeastern counties, the Hungarian state has now moved on to larger-scale projects in southern Transdanubia and the Southern Great Plain. Yet, local actors are still very weak and inexperienced in programming and budgeting, in part, because the government act that created them called for "voluntary" regional groupings. Moreover, while the embryonic regional structures have been able to process Phare monies for pilot projects, total spending has been less than 0.1 percent of Hungarian GDP. The EU structural funds, by contrast, presume channeling up to 4 percent of national GDP through such organizations. Evidently, aspirant members have significant work ahead to prepare for the *acquis* in this area. But because regional policy is largely a direct-effects domain, the imitation of foreign practices has been slow and partial.

By contrast, in consumer protection, the rather slavish imitation of prevailing EU language often has seemed the best recourse. This case is interesting because, unlike regional policy, there are many EU directives that require transposition into national language. Where regional policy requires national elites to build *structures*—that is, competent regional policy and planning bodies—the domain of consumer protection obliges those elites to first make *rules*. For example, the screening of EU legislation on consumer protection showed significant differences between existing Czech laws and EU legislation.[22] Of the sixteen pieces of relevant EU legislation, all but one was judged still to be in need of additional work. In Hungary, the hodge-podge of laws that made up the domain of consumer protection could build on a firmer Communist-era legal basis than in the Czech Republic (Tatham 1997). Even here, however, the Hungarian equivalent of the EU's prohibition on unfair contract terms was more limited in scope and placed the burden of proof on the injured party rather than, as in the EU directive, on the producer of the good or service in question. Not until 1997 did subsequent legislation move closer to full harmonization with EU directives.[23]

Health-care policy is also an institutional arena where CEE elites have clearly looked to Western models, especially those from Western Europe. Yet, perhaps because of the diversity of institutional practices in Western Europe or because of the obvious struggles the various national systems have in controlling costs, health care generally has not been an arena where CEE elites have slavishly imitated Western structures. Further complicating the use of Western templates has been the incommensurability of advice on broad social policy given by a range of international organizations, including the World Bank, International Labor Office, International Monetary Fund, OECD, the Council of

Europe, and the EU (Deacon and Hulse 1997). As a result, the process of organizational construction has included more cases of isolated, adaptive borrowings from different Western models. We can see this process of continuously negotiated inspiration in a review of some of the structural changes in Hungarian and Czech health-care systems, each of which underwent major revisions in the post-1989 period. The fact that the last socialist government in Hungary and the first Czechoslovakian government both looked to Western health-care models implies that these models were attractive somewhat independent of the regime type considering them.

In Hungary, the first crucial step was taken by the last socialist government in 1989, which separated the health system from the general fund and sought to institute quasi-corporatist arrangements for their funding and oversight. The precise roots of this move, and thus of Western antecedents, are difficult to pin down; as one of the Roundtable participants on the committee charged with health policy has recalled, the idea of neocorporatist oversight "just conquered brains. It was in the air."[24] Under the first postsocialist government, a fee-for-service reimbursement system was introduced. Hungary adopted and then heavily adapted the institution of so-called diagnostic resource groups (DRGs). These DRGs, which set insurance fund payments to hospitals for groups of related medical conditions, are widely used in the United States, but are also being used now in European countries such as Norway, Sweden, Portugal, and Austria. Indeed, there is some indication that German enthusiasm for DRGs may have contributed to German consultants' advocacy of their use in Hungary. The DRG system was adapted in at least three ways. First, account had to be taken of the much higher use of technology and longer stays in hospitals in the United States than in Hungary. Second, Hungarian hospitals had to build into the DRGs the employment costs of doctors since those charges are typically billed separately in U.S. hospitals, where doctors often have "privileges" without being employees. Third, DRGs were adapted to take account of different epidemiological patterns in Hungary. Again, some adaptations of the DRGs apparently came by way of German experience. Since DRGs have the potential to invite "overcoding," the German state of Bavaria has used a capped fund for physician fees so that as use rises in a particular category, average reimbursement rates fall. But what was a regional system for physician fees in Bavaria has been used as the national model for Hungarian DRGs, and has apparently made a contribution to cost control problems faced by the funds.

In the Czech case, health care was also an area of major discontinuity with past practices—significantly more than in social services or education, to name two other social policy domains. Initially, the then-Czechoslovakian state moved in January 1992 to a General Health Insurance Office with the state as the dominant shareholder. As Olga Vybomá (1994) has argued, such a monopoly was hard to justify as "natural" when cost calculations were so unclear, and this opened space for Czech parliamentarians to invoke Western models to suggest that a competition of health insurance companies would be key to dampening cost pressures. Within a year, the parliament allowed a plurality of private insurers through the Sectional, Professional, Corporate, and other Health Insurance Offices Act. As in Hungary, the Czech health-care system has introduced fee-for-service methods of payment in which "points" are distributed for each procedure. Yet, unlike in most Western societies where fee-for-service systems are used, there were no provisions made for copayments so that insurance companies lost an important cost control lever, and health-care costs increased dramatically.

Finally, competent public administration might be the single most important factor differentiating cases where public officials engage in careful experimentation with Western models or lurch haphazardly from one to the next (Dorf and Sabel 1998; Locke 1995: 15–25). The quality of public administration seems to vary cross-nationally more than by policy domains within a given nation.[25] Thus, notwithstanding the common challenges of low pay, constant personnel turnover, and inadequate interministerial coordination, some public administrations seem much more likely to be able to implement the *acquis* than others. The situation is dire even among some countries that are favorites for early entry into the EU. And despite a keen awareness of the problems, the Commission has not been notably successful in promoting change. For example, an external review of those Phare programs designed to promote "public administration reform" in the Czech Republic for the period 1995–97 concluded that a full two and a half years after the starting date of the project (and only six months before its conclusion), none of the nearly 1.4 million ECU budgeted had yet been disbursed even though 83 percent had been committed. Citing "serious delays" and a "limited connection with the original objectives" of the program, the external evaluators rated the complex of programs "highly unsatisfactory."[26] The publicity given much of the ineffective Phare programming has led some critics inside the European Parliament to call for efforts to decentralize Phare. Yet, in the Czech Republic even this step might well founder if the significant public administration problems leave bureaucrats unable to formulate a basic reform plan.

In Hungary, again, the situation is more promising (Illner 1997). With a comprehensive civil service law in place and, at least under the last two governments, growing levels of interministerial cooperation, the Hungarian civil service seems much better placed to implement the laws it passes. Interestingly, some observers link the rise of better interministerial cooperation to the task of responding to the EU's 160-page questionnaire to prospective applicants.[27] Indeed, Hungary produced a nearly 5,000-page response, one that would not have been possible for individual ministries in isolation (Böröcz 2000). The Hungarian ministerial bureaucracies seem much more involved in drafting legislation than do their Czech counterparts. Indeed, in Hungary the approximation is a process led by the executive and its ministries and flanked by crucial judicial decisions. In this respect, the Hungarian Parliament seems to have taken a backseat.

Conclusion: Imperialism, Experimentalism, Scaffolding

The priest has heard many of the various confessions, and some of the penitent, in a reversal of the usual order, have been paid handsome indulgences as a reward for revealing their weaknesses. On paper, large changes are afoot. In practice, change is less certain, for such changes do not come without costs. One cost is exclusion. Alongside the necessarily inclusive screening process, fitful negotiations to prepare the EU for enlargement go on over the heads of the aspirant members. As the Czechs say, many discussions are "about us, without us." The December 2000 Nice Summit just reinforced this long-standing pattern. A second dilemma for national elites is that institutional convergence costs money, and not all costs are borne by Brussels. Politicians who have won elections based on a set of narrower promises are loath to spend large sums on changes to support the broad goal of EU membership, especially initiatives whose fruition lies many years down the road. And finally, yielding sovereignty to Brussels limits the room for maneuver that parties have used to build their own profiles. Given the thin connections they have to their voters, they are even keener to avoid or ceremonialize potentially embarrassing EU monitoring.

This paper began with a claim that a "loose coupling" between an organization's public face and its daily work can be functional in institutional environments where myths are prominent. In the CEE context, however, the result of such dualism is also likely to be growing organizational complexity at a time when social interests are still not well formed and state actors are sometimes remarkably incompetent. So is this glass half empty or half full? Stepping back, there seem to me three potential ways to characterize the meaning of the EU's institutional tutoring and monitoring.

First, the process might be cast as EU imperialism (Hartnell 1997). If the EU is acting as an imperial power in the region, however, then it is as a fairly weak and fragmented one. Its actions seem able to give concrete shape to the legislative agendas once they are broadly defined by national elites. But unlike the occupying armies that have so often reshaped institutions in this region, the EU lacks the power to reach down inside societies and radically shift their domestic agendas in new directions. Indeed, if anything, the EU struggled far too long to define a way to help in the region while attempting to keep at bay the states' desires for membership. In the context of long-standing declarations from CEE states that they wanted to join the EU, the EU refused to emphasize harmonization. In part, this choice was no doubt motivated by a fear of giving rise to the impression that institutional conformity with the EU would bestow on aspirant states the right to become members. As the Commission continues to emphasize right up to the present moment, membership is a political decision for which such conformity is a necessary but not sufficient condition. There has indeed been a significant recent shift in EU policy toward promoting accession—the target date of 2004 emerged from the Nice Summit—but if imperialism this be, then a reluctant and recent one.

Second, it is not wholly convincing to speak of CEE as a mere testing ground for new ideas, as do, for example, Deacon and Hulse (1997: 60). While it is undoubtedly true that different agencies and their different consultants give conflicting, often incommensurate advice, the EU, by virtue of the desirability of membership that it controls, has a weight far disproportionate to the other agencies. In the past year or two, it has also demonstrated a newfound willingness to impose tough conditions on aspirant member states, and has not been shy about pointing to institutional deficiencies in various policy domains. In addition, the financial contribution that the EU, through its Phare program, now makes in the region dwarfs any new spending coming out of the other agencies. Emphasis on the disproportionate weight of the EU does not mean that these other agencies have no effect or that the image of CEE as a testing ground for novel ideas is misleading. Other agencies undoubtedly do look to the region as a potential testing ground. But, to return to the theme of transfer as the junction of internal and external forces, they must contend with the desires of political elites in the region, many of whom have little enthusiasm for such experiments. It is, after all, not only in Eastern Germany that the slogan "*keine Experimente!*" won many hearts and minds.

Rather than seeing new structures in the region as the result of imperialism or experimentation, I wonder whether we might come to regard them as scaffolding. That is, to what extent might the weakly organized consumer groups be able to use the new legislation as focal points around which to organize? And to what extent can the nascent regional planning bodies use the structural funds to build administrative competence? The virtue of this perspective is that it brings together questions of design and questions of political power and social structure. If this notion of transfer as productive of a potentially useful "scaffolding" is correct, then it is important to note again, and finally, the roots of the transfer process in an *idea* about rejoining Europe. The Commission has emphasized a particular variant of the idea of "rejoining Europe," one that underlines the need for members to implement the *acquis* from the start and without backsliding. Acting as gatekeeper, the Commission also has taken the idea of rejoining Europe and attached to it a list of specific institutional and procedural conditions. In so doing, it has made the romantic idea both more concrete and more bureaucratic. Further, in institutionalizing the idea, the Commission has tried to emphasize that there should be a very small gap between formal rules and actual practices. But having finally moved to allow some CEE states to enter, the council will have to decide how strictly to insist on the Commission's principles. It will do so knowing full well that if the idea of "rejoining European institutions" should fail, then alternative ideas will likely gain ground. Currently, what might be called "cosmopolitan skepticism" about the wisdom of joining Europe is dominated by two general camps—those neoliberals who fear that West European socialism is being reimported through the back door via Brussels and those social protectionists who fear that CEE economies and polities are not yet prepared for the rigors and risks of full participation in European structures. Should either or both of these camps make common ground with nationalist groups—the noncosmopolitan skeptics, as it were—then the EU will have significantly misplayed its hand.

Notes

1. Peter Hall (1997: 183–86) has identified the role of gatekeepers and the process of institutionalization of ideas as two areas in need of attention in better specifying links between "ideas" and "interests" approaches to political economy.

2. I borrow the word *design* from Pickel and Wiesenthal (1997). Pickel, in turn, links his use to Karl Popper's term *holism* (21).

3. For more on this unhelpful dichotomy, see Jacoby (1999a).

4. In this, my approach is far closer to what Ira Katznelson (1997) has labeled "configurational" approaches to comparative politics.

5. This section builds on the argument introduced in Jacoby (1999b).

6. Select parts of the *acquis* had long constituted informal targets for many ministerial elites in the region, and some governments (e.g., Hungary) had long had procedures for checking the compatibility of new laws with the *acquis*.

7. Indeed, in the mid-1990s, the Commission's Hans van den Broeck reportedly said this to Czech Prime Minister Václav Klaus during a formal dinner at the Davos Forum.

8. Though national leaders from each have been assured that these five need not join as one group in case some are deemed ready well before others. Cyprus, the final "in," is not considered in this paper. At the Helsinki Summit in December 1999, the EU opened formal negotiations also with the former "pre-ins" (Bulgaria, Slovakia, Latvia, Lithuania, and Romania) and with Turkey.

9. Just how much they rely on CEE informants can be gauged from Böröcz (2000).

10. Interview with Michael Leigh, Commission negotiator with the Czech Republic, Brussels, 8 July 1998.

11. The theory holds that the "myths generating formal organization . . . are rationalized and impersonal prescriptions that identify various social purposes as technical ones and specify in a rulelike way the appropriate means to pursue these technical purposes rationally" (44).

12. Mainstream international relations scholarship thus suggests point that elites in new democracies often seek insurance against the great uncertainties they face. See Moravcsik (2000).

13. Because NATO commitments oblige a nation to coordinate among several ministries (especially defense, foreign affairs, and finance), the prospect of NATO expansion has also visibly thickened interministerial coordination in some CEE states.

14. Note especially the EU's warnings to the Czech Republic that including the representatives of labor in a range of policy deliberation processes is "part of the *acquis*." Uniting Europe, 9, 1 June 1998.

15. E.g., the otherwise excellent study by Deacon and Hulse (1997).

16. Quotation from the Hungarian Accession Partnership, 1998, 1, 5, 6.

17. Interview Bertin Martens, Phare Evaluation Unit, Brussels, 6 July 1998; Pavel Cernoch, Delegation of the EU to the Czech Republic, Prague, 12 July 1999.

18. Depending on the pace of enlargement, by 2006 up to 30 percent of total EU structural fund spending could flow to CEE countries.

19. Such reluctance may partially reflect the memory of the Czechoslovak Communists' extreme regional redistribution policies (Blažek 1997).

20. For an extended discussion of the impact of EU regional policy "norms" on Czech regional policy, see Jacoby and Cernoch (2001).

21. When the Klaus government finally agreed to allow regional bodies, it inflated their number so that no one region could develop a large power base. Thus, from the eight regions in the Communist-era territory of the Czech Republic were made fourteen regions. With this distribution set, regional policy advocates then moved to coordinate the fourteen through eight informal regions for purposes of dealing with the EU. Interview Jaroslav Dupal and Miloš Červený, TERPLAN, Prague, 21 July 1998 and July 1999. See also Martin Hamp et. al. 1999; Blažek and Boeckhout, 2000.

22. Though the Czech Republic declined to ask for any derogations. Interview, Josef Tržický, Prague, July 1999.

23. Tatham 1997: 276–79. See also Hungarian Parliament (1997).

24. Interview with Ivan Csaba, Budapest, July 16, 1998.

25. This is the implicit message of European Community Studies Association (1993). See also Nunberg (1999).

26. OMAS Consortium (1998) T4. Clearly, some Czech governments have seen it in their interest to keep civil servants without tenure and thus more open to government intrusion and control.

27. Interview with András Inotai, Budapest, 14 July 1998.

Chapter 8

Global, Transnational, and National Change Mechanisms: Bridging International and Comparative Approaches to Postcommunist Transformation

Andreas Pickel and Jacqui True

Contemporary changes in the global political economy have played a crucial role in postcommunist revolutions and transformations since 1989. Yet, the nature and significance of these global forces in East European transitions have not been systematically mapped by scholars of comparative transformation. Conversely, international relations scholars have paid scant regard to Eastern European change processes since the collapse of Communism. This is indeed an irony when international openness, external vulnerability, and regional and global pressures have all greatly intensified in Eastern Europe in the 1990s. The lack of congruence between the theory and practice of postcommunist transformation is an anomaly akin to the one Barbara Stallings observed in the 1980s with respect to the theory and practice of economic policy change in the Third World: "just as international variables became especially important in the 1980s, they disappeared as the key factor from theories of development" (1992: 43).[1] At the same time, global policy formulas alone clearly do not determine the course of transformation in individual nation-states, and international relations analysts can overrate the ability of external forces to transform Soviet-type economies into capitalist economies. What is thus insufficiently studied, and indeed undertheorized, is the interplay between national and transnational forces in the transformation process. One of the reasons for this scholarly neglect, we contend, is the strength of disciplinary and subdisciplinary boundaries in the social sciences. In this analysis, we focus on the division of political science into the subfields of comparative and international politics, and of political economy into comparative and global.

The task of this essay is to contribute toward a new approach and conceptualization of postcommunist transformation that seeks to bridge what, along with others, we consider a misleading conceptual dichotomy and unfruitful academic division of labor (cf. Caporaso 1997; Hermann 1998; Jacobsen 1996; Jordan 1997). We argue that a proper understanding of these multilayered systemic change processes requires an explicit and systematic attempt to capture the specific interactions of global, transnational, and intranational change processes. In the following section, we continue to outline the nature of the problem in the postcommunist transition context. We then briefly explain our methodology and our distinction between global, transnational, and intranational mechanisms. We cite major instances of these three types of mechanisms and some representative studies in each category. Finally, we present short case studies of combined change mechanisms in the Czech Republic, East Germany, and Cuba in which we apply and illustrate our approach.

Approaches to Postcommunist Transformation

The lack of careful analysis of global factors and their particular reception in postcommunist transition countries, in a nutshell, can be attributed to two causes: (1) the dominance of neoliberalism in the wake of the fall of state socialism,[2] and (2) the persistent "great divide" between comparative politics and theories of international relations, despite the burgeoning of critical theory (Agnew 1994; Cox 1991; Rosenau 1997), comparative political economy (Hollingsworth and Boyer 1997), and institutionalist perspectives that to some extent bridge them (Gourevitch 1978; Keohane and Milner 1996; Campbell 1993; Evans et al. 1993). Each set of perspectives and approaches comes with its own particular blinders.

Comparativists' Blinders

Scholars of comparative institutional design, largely from sociology and political science, point to domestic factors such as state capacity, the design of institutions and policy, and the strength of state-society networks and civil society to explain transition success or failure. Other scholars who emphasize the primacy of domestic factors in shaping transitions use path dependency and Leninist legacy approaches. They focus more on the negative effects of *nomenclatura* elites and previous state socialist institutions that persist after communism. Postcommunism is not a tabula rasa in their view, and the relative success or failure of the transition from socialism depends on the adaptation of former socialist networks and informal institutions, as well as the transformation of practices and mentalities associated with past Communist regimes.

There is no approach to postcommunist transformation that approximates the radical contribution of 1970s dependency analysis to Latin American (under) development. This is a stunning absence. While some analysts have suggested that neoimperialism is emerging in postcommunist Eastern Europe, they have not developed a coherent theoretical approach (Gowan 1995) or adequately empirically supported their claims yet (Altvater 1998). Scholars giving primacy to domestic variables have also suggested that global economic models, regional integration in the European Union, and membership in and ratings by international organizations are significant forces determining comparative outcomes of Eastern European transitions (Offe 1997; Hellman 1998b). Beverly Crawford and Arend Lijphart (1995), for example, discuss both endogenous and exogenous influences in postcommunist transitions, but exclude the possibility of an approach that analyses but does not prejudge the impact of global pressures. They conceive only two ideal-type approaches to postcommunist transformation; *legacies of the past* and *imperatives of liberalization*. The former domestic set of factors are construed as having a mostly negative impact, while the latter internationally driven set of factors is generally analyzed as having positive effects in postcommunist societies.[3]

This failure to link the analysis of postsocialism with the debate on the effects of economic globalization and to theorize the interaction between "domestic" and transnational dynamics in postcommunist transformations is exacerbated by the disciplinary divide between comparative politics and international relations. Comparative political economy itself is based on a sharp distinction between internal-external, inside-outside, and domestic-international, with the former remaining most central for a full understanding of the diversity of transformation processes. New institutionalists argue that the largely ideological and faddish discourse on globalization and transnational mechanisms exaggerates the significance of global determinants of national change (Wade 1996; Weiss 1998; Whitley 1999). When it comes to explaining the transformation processes in postcommunist countries now and in the near future, the primacy of the national level in general, and the nation-state in particular, remains beyond doubt for most comparativist authors. They argue that global forces, whatever their strength, interact with and are filtered through nationally based political and cultural—and of course economic—institutions and in the process produce a significant range of outcomes. Both historical contexts and strategic decisions and actions of domestic actors are seen as decisive in producing these varied outcomes. Comparative perspectives are concerned most significantly with what global forces and structures contribute to internal transformation and how they manifest themselves "on the ground." In general they argue that while economic globalization qua world market integration is a serious practical problem for postcommunist countries, it is neither as historically unique nor as theoretically problematic as the domestic transformation of a Soviet-type economy into a capitalist economy.

International Relations Blinders

For international relations scholars who study the global political economy, however, dichotomies such as internal-external, inside-outside, domestic-international are largely misnomers. As Susan Strange (1994: 32) aptly put it, "even the best work in comparative politics tends to focus on the similarities and differences—more often the differences—between individual states or national systems of decision-making than on the common factors emanating from the world economy, such as the greater mobility of capital, of technical know-how, of disease, and of ideas." State socialism in Eastern Europe and the former Soviet Union collapsed as a result of the greater dynamism and gradual encroachment of the capitalist world system (Cox 1991; Kolodziej 1997; Verdery 1996), or it is argued, as a result of Soviet military overstretch (Lebow and Risse-Kappen 1995; Keohane, Nye and Hoffman 1993). The transition from a Soviet-type command economy to a capitalist market economy is thus shaped in the last instance by the imperatives of global integration. All the countries in this region share a common set of transition choices and constraints in the context of the structural power of global capitalism. Since the collapse of Communism, transnational mechanisms have intensified and expanded exponentially such that the "identities of cities, regions, and nations are [increasingly] more a matter of global interconnections than of internal linkages" (*Review of International Political Economy* 1994: 4). Global production, finance, knowledge, and security structures are the decisive—transnational—determinants of national change, since unlike solely domestic or national factors, they define and govern the framework within which East European transitions from communism can and must occur.

The a priori decision in favor of a global or a comparative perspective poses a major obstacle to our understanding of postcommunist transformations. The question of the relative importance of transnational and intranational factors cannot be settled by theoretical reason alone since it is, to a considerable extent, an empirical question. However, to be able to examine the empirical question in a systematic and theoretically informed fashion, we require a conceptual and theoretical apparatus that does not unduly prejudge the answer. This is a central weakness of both comparative and international perspectives. Here, we briefly introduce our systemic framework that allows us to search for particular *combined mechanisms* of transformation. Our methodological assumption is that each case of systemic transformation needs to be investigated as a particular combination of typical or general *mechanisms*—combinations that may be more or less unique.

Beyond the Great Divide: Toward a New Methodology

To understand change processes occurring *within* and *across* nation-state systems, such as postcommunist transformation, we need to examine systematically the following dimensions of change:

1. The structures of the global system within which the transforming systems are embedded and act.
2. The major actors—both state and nonstate, formal and informal—that act in the global system in ways that significantly affect national transformation processes.
3. The structures of the transforming national system within which and on which both transnational and intranational actors work.

The division of labor in political science assigns responsibility for major actors in the global system to the field of international relations, and for the structure of national systems to comparative politics. The structures of the global system are perceived and invoked ("globalization") but usually not systematically theorized by either subdiscipline (exceptions: world systems theory, unequal exchange, dependency, and historical sociology).[4] Global-national relationships are often overlooked or insufficiently conceptualized as a result of mainstream social science's disciplinary ontologies and methodologies, as seen in the perennial levels of analysis and structure versus agency debates in international relations (see Waltz 1979; Wendt 1987; Dessler 1989, Hollis and Smith 1991). As a result, it is theoretically and conceptually difficult to map these interrelated change processes.

Given the dearth of analytical frameworks capable of systematically capturing the complex interactions between "internal" (national) and "external" (transnational and global) transformation processes[5], we adopt systemism (Bunge 1996, 1998) as our fundamental approach to the problem.[6] Systemism is an alternative to both individualism and holism. It accounts for both individual agency and social structure. It postulates that everything is a system or a component of one. It models every system in terms of composition, environment, and structure. It breaks down society into four major subsystems—biological or kinship system, economic system, political system, and cultural system.[7] It can be applied at subnational, national, and transnational levels of analysis. Above the level of societies organized within nation-states, there are regional "supersocieties" (e.g., EU) as well as an international society of states (Armstrong 1998). It is important to note that, unlike Parsonian systems theory, *systemism is not a theory but only a framework or approach*, "just a skeleton to be fleshed out with specific hypotheses and data" (Bunge 1996, 265). As such, it is not "static" or blind to processes of conflict and change—a common criticism leveled at systems *theories.*

We propose the concept of *mechanism* to get at the interrelations—making for either continuity or change—between all three dimensions discussed above.

1. Global *mechanisms* refer to the way the structure of the global system affects its composite elements (states, markets, multinational corporations, international organizations) and is, in turn, affected by them.
2. *Transnational mechanisms* refer to the interactions between systems and actors in the global system (including, but not confined to, states and international relations) that transcend the national system.
3. *Intranational mechanisms* refer to the interactions between subsystems and actors embedded and contained in the national system.

Our argument is that postcommunist transformation processes should be approached as *combined change mechanisms* composed of global, transnational, and intranational mechanisms. Mechanismic explanation is not to be confused with mechanical explanation.[8] It differs from most standard modes of explanation employed in the social sciences: the neopositivists' "covering law" model of scientific explanation, the interpretative approach of the hermeneutic or *Verstehen* school, as well as functional and teleological modes of explanation.[9] The mechanism of every major social change is likely to be a combination of mechanisms of various kinds coupled together (Bunge 1998: 417). Postcommunist transformations, like any sweeping and profound social changes, affect all areas of society. Thus, they are likely to be biological, psychological, demographic, economic, political, and cultural—either simultaneously or in succession. Here, the task of our mechanismic mode of explanation is to identify how global, transnational, and intranational mechanisms combine in individual cases and to elucidate the configurations of mechanisms at work in particular transformation processes. In contrast to the voluntaristic and individualistic assumptions that figure prominently in much of the neoliberal transformation literature, our approach does not equate change mechanisms with reform policies. Eschewing the structuralist assumptions that are assigned dominance in much of the critical and culturalist literature, our approach does not reduce change mechanisms to "deeper structural factors."

Below, we introduce a list of general mechanisms at global, transnational, and intranational levels that we consider to be of primary importance in postcommunist transformation. Our conceptual catalogue aims to be comprehensive, though clearly not exhaustive, and to suggest some representative studies of each set of mechanisms. The case studies of the Czech Republic, East Germany, and Cuba that follow provide examples and illustrations of these and of some combined mechanisms.

Global mechanisms refer to the way the structures of the global system affect its composite elements—for example states, markets, cultures, multinational corporations, and international organizations—and are in turn affected by them. Following Susan Strange (1988, 1994), we distinguish four key global structures: production, security, finance, and knowledge. In the realm of production, competition for world markets is assuming strategic importance over production for local needs in Eastern Europe. Global forces increasingly shape postcommunist economies and social structures as states limit their control over monetary policy, taxation, and national regulation to compete for investment and markets. Financial integration and the transnational mobility of capital and credit, for instance, are undermining the ability of states to protect domestic employment and social welfare. Philanthropist and investor in the region, George Soros (1998) has also stressed the deleterious consequences of global financial speculation and instability for the development of postcommunist "open societies." Further, in terms of global knowledge structures, the diffusion of Western neoliberal ideology and policy has provided the momentum for radical transition strategies (Balcerowicz 1995; Szacki 1996; Greskovits 1998). Following global (typically Anglo-American) models, elites in Eastern European countries have initiated privatization and other reforms. The colonization of academic knowledge in post-1989 east-central Europe by American social science has also been observed (Hada and Voros 1996). In addition, the military force of the United States, the remaining superpower, and its transatlantic strategic institutions have underwritten the prevailing global liberal institutions and reintegration of the old East bloc. American hegemony during and after the cold war has largely determined the structure through which other states and their political economies may relate to each other. The eagerness of the majority of central and Eastern European states to join the NATO alliance only underscores this structural power.

Transnational mechanisms refer to the interactions between systems and actors in the global system (including, but not confined to, interstate relations) that transcend the national system (see Risse-Kappen 1995). Scholars of postcommunist transformations have analyzed a number of these systems and actors. Several studies have assessed the entry of multinational enterprises and joint ventures into East European markets and their impact on production, consumption, and regional/global integration (Thornton and Mikheeva 1996; Cyr 1997; Hardy 1998; Comisso 1998; Eichengreen and Kohl 1998; Grabher 1994). Other authors have focused on the role of intergovernmental and transnational business elite networks in the design of institutional reform (Greskovits 1998; Von Zon 1998). In her book *Collusion and Collision*, anthropologist Janine Wedel (1998), for example, suggests a framework for examining emergent "transactor" relationships between East European *nomenclatura* networks and American elite groups in the transition. Scholars have also investigated transnational mechanisms with respect to professional associations, the scientific community (Evangelista 1999), and human rights, environmental, and women's organizations in global civil society (see Chilton 1995; Skilling 1989; Henderson 2000; Jancar-Webster 1993). These movements, which are known to have supported independent movements during Communism, have also been key forces in rebuilding "civil societies" in Eastern Europe since 1989. Tourists and travelers, migrants and émigrés who returned to Eastern Europe after the revolutions have been vital forces in its economic and social transformation as well. Additional transnational mechanisms discussed in the transitions literature include the influence of cultural associations, such as the Goethe Institute, Alliance Française, and the United States Information Agency in East European cities (Fawn 1995), religious leaders and religious organizations, especially the pope and the Holy See in Poland (Eberts 1998), and major banks such as Deutsche Bank. Linkages between *nascent global* cities in the region, Warsaw, Moscow, Prague, and Budapest, and *powerful* global cities, New York and London, are also discussed, as are the emergence of subnational regions and cross-border areas with Western Europe (Jessop 1995).[10] Much of the current transitions literature is of course taken up with preparations for the enlargement of the European Union and consequent regional reorientation and transformation of Eastern European political and economic institutions (Lemoine 1998; Kyvelidis 2000; Jacoby in this volume). Finally, the major multilateral institutions (NATO, the United Nations, the World Bank and International Monetary Fund, and the OECD) have obviously also been important transnational actors in the transitions. Competition among these international organizations has not only dominated macroeconomic policy formation, but also, as Bob Deacon (1997) argues, the restructuring of social policy across the region (Müller 1999).

Intranational mechanisms refer to the interactions between subsystems and actors embedded and contained in the national system. Most studies of postcommunist transformation focus on particular, key intranational mechanisms in their explanation and understanding of systemic change. Some scholars have stressed the strength of civil society/state or social cohesion as a crucial variable (see Hann and Dunn 1996; Ekiert 1996). Anticommunist ideology, for example, has been noted as central to the extraordinary political legitimacy in the early days of the transition in spite of widespread economic depression and relative deprivation after market liberalization and stabilization. Other scholars argue that the relative success or failure of transitions depends on national political economy dynamics such as the balance between market and state coordination (Crawford 1995), the institutional design of politics and economics (Elster, Offe, Preuss 1998), and a country's historical experience with markets and democracy and/or its previous level of economic development (Berend 1999). The strength or learning capacity of the state in the transition is considered a critical determining factor by comparativist George Schöpflin (2000), whereas J. Higley, J. Pakulski, and W. Wesolowski (1998) stress the quality of postcommunist elites and political leadership, and Herbert Kitschelt et al. (1999) the nascent postcommunist party system. Last, some major area scholars regard the dynamics of political identity, especially ethnic identity (Tismaneanu 1998) and class social structure (Eyal, Szelenyi, and Townsley 1999), but also gender and generation (True 2000) as crucial factors in enabling and constraining postcommunist transformations.

We acknowledge that studies of each individual set of mechanisms make significant contributions to our understanding of major dimensions of postcommunist change. However, our argument is that transformation processes can be more fully explained only if they are systematically theorized and empirically examined as *specific combined mechanisms of all three types of mechanisms—global, transnational, and intranational.* The following section offers three case studies to illustrate this argument.

Combined Change Mechanisms in the Czech Republic, Germany, and Cuba

Our case studies, despite their shared purpose of illustrating the crucial importance of explanation in terms of combined mechanisms of global, transnational, and intranational mechanisms, have divergent points of departure and slightly different formats. Our study of the Czech Republic begins by stressing the powerful influence of global and transnational mechanisms in the country's transformation processes, only to proceed to show how their particular configuration with intranational mechanisms produced specific Czech paths of economic and cultural transformation. In the Czech study, we make an attempt to illustrate with very specific examples how our general and somewhat abstract argument plays out empirically. By contrast, our studies of East Germany and Cuba take a more general, macro perspective to flesh out our theoretical argument. Here, we begin by noting the widely recognized power of intranational mechanisms (German unification and the staying power of the Castro regime, respectively), only to argue subsequently that it was their particular configuration with global and transnational mechanisms that produced the specific East German and Cuban transformation paths.

Domesticating the Global in the Czech Republic: The Case of Cultural Transformation

The transition from Communism in the Czech Republic has involved the simultaneous destruction of transnational linkages to the Soviet Union and Comecon and the creation of new transnational linkages to the West, particularly to European Union countries, NATO, and the global market. On the face of it, the postcommunist Czech Republic appears to be shaped more by global interconnections than by domestic. These intensified global linkages include the flows of international trade, assistance, foreign capital, and foreign experts associated with the liberalization and privatization of the Czech economy and regional integration with European Union elite networks and institutions. In the following analysis, we focus on a specific dimension of cultural transformation.

There have been large increases in private consumption of durable and luxury goods, in spite of an unprecedented fall in national income and output in the

Czech transition. Western imports make up the bulk of this postcommunist "conspicuous" consumption. Czech imports amounted to approximately U.S. $27 billion in 1997 compared with around U.S. $5 billion in 1988. According to several market studies, Czechs generally prefer foreign-made goods; Sony and Panasonic over the Czech electronic brand Tesla, goods made in Switzerland, the United Kingdom, the United States and Germany over those made in the Czech Republic.[11] In addition to consumerism, external influence in the Czech transition has involved the spread of Western business practices, new forms of communication and culture. This influence is diffused by "fly-by" foreign consultants and experts who pass on management practices, scientific knowledge, and other information to local elites, local resident expatriates (estimates of Americans living in Prague alone range from 20–40,000), the nongovernmental sector—the majority of which is American or foreign funded,[12] and foreign media ownership—over 50 percent of the Czech press is foreign owned.[13] The growth of Internet servers in the Czech Republic is also an indicator of global linkages. There are now 4.34 Internet hosts per 1,000 people and approximately 6–9 percent of Czech citizens currently have access to the Internet (over 200,000 in 1997), mostly in the 15–35 age range. The publishing and movie industries have been deregulated since 1991 and are also sites for foreign influence since they are dominated by mass-market imports from Western Europe and America. Moreover, cultural activities such as music and theater have become increasingly commercialized with the large influx of foreign tourists and loss of state funding.

Global and transnational linkages to the Czech Republic have intensified and expanded since 1989 and would appear to be a major factor determining the course of postcommunist transformation. However, no explanation of Czech transformation processes would be adequate without considering their unique interaction with intranational mechanisms and domestic politics. In the following example, we want to show how global integration, as exemplified by the globalization of American culture, is best understood as a combined mechanism. Indeed, in the postcommunist Czech Republic, integration with Western institutions and global markets has increased intranational networking in key instances and has actually produced a greater sense of local agency and identity.

As in other arenas of transformation, a combined mechanism of change is evident in the realm of culture. Global cultural flows are received differently and shaped by distinct national contexts. The cases of two multinational enterprises in the Czech Republic that specialize in women's journals, Harlequin Enterprises and *Cosmopolitan* magazine, illustrate this point. They show how cultural globalization is having a positive impact on Czech gender relations by empowering women as individuals and consumers. In a nutshell, not only do these American-owned journals persuade women to consume, they also encourage their role as citizens by responding to nonconsumer concerns such as physical safety, employment discrimination, and political education. Harlequin and *Cosmopolitan* inadvertently reveal how national social and cultural transformations result from even the most seemingly trivial penetration of American imports and global advertising media.[14]

In 1997 Harlequin Inc. made U.S. $81.3 million in profits, with sales of 165 million books in twenty-three languages in more than 100 countries. Owned by Torstar Corporation, Harlequin is the global leader in serial romance publishing. It is the second largest foreign publisher in Poland, and has operations in Hungary, Bulgaria, and Russia. Since 1992 Harlequin—Czech Republic has sold romance novels to an estimated one in four Czech women; that is, 256 titles per year in Czech translation from English and 35 million books for a population of 10 million. This is the result, not of global strategy, but of a highly strategic, *local* marketing plan.

Some of the ingredients of this plan include; introducing both Valentine's and Mother's Day celebrations to the Czech calendar to replace International Women's Day on 8 March, which used to be the day for celebrating women during the Communist era. After the fall of the regime, people stopped celebrating this holiday. Since 1994, however, Czech-Harlequin has promoted Valentine's Day as a celebration of romance, love, and women, sponsoring television specials and media events. Czech-Harlequin also has a social conscience. The director, Dagmar Degrínová, acknowledges the poverty and difficult living conditions of her readers. So, in 1995 she initiated a social program to support battered and abused women, funded by 1 percent of net profits. She also provided a radio program and drop-in center at Prague headquarters for women seeking counseling and advice. All of these activities are unique to Harlequin in the Czech Republic and are not shared by Torstar Corporation's other country operations. In the Czech context, Harlequin has become as much a women's social forum as a book club or consumer luxury.

In an unintentional way also, Harlequin romances have actually popularized questions about gender relations in the public domain. The novels in translation diffuse the changes in sexual and gender roles that feminism has evoked in North America over the past two decades. Former Czech-Harlequin translator Eva Hauserová has actually gone on to write the first popular books that describe a variety of Western-style feminist ideas for the benefit of Czech society. She has no qualms about calling Harlequin feminist, although we might question it. Director Degrínová believes that Harlequin books have helped promote a revolution in values, in her words "a return to what is natural; personal lives, strong families and human relationships over socialism and ideology." In her view, the former regime sacrificed "women's position in society and their rights as mothers, while femininity was given up for careers" (personal interview, 28 April 1998). Innovative in its profit making, Harlequin has also opened up a new space for women to express themselves in the nascent Czech democracy. Harlequin's success in Eastern Europe demonstrates how discourses associated with anticommunism and those associated with Western consumerism work off one another in complex ways, provoking new potential for social and democratic change.

Cosmopolitan magazine, published by Hearst Corporation, is a U.S.-based global enterprise. It is the world's best-selling women's magazine. It has a circulation of 2.75 million in the United States and 4 million readers abroad, who buy one of thirty-six foreign editions. The *Cosmopolitan* woman exudes independence, sexual freedom, and glamour. If anything suggests a global wave of American feminism, *Cosmopolitan* does through its assumption of sexual liberation and women's economic independence. In emerging markets, such as the Czech Republic, *Cosmopolitan* provides an outlet for an advertising onslaught, and is thus a trailblazer for fashion, beauty, and other gender-specific consumer industries. But while *Cosmopolitan* is at the forefront of global market expansion with its emphasis on female freedom and beautification, it has a distinctly indigenous face in its Czech market. For one, the female face of *Cosmopolitan*'s Czech editions is certainly more feminist than its American alma mater. Czech *Cosmopolitan* regularly features articles about such issues as sexual harassment and discrimination against women in the labor market; it conducts interviews with prominent Czech women activists and suggests strategies for political lobbying in the Czech Republic and in the EU.

Editor Anaztázie Kudrnová has written monthly editorials that have pressured the Czech government to take action on domestic violence and to draft special legislation to legalize homosexual partnerships. Actually, after *Cosmopolitan* ran an article on all the ways in which women could lobby their politicians, the Czech Parliament was inundated with telephone calls from women, and was querulous as to what this *Cosmo* article had sparked! Editor Kudrnová is consistently critical of the status of women in the Czech Republic. In January 1998, for example, she commented on the use of female bodies to sell all kinds of commodities in the new Czech marketplace. Further, she related this to the gender discrimination faced by women in the nascent labor market. Following this editorial Kudrnová encouraged readers to write in with their experiences of discrimination and harassment at work. A subsequent issue featured a lengthy article describing some truly horrific reader experiences. Kudrnová and her staff appear to be pushing the limits of *Cosmopolitan* in the interests of shaping a new feminist awareness in the postcommunist Czech Republic, where the local media have been largely hostile to discussions of feminism. Further, they are doing this in an American-owned publication, not in one of the umpteen local women's magazines, the majority of which shy away from serious issues and from questioning traditional gender roles.

But *Cosmopolitan* is also Janus-faced, and only ambivalently Czech. Approximately half of its contents are local; the other half is translated from English without regard to the specific issues faced by Czech women. The same cover girl as the American version appears on all Czech editions of *Cosmopolitan*. But this universal cover masks the two faces of the magazine as found in the Czech Republic. One face looks approvingly on women as a group that deserves and is desirous of social change in their public and private lives. The other face teases them, enticing them to join the new class of consumers and promises fulfillment through makeup, diets, and the possession of luxury commodities. Two-faced, the magazine presents feature articles that question the objectification and social marginalization of Czech women cheek-by-jowl with advertisements vigorously cultivating a new market of women consumers.

The cases of Harlequin and *Cosmopolitan* have a number of implications for analyzing postcommunist transformations. One way to look at them is to see them as yet another instance of Coca-Cola capitalism or global cultural imperialism. That is the classic knee-jerk response to globalization—the wall comes down and all the cultural detritus of the West comes oozing in. While acknowledging elements of this, a more subtle reading, and a more fruitful one for scholarship, is to notice the differences in the way the respective national or local culture responds to external influences and the potentially positive aspects of this. What the cases of Harlequin and *Cosmopolitan* have in common is that they both have had to adapt the form, and to some extent, the content of their "American" product to be successful in a postcommunist society. It is their very domestication that has liberated spaces for women's expression in the Czech Republic. That is, Czechs have a degree of agency in their reception to and adaptation of global culture. Any intelligent reader looking at the U.S. *Cosmopolitan* magazine will see immediately that it is schlock, selling products primarily through sex and by conditioning women to view themselves through the approving and disapproving male gaze. In stark contrast, in the Czech Republic, the editors have deliberately used *Cosmo* as a site for popularizing feminist thinking —and made it a commercial success. Czech-Harlequin and *Cosmopolitan* suggest that postcommunist transformations cannot be comprehended simply as internal or external processes that homogenize or threaten cultural identity and everyday life across the globe. Rather, we need to specify the combination of change mechanisms in each country case that influences the nature and direction of the economic, political, or cultural change.

Globalizing the Domestic: East Germany and Cuba

Comparativists treat each postcommunist country as a distinct case with its own internal dynamic. External forces, such as economic globalization or regional political integration, may be acknowledged in general terms as "triggers" or "intervening variables," but are rarely systematically analyzed from a transnational and global viewpoint. To further illustrate our argument in favor of combined mechanisms—particular configurations and interactions of global, transnational, and intranational mechanisms—let us look at two country cases that at first glance would seem to justify the comparativist's almost exclusive focus on intranational structures and actors. East Germany's postcommunist transformation began in earnest only once a general timetable for unification with West Germany had been set. Henceforth, the transformation of East Germany became a national affair for the enlarged Federal Republic of Germany. Cuba, although subject to powerful transnational forces, specifically the United States' relentless opposition to the Castro regime, precisely for that reason would seem to be understandable as a particular transformation case only in terms of internal factors that explain the political regime's capacity for survival against tremendous odds. Yet, as we argue, the particular national transformation paths of both cases cannot be fully explained without taking into account the major interactions of global, transnational, and intranational mechanisms.

As analysts of the German Democratic Republic (GDR) and Cuba have always been well aware, internal developments in those states were particularly closely linked to the larger cold war context. As creatures of the cold war, the societal transformation paths the two states followed under Communist rule were in large part due to dominant political structures of the world system. The collapse of the Soviet political and economic order liberated Eastern Europe from Soviet domination, but at the same time exposed it to a different set of global power structures. The old regime's collapse (GDR) or survival (Cuba) and the country's mode of integration into these economic, political, and cultural structures therefore becomes crucial for the course of postcommunist transformation.

East Germany

The collapse of East German Communism was above all a product of the Soviet-bloc changes initiated by Gorbachev's reforms in the late 1980s. This is not to deny that intranational processes played a crucial role in the chain of events leading to the demise of the GDR. But there is no evidence that the combined change mechanism for the East German case would have worked in a similar fashion had it not included these particular transnational and global mechanisms. Indirect historical and comparative evidence seems to support this point. The internal transformation dynamic of the Prague Spring, as that of earlier manifestations of popular resistance against Soviet-backed Communist rule in East Germany, Hungary, and Poland, was successfully suppressed by antireformist Soviet leaders and their local allies defending the hegemonic power structures in the Soviet bloc. All Communist countries that were not part of this transnational political structure, and were therefore not affected in the same way by its implosion—China, Vietnam, Yugoslavia, and Cuba—have followed fundamentally different transformation paths.

The conditions for the possibility of East Germany's transformation by unification have included at least three fundamental global and transnational mechanisms. First, West Germany's position in the global economy has made it possible to treat the problem of economic feasibility of unification as a minor issue. Second, the geopolitical realities of the emerging post–cold war world made unification politically conceivable for the first time in almost four decades. Third, Germany's transnational linkages with the EU, the United States, and the Soviet Union made unification politically feasible. In the absence of any one of these global and transnational mechanisms, transformation by unification would have been highly unlikely, while in the absence of all of them, it would have been all but impossible. These three sets of mechanisms qua conditions of course do not in themselves constitute an adequate explanation of East Germany's transformation path. However, without explicitly incorporating these transnational and global mechanisms in an account of combined mechanisms, no general explanation of collapse or transformation would be adequate.

Granted that collapse and unification were so decisively conditioned by global and transnational mechanisms, the comparativist might retort, was East Germany's actual transformation significantly shaped by supranational forces? The bulk of the literature pays basically no attention to such forces, and actually tends to treat the East German case as unique and of little comparative interest.[15] The West German government (and subsequently West German intermediary organizations from professional associations to trade unions and employers associations) did indeed take control of the East German transformation process as a "quasi-external" collective actor to an extent unparalleled in any other transforming country. Nonetheless, we will argue that it would be wrong to tell the (East) German transformation story as overwhelmingly an intranational process. Three factors in particular are important to discuss. The first is that the logic of nation-state building, of which we take unification to be an instance, follows a global and transnational logic in addition to the more commonly perceived intranational logic. Second, the fact that many global and transnational mechanisms affecting the East German transformation process were or seemed to be largely mediated by West German institutions and actors tends to obscure their existence and functioning. Third, the process of transformation by unification was embedded in a transnational and global context that directly affected the actions of West German mediating institutions as well as the West German and East German populations. Let us explore all three dimensions in somewhat more detail to illustrate our claim that it is only the combined mechanism of intranational, transnational, and global mechanisms that adequately explains the transformation process in individual countries.

The logic of nation-state building (cf. Chirot 1995), of which we take unification to be an instance, follows a global and transnational logic in addition to the more immediately perceived intranational logic. While unification remained a distant goal, the cold war order had in effect subordinated the primacy of the nation-state to the imperatives of superpower competition in a bipolar global system. Only with the decline of that order could the primacy of the nation-state (and with this: the demand for unification) be seriously reasserted. The nation-state imperative as a global political principle and basic structural feature of the world system is always and everywhere embedded in a particular transnational setting. In the case of German unification, this was the European Community (see further below), as well as the concerns and fears the specter of a reunited Germany evoked in neighboring states, both East and West. The nation-state imperative had to be worked out and negotiated in and through this transnational set of mechanisms.

Early nationalist sentiments especially among the East German population, which would appear to be a "natural" complement of nation-state rebuilding, quickly turned into a major source of friction and disappointed hopes on both sides. The persistent cultural divide between East and West since unification is usually explained in purely intranational terms—in particular the grossly unequal power structures (real and perceived) between East and West Germany in the transformation process and the way this made political, economic, and cultural integration of the two societies into a rather one-sided, almost colonial affair. While true, this "internalist" explanation does not go nearly far enough. It was precisely the historically evolved embeddedness of the institutions and people of the old FRG in the Western world that made this intranational dynamic so problematic. West Germany had developed transnational political and economic linkages from European integration to leading world market presence, as well as numerous transnational cultural linkages shaping the increasingly "postnationalist" and postmaterialist identities of West Germans. They represent a major part of the context in which nationalist sentiments that under different circumstances might have underwritten German unification have actually appeared as quite anachronistic, fit to be instrumentalized only by radical right-wing organizations and movements. The cultural divide between East and West in Germany reflects to a large degree the significance of transnational political, economic, and cultural linkages in West Germany and their general absence in the GDR as a result of its historical relative isolation and material backwardness. In other words, it is to a large extent the transnational elements of West Germany's post–World War II "national character" that make the integration of the two societies so difficult.

The fact that global and transnational mechanisms affecting the East German transformation process were or seemed to be largely mediated by West German institutions and actors tends to obscure their existence and functioning. There can be little doubt about the great importance of the broad range of intranational mechanisms in East Germany's transformation by unification (Pickel and Wiesenthal 1997). From the West German government's virtually exclusive role in formulating the political terms and conditions of the unification process, the FRG state bureaucracy's implementation of the transfer of all state institutions, to the incorporation of the East into West Germany's extensive structure of parastate organizations, the absolute primacy of intranational mechanisms appears self-evident. What then were the global and transnational mechanisms that have affected the transformation process via the dominant West German actors?

Perhaps the single most important and underestimated transnational mechanism in the transformation process was East Germany's integration into the EC. As one analyst notes, "GDR integration proceeded with little friction, and it can be termed one of the most successful aspects of the unification process. The approach taken by the [European] Commission and the German government embedded unification in the European integration process and legitimized it from a European perspective" (Falke 1994: 185). It entailed "German willingness to forgo major claims on the EC budget to finance reconstruction in the five new *Länder* and not to insist on a special regulatory treatment there. . . . [as well as] close coordination of every step between the Commission and the German government" (185). Thus, the radical economic transformation process, beginning with the Monetary, Economic, and Social Union between the FRG and the GDR in July 1990, exposed the East German economy to a major—not just national, but global—integration shock. To make unification possible in the European integration context, the German government had to give up any policy tools for protecting the East German economy in the transition period. Instant opening up to the world market and the rapid privatization strategy pursued by the Treuhand agency transformed the region into an economic wasteland and perpetually dependent periphery, albeit at a high level of individual consumption and social protection. For East Germans this has also meant instant access to the transnational political structures to which the FRG belongs. And "instant globalization" has markedly improved East Germans' cultural opportunities from travel to access to popular culture.

The process of transformation by unification—apparently a largely intranational affair—was therefore embedded in a transnational and global context that directly affected the actions of West German mediating institutions and the West German and East German populations. As an example of the former, consider the effect of the world market on the transplanted system of industrial relations in East Germany. Given their generally lower level of productivity, many East German enterprises would be unable to survive without violating the nationwide collective agreements that, among other things, set uniform wage rates. The mediating institutions—trade unions and employers federations that had a common interest in extending their industrial relations system unaltered to the East—have been forced to tolerate infractions in the East on a scale that is threatening to undermine the integrity of the national system. As an example of transnational mechanisms affecting directly West German and East German populations, consider again the cultural backlash against unification. West Germans perceived, to some extent correctly, that the East Germans' "worldliness" and "modernity"—that is, their transnational integration and sophistication—were significantly below general Western standards. Thus, in addition to political and economic "backwardness," East Germans were seen to suffer from cultural underdevelopment—a view that among West Germans produced individual reactions from arrogance to pity. Lack of acceptance as equals produced in turn a collective cultural response from East Germans as they rediscovered their separate collective identity. The cultural conflict between East and West is therefore not simply due to the nature of intranational mechanisms, but rather to the way intranational and transnational linkages come together in a peculiar combined mechanism.

Cuba

The survival of Cuban Communism (more accurately, Castro's political regime) at first glance also seems to contradict our strong emphasis on global and transnational factors.[16] It continues to be surprising to many observers that the regime managed to survive the early 1990s after its lifeline to the Soviet Union was cut and the pressure from the United States further increased. Cuba lost its particular niche in the global structure with the demise of the Soviet bloc, while facing the relentless opposition of the remaining superpower in its attempts to integrate into the global capitalist market. What if not internal factors could possibly account for the regime's staying power? Even if we go beyond the simplistic ideological argument that regime repression alone is what keeps Castro going and include a broader perspective on the sources of legitimacy and political stability in Cuba, our explanation will remain inadequate without incorporating transnational mechanisms. Somewhat counterintuitively, it is precisely the aggressive U.S. foreign policy approach—given impetus by the Cuban exile faction in Miami and those multinational U.S. companies whose property was nationalized in Cuba—that helps shore up the Castro regime. The combined mechanism is, in short, the reinforcement of the intranational linkage between Cuban nationalism, socialism, and Castroism by U.S. foreign policy (the transnational linkage). It strengthens whatever legitimacy the regime has left in spite of the deteriorating social and economic conditions and weakens potential reformist opposition. This is how the transnational mechanism hooks up with, and to some extent counteracts the direction of, the intranational mechanism, i.e., the undermining of regime legitimacy as a result of deteriorating economic conditions and growing social polarization. Other transnational mechanisms contribute to the combined mechanism explaining regime survival—such as the inability on the part of the United States to keep other capitalist countries from investing in and trading with Cuba, remittances from Cuban émigrés in the United States, Cuba's various links with Latin America, the regime's reputation especially in the Third World, etc.

At the same time, it is a different set of transnational mechanisms, i.e., those associated with global capitalism, that serves to undermine the social structure and political legitimacy on which the regime is based. The legalization of the U.S. dollar and the growing importance of the tourist industry and other large-scale economic ventures with foreign participation link Cubans to the outside world in many different economic and cultural ways. Internally, they give rise to a new class structure that is largely determined by degree of access to these transnational linkages. Thus, for example, workers in the tourist industry earn significantly higher incomes than professionals in the public health and education sectors. At the same time, systemic transformation in Cuba is less dramatic and visible than in Eastern Europe. In fact, both Castro and his most committed opponents abroad deny that any such systemic transformation is under way. Both sides share a common view of what would qualify as systemic transformation—namely, counterrevolution (Castro) or a transition to capitalism and electoral democracy (his opponents). Evidence tells us that systemic transformation does not necessarily require prior or simultaneous political regime change (historical: Japan's Meji Restoration; comparative: China's marketization). However, the denial syndrome points to another crucial transnational mechanism in Cuba's transformation: the potential political cost of more rapid liberalization in the context of the highly antagonistic U.S.-Cuban relationship. Conversely, the political limitations imposed by the United States on Cuba's world market integration on more favorable terms undoubtedly has had a fundamentally adverse effect on the country's transformation in more narrow economic terms. These are some major elements of the combined mechanism determining Cuba's transformation path.

Concluding Comment

The reader may have noticed that our case studies, despite their shared purpose of illustrating the crucial importance of explanation in terms of combined mechanisms of global, transnational, and intranational mechanisms, had divergent points of departure. Our study of the Czech Republic began by stressing the powerful influence of global and transnational mechanisms in the country's transformation processes, only to proceed to show how their particular configuration with intranational mechanisms produced a specific Czech path of cultural transformation. By contrast, our studies of East Germany and Cuba began by noting the widely recognized power of intranational mechanisms, only to argue subsequently that it was their particular configuration with global and transnational mechanisms that produced the specific East German and Cuban transformation paths. This divergence in starting points reflects our respective subdisciplines of origin: international relations and global political economy for the author of the Czech case study (True), and thus the attempt to move beyond the conventional views and assumptions of that tradition by systematically incorporating intranational mechanisms; comparative politics and political economy for the author of the East German and Cuban case studies (Pickel), and thus the attempt to incorporate systematically global and transnational mechanisms. Thus, even in our attempts to break out of our subdisciplinary perspectives, we have in a certain way (even if dialectically) reproduced them. If nothing else, it underscores the depth of the divide separating the two scholarly traditions and communities at a time when this separation appears more anachronistic than ever.

Notes

1. Stallings argues that both intellectual critiques and orthodox global economic and ideological trends led to the demise of dependency analysis and its study of the negative impact of the capitalist world system and powerful international actors on developing economies. As such, "it is rarely even mentioned today" (1992: 48).

2. There are some notable exceptions to this general lack of analysis of global forces in postsocialist transitions. See especially, Bönker (1994); Deacon (1997); Greskovits (1998); Henderson (1998); Mygind (1998); Von Zon (1998); and Kummel (1998).

3. Comparative analyses of postcommunist transformations often do take into account global and transnational dimensions. Conceptualizations of the global system tend to be somewhat superficial or ad hoc since the analytical focus remains above all on the national system. Notwithstanding their significant contributions to examining intranational change processes, this applies to, among others: Bartlett (1997); Burawoy (1996); Cortell and Peterson (1998); Crawford (1998); Fish (1998a, b); Grabher and Stark (1997); Poznanski (1998); Stark and Bruszt (1998); Stoner-Weiss (1999); and Task Force on Economies in Transition (1997).

4. Historical sociologists such as Theda Skocpol (1988) and Charles Tilly (1992) have integrated ostensibly internal and external dynamics in their comparative studies of war and social revolutions (see Hobden 1999). Recently, international relations scholars, attempting to bridge the disciplinary divide, have used the rational choice concept of two-level games to show how national-level elites mediate policy change at both the national and international levels (Evans, Jacobson, and Putnam 1993; Garrett and Lange 1995; Keohane and Milner 1996).

5. The framework that perhaps comes closest to bridging the national-global divide systematically is a more orthodox neo-Marxist perspective (cf. e.g., Panitch 1996; Radice 1999).

6. For an analysis employing a systemic approach in the context of sustainable development, see Köhn (1998). For systemic approaches to postcommunist transformation, see Kolodziej (1997) and Mygind (1998).

7. This framework is thus at odds with most conventional approaches in economics and political science that are based on a "sectoral" model of society, i.e., a narrow delineation and definition of their subject matter.

8. The concept of mechanism should also not be confused with the concept of system. "Note that our definition presupposes a distinction between system and mechanism: the latter is a process in a system. This distinction is familiar in natural science, where one is not expected to mistake, say, the cardiovascular system for the circulation of the blood or the brain with mental processes. But it is unusual in social studies " (Bunge 1997: 447). "Mechanism is to system as motion is to body, combination (or dissociation) to chemical compound, and thinking to brain" (449).

9. For examples of explanation employing the concept of mechanism, see e.g., Tilly (2001) and Grandori and Soda (1995) in the context of interfirm networks; Rona-Tas (1998) in the sociology of postcommunist transformation. For counterexamples, see any number of variable-oriented analyses that either start from, or are limited to, inductive searching for correlations between outcomes and their presumed causal factors (see, e.g., Fish 1998a).

10. As Michael Illner (1994) argues, a new form of regional polarization along the East-West axis is emerging. Regions with the highest development potential are those with higher levels of private business and foreign direct investment and also with notable, transborder linkages.

11. However, the protracted economic recession in the Czech Republic has recently produced a 10 percent fall in consumer spending and growing skepticism toward the American or Western market model.

12. *Odpovědi Na Otázky Neziskový Sektor v České Republice (Responses to questions about the non-profit sector in the Czech Republic)*, Prague, Czech Republic, 29 November 1997.

13. The major Czech newspapers are under German ownership, while television is dominated by Nova T.V.—until recently a solely U.S.-owned channel that captures more than half of Czech viewership, and attracts over 70 percent of TV advertising revenue. Over 60 percent of its programming is American, French, or British, and 10 percent of its airtime is devoted to ads, in contrast to the 1 percent on the two Czech public channels. Before Nova's launch it was expected to break even within three years. Due to strong advertising sales, however, it was profitable in just nine months (Madden 1996: 14).

14. For a more detailed elaboration and documentation of these cases, see True (1999).

15. While one of us has argued that East Germany is indeed of great comparative significance in the transformation debate (Pickel 1997c), this argument did not include any systematic account of the significance of transnational factors. For the significance of the East German case for Eastern European transformation in the context of EU expansion, see Jacoby (2000).

16. For a more detailed analysis of Cuba's transformation, see Dilla (1999); for a comparative perspective, see Pickel (1998).

Chapter 9

Economic Transformation, Moral Resources, and the State in Postsocialist Societies: On the Comparative Analysis of Transformation Paths in Central and Eastern Europe

Melanie Tatur

It has almost become common sense that politically defined and culturally embedded institutions are of considerable significance for economic productivity and growth. There is no longer any shortage of references to "political frameworks," "frames of interest perception," and "values" in analyses of the economic transformation of postsocialist societies. Nevertheless, many conceptualizations of economic transformation are still bound up with the economistic traditions of political economy and with its rational choice assumptions, to the extent that "transformation" itself is not conceptualized institutionally. Economic transformation is referred to as a strategy and a politically led process toward the desired institutional order of private property rights and the market. However, scant attention has been paid to the institutional arrangement mediating this process, as well as to its political-cultural dimensions.

I begin by taking up the concept of "political capitalism" proposed by Jadwiga Staniszkis (1995). I develop the term into a conceptual apparatus that enables us to proceed to comparative analyses of transformation paths in central and Eastern Europe. I attempt to define various forms of political capitalism related to different types of state, and relate these to the patterns of social integration prevailing in the respective societies. The chapter thus represents an attempt to amplify Staniszkis's concept and provide it with a cultural dimension; in my own conceptualization, this dimension is the decisive factor influencing the diversification of transformation paths.

I develop my analysis in the following steps. In the first section, I try to define *transformation* and *political capitalism* with the help of the theory of property rights as employed in the field of economic history (North and Thomas 1973; North 1990b). The result is a politically defined concept of economic transformation emphasizing the relationship between state and society. In the next section, I broaden the concept by shifting the perspective and bringing in discourses from the globalization debate about the political conditions of economic competitiveness (Pyke et al. 1990) and considerations related to the cultural preconditions for efficiency in democratic institutions (Putnam 1993). The cultural dimension of political capitalism I emphasize referring to a concept of social capital in terms of individual competences and social patterns (Putnam 1993; Fukuyama 1995) rather than in terms of individual strategies (Coleman 1990). To Putnam's distinction between "amoral familism" (Banfield 1958) and "civil community" I add a concept of tribally fragmented morality or "familism" (Fukuyama 1995). After summarizing the argument up to this point by means of an ideal-typical construction of the concepts of "criminal," "political," and "democratic" capitalism, I attempt in the third section to add a dynamic element to this initially static schema by looking at diverse transformation regimes mediating diverse transformation paths and leading to different social-structural consequences, and in this way to comprehend *political capitalisms* as modes of transformation.

"Socialism," "Democratic Capitalism," "Political Capitalism"

Two perspectives can be distinguished in the social-scientific discussion of "transformations" in central and Eastern Europe until the mid-1990s. In 1990 the new democratic elites formulated the *project* of creating an open society, which involved establishing a new democratic order and a market economy from above by means of political strategies and the introduction of new legal systems. This perspective also found expression in scholarly debates, as political scientists considered transformations in terms of political and legal strategies. The reference to social context led to reflection on the dilemmas inherent in the project of democratic transformation of socialist society (Staniszkis 1991a; Offe 1991). Economists debated "shock therapy" versus "gradualism," again emphasizing political strategies (Balcerowicz 1995; Poznanski 1995). In this debate neoliberal monetarists argued in favor of a "shock" whereas institutionalists emphasized the state's role in a gradualistic transformation. The paradox is that liberals turned out to be the better institutionalists, because they were much more aware of the specific character of the socialist state and the necessity of decisive institutional change. To introduce the price mechanism and instruments of macroeconomic regulation, the Polish neoliberal reform package designed by Lezsek Balcerowicz introduced a sudden change in the rules of the game. By contrast, the institutionalist argument for a gradualist approach and interactive interest mediation did not take into consideration the neopatrimonial character of the state or the respective form of a clientelistic type of interest articulation.

At an early stage, however, sociologists such as Staniszkis and David Stark (1990, 1996) argued strongly against the implicit assumption that the old order had "collapsed," criticized what they saw as an illusory belief in a political-legalistic method of implementing institutional change, and drew attention to elements of continuity in the middle of change. Referring to the Hungarian case, Stark argued that the most one could speak of was the dissolution of the old order's political facade. It should not be supposed that this left a societal vacuum. Rather, what could now be observed was the social fabric of informal relations, rules, and routines that had sustained socialist society. Transformation, argued Stark, should be understood as a gradual *evolution* of the socialist order rather than a project of change. Staniszkis, on the other hand, saw in the Polish case a more contradictory mixture of continuity and change. Like Stark, she identified continuities in the dimension of informal standards of behavior and networks of relationships, and pointed out that these made it possible to get around institutional innovations imposed "from above." At the same time, she demonstrated that the introduction of new democratic rules and macroeconomic standards had altered the significance and function of the inherited models and actor constellations, and most important of all had initiated a new dynamic of change.

The differences between these analyses may seem minimal, but they are only superficially a matter of country-specific features. Stark and Staniszkis are in agreement to the extent that they treat transformation as an evolution of socialist society, but they differ sharply in their evaluations of *continuity in the midst of change*. Stark (1996) speaks of the development of a "mixed economy" characterized by "hybrid forms of property" and "cooperative networks," and sees similarities with certain phenomena observable in highly developed capitalist economies. Staniszkis, on the other hand, analyzes the constitution of political capitalism as a specific postsocialist formation whose "hybrid forms of property" and informal links between economic and political administrative structures bear no more than a superficial resemblance to the corresponding phenomena in modern Western societies. In reality, the function of these structures is to transfer state resources, to externalize the costs of private profit making with the help of state institutions, or to monopolize access to a financial infrastructure guaranteed by the state. In Staniszkis's analysis, political capitalism is a mode of transformation, or, to be more accurate, an institutional model by means of which economic actors and capital can be created.

Anders Aslund's analysis is very similar to Staniszkis's. In the Russian case, Aslund (1995, 1996) sees various forms of "rent-seeking"—i.e., a continuity in the mechanism of central redistribution of resources that under the new conditions serves to facilitate private accumulation and the concentration of capital. Aslund classifies these rent-seeking mechanisms as transitional phenomena and hopes that the final outcome will be a reorientation toward profit seeking in competitive markets. Staniszkis also treats political capitalism as a transitional formation. However, this institutional model of adaptation will in her view exert a lasting influence on the future social structure, which will take the form of a more or less peripheral capitalism. She develops this suggestion with the help of a historical analogy. In the sixteenth century, the Polish landowning aristocracy came into contact for the first time with the west European cereal market, and was able to defend its interests as a social group by falling back on the institution of serfdom. The result was a path of development that condemned the country to a peripheral position. In much the same way, falling back on the socialist institutional model currently enables local elites to shore up their positions in the new conditions under which these countries are being integrated into the world economy, but the institutional regress means that these societies' development potential is blocked (Staniszkis 1995).

In my view, these divergent assessments of the relationship between continuity and change in postsocialist societies can be traced back to more fundamental differences of opinion about the socialist order in its mature phase. Stark's analysis is close to that of the Hungarian social scientists and economists who were heavily influenced by the technocratic reform policy pursued from the 1960s onward. Socialism is seen as a system based on centralized mechanisms of redistribution, and the reforms launched in the early 1960s as a constant process of reconstructing this form of economic organization by incorporating market mechanisms and combining "bureaucratic" and "market-type" forms of coordination (Kornai 1992). The consequence of these modifications in the system's regulation was, according to Stark (1990), that managers of state enterprises acquired property rights in all but name, and a new order involving market coordination and managerial control emerged within the framework of the old system.

For Staniszkis, socialism was a state-political order rather than a type of economic organization. Its constitutive feature was not the economic mechanism of central redistribution but the political atomization of society and the replacement of society by administrative structures. This not only produced functional problems in the economic sphere but also created a quite different logic in the reproduction of society as a formation. Where capitalist society is based on a logic of wealth and exploitation, the socialist system's logic is the reproduction of power and dependency (Staniszkis 1992). The American sociologist Andrew C. Janos (1991) has put forward a similar analysis of the Soviet order as a "military state" in Herbert Spencer's sense of the term. One could express this slightly differently by saying that it was a formation based on the reproductive logic of state building (Tilly 1990) rather than that of capital. This certainly does not mean that the socialist system was simply identical with the totalitarian power apparatus that enforced it, but it does mean that the primacy of political power and political stability was also institutionalized in mature, post-Stalinist socialism. This form of socialism was, according to this analysis, a self-supporting network of relationships that reproduced human beings socialized by the state via daily routines, patterns of thought, and interests.[1] Seen from this perspective, post-Stalinist reforms were "dearticulations" of the system (Staniszkis 1991b), that is, the incorporation of extraneous elements that did not signify the beginning of a mixed economy because they remained subordinated to a systemic logic that still prioritized domination.[2]

The final reason for Stark and Staniszkis's divergent assessments of the relationship between continuity and change lies in their differing implicit assumptions about the constitutive conditions of Western *democratic capitalism.* Both authors refer to the property rights school, but they interpret the assumptions and findings of this school differently. Stark continues to treat the economic order as an organizational apparatus and coordination mechanism, and property rights as discretionary powers in the hands of various actors: when he refers to the de facto property rights acquired by Hungarian management from the 1960s onward, when he speaks affirmatively of a "recombination" of property (Stark 1996), or when he equates the new hybrid property forms and hybrid networks with those of a modern, cooperative capitalism. He fails to take into account the fact that even the Hungarian management remained subordinate to the *nomenclatura* right up until 1989, and that the political system served to maintain the party's privileges—as it did elsewhere. The correct conclusion to draw would be that discretionary powers in reformed Hungarian socialism were concentrated in the hands of the economic administrative apparatus to a greater extent than in other countries, but not that property rights formed the institutional basis of economic relations.

The institutionalization of property rights was, however, decisive for the emergence of the Western world and the economic dynamic that characterized it. In this context, property rights meant rights, i.e., the judicial embedding of economic power and the political constitution of systems of economic incentives by a regulative state withdrawing from an economic sphere that would henceforth be considered private (North and Thomas 1973). What was new about the historical discovery of property rights was not the English aristocracy's discretionary powers, but the fact that these powers were judicially embedded and sanctioned by the state. The institutional innovation, therefore, was the reconstitution of the state as a public order that both opened up and institutionalized a societal space permitting private economic activity (North and Thomas 1973; North 1990b). Property rights that were long-term, exclusive, and transferable made it possible to relate the costs and benefits of economic action, thus creating a structure that stimulated the expansion of the market, the reduction of the transaction costs, and endogenous economic growth. The strength or weakness of the property rights that served as the basis for economically successful or unsuccessful paths of development is not, therefore, dependent on property and control, but on the political and social order. North uses the cases of England and Spain, and the United States and Latin America, to demonstrate the constitution of two diverging political-economic orders and so of two institutionalized paths of development. In England, the crisis of state financing in the sixteenth century was resolved by means of a settlement agreed between the crown and the other estates and an institutional innovation. The rule of law, which was secured via Parliament and the judiciary, guaranteed property rights and also a system of incentives that favored the expansion of markets, profit-seeking orientations, and endogenous economic growth. In Spain, on the other hand, the model that established itself was one that subordinated economic activity to the interests of the state exchequer, as enforced by means of decrees and direct intervention. This led to the expansion of the state apparatus, an economic orientation toward rent-seeking, and economic decline. In his explanation of these two models, North not only contrasts two types of political order but also shows how far different institutions are able to reproduce themselves and the element of path dependency in economic change that results from this. Institutional options that were initially quite contingent subsequently defined orientations and the balance of forces and became systemic and social-structural facts.

Seen from this perspective, economic transformation is not a matter of the introduction of "market coordination" and private property, but rather the institutionalization of property rights as the drawing of institutional borders between spheres of public and private action. This is achieved by means of law and a democratic order.

Global Capitalism, the Efficiency of Political Institutions, and Social Integration: The Conceptualization of "Political Capitalism"

In the first section, I followed North and Thomas in treating the institutionalization of property rights as the beginning of a process of differentiation between state and society. I also advocated treating this development as a normative point of reference in the analysis of economic transformation processes. Needless to say, this does not mean that postsocialist developments can simply be measured against the model of bourgeois society that came into existence in the eighteenth and nineteenth centuries. Classical bourgeois society was a space pacified by the state's monopoly of violence and regulated by state-sanctioned institutions, which made possible broader social—both economic and political—interaction between private persons. This is certainly not an adequate model of democratic capitalism in twentieth-century conditions, in which the space of bourgeois society has been incorporated by an organized capitalism.

Should we not therefore conclude that Stark is right to identify the institutional forms taken by postsocialist political capitalism with those of highly organized and cooperatively integrated postmodern economic actors? Is he not right when he says that the characteristic features of actors able to assert themselves successfully in the global economy are their embedded status within a complex infrastructure set up by the state and the integration of economic and political power?

Since the 1980s there has been a paradigm shift in the discussion about the current and future roles of the state. This has been based on a new awareness that with the internationalization of capital markets and *globalization* of competition, it is no longer possible to pursue a national, state-based policy in the Keynesian sense. The options available for autonomous action at the state level are becoming more and more restricted. The recent debate about the state has been less interested in its internal regulative functions than in its intermediary role in relation to the interactions between societal actors in an open, increasingly debordered, truly global economy. This debate has gone on to examine the ways in which business activity is politically and societally rooted in state institutions and cultural contexts that are increasingly significant as aspects of competitive and developmental advantage.

In a study published in 1990, Michael E. Porter drew attention to the fact that enterprises are socially embedded, and that productivity can be improved with the help of inter enterprise *networks* and also of networks linking enterprises with state or nonstate providers of services. Similarly, studies of new industrial districts in northern Italy (Pyke et al. 1990) have looked at new forms of regional cooperation that amount to a specialized division of labor, the fusion of certain enterprise functions, and the development of a common infrastructure. In both cases, the competitive advantages observed are the results of cooperation. The clusters described by Porter are to be found for the most part in highly developed branches of industry, in scientific institutions, and in areas where specialized technical know-how is transferred and pooled. As far as the forms of cooperation in new industrial districts are concerned, the actors are local, small- and medium-sized firms and local political institutions. Improvements in productivity were the direct result of cooperation and the capacity to cooperate. It is, however, important to note that while both of these approaches deal with informal cooperation between state and private economic actors and the intensification of these contacts, they locate this model in an extremely competitive environment. Moreover, the intensification of cooperation is not to be confused with any relaxation of the rule of law and the distinction between political and economic institutions.

Is it possible to compare the competitive advantages achieved with the help of political capitalism with the resources identified by Porter and discussed in the studies of industrial districts? Stark himself has referred to cross-ownership of state and private actors and the personal links between politics and economics and associated those institutional features with a transformation of the state into a central debt-management institution (Stark 1996). However, this means that the result of the "recombination" of property cannot be treated as identical with the new forms of cooperation emphasized by Porter and the industrial district studies. The competitive advantages enjoyed by postsocialist actors and networks rest on exclusive access to information and financial resources, that is to say, on political privileges, and on the opportunities this provides to pass costs on to society. This means that in political capitalism, one of the basic institutional patterns of the socialist political economy is reproduced. The main characteristics of this economy were redistribution according to political criteria and the formula of state property, which stood for a fragmentation and diffusion of property rights. Formal state property was realized via the state administration as a hierarchy of control. This system was bureaucratically regulated to a degree that varied from country to country, but in each case it was subordinated to the prerogatives and cadre policy (the *nomenclatura*) of the political power center. Formal and informal opportunities to gain access to state property were distributed in different ways via the apparatus that administered production, and in ways that also varied from country to country. However, rights of disposal defined in this way were never institutionalized as property rights that constituted personal responsibility. "Political capitalism" refers to privatization mechanisms and forms of private property that, via the activation of a deformalized, political type of capital, serve to reproduce institutionally weak property rights and inherited orientations toward state rents. The competitive advantages derived from such institutions rest not on improvements in productivity achieved through innovation and cooperation, but on passing on costs to the state and society.

In other words, the function of more or less institutionalized forms of cooperation and linkages between market actors, and between economic and political actors, cannot be deduced simply from the forms of cooperative organization. Modern competitiveness is not only a consequence of the embedding of enterprises in cooperative networks and a developed political infrastructure. Network functions and the contribution of the infrastructure must be seen in the context of the political institutions' own capacities.

Putnam's 1993 book synthesizes a large number of empirical studies of the functioning of regional and local administrations in Italy. Putnam presents his findings as a study of the *efficiency of democratic institutions* and the way in which efficient political institutions rely on being socioculturally embedded. His thesis can be summarized as follows: economic development depends on efficient political institutions, and these in turn depend on active civil communities.

Putnam's work can be seen in combination with my own argument as an explanation of the sociopolitical aspects of Porter's thesis and of the industrial district studies. Putnam offers a change of perspective insofar as he makes the local society, rather than the enterprise or a network of enterprises, his point of reference for the question of competitiveness. But we can also treat Putnam's book as a historical extension of the work that has examined the significance of institutionalized property rights for economic growth. He poses the question of the efficiency conditions of democratic political institutions in the context of intensifying interdependence between politics and economics. To the extent that the formal borders between private interests and the public sphere tend to fade, the significance of cultural regulation increases. The transaction costs of economic activity are reduced to the extent that democratic state institutions, and so property rights, are institutionalized efficient, that is, the validity of such rights becomes less dependent on the state's threat to use violence, and increasingly informally guaranteed by virtue of being culturally anchored in civil communities.

We have already seen how North, using the examples of relationships between state and society in England and Spain, contrasts different kinds of politically defined development paths. Putnam proceeds in a similar way by showing how in northern Italy, in sharp contrast to the south of the country, institutions of civil urban culture have, in the course of postwar development, reproduced and determined both the efficiency of political institutions and competitive economic advantages. Putnam uses the concept of civil community to translate the institutional model of civil society into the categories of social capital[3] and cultural competences. He contrasts the civil community with a Mafia-type clientelism. Civil community is characterized by engagement on the part of the citizens, motivated by the idea of an imagined community and an abstract public good. Citizens conceptualize their relations in institutional terms, as regulated by rules and based in equal rights. Their engagement is realized and reproduced in the form of solidarity, trust, and tolerance, by means of horizontal associations. Putnam contrasts this with "amoral familism" (Banfield 1958), which treats social relations as forms of personal dependency between patron and client or boss and petitioner, sees these as hierarchical and concrete, and is articulated as opportunism based on an absence of trust in the reciprocity of relations and obligations. Both Banfield and Putnam see amoral familism as the basis of a quasi-integration on the lines of a Mafia. The specific feature of this pattern is violence. In the absence of any normative standards personal relations are regulated by nothing more than opportunism and the law of the jungle. According to Putnam, what is decisive for the efficiency of political institutions and the scale of economic transaction costs is on the one hand the "moral resource" of public spirit (in a civil community), and on the other hand the extent of opportunism.

These diverse models of integration—civil community and amoral familism—are reflected in political life either as an orientation toward political programs and general rules of communal life or as an orientation toward individuals, who are seen instrumentally in order to pursue personal interests (positions, licences). The first model of political culture is associated with a high degree of transparency, relatively equal opportunities for social advancement, and fairly narrow social distances. The second model, the culture of clientelism, is associated with a lack of transparency in political decision making and an elitist and extremely hierarchical social structure.

The significance of these findings for our assessment of political capitalism is that the social capital of civil community is related not to the existence of social networks as such, but to the moral resources of normative integration. Postcommunist networks can therefore be understood as instances of the exact opposite of civil communities. As institutional successors to the *nomenclatura*, they rest on personal loyalties and opportunism and are motivated by the pursuit of personal interests. However, this still does not allow us to proceed on the basis of a straightforward antithesis between corrupt postcommunist power elites and societies that have preserved their integrity. Nor are the bipolar concepts of amoral familism and civil community adequate ways of conceptualizing integration models in socialist, and postsocialist, societies.

Polish sociologists demonstrated during the 1980s that Polish peasant families applied one set of standards to their "own people" and a different set to "strangers." Like Banfield, they found a narrowing of societal space, and interpreted this as an expression of social disintegration (Tarkowska and Tarkowski 1990). Studies of other environments showed that familial models of interaction existed within all social strata in Communist Poland, and that the circle of social contacts mediated via networks became wider at higher levels of education and in the upper social strata. The most atomized category was that of unqualified workers of peasant origin, who had lost contact with their villages but not yet established new contacts in the urban environment. This category had been profoundly affected by the pattern of Stalinist industrialization, in which massive migration of peasant laborers to the cities degraded the traditional working-class environment. The academic intelligentsia enjoyed the widest circle of contacts, and qualified workers in the second generation occupied an intermediate position but had become assimilated to the intelligentsia's life-style with its orientation toward social contacts (Makarczjk 1978, Wnuk-Lipiñski 1985). Analyzing the symbolic construction of social reality corresponding to this pattern of social integration Wincent Narojek (1982) characterized socialist society as "tribal" society.

Recalling Banfield's formulation, one could speak by analogy of an "amoral tribalism" or "moral familism," in the sense that we are dealing here with a *fragmented morality*. There is no unique normatively integrated societal space, but rather a fabric of networks, each of which is internally integrated in accordance with moral standards, but whose contacts with the (anonymous) outside world are characterized by opportunism.

For the purposes of the present analysis, a sharper conceptual distinction seems useful. The reduction of social integration to the core family in the sense of Banfield's amoral familism means that we are dealing with an anomic order, in that relations within the traditional family are stabilized not normatively but by means of status (patriarchy) and obligations related to persons (relatives). Status and emotional attachment, rather than shared values and norms, are here the basis of feelings of belonging. The forms of amoral tribalism/moral familism mentioned above, on the other hand, are indications of fragmented morality and not of anomie. Families and clans can be internally integrated in a normative way. This is true in the case of a modern core family or a modern extended family where status (patriarchy) tends to be replaced by rules and shared norms. This is also true for those clanlike networks that are not based on power but rather on the reciprocity of personal relations and thus produce moral obligations toward persons. These networks can stabilize and enforce norms, namely, if the networks are embedded in specific milieus and subcultures. They can be sharply distinguished from Mafia structures, i.e., anomic relations based on violence. Taking up Fukuyama's distinction between low trust societies and high trust societies (Fukuyama 1995) we can say that amoral tribalism/moral familism refers to low trust societies whereas amoral familism and Mafia refer to "no trust" structures. Fragmented morality thus refers to personalized trust and norms that are functioning exclusively and not universally. What is the problem here is not subculture integrating a group or a segment of society, but the fact that a medium for societal integration is missing. In modern Western societies this mediating structure used to be the nation (Gellner 1983). In the context of globalization, civil society and public spirit (Gellner 1994) seem to be a more abstract and general, and thus more appropriate, normative reference point and medium. As far as the state is concerned, the amoral familism model involves the dissolution of the monopoly of violence in a criminal state or a straightforwardly anarchic system of competition between gangs. The fragmented morality of neotribalist integration is connected with a personalization of social relations and can be understood in terms of "civilizational incompetences" (Sztompka 1993, 1994) and obstacles to civil society and the rule of law because it encourages the formation of cliques and a clientilistic political culture.

In historical terms, the amoral familism model came into being both inside different fragments of the apparatus (especially the political and security apparatuses) and in criminal milieux, which frequently worked hand in hand with this apparatus. Culturally integrated networks gave rise to the political and cultural opposition movements, intellectual and traditional milieux. But normative standards also functioned in the various groupings of the professional *nomenclatura*.

In addition, socialist conditions had given rise to forms of interaction that, to different degrees in different societies, went beyond the familistic model and introduced elements of civic culture. I am not thinking here of the "second economy" as an "alternative society" (Hankiss 1991), because this is more likely to have functioned as a field in which opportunistic atomization prevailed.[4] Rather, I am referring on the one hand to movements such as Solidarnosc or Sajudis, whose moral fundamentalism or national ethos was able to overcome the segmentation of society at the symbolic level by offering society an imagination of itself as a community and a conception of the abstract public good. And I think on the other hand of various forms of civil self-organization such as the "social" organization of shopping queues,[5] the organization of "social" neighborhood watch schemes for housing estate car parks, and the way in which communities of allotment owners took on social functions.[6]

Let us summarize the argument so far. Assuming that the economic constitution of a society is politically determined via the character of the state and the prevailing type of social integration, amoral familism can be associated with a criminal, Mafia-type economy and civil competences and communities understood as necessary preconditions of democratic capitalism. It is more difficult to evaluate the fragmented morality of tribal network structures. One reason for this is the fact that these structures are not a clearly defined ideal type, but a whole spectrum of relations whose political functions differ depending on the range and concrete features of the normative integration they provide. A second reason is that normatively integrated networks perform different functions in different types of economic organization. Francis Fukuyama has identified "familism"[7] as a moral resource available to flexible small businesses in northern Italy or the Chinese diaspora (Fukuyama 1995). Private assistance and the backing of relatives and friends were also economic preconditions for the rise of small businesses in Poland, which were cut off from the services provided by the banking sector. On the other hand, the dominance of groups such as the Vietnamese in some areas of the postsocialist bazaar economy demonstrates not only that ethnic communities provide social capital, but also that these communities are exclusive ones. Fukuyama has also pointed out that familistic integration models weaken the formal rationality of associations and corporate organizations and do little to stabilize large bureaucratic enterprises with efficient corporate governance. I have already mentioned the problem of the personal linkages between new political institutions and economic actors in the postsocialist context, and argued that they undermine the desired institutional differentiation of politics from economics while being sustained by opportunistic attitudes. If we associate familistic orientations and the fragmented morality of tribalist integration with the organizational type of political capitalism, we are working with a less precise definition of this term.

I suggest that we can think of "political capitalism" as a type of societal organization that manifests itself in specific forms at different points on a spectrum between polarized ideal types of "criminal capitalism" and "democratic capitalism."

Table 9.1 and the argument so far should make clear the assumptions on which I have based the construction of my concepts. I assume that the way in which the state is transformed, and so the new type of political power that constitutes itself, is of decisive importance for the economic functioning of the new

Table 9.1:
Three Types of Societal Organization

	Criminal Capitalism	***Political Capitalism***	***Democratic Capitalism***
Economy	Extraction, redistribution, protection money, "markets" organized through violence and controlled by Mafia structures.	Extraction /production, externalization of costs, rent-seeking, monopolization of markets.	Production, improvements in productivity.
State	Anarchy/law of the jungle (no property rights, no way of enforcing contracts).	Fragmented and partial monopoly of violence, weak rule of law, weak property rights, weak enforceability of contracts	Monopoly of violence, rule of law.
Politics and Society	Atomization, social vacuum.	Oligarchy, patronage politics pursued by oligarchic party apparatuses anchored in a "hybrid" economy. Clientelism as a form of interest articulation, a weak public sphere, and limited political transparency.	Democratic institutions, parties and associations, with mediating functions anchored in a differentiated society. Activity in civil society, a strong public sphere, and strong political transparency.
Moral Resources	Anomie, amoral familism, opportunism.	Tribally fragmented morality, personalization of social relations, concrete community, ambivalent moral resources, opportunism.	Civil community, generalized trust, abstract community, strong moral resources, limited opportunism.

order. I assume also that the efficiency of state institutions is to a large extent the outcome of cultural patterns of integration and perception. In other words, I treat the moral resources and social-cognitive competences of societies as factors that directly determine the diversification of economic relations. Both criminal and democratic capitalism are ideal-typical constructions, abstractions rather than pictures of historical reality. An economic order without any moral resources, which serves exclusively the purposes of extraction and the reproduction of power based on violence, can hardly be imagined as a social reality. The same can be said of an economic mechanism that is embedded in a normatively integrated and democratic society and whose economic content is the expansion of production. Actual historical configurations are always differently weighted mixtures of these ideal types. My table, therefore, functions as a model to be referred to in the analysis of historically concrete societies.

Transformation Paths

The revolutions in Eastern Europe can be understood as a break with three axioms that were constitutive of the socialist system: the party's political prerogative, the state property taboo, and the political closure of the socialist economies from the world market. Referring to the new context of democratization, privatization, and economic opening, the concept of political capitalism is designed to help in describing the form taken by the process of adjustment and the character of the institutional change. In this way it serves as a tool for the analysis of the relationship between continuity and change. It refers to the extent to which the logic of the reproduction of power remains built into the new capitalist order and becomes an instrument of transformation and a factor determining the shape of the new social structure.

It is possible to identify phenomena associated with political capitalism in all postsocialist societies, but there are clear differences between the directions taken by institutional change in different cases. Before summarizing these developments in tabular form (at the end of this section), I illustrate them with the help of country-specific sketches.

Poland, Hungary, and Czechoslovakia/Czech Republic

In the cases of Poland, Hungary, and Czechoslovakia we can identify different phases and country-specific features of political capitalism. In both Poland and Hungary, a series of legislative measures passed in the second half of the 1980s created the conditions for "spontaneous privatization." Soft financing of state enterprises and the formal and/or personal linkages between state actors and private business opened the way to various forms of rent-seeking, and so to the transfer of state resources into private hands (Staniszkis 1991b: 31–68).

In Poland, these informal transfers were blocked after 1989 under the governments formed by the Solidarnosc elites. Privatization was subjected to fairly far-reaching political controls, which was possible because the new government was able to exercise power and act autonomously toward existing administrative interests on the basis of a symbolic reform consensus supported by broad segments of the population (Tatur 1995). In addition, privatization in Poland was a conflictual process in which the workforces or their representatives (workers' councils and trade unions) also participated (Kloc 1996). This may also have been an obstacle to rapid restructuring in some enterprises in the traditional industries where Solidarity had its roots[8], but the existence of competing power centers also provided an instrument by which management could to some extent be controlled and flexible adjustment processes via conflicts could occur. At the political and enterprise levels, symbolic consensus and conflict were at this time the characteristic ways in which Poland carried through institutional change (Deppe and Tatur 1995, 1996). Disregarding the new government's preference for privatization by sale in the initial phase, "liquidation" became the most important method of privatization, meaning that parts of enterprises were sold to outsiders or the workforce, or leased (World Bank 1996: 52f.; Jarosz 1994). The distinctive feature of this form of "insider takeover" was not only that by acquiring property members of the industrial middle class were among those to benefit from restructuring, but also that the new firms became independent of the old, liquidated structures. The industrial growth that began as early as 1992 was kept going by an expanding private sector, which, as a consequence of this privatization policy and the monetarist stringency of government financial policy, was largely cut off from any possibility of obtaining state subsidies. The intention was to detach both private and commercialized state enterprises from the state, and thereby to block rent-seeking behavior and to enforce structural adjustment as a process of "creative destruction" (Schumpeter 1992). In Poland, therefore, "spontaneous" transformation of political power into economic capital was, in the period immediately after 1990, forced to a large extent to take place in the form of illegal or semilegal "affairs" in the area of foreign trade or in the banking system.

As a result of political instability, general privatization in Poland was delayed. The change in government after the election of 1993 did not bring a fundamental shift in economic reform policy. However, it resulted in the cutting down of the privatization program and emerging preferences for a "commercialization" of relevant parts of state industry. The new policy involved the setting up of holding companies, especially in the coal industry. In addition, new hybrids were organized around foreign trade and financial institutions, and frequently closely linked with the postcommunist parties. Financial institutions whose loans were guaranteed to varying degrees by the state therefore became part of the agenda of political capitalism. The 1997 election campaign emphasized the postcommunist party's patronage policy and the "slow down" of reforms. The new government of liberal and Solidarity elites in fact introduced new reform programs (territorial reform and decentralization, education, health and social insurances). Although privatization was speeded up, a significant state sector remained, and so did complaints about patronage and party clientelism. Due to the initial rupture, the equilibrium of the Polish transformation regime was characterized by comparatively open markets and resulted in dynamic growth. The political polarization of Polish society meant that changes in governments were associated with a circulation of elites and shifts in the reform program. Finally, external factors influenced the transformation regime. Foreign investment, especially in the banking sector, put the hybrids mentioned above under pressure and EU demands forced a speeding up of the old state industry's restructuring, thus weakening the agenda of political capitalism.

In the Hungarian case there has been no comparable break in transformation policy, and the year 1990 does not mark the same fundamental turning point as in Poland. Although the conservative government made initial attempts to assert political control over and the right to take initiatives on privatization policy, these attempts proved unsuccessful. Despite the fact that formal competences were placed in the hands of the State Property Agency and the workers' councils were legally entitled to initiate privatization processes, management remained even after 1990 the most important actor in the economic restructuring process. In practice, leading managers initiated and dominated the privatization process, even though they were now forced to negotiate with the state's property administration. The power of management was strengthened further by the failure of the attempt to centralize the whole process (see Frydman et al. 1993: 130ff.). This policy reflected both the weakness of the conservative government and the absence of any counterweight in the enterprises themselves. Although the workers' councils enjoyed a number of formal rights, they were insignificant in a situation in which the workers themselves had been depoliticized. Stark described the privatization process as a "recombination" of property: private companies were set up as satellites orbiting around state-owned mother concerns, and the creation of holding companies and conglomerates was encouraged by cross-shareholdings in institutional property, which were characteristic here (Stark 1996). In sum, the result of privatization was a hybrid structure in which state and private actors were much more closely interconnected than in Poland, either because private businesses and state enterprises were being run by the same people,[9] or through formal institutional links of the properties owned by state and private actors. In this institutional environment, rent-seeking took the form of state subsidies to offset debts.[10] H. L. Baer and C. W. Gray suggest that the weakness of the credit institutions was a precondition of "spontaneous privatization" by the management (Baer and Gray 1996: 81ff., 100).

In Hungary it was the new government of postcommunist socialists and liberals that introduced a delayed shock therapy after 1994. To stabilize the budget it cut down social expenditures and wage incomes. As far as the agenda of political capitalism was concerned the government weakened the structures described by Stark indirectly. Aside from the widespread management buy outs, in Hungary the dominant form of privatization was sale to outsiders with an extremely significant role for foreign investors (see World Bank 1996: 53). Since 1995, privatization in Hungary has also proceeded rapidly in the banking sector with a dominant position for foreign investors. The high level of foreign investment and the associated improvements in productivity are seen as a future source of growth. In fact Hungary recovered from stagnation at the end of the 1990s.

Hungarian politicians and economists looked for the causes of the country's economic growth problems during the first half of the 1990s in the sphere of economic rather than institutional policy. My own explanation is that Hungary is characterized by a high degree of continuity in structures of political capitalism. It is this factor, and not the "inflated welfare state" (Kornai 1996) that explains certain developments usually seen as resulting from mistakes in economic policy, and that also explains the Hungarian economy's initially low levels of growth. This continuity in institutional models must in turn be seen as a result of the political weakness of a society that, after the traumatic experience of the crushing of the 1956 revolution and the subsequent terror, was successfully incorporated into the technocratically reformed system during the 1960s and, at least in its middle and lower strata, atomized.

However, the weakness of society was balanced in Hungary by the strength of external factors. In Hungary the reform regime's equilibrium was strongly influenced by the dominant position of foreign capital. This resulted in a kind of segmented economy with an international sector, the representatives of which negotiate directly with the government and thus need not be included in the national system of interest mediation (Greskovits 1998). This, too, can be considered as a kind of political capitalism—however not of the postsocialist but rather of a different and global type.

In Czechoslovakia, the late and brief mobilization of the Czech "velvet revolution" led to the collapse of a Communist regime that was still controlled by the political elite of "normalization." Technocrats from inside the state apparatus had not emerged here as "reform Communists." Democratic counterelites were even weaker than in Hungary, and with the implosion of the old regime the small group of dissidents were backed by professionals that had been rather loyal to the system. The membership of the ODS Party led by the "neoliberal" Vaclav Klaus was recruited from this stratum of technocrats that in Hungary and Poland formed the backbone of "left" postcommunist parties. The reform program introduced by the "right" government of Klaus was intended to be radical and quickly introduced liberalization and a mass-scale voucher privatization (Kosta 1997). What in fact emerged in the Czech Republic was a postcommunist type of financial capitalism. Shares of privatized enterprises were held by investment funds closely related with commercial banks that were linked to a national property fund and the consolidation bank, both controlled by the ministry of finance. This formalized structure corresponded to the old centralized economic apparatus within which enterprise managers enjoyed only limited autonomy and power and central networks turned out to be dominating (Stark and Bruszt 1998). In contrast to the rhetoric of "people's capitalism," voucher privatization created a form of political capitalism. When economic indicators worsened dramatically after 1996 the explanations offered by Czech commentators included both the boom in wages and consumer demand, and what was perceived as formalism in the restructuring of property relations. Voucher privatization was less closely connected with microeconomic restructuring than the measures taken in Hungary and Poland, and led to a concentration of economic power in the hands of the newly created and not very transparent investment funds. These funds functioned simultaneously as investors and creditors. It emerged that they had obtained some of their wealth quite illegally and then transferred some of it abroad. These transactions were also believed to have played a part in the collapse of various banks during the course of 1996. A large number of legal loopholes made possible a variety of corruption affairs, especially where the state banks and their credit policies were concerned (Manochin et al. 1996: 255–61). There was criticism of the absence of any effective corporate governance to oversee the management of these funds, which left small investors with no means of redress when their schemes failed. The bank crisis and related affairs discredited the privatization,[11] and the corruption affair of the ODS Party revealed an enormous degree of party clientelism and of cynicism of the new elite. Elections in 1998 resulted in formation of a minority government by the Social Democratic Party. The political regime introduced by the "opposition-contract" openly referred to a system of party patronage. It was not the pressure of a strong opposition but rather that of the EU and other external actors that forced the government to react to the symptoms of crisis and to amend legislation governing investment funds, companies, and the banking system to introduce a stricter separation of commercial from investment banks. There is also external pressure to open the bank sector for foreign investors.

Two things should have become clear from the foregoing brief sketch. First, it is possible to discern a variety of developments even within the group of central European countries at the forefront of reform, in particular different strategic agendas and different groups functioning as the bearers of political capitalism. Second, despite the fact that one can identify differently camouflaged forms of rent-seeking in all three countries, it is clear that what we are seeing is not only a transfer of power but also a transformation in the form taken by power, and a gradual rationalization of political capitalism. The equilibrium of transformation regime that initially is defined by endogenous factors (character and strength of old and new elites and networks, strength and weakness of civil society) tends to be influenced by external pressures reducing the initial divergencies and shifting the transformation regime to a more open and democratic type of postsocialist capitalism.

Southeast Europe

The institutional change under way in southeast Europe involves different time scales, different approaches, and different consequences of political capitalism. Romania, Bulgaria, and Albania experienced no earlier phase in which alternative societal actors or orientations came into being—either in the shape of a significant democratic opposition or of a spontaneous privatization and technocratic modernization of the respective *nomenclatura* elites. When the system collapsed, it left atomized societies and power elites that thought in extremely Machiavellian terms. In both Romania and Bulgaria, political capitalism has taken on more strongly extractive, illegal, and criminal features and has been economically more destructive than in the central European countries discussed above. Even so, economic destruction has also followed a certain logic insofar as it has served the redistribution of resources according to political privilege. This is what happened in Romania and to an even greater extent in Bulgaria. In both cases the postcommunist elites pursued "gradualist" policies that destroyed any possibility of financial stabilization and resulted in a social catastrophe, while at the same time creating concentrated capital and effective criminal economic organizations. The "neoliberal" shock therapy first introduced in the second half of the 1990s in these two countries therefore encountered a social structure much more polarized than it was in 1990, consisting of strong and vigorous economic power elites and populations that have been pauperized to an extreme degree.

Albania has been an extreme case. Here a highly criminalized postsocialist redistribution economy, by all accounts supported by foreign Mafia organizations making use of Albanian financial institutions to launder their money, was able to use savings pyramid schemes much more successfully than anywhere else as a way of persuading the population to part with what little money it had. When the whole house of cards collapsed and the scale of the fraud became apparent, the organizers of the pyramids succeeded in turning popular anger against the powerless government, reducing the state's security apparatus to impotence and bringing the latent anarchy into the open. An equally extreme case is Serbia, where a government able to rely on the state security apparatus and large state-run industrial concerns could use several phases of deliberately provoked hyperinflation to destroy the savings of a population that was at the outset relatively prosperous. In Serbia, the state itself became more and more openly criminalized in the course of the war. Notwithstanding the apparent contrast between the anarchic implosion of the Albanian state and the exceptional continuity of the state apparatus in Serbia, these two countries had two features in common: power was exercised in an extremely violent form, and the atomized and powerless population saw its resources extracted in a manner that was economically very destructive. Serbian economists have spoken in this connection of an "economy of destruction" (Dinkic 1995).

Russia

Developments in Russia have also followed a different course from that of central European political capitalism. As in southeast Europe, privatization took place in Russia in a predominantly anarchic environment unregulated by law and was accompanied by hyperinflation, which once again facilitated the redistribution of resources. The Russian model of political capitalism resembles that of Albania and Serbia, rather than the central European countries, in respect to the strong tendency toward violence that has characterized its economic relations. In Russia, the center of the state security apparatus maintained itself as a coherent unit. However, the apparatus as a whole underwent fragmentation rather than dissolution. The unmistakable and unique features of Russian political capitalism are economic conglomerates more or less owned by the state and rooted in the energy, financial, and military-industrial sectors. These hybrid economic actors are believed to control over 50 percent of total Russian economic potential (Slay 1997: 35). There is a tendency for these oligopolistic and monopolistic economic actors to take the place of the state. They do this by using the fragmented security apparatus and the central political institutions as power bases that can be played off against one another, and by manipulating the state's redistribution machinery in their own shared interests.

These large conglomerates are also prototypes of a new model of structuration. The sociologist Vladimir Shlapentokh (1996) has written of the formation of organizational "roofs," under which "quasi-markets" equipped with financial agencies, trading agencies, and private armies are organized vertically. Shlapentokh describes this new formation as an instance of "early feudalism." In my view there is a specifically Russian feature that distinguishes these hierarchically organized conglomerates from similar organizations in East Asia: the violent nature of the Russian type of integration and its isolation from the surrounding society, which reflects the fact that no moral resources are available that could integrate that society. The economic function of this segmented power structure cannot be equated either with "creative destruction" or with a pure "economy of destruction." Rather, we are clearly dealing here with an infrastructure based on extractive industries or "basic factors." At the beginning of the 1990s, M. Burawoy and P. Krotov (1992, 1993) argued on the basis of a study of the Russian wood industry that a "neo-mercantilist" structure with purely extractive functions had been established.[12] One can agree with the authors that Russian political capitalism is functioning so as to marginalize the country's society and national economy. However, it would be a mistake to see either the Russian politicians or the energy concerns as puppets of Western interests. The "colonization" process is internally driven. It is leading not only to the marginalization of Russian society, but also to an extreme concentration of economic power. The conglomerates emerging around Russian financial and energy concerns are not just local, parastate organizations but also offensive players in the global game.[13]

Table 9.2:
Institutional Frameworks as Modes of Transformation

	Criminal Capitalism	*Political Capitalism*	*Democratic Capitalism*
Transformation of the state monopoly of violence	Dissolution of the monopoly of violence; implosion into criminal bands or the criminalization of the state	Segmentation of the state	Transformation into a state governed by the rule of law
Transformation of the logic of the reproduction of power	Continuity in the rationality of power, an economy of destruction	Transformation into an extractive economy	Transformation leading to economic rationality, productive destruction, improvements in productivity
Societal context	Atomization	Segmentation	Integration
Transformation of the socialist middle stratum	Dissolution of this stratum (if present), emergence of a criminal power elite and pauperized masses (90 percent of the population)	This stratum dissolved to a considerable extent, emergence of a power elite and a small, rich stratum of businessmen, pauperized masses (60 percent of the population)	Fairly broad old and new middle stratum, pauperization of a significant part of the population (30 percent)

Social-Structural Consequences

The different forms of political capitalism I have summarized have identifiable social-structural consequences. Comparative studies conducted in 1993 and 1994 show a clear divergence between developments in central Europe on the one hand and Russia on the other (Domanski 1996). Bulgaria emerges as a third, intermediate type. In Russia the old socialist middle class—intelligentsia, professionals, technicians, and qualified and unqualified workers—experienced both relative and absolute social degradation, with most of its members now living below the poverty line. The winners, that is, the new stratum of business[14] that in Russia have a distinctive *nomenclatura* background together with a narrow group of self-employed, live a large distance from the rest of society and provide a fragile social underpinning of the new economic power structures. In central Europe, a new stratification model has replaced the socialist one. This model correlates education and qualifications with income, which was not the case in central Europe during the 1980s and is not the case in postsocialist Russia either. Further studies conducted in Poland in the mid-1990s confirm the rise of this new middle stratum. They also show that the highly qualified professionals and the self-employed form a group with a strong societal engagement and liberal orientations (Domanski 1997).

In table 9.2, I attempt to present the above comparisons and analyses in systematic form. The ideal-typical categories of criminal, political, and democratic capitalism can now be seen as models to be referred to in the analysis of the direction of change.

Conclusion

This article began by putting forward the thesis that the socialist order should be understood not as an economic system but as a social formation within which power expanded according to a contradictory and self-destructive logic. The transformation project, understood as a transition to the market and democracy, should therefore be modeled as a reconstitution of the state, an institutionalization of strong property rights, and an institutional differentiation of the distinctive rationalities of politics and economics. The concept of political capitalism serves to identify a hybrid institutional framework mediating the transformation paths and defining them.

In my comparative sketch I have looked in more detail at the different forms taken by political capitalism. I referred to different arrangements of actors, networks, and institutions rather than political strategies. The degrees of political mobilization and integration or atomization and demoralization of society as an explanation for divergent types of equilibrium—as far as endogenous factors are taken into consideration—was suggested rather than demonstrated. In this respect this article represents no more than an initial step in the development of categories to be used in the comparative analysis of transformation processes in Eastern Europe.

I understand the rationalization of economic and political relations as an emancipation of civil society. It should be possible to develop further the categories suggested here, in such a way that they could be used in the comparative analysis of countries and subregions in Eastern Europe. My methodological conclusion is that further work along these lines should pay particular attention to cultural norms and the symbolic construction of social relations.

These categories should also be applicable to political and economic orders outside the former Eastern bloc. As the concepts used in research on Eastern Europe no longer need to be developed exclusively for this region, the region itself loses its structural uniqueness and the extent of the systemic change that has already occurred becomes fully visible. An examination of Latin America,

Turkey, and Southern Asia makes it clear that there are other parts of the world in which the regulative rule of law and civil society cannot be assumed unconditionally. The conclusion is clear: it is time to bring society back in.

Notes

1. This analysis also enables us to respond to the argument of János Kornai (1996), who sees "consumer orientation" and "welfare state paternalism" as the main features of Kadar's "goulash communism" and explains this policy as a response by the power elite to the trauma of the 1956 revolution and to existing popular value orientations and expectations. A more convincing explanation is that this policy was an expression of the dominant (paternalist) rationality of rule. The problem with goulash communism was not, as Kornai would have us believe, that the population's expectations were too high, but the fact that a politicoeconomic apparatus whose main interest was its own reproduction depended on those expectations and could not satisfy them—or could do so only at the cost of a heavy debt burden.

2. Examples of "dearticulation" would include: the Polish and Hungarian policies of permitting opening to the world market while retaining a state monopoly on foreign trade and the state banks' monopolies; the legalization of the private sector in Poland in the mid-1950s and in Hungary in the 1960s (although these sectors remained embedded in the state apparatus, and were kept dependent on the state economy by means of supervision, the allocation of licences, and their existence in the interstices of that economy). Another example was the formation of an opposition whose status remained informal, i.e., without legal safeguards (Staniszkis 1992).

3. Putnam refers to Coleman here. Although both Putnam (1993) and Coleman (1988) relate social capital to transaction costs, their points of reference are different: Coleman refers to the individual actors' strategies and to the costs of transactions these actors face. Putnam refers to society and the social framework and the cultural context of individual action. Social capital and transaction costs are treated as a feature of the structure of interaction.

4. It is difficult to see the second economy as a space in which it was possible to experiment with behavior conforming to market expectations. First, economic actors operating in niches within the state economy were dependent on that economy and on the goodwill of the administration, and so were trapped within existing power relations. Furthermore, the second economy was characterized by "grey," criminal forms of behavior, even in countries such as Hungary and Poland where it was to a considerable extent legalized. There has been a tendency to idealize this economy, particularly in its Hungarian form, and to treat it as a form of bourgeois society. This view fails to see that in bourgeois society the figure of the "bourgeois" relied on the "citoyen" to be able to act as a bourgeois; in other words, he could only be a "bourgeois" if he was a "citoyen" as well.

5. Queues would form a committee, which was responsible for keeping a note of the names of those waiting and for checking the queue at set intervals. The objective was to ensure that those waiting did not need to spend several days queuing in front of a shop selling furniture or refrigerators, but could simply report at intervals to those responsible for the list.

6. Members of these allotment associations came together to organize social services and facilities such as clubhouses. Descriptions of this well-ordered, petty bourgeois world can be found in the stories of Bohumil Hrabal.

7. Fukuyama uses this term to refer not to the amoral familism of the Mafia, but to forms of social integration that correspond to the model of tribally fragmented morality as described above.

8. The Gdansk shipyard, the Ursus tractor works, and the coal-mining industry are often cited as cases in which Polish trade unions played a conservative role. In each case there were a number of factors involved, but strong unions were certainly able to block a policy of rapid structural adjustment and behaved, under new conditions, in much the same way as the earlier plant management had done by playing for time and hoping that state assistance would be forthcoming.

9. In 1993 40.4 percent of top managers in Hungarian state enterprises had their own private business. In Poland, the figure was only 7.2 percent (Hanley et al. 1996: 35).

10. Comparative studies of banks' strategies and their roles as actors in corporate governance have shown that state refinancing policy in Hungary, under both the conservative and the postsocialist governments, was much more generous than in Poland (Baer and Gray 1996: 81ff.).

11. Opinion polls showed that "entrepreneurs" came to be associated with "swindlers," and that the initial high degree of trust in economic transformation melted away rapidly (Manochin et al. 1996).

12. These authors go on to draw unconvincing conclusions, employing antiliberal rhetoric and implicitly putting forward the political proposal that the Russian centrists and the production sector, which after all means the heavy and arms industries, should be supported (Burawoy and Krotov 1993). It is not the reformers' neoliberalism that leads to the policy of extraction, but the elites' opportunism and above all the powerlessness of society. There is no reason why a policy more oriented toward the interests of the military-industrial complex should lead to restructuring of the productive apparatus that would be more rational from the point of view of society. On the contrary, an opportunistic strategy pursued by the relevant segments of the power elite could, as the Serbian example indicates, have consequences that are much more dangerous in terms of world politics and would do very little to benefit the population of Russia.

13. Gazprom, for example, controls over 25 percent of global gas reserves.

14. The incomes of businessmen employing additional staff are approximately three times higher than those of the other categories, and those of the self-employed four or five times higher (Domanski 1996: 82).

Chapter 10

Transformation Process, Modernization Patterns, and Collective Identities: Democratization, Nationalism, and Religion in Postcommunist Germany, Poland, and Russia

Willfried Spohn

After the decade-long transformation processes in the postcommunist societies in central-eastern, southeastern and eastern europe, two distinct phases of transformation or transition research can be roughly distinguished. In the first phase—under the imminent impression of the collapse of the Soviet Communist order and the incipient postcommunist transformation processes—a revival of the classical modernization theory took place. Within this theoretical framework, the postcommunist transformation processes were basically conceptualized and analyzed as forms of catching-up modernization in the direction toward Western constitutional democracy, market capitalism, and welfare state.[1] In the second phase, now under the impression of varying and crisis-prone transformation processes in the different East European regions, a growing critique of the evolutionist and system-functionalist premises of the revived modernization theory developed. As a consequence, a neomodernization paradigm has been formulated, emphasizing the historical contextuality, the agency and reflexivity of social actors, and thus the path dependence and contingency of the postcommunist transformation processes (Müller 1992, 1995, 1998a; Tiryakian 1995).

What can be generally said about the changes in the modernization framework for transformation research holds also true for the more specific transition research on political transformation processes or so-called transitology. Also here in the first phase, the framework of a political catching-up modernization process was predominant. The basic premise was that in the context of the third democratization wave the Western type of democracy would be institutionalized in Eastern Europe, too. Accordingly, the transition models developed for the explanation of the democratization processes in southern Europe and Latin America were now transferred to postcommunist Eastern Europe (Schmitter and Karl 1994; Przeworski 1991). Also here in the second phase, there has developed a growing critique of the evolutionist and normativist premises, emphasizing again the historical context, the agency and orientations of political actors involved, and accordingly the empirical variation and contingency of the postcommunist democratization processes. From this perspective, there has also emerged a clearer distinction between the transition phase proper and the consolidation of different democratic regimes as well as the recognition of the possibility of nondemocratic reversions and authoritarian developments.[2]

One crucial experience leading to the theoretical revisions in transformation research has been the unexpected revival of nationalism and the related development of ethnic-national conflicts—particularly in the form of violent warfare in the Balkans and the Caucasus, but also of rather civilized conflicts in east-central Europe.[3] This has led to a growing realization that a mere analysis of transition processes of the political system regarding the main political institutions and actors does not suffice, but that also an analysis of the processes of state formation, nation building, and collective identity construction is needed (Barkey and Hagen 1997; Rudolph and Good 1992). Accordingly, a direct application of the theoretical models tailored for the transition processes from authoritarian regimes in southern Europe and Latin America has been called into question due to the different starting bases of transition from the post-totalitarian and postimperial types of political regimes, state formation, and nation building in postcommunist Eastern Europe (Bunce 1995). As well, a mere functionalist explanation of the revival of nationalism grounded in power interests of political elites and power inequalities due to socioeconomic unevenness does not suffice. Rather, as already seen by modernization approaches to non-Western world regions, processes of democratization require parallel processes of state formation and nation building, to integrate politically and homogenize culturally the historically pregiven ethnic mixture of populations (Deutsch 1953; Eisenstadt and Rokkan 1973). In postcommunist Eastern Europe, the processes of state formation and nation building have developed by no means in a parallel way, and the frequent structural unevenness between both processes has considerably impeded the consolidation of democracies (Brubaker 1996; Dawisha and Parrot 1997a, b; Linz and Stepan 1996: 16–37).

A second conspicuous phenomenon, equally unexpected on the backdrop of the long impact of the atheist Communist regimes, has been the widespread, though varying revival of religion in the postcommunist Eastern European regions.[4] From the secularist premises of the predominant transition theories (following secularist modernization theories), the factor religion in the postcommunist countries has been left to the sociology of religion, rather than analyzing, on the basis of its results, the varying interrelationships between religion, nation-state formation, and democratization. The factor religion both as cultural value system and as institutional order first contributed decisively to the delegitimization of the Soviet system of domination; and it has now an important, though varying impact—depending on the degree of secularization or revitalization of religion—on the different postcommunist transformation processes. Religious organizations and cultures, here, represent important components of the developing civil societies, have a direct or indirect influence on the political system, state apparatus, and legal order as well as on social institutions and cultural mentalities, thus shaping social and national identities.

The intention of the following comparative analysis is to outline the structural interdependence of democratization processes, collective identity formation, and patterns of religion and secularization in the three postcommunist transformation cases of East Germany, Poland, and Russia and to propose a historical approach for explanation. For this purpose, I start with a comparative sketch of the configurational development of political transformation, nationalism, and religion in the three cases and present a comparative historical-sociological approach for explaining the three varying transformation constellations. On this basis, I then characterize the empirical religiopolitical dynamics in the three transformation cases, and finally summarize the comparative results. I should add that the analytical selection of the three cases of East Germany, Poland, and Russia has—aside from personal priorities—also systematic reasons. Though all three cases as postcommunist transformation societies have some structural similarities, they differ enormously regarding the political, national, and religious components and thus demand a systematic explanation of their differences. Finally, I should emphasize that the explanatory approach here developed is comparative historical-sociological, i.e., it attempts to explain the varying contemporary empirical trends in the context of long-term historical trajectories regarding both the case-specific precommunist constellations as well as its communist legacies.

Democratization, Nationalism, and Religion

From the perspective of the predominant transformation theories, the main reasons for the collapse of Soviet Communism have primarily been seen in structural causes such as the overuse of economic resources in the context of political-military bloc competition, the increasing economic inefficiency of the state-administered economies, and the obstacles of the post-totalitarian regimes for democratization. Within these lines of argumentation, however, it has been overlooked that the collapse of Communism was also the result of a growing legitimacy deficit of the Communist order in the Soviet Union and in parallel ways in the east-central European societies. Of crucial importance since the Brezhnev era was the fading belief in the principal economic superiority of the Communist system and the higher political freedom potential of the people's democracies as well as the growing longing for political, national, and religious self-determination. Reinforcing each other, the growth of demands for freedom, the revival of nationalism, and the revitalization of religion represented parallel processes in the later phases of Communism. In different variations, these processes first undermined the legitimacy of the Soviet Communist order and then developed their specific cultural dynamics in the postcommunist transformation period. Thus, in theoretical terms; the revival of nationalism and the revitalization of religion are not simply political or cultural reactions to the crisis-prone transformation processes, rather they represent constitutive dimensions of both the erosion of the Soviet Communist order as well as the postcommunist transition and transformation processes.

The most visible case for this three-tiered configuration of democratization, nationalism, and religion, to begin with, is Poland. In the post–World War II era, the established Communist regime did not suppress the Catholic Church as the representation of the Polish nation to the same degree as it was the case with religion in other central and Eastern European Communist regimes.[5] Instead, the Polish Catholic Church played a crucial role in both society and politics in securing an important space for independent education at schools and universities as well as developing into the main counterpole against the Communist regime. In particular, the resistance of Cardinal Wyszynski and the election of Karol Wojtyla to Pope Paul II contributed to this emerging dual power structure. Under the shield of the Catholic Church, some space for intellectual freedom and civil society was preserved and then considerably widened by the formation of the social-Catholic Solidarnosc movement as the main carrier of the revolutionary change of Polish state and society in 1989–90. Thus, the societal dynamic of this revolutionary breakthrough was not only democratic and capitalist, but also national and Catholic. As a consequence, the influence of the Catholic Church became particularly strong in the postcommunist transformation period. This can be seen in the growing presence of the Catholic Church in state and society, such as its direct political intervention in the issues of abortion legislation and religious school education or its active evangelizing policy, resulting in a substantial influence on national, social, and political movements and parties. In the early transition phase, this influence of the Catholic Church was represented not only in the social-Catholic Solidarnosc movement led by Lech Walesa, but also in the liberal-Catholic Freedom Union under Tadeusz Mazowiecki and the conspicuous adaptation of the postcommunist, Social-Democratic Party currents to national-Catholic value orientations. All this happened on the backdrop that the Polish nation after World War II had become a religiously and ethnically homogenized society with only a weak impact of secularization and a strong liaison of Catholicism and national identity (Poian-Srednicki 1982; Kriedte 1997; Luks 1997).

The most complex case is post-Soviet Russia as the former center of the soviet Communist empire. Here, the Communist reform movement under Gorbachev originated from the core of the Communist elite, even though *perestroika* was based on widespread dissident sentiments in state and society (Linz and Stepan 1996: chap. 19; Petro 1995; Sakwa 1996). However, this Communist reform movement was inspired by a utopian communism—in a certain parallel to human socialism in the Prague spring—rather than by a Western orientation toward democracy and market capitalism (Hanson 1997b; McDaniel 1996). This came to the fore only after the failure of Gorbachev's experiment and the destruction of the Soviet empire through Yeltsin's nationalist-democratic revolution against the Communist *nomenclatura*. At the same time, Yeltsin's revolution was based on growing Russian nationalism linked to a conspicuous revitalization of Orthodox Christianity. In the Russian case as well, the combined revival of nationalism and religion was not a result of the crisis-prone transformation process. Rather it had deeper roots as a long-term reaction to the ideocratic suppression of nationalism and religion under the Soviet regime (Dunlop 1983; Lane 1978; Pospielovsky 1984; Petro 1995). In the Brezhnev era, the first signs of a renewal of religion and nationalism had emerged in the Samizdat press as a reaction to the moral crises of Russia—the most prominent voice was certainly Alexander Solshenytsin. Since then, some representatives of the Orthodox Church have demonstrated a stronger independent attitude toward the Soviet state while the repression policy against religion by the Soviet state gradually weakened. As a consequence of Gorbachev's *perestroika*, religious freedom became finally restored in 1988 on the occasion of the 1,000-years celebration of the foundation of the Orthodox Church. In the context of the collapsing Soviet order, an enormous revival of national sentiments and of religious life has taken place. The revival of nationalism is not only characteristic for the formation of right-wing and right-radical parties, but it is also an important current in the Western-liberal camp and the Communist Party (Hanson 1997c). The parallel revitalization of religion is indicated both by the strong renewal of religious life—particularly in Orthodox Christianity, but also in Catholicism, Protestantism, Islam, and Eastern Asiatic sects—and its growing political function in public life and its increasing impact on political parties from the right to the left (Furmann 1998; Greeley 1994). Thus, also in post-Soviet Russia, there has been a close link between processes of democratization, nationalism, and Christian Orthodoxy.

A special case, finally, seems to be East Germany—not least because the collapse of Communism soon turned out to be equivalent to the dissolution of the East German state and its incorporation into the federal-democratic order of West Germany (Merkl 1993). Nevertheless, also in this case, a comparative analysis of the interrelationships between democratization, nationalism, and religion is a worthwhile enterprise. Also in the GDR, in a certain parallel to the Soviet Union, the reform of the Communist system was limited to a movement within the political elite. Not least because of the adjacent Federal Republic of Germany, however, the reform movement was relatively weak and emerged only very late in the context of the already collapsing GDR regime (Joppke 1995). The main basis of the GDR revolution was not the dissident citizens' movement, but a unifying German nationalism oriented to West German democracy and social market economy on the basis of a common national history (Spohn 1995). This common basis was also the decisive precondition for a unified German nation-state in the form of an expanded Federal Republic. Whereas the link between the democratic transition and a West German-oriented national identification is an obvious connection, the interrelationship between religion and nationalism in strongly secularized East Germany is less clear. Nevertheless, this religio-national interrelationship exists in two ways. On the one hand, particularly the Protestant Church played an important role in the GDR revolution, both in a direct way as a space for communication and protection and in an indirect way in its pacifist, ecological, and cultural impact on the dissident movements (Rendtorff 1993). It would be an exaggeration, however, to label the GDR revolution a "Protestant revolution." On the other hand, again Protestantism in a transformed secularized form played an important role in GDR socialism. By contrast to the Polish Communist regime, but in a certain parallel with the Soviet Union, GDR society was characterized by a relatively high identification with the imposed state socialism and, through this identification, the historically well-advanced secularization process in East German Protestantism further progressed considerably (Goeckel 1990; Pollack 1994). On this historical basis, the democratic transition and consolidation process in East Germany has been divided in two parts. On the one hand, East German collective identity has been linked to a secularist orientation to West German society. On the other hand, important parts of East German collective identity have remained tied to socialist values based on transformed Protestant secular-religious and cultural-humanist traditions. The first part integrates clearly and positively into the West German dominated federal-democratic German nation-state; the second part as a social milieu supporting the postcommunist PDS, however, is integrating rather negatively.

A Comparative Historical-Sociological Explanatory Approach

As outlined, the three transformation constellations in East Germany, Poland, and Russia show positive interrelationships between democratic orientations, national identities, and religious value systems—though as different figurations determined by specific societal contexts. In Poland, a broad spectrum of democratic orientations (including partially postcommunist currents) combines with a strongly Catholic national identity. In Russia, the development of a postcommunist or post-Soviet democracy (with all its limitations) goes hand in hand with a significant and growing strength of nationalist and Christian Orthodox value orientations. And in East Germany within unified Germany, as well, democratic and German nationalist orientations are related positively to religious value orientations—though as a result of the high degree of secularization only in a very limited way, whereas the secular-religiously transformed socialist legacies remain an important cultural basis for an East German counteridentity.

For an explanation of the three differing constellations of nationalism, religion, and secularism in the postcommunist societies under comparison, the predominant methodological orientation in transformation research to socioeconomic and political-institutional processes of system change do not suffice. Rather, two additional methodological premises have to be included in transformation theory as well. First, to explain cultural processes such as national and religious identity formation, the cultural dimension of societal transformation has to be analyzed on its own terms, before statements on the causal relationships between the different societal dimensions are possible. Second, not only the revolutionary break, but also the historical preconditions of postcommunist transformation societies, i.e., the specific forms of precommunist modernization patterns as well as the communist modification and reconstruction of these modernization patterns as starting points of postcommunist transformation processes have to be taken into account (Spohn 1998).

From such a historical-sociological perspective, the explanation of the contemporary varying figurations of democratization, nationalism, and religion has to consider two long-term historical-structural processes that are of particular importance: state formation and nation building, on the one hand, and religious development and secularization, on the other.

Processes of political modernization such as democratization of the political system, constitutionalization of the state, and pluralization of the political culture are dependent on an established framework of state formation and nation building (Tilly 1975; Mann 1986; Linz and Stepan 1996). In a comparative European perspective, the processes of state formation and nation building in the three cases of Germany, Poland, and Russia do not move simultaneously on an evolutionary plane—as assumed in evolutionist versions of modernization theory—but they develop in different time zones or developmental figurations. Following the developmental typologies of Stein Rokkan, Ernest Gellner, and Anthony Smith, the state-led form of nation building in Western Europe contrasts with the national unification of fragmented regions in Germany, the peripheral form of nation building in Poland, and the empire-contracting form of nation-building in Russia. Accordingly, the figurational combinations of state formation and nation building in specific trajectories determine also the formation of national identities (Gellner 1993, 1994; Smith 1986). Again in a comparative European perspective, the processes of religious development and secularization in these three cases do not follow a coevolutionary development of modernization and secularization—as presupposed in the classical secularization thesis. Rather, they depend on specific developmental figurations. Following here the comparative analysis of the European civilization by Shmuel Eisenstadt and the general theory of secularization by David Martin, the secularization patterns are particularly determined by the predominant types of religion in a national society and their relationship to the state (Eisenstadt 1987; Martin 1989; Spohn 1997). In the three cases of Germany, Poland, and Russia, accordingly, the dominant forms of religion (Lutheran-pietist Protestantism, antemural Catholicism, and Orthodox Christianity) with specific relationships to the state and particular secularization patterns are of crucial importance as cultural bases of the religious and secular components in national identity formation. In the following, I compare the different historical trajectories of state formation, nation building, religious development, and secularization patterns as preconditions for the contemporary constellations of democratization, nationalism, and religion in the three postcommunist societies under analysis.

In Germany, the process of nation building did not develop in a given state framework as in Western Europe, but within a federation of regional dynasties under the growing hegemony of Prussia as the strongest absolutist state and on the basis of a linguistically and culturally defined nation (Breuilly 1992; Giesen 1993; Lepsius 1991; Spohn 1995). Hence, the structural convergence between nation and state was accompanied by strong conflicts between small German and great German solutions as well as between state centralization, federal decentralization, and constitutional democratization. The Kaiserreich contained these structural conflicts through the construction of a semidemocratic, authoritarian national state, but at the same time the lack of democratization limited substantially the degree of national integration. The Weimar Republic then created a democratic political regime, but it collapsed basically as a result of the lack of congruence between state and nation. It was finally only the reconstruction of Germany through territorial concentration, national division, and reunification that a basic congruence of state and nation became realized. With it, the democratic-constitutional institutions have a firm framework of a nation-state—first established in West Germany and now also transferred to East Germany. The one-sided form of this institutional transfer, however, contributed considerably to the East German national ambivalence vis-à-vis the unified nation-state order, articulated in the growing impact of the postcommunist camp on the German party system.

On the other hand, the religious structure in German lands was constituted by the confessional dualism of Protestantism and Catholicism and shaped through the basic institution of the state church in the form of a religious "duopoly" (Martin 1989: 168–208). With German unification in 1871 this confessional dualism and related church duopoly became dominated, due to the hegemonic role of Protestant Prussia, by Lutheran-pietist Protestantism. Under these conditions, the institutional secularization as separation from state and church was relatively weak, whereas the cultural form of secularization in the sense of anticlerical and antireligious estrangement from church and religion was relatively strong, primarily in predominant Protestantism and less so in minority

Catholicism. With regard to nation building, this religious dualism had disintegrative consequences, exacerbated additionally by the semidemocratic authoritarian form of regime. Only with difficulties did this religious dualism become mediated by secular-religious forms of cultural humanism and Marxist socialism in the nineteenth century and then by chiliastic national socialism in the twentieth century (Spohn 1996; forthcoming). As a result, first in West Germany and now also in East Germany, a secular nationalism or civic religion with some interconfessional underpinnings has become characteristic. In such a historical perspective, it was crucial for the interrelationship between communism and nationalism in East Germany that the GDR was essentially built on the territory of former Prussia—a historically predominantly Lutheran-pietist, but culturally already strongly secularized region. Here, in contrast to most other Communist societies in central and Eastern Europe, the original identification of a larger part of the population with the emerging socialist ideocracy was relatively strong and thus contributed to the further advance of secularization. The cultural basis for the then-growing delegitimization of GDR socialism was a rather secular form of German national identity, even if East German Protestantism played within it an important role. As compared to the West German part of unified Germany, in contemporary East Germany the Protestant and interconfessional components are relatively weak, whereas the secular-religious socialist components as a basis of an East German national identity are relatively strong.[6]

In Poland, by contrast not only to Western Europe, but also to Germany, the process of nation building could not develop within an independent framework of state or protostate formation, but rather was dependent on the surrounding processes of empire-building. Poland represents a—for east-central Europe typical—case of peripheral nation state building (Davies 1982; Stokes 1989). In Poland, the process of nation building experienced a crucial turning point with the three-tiered partition of the Polish-Lithuanian Commonwealth by the surrounding empires, Prussia, Hapsburg, and tsarist Russia. Under those peripheral conditions, first the Polish nation came into being and then much later, with the collapse of the imperial powers in World War I, the corresponding state order followed. At the same time, the regaining of national independence was confronted with a high degree of ethnic-national heterogeneity and regional diversification and enabled the authoritarian reversal of the democratic order by the Pilsudski regime. In addition, the phase of national independence of Poland between the consolidating Stalinist Soviet Union and rising Nazi Germany was only short-lived, and the course and outcome of World War II prepared a renewal of Poland's peripheral form of nation-state formation. This time, however, a strongly homogenized Polish nation combined with the formation of a dependent, but unitary Polish state. Thus, even if in modified form, Polish nation-state formation under Soviet Communist rule continued the traditional loyalty to the nation against the state, and this Communist legacy has made its impact on the prevailing orientations to civil society and the low identification with the state and the party system in postcommunist Poland.

Regarding the religious structure, on the other hand, the specific Polish path of peripheral nation-state building has undermined the possibility of the organization of a monopolistic state church as in the West and south European Catholic countries. Instead, the Polish Catholic Church has developed under the conditions of imperial dominance into a cornerstone of the Polish nation, reducing considerably at the same time the forces of secularization (Casanova 1994; Davies 1982; Majka 1972). On this basis, the originally predominant secular, liberal, and romantic currents of Polish nationalism weakened against the growing Catholic influence during the nineteenth century. As a consequence, the reconstituted independent and sovereign Polish nation-state after World War I was dominated less by Jozef Pilsudski's aristocratic-secular nationalism and more by Roman Dmowski's Catholic integral nationalism. Again, the interwar period was too short to allow for stronger secularization processes. Instead, the renewal of peripheral nation building under Soviet Communist rule led to an unprecedented link between Polish nationalism and Catholicism. As a corollary, the process of secularization remained very limited until the final collapse of Communism and has gained some strength only in the contemporary postcommunist phase. This explains the strong weight of the Catholic against the secular components in present-day Polish national identity (Casanova 1994: chap. 4; Poian-Srzednicki 1982).

Russia, finally, contrasts to Western Roman Europe including Germany and Poland in that the process of nation building until the present has remained embedded in an imperial framework (Barkey and von Hagen 1997; Bakka 1994; Gellner 1991; Eisenstadt 1992; Rudolph and Good 1992). Accordingly, the autocratic regime of the tsarist empire differs crucially from the Western and central European absolutist states, and processes of constitutionalization and liberalization as autocratic reactions to the revolutionary pressures in 1905–6 and in 1917 remained clearly limited. The October revolution suppressed these starting processes of democratization and renewed the autocratic imperial state structure —though in a specific ideocratic-totalitarian form. However, even this autocratic totalitarianism was unable to suppress or destroy an alternative Russian political culture either in the underground or abroad that remained oriented toward a Russian-nationalistic, Christian Orthodox, and autocratic form of democracy (Neumann 1996; McDaniel 1996; Petro 1995). After the collapse of the Soviet Communist regime, this alternative political culture is one of the important foundations of the post-Soviet forms of political change.

Even the dissolution of the Soviet Union has not yet completed the contraction process from empire formation to nation building as in the similar cases of the Habsburg and Ottoman empires after the First World War. On this basis, until the present also the forms of Russian identity formation have oscillated between national and imperial poles. In the tsarist empire of the nineteenth century, this dualism was expressed as an opposition between a Western-oriented liberal constitutionalism and an Eastern-oriented pan-Slavic autocratism (Curtiss 1960). One cornerstone of the imperial order was the Christian Orthodox Church that in its self-image as the Third Rome was closely related both to the autocratic state as well as to missionary pan-Slavism. As a reaction to the monocratic caesaro-papist structure, a nihilistic atheism developed within Russian populism and Marxism at the end of the nineteenth century (Beryaev 1960). But this secularist reaction was basically an elite phenomenon of the Russian intelligentsia rather than a cultural process of societal secularization in the Western European sense. As a corollary, the secular components of imperial-national identity formation were quite weak. The institutionalization of the Soviet state through the October revolution did mean both the preservation of an imperial order as well as the establishment of an atheistic ideocracy. It represented a chiliastic secular-religious form of charismatic domination (Walicki 1995). Certainly, this secularist ideocracy had also a deepening secularizing impact on Soviet society. However, since this process of secularization had been largely imposed on society from above in the form of an ideocratic totalitarianism and combined with political repression of the Orthodox Church and other religious communities, cultural secularization in the Soviet Union in contrast to the GDR remained limited and ambivalent.[7] Instead, there emerged a religious countermobilization against ideocracy that contributed essentially to its delegitimization. Even though this religious revival consists of many religious currents, hegemonic Christian Orthodoxy motivates also the revitalization of nationalistic and imperialistic orientations—at least in the Russian core ethnie in contrast to other nationalities in the former Soviet empire (McDaniel 1996; Neumann 1996; Petro 1995).

Three Postcommunist Development Dynamics

To summarize the above developed historical-sociological explanatory approach: the varying positive relationships between democratization, nationalism, and religion in the three postcommunist societies under comparison are the result of different historical developmental figurations of nation-state formation and religious development or secularization as well as their respective reconfiguration under the Soviet Communist order. On the one hand, the different time zones of state formation and nation building matter: Germany in contrast to Western Europe experienced a belated, but quasi-sovereign unification of the nation-state only temporarily interrupted by national division; Poland followed until the end of the cold war, only briefly independent in the interwar period, an even more belated and peripheral form of nation-state building; and Russia until the collapse of the Soviet Union remained embedded in an imperial order that even in the present has not yet completely eroded. On the other hand, the different religious forms and secularization patterns matter. In Prussia/Germany, there developed a predominant Lutheran-pietist Protestantism with a close relationship to the authoritarian state and as a corollary a strong cultural process of secularization—a cultural basis also of GDR Communism. In Poland, there evolved an antemural Catholicism with a close relationship to the nation and therefore a considerable limitation to the process of secularization—an osmosis even deepening under Communist rule. And in tsarist Russia, there existed originally a close bond between Christian Orthodoxy and the autocratic state, provoking radical secularization, and then in Communist Russia, a reversed bond of atheistic ideocracy and totalitarianism motivated a marked religious revival. As a result, contemporary East Germany is predominantly shaped by a secular national identity, Poland by a strongly Catholic collective identity, and Russia by a combined Orthodox/secular national-imperial identity.

Under the postcommunist conditions of transformation, the historically structured constellations of democratization, nationalism, and religion in East Germany, Poland, and Russia are now subject to new constellations of societal and cultural forces. The resulting developmental dynamics within the three postcommunist transformation societies can be described from the perspective of the following guiding questions. First, which types of democratization, of transition and consolidation, or authoritarian reversal develop and on which type of political culture are they based? Second, what impact do the different types of nation building and related forms of national identity have on these forms of democratization? Third, what role do the types of religion and secularization play in these processes: what impact does organized religion have on the political-institutional power balances and in which ways do the forms of religious or secular culture shape postcommunist political culture? From the perspective of these three main questions I characterize the three transformation constellations in East Germany, Poland, and Russia and in the conclusion compare their developmental dynamics.

Regarding the democratization in East Germany, due to the rapid collapse of the GDR and quick German unification, it is only possible to speak of a very short transition phase. As a result of the almost total transfer of the West German political institutions from the constitution and the legal order to federal democracy and the multiparty system, the consolidation of democracy in an institutional sense was basically completed already in 1990, the year of German unification. Nevertheless, similar to other east-central European transformation societies, the Communist legacy had an impact on the East German democratization process and led to a corresponding discrepancy between the Western and Eastern parts of the unified German political system (Merkl 1999; Zapf 1996). Thus, in the postcommunist decade in East Germany, there developed a dominating, though regionally varying, three-party constellation of Christian Democrats (CDU), Social Democrats (SPD) and Postcommunists (PDS), whereas the radical right-wing parties as well as the combined party of former GDR dissidents and Greens did not play any significant role (Olsen 1998). Of particular importance here, again with regional variations, is the growth of the postcommunist PDS, combining a tradition of German left-wing socialism with specifically East German interests and mentalities. At the same time, in East Germany the degrees of political organization and participation are considerably lower than in West Germany and thus show a certain parallel development to other east-central European societies regarding the relative weakness of civil society or a pluralistic participatory political culture (Barnes and Simon 1998; Rose et al. 1998; Seifert 1994).

One of the crucial reasons for the growing political importance of the PDS is its role as an East German milieu party that is able to mobilize the GDR-shaped socialistic life-worlds, their social interests, institutional networks, and cultural mentalities. Another reason is that the PDS is able to articulate elements of the East German national identity that constituted an important basis for the East German revolution, but then—due to West German dominance—were unable to play a legitimate role in German unification. The formation of an East German identity, therefore, does not primarily represent an ethnic-regional sentiment and loyalty. Rather, it articulates a specific political culture shaped by GDR legacies while at the same time being based on a common German identity comprising Eastern and Western Germany (Krisch 1999). This political culture is closely related to the humanist-atheist value systems that were the ideological core of the German Marxist labor movement as well as of GDR-socialism (Spohn 1991). By contrast, the Christian Democrats and the Social Democrats represent East German religious as well as secular mentalities and social milieus that in GDR times were on the victims' and losers' side, but that now belong to the relative winners of German unification. The political-cultural dualism within the East German society will stabilize also in the future as long as the social-moral milieus in their secular-religious and religious varieties will be reproduced. In the long-term, however, one can assume a further secular pluralization and parallel melting away of the socialist-atheistic as well as the confessional-religious milieus and, accordingly, an undermining of a specific East German identity in opposition to West Germany. In this process, it cannot be ruled out that the PDS will be able to establish itself as an all-German party, thus contributing in its way to national integration.[8]

By contrast to the East German special case, the process of democratization in Poland needed a longer transition phase before the contours of the Polish post-communist democracy became stable (Linz and Stepan 1996: 255–92; Michta 1997; Szczerbiak 1998). The main reason for this was the constitutionally anchored very strong position of the president in the person of the charismatic Solidarnosc leader Lech Walesa, on the one hand, and the enormous fragmentation of the Polish party system resulting institutionally from the absence of a minimum 5 percent threshold for parliamentary representation on the other. These two transition problems, however, were gradually solved. After introducing a 5 percent clause in the Sejm elections of 1993, two dominant party blocs emerged: (after its incipient fragmentation) the Solidarnosc camp *Akcja Wyborcza Solidarnosci* (AWS) and (after its postcommunist transformation) the

Social Democracy of the Republic of Poland (SLD), complemented by the liberal Freedom Union (UW, since 1994 UD) and the conservative-nationalist agrarian party, the People's Peasant Party (PSL). On the other hand, the election of the postcommunist president Alexander Kwasniewski enabled the constitutional reduction of the presidential power position. The presidential change in 1995 as well as the government change after the Sejm elections in 1997 between the two dominant party camps—though they are not unified party formations—can be taken as indicators for the consolidation of the Polish party system. However, this consolidated democracy is based on a political culture in which the antipolitical attitudes of the civil-society-oriented rebellion against the Communist regime are still present. Participation degree in the national elections is on the whole very low, the number of parties are still very high, and the loyalty to particular parties as well as the consolidation of political cleavages still remain low (Barnes and Simon 1998; Rose and Haerpfer 1998).

A crucial precondition of the relatively smooth process of transition and consolidation of Polish democracy has been the high degree of national homogenization and integration of Polish society. By contrast to the interwar period, in which the Polish society was characterized by a high number of ethnic-religious minorities, the Polish society of today consists of 95 percent Catholic Poles, whereas the German, Jewish, and Ukrainian minorities play only a marginal role (Davies 1982: vol. 2). At the same time, the major parts of the Polish political system, the social-Catholic Solidarnosc camp as well as the secularist postcommunist Social-Democratic camp, count as legitimate pillars of the Polish nation, because Polish Communism after the war became increasingly fused with Polish Catholic nationalism (Walicki 1990). This high degree of national integration allowed for the social-democratic transformation of the Communist camp as well as the emancipation of the Solidarnosc camp from the Catholic Church and thus the transformation of an ideological dualism into a legitimate form of democratic competition. Certainly, the degree of religiosity in the Polish postcommunist society continues to be very high (Borowik 1998). In 1994, as many as 86 percent of the population declared themselves as being religious and 64 percent as practicing this religious belief. At the same time, however, the part of the Polish population that criticized the influence of the church as too high rose to 45 percent and the part that rejected the authority of the Catholic Church in life conduct increased to almost to 50 percent. As a reaction to the religious monopoly and political power of the Catholic Church, there now emerges a stronger tendency toward secularization in the sense of both defection from the church and privatization of religion. Both cultural tendencies are principally conducive to the pluralization of political culture as an important basis of stabilizing the democratic institutions (Aniol et al. 1997; Hetnai 1999).

In contrast to the processes of postcommunist transition and consolidation of democracy in Poland, the post-Soviet development in Russia can merely be conceived of as a catching-up process of political modernization in the Western sense. Instead, the post-Soviet semipresidentialism has to be seen as an equilibrating mixture of democratic and autocratic elements (Hanson 1997c). Although since Yeltsin's revolution in 1991 a competitive democracy with a democratic constitution and a pluralistic party system has existed, two main political sources have supported the tendency toward strengthening the simultaneous autocratic components. On the one hand, the president has an enormously strong, though not unconditional, executive authority above parliamentarian control. It was institutionalized in the constitution right after Yeltsin's coup against Gorbachev, renewed in Yeltsin's battle against the Communist-Nationalist parliamentarian majority in 1993, continued in Yeltsin's reelection in 1996, and now is laid into the hands of Yeltsin's successor, Putin. On the other hand, the party system—though since the introduction of a 5 percent clause considerably less fragmented than the Polish one—became dominated after the two parliamentarian elections in 1993 and 1997 by two political ideological camps, Zhuganov's neocommunist party (CPFR) and Zhirinovski's right-wing liberal-democratic party (LDPR). This political composition of the Parliament first limited severely the reform-oriented parliamentarian basis of Yeltsin's rule, then led him to incorporate more strongly the nationalist camp, and this reformist and nationalist coalition is now also the parliamentarian basis of the Putin administration. This conflictual opposition between the autocratic authority of the president and the parliamentarian dominance of two ideological antisystem party camps is the structural core of the Russian semipresidentialism. At the same time, this semipresidentialism is based on a political culture that on the whole—with the exception of the CPFR and the LDPR—is characterized by a low degree of party loyalty and political participation and a high degree of personalistic clientelism and charismatic populism. In addition, due to the territorial vastness of the Russian Federation and the power loss of the center against the regional peripheries, there is strong political fragmentation of regional party systems (Miller et al. 1998; Petro 1995; Sakwa 1996).

This first conflicting but now stabilizing mixture of an autocratic democracy rests on several crucial constitutive elements of Russian society. First, there is the enormous territorial extension and dispersion of the dominant Russian ethnic core that has resulted in the low degree of ethnic-national homogenization within the Russian Federation and the widespread irredentist Russian populations outside the Russian Federation in the newly independent nation-states (Brubaker 1996). This ethnic-demographic dispersal of the Russian population—in an obvious parallel to the German-speaking population until the population resettlements in and after World War II—is the ethnic-territorial basis for the continuing ambivalence between a small-Russian national and a great-Russian imperial identity. Second, the cultural core of this national-imperial ambivalence is the Christian-Orthodox tradition that historically was closely intertwined with Russian pan-Slavism and tsarist autocracy, and with its contemporary revitalization in the postcommunist period, contributes to this national-imperial oscillation in collective identity formation (McDaniel 1996; Petro 1995; Sakwa 1996). The religiosity in Russia rose from 25 percent in 1988 to 34 percent in 1991 and 47 percent in 1996 and is now stabilizing on this relatively high level (Käakkinnen 1997; Greeley 1998). This enormous growth in religiosity has been caused first and foremost by the revitalization of Orthodox Christianity, but also Protestantism (in the form of evangelical sects), Catholicism, Islam, and new religious movements contribute to this development. The conspicuous increase in religiosity does not mean that the atheistic secularism as a cultural legacy from Communist times has completely disappeared, but it is characteristic that also here the atheistic rejection of Christian Orthodoxy has almost disappeared and the trust in the Orthodox Church has considerably increased. Third, this revitalization of Orthodox Christianity is revealing not only in the sphere of cultural life, but also in its increasing influence on national culture and the political sphere. The Orthodox-Christian culture has regained a public function in the educational system, the public sphere, and political parties from the right to the left. However, this revitalization of religion in the private and public spheres goes together only in limited ways with a pluralization of the political culture. The major reason for this is that Orthodox-Christian religiosity is traditionally shaped by spiritual-ritualistic components in cultural terms and that the Orthodox Church is again trying to limit religious differentiation with the help of the state in institutional terms. In these ways, Orthodox Christianity is supporting the autocratic-collectivist tendencies in the Russian political and civil society (Petro 1995; Sakwa 1996; White et al. 1994; White et al. 1998).

A Comparative Conclusion

On the backdrop of the renaissance of modernization theory in transformation research I have attempted to outline a comparative historical sociological approach to the varying processes of democratization in central and Eastern European societies. Rather than conceiving of postcommunist democratization as a catching-up modernization process toward a Western model of democracy, I have tried to show that the nature and direction of this process is dependent on the sociopolitical and cultural contexts in which it occurs. In such a historical perspective, the precommunist foundations and the Communist legacies in state formation and nation building as well as in religious development and secularization are of crucial importance for the constellation-specific and path-dependent developmental dynamics of democratization.

In comparing the three postcommunist processes of democratization in East Germany, Poland, and Russia, the differences in the collapse of Communism, the transition process, and the consolidation of democracy are quite considerable. The crystallizing forms of democracy, however, are not simply variations of an ideal-typical Western democracy; rather they represent path-dependent types of democracy. Regarding East Germany, the political system developing under the general conditions of unification with West Germany can be categorized as a state-regulated form of postcommunist democratization. In postcommunist Poland, by contrast, the crystallizing political system can be seen as a civil-society-centered form of democracy. And in Russia, one can speak of a quasi-autocratic, semipresidentialist form of democracy. Whereas the forms of consolidated democracy in East Germany and Poland can be classified on a general definitional plane as variations of Western competition democracy, this is not possible in the Russian case. It is therefore not sufficient—as often is done in transition research—to establish analytically the conformity or deviance of postcommunist political systems as measured against the Western ideal-type, but it is necessary to explain the varying types of consolidating democracies in postcommunist Eastern Europe.

Regarding the cluster of political factors relevant for explaining the varying forms of postcommunist democracy, the specific institutional forms of the state and the nation as well as their cultural counterparts of political culture and national identity are of special importance. In the East German case, despite the complete collapse of the GDR state and its thorough reconstruction under West German auspices, there is a strong continuity of a regulated stateness on the basis of an ethnically and culturally defined nation. Accordingly, the East German political culture—in a certain analogy to postwar West German political culture—displays patriarchal and authoritarian features rather than pluralistic and participatory ones. In the Polish case, by contrast, the gradual transition and consolidation process of democracy is shaped by a low degree of stateness, but on the basis of a highly integrated nation. As a corollary, the political culture is less politically institutionalized, more personalistic than participatory. And in the Russian case, the crystallizing form of semipresidentialism shows a strong continuity with an autocratic form of stateness in the context of a nation still oscillating between an imperial and an ethnic definition. Accordingly, the postcommunist culture is characterized by collectivist-clientelistic and charismatic-personalistic features.

Regarding the cultural bases of the differing forms of consolidating democracy, the specific institutional and cultural forms of religion and secularization play an important role. East Germany is a strongly secularized society, in which traditionally predominant Lutheran Protestantism has only a marginal and even further eroding status. But this high degree of secularization is not identical with a pronounced cultural pluralism; rather the postcommunist reproduction of the GDR-specific secular-religious social-cultural milieu supports a defensive and only slowly eroding camp mentality within the political culture and national identity of the East German society. For Poland, conversely, a strong institutional power of the Catholic Church within an only weakly secularized society is still characteristic. But here, the accelerating secularization process will be accompanied by an institutionally and culturally growing process of pluralization, supporting with it a further stabilization of political democratization. In Russia, finally, there is an inverse process of institutional and cultural revitalization of Orthodox Christianity. This process represents, on the one hand, a crucial element of post-Soviet democratization and pluralization. But this process also supports, on the other hand, countertendencies to a Western model of civic democracy on the basis of the strongly autocratic-collectivist, ethnic-nationalist, and charismatic-chiliastic components of Russian political culture and collective identity (McDaniel 1996; Neumann 1996).[9]

Finally, to translate the interpretive results of my comparative analysis to the methodological problematique of transformation theory: my historical-sociological approach starts from the basic premise that the transformation processes in postcommunist societies do not follow either a transformational logic of system change or a transformational contingency of collective agency; rather transformation processes are determined by particular developmental trajectories with interrelated social structures and social actors as well as with changing internal components and external conditions. These developmental trajectories encompass the precommunist formations in the modern era as well as their Communist reconfigurations as historical foundations of the contemporary processes of societal transformation and crystallizing consolidation of specific postcommunist figurations. These developmental and transformational trajectories are constituted not only by political institutions and socioeconomic structures, but also by cultural—institutional as well as mental—dimensions. These formative influences on societal development and social change essentially constitute what Shmuel Eisenstadt has coined "multiple modernities" and related diversity of multiple modernization paths (Eisenstadt 1998; Tiryakian 1997). My intention here has been to follow this approach in a comparative analysis and interpretation of three transformation constellations of democratization, nationalism, and religion in postcommunist East Germany, Poland, and Russia.

Notes

1. See Zapf 1971 on classical modernization theory, Alexander 1994 on the recent renaissance of modernization theory, and Zapf 1996 on the application of modernization theory in transformation research.

2. For a critique of transitology, see Bunce 1995 and Marckwick 1996; for a theoretically oriented comparative analysis, see Dawisha and Parrott 1997a, b; Linz and Stepan 1996; Rubin and Snyder 1998.

3. On ethno-nationalist conflicts, see Brubaker 1996. Generally on the new theories of nationalism, see Alter 1995; Anderson 1983; Armstrong 1982; Balakrishnan 1996; Calhoun 1997; Gelnner 1983; Greenfeld 1993; Smith 1986, 1992 and, as an overview, Hutchinson and Smith 1995.

4. On the relationship between nationalism and religion in the postcommunist societies of central and Eastern Europe, see Casanova 1994: chap. 4, 1998; Dunn 1987; Khazanov 1996; Michel 1994; Ramet 1991; Ramet 1998; Stölting 1990; de Swatos 1994.

5. On the opposition of the Catholic Church and the Communist regime in Poland, see Ash 1993; Casanova 1994: chap. 4; Jerschina 1990; Koblinska and Lawaty 1994; Michel 1994; Michnik 1993; Micewski 1984; Morawska 1995; Schoepflin 1992.

6. The best and most comprehensive study is Pollack 1994; however, in my opinion, the importance of the secular-religious socialist identity in the GDR is not sufficiently developed.

7. Martin (1978: 209–43) interprets the Russian-Soviet secularization pattern as a secular monopoly, but he overstates the cultural secularization tendency and thus underrates the religious countermobilization. Cf. Spohn 1997.

8. Even the best studies on the emerging relationship between Germany and Europe do not adequately analyze this peculiarity of East German identity, its cultural bases and its impact on United Germany. Cf. Katzenstein 1997; Markovits and Reich 1997.

9. Casanova (1998), in his fine analysis of the religious situation in contemporary Ukraine, argues that Ukraine is developing toward the American pluralist model more than other European countries. This thesis, in my view, seems to be overstated. In the case of the United States, religious pluralism is based not only quantitatively on the number of different religious orientations, but also qualitatively on the plurality of institutionally independent religious communities and in addition is often embedded in ethnic networks. By contrast, in Ukraine there are two large dominant churches plus a diversity of small sects. The Greek-Orthodox Uniate Church represents a religious monopoly and the Orthodox Church is currently differentiated in four currents, but all with monopoly-like claims. This situation corresponds to the German religious duopoly in the nineteenth century rather than to the American pluralism in the nineteenth and twentieth centuries. In a parallel to Ukraine, Russian Orthodox Christianity and its currents are not similar to Western Christian pluralism, because they rest on differentiated religious orientations rather than on differentiated religious institutions.

Chapter 11

The Path-Dependence of Transitology

Béla Greskovits

This is an essay in the short history of social thought on East European transformations. I shall present the structure of the discourse on the likely economic, social, and political dynamics under postcommunism. I shall also point to the historical and theoretical roots of the competing concepts and assess the contribution of transitology to our understanding of social change. While reviewing various interpretations of Eastern Europe's transformation I identified two important axes of the debate: the political consequences of capitalist expansion and the impact of the Communist legacy on the viability and specificity of East European democratic market societies. I shall use these axes as a simple framework to analyze the nature of the discourse. Specifically, I shall structure the transformation debate according to the participants' answers to the following questions: (1) Is economic liberalism a prerequisite of, or a threat to, political freedom and democracy? (2) Is the communist legacy a liability, or an asset, from the viewpoint of the emerging market society? In section 1, I shall introduce four frequently advocated but mutually contradicting theses on the perspectives and the sources of viability of the postcommunist market society. Studying the origins of rival views I argue that they are not entirely new, rather in essence each of them had been advocated earlier in different historical contexts. Based on Albert O. Hirschman's tableau of theories (Hirschman 1992) in section 2 I shall demonstrate that the manner social scientists think about postcommunism has much in common with the ideas of their predecessors who faced the emergence of capitalism over the past centuries.

This observation invites further inquiry: what explains the continuity of the major views? Even more puzzling, what accounts for the continuity of conceptualizing capitalism in antinomies? Why did the debate on the perspectives of capitalism and on the nature of its strengths and weaknesses remain open over the past centuries? Why did the rivalry with no less vigor reappear in the new historical case of postcommunist market society? Is it the systemic context, the contradictory systemic identity of capitalism which is responsible for the lack of consensus on some of its core attributes? I do not think it is. Instead in section 3, I shall show that socialism in its time was no less controversial for social scientists. One conclusion is that neither the specific historical nor the specific systemic context of capitalist expansion can account for the prevalence of competing interpretations. Rather the latter is the standard way social scientists think about systems and systemic change in general. A second conclusion of my forthcoming analysis is that the irreconcilable antinomies allegedly characterizing various systems and specifically the market society may be exaggerated and magnified by the theoretical lenses through which scholars study their material. The last thing I ask is why social scientists prefer to stick to sharply conflicting concepts rather than strive for reconciliation with their opponents. Partly, one can view this as unproblematic, as a normal standard of intellectual accumulation. However, my argument developed in section 4 asserts that the trench-war between rival views of postcommunist market society also reflects the impact of new psychological, political, and institutional factors specific to the mass-production of social science ideas toward the end of the twentieth century. In section 5, I conclude and mention some questions for further research.

Four Conflicting Interpretations of Postcommunism

Social science discourse on the likely economic, social, and political dynamics under postcommunism, the viability of postcommunist market democracy, and the nature of the obstacles it encounters has been divided from its birth. For the purpose of mapping the discourse I chose four influential, frequently asserted but mutually contradicting theses, which I call the free market road to freedom thesis, the impossibility theorem, the Leninist legacy thesis, and the communist assets thesis, respectively. Below I shall present the four theses, take a closer look at the logic of each argument, and compare their assessment of the main obstacles to successful economic and political transformation and their suggestions for overcoming the difficulties.

The Free Market Road to Freedom Thesis

The free market road to freedom thesis shares the widely held belief that under capitalism the democratization of the polity goes hand in hand with the marketization of the economy. While it is a commonplace of western political discourse to see democracy and capitalism as virtually identical (Rueschemeyer et al. 1992: 1), this thesis in the context of postcommunist transformation puts the stress on only one of the possible causal links involved: the causality between successful marketization and successful democratization. Advocates of the thesis—mainly economists, East European top economic policymakers, and their Western advisors—assert that political freedom and democracy under postcommunism are the outgrowth of economic freedom. In other words, economic liberalism breeds political liberalism.

The logic of the argument is as follows: the durability of the new democracies will depend to a large extent on their economic performance. Both increasing material welfare and declining inequalities are seen as important factors of democratic stability. Economic growth generates higher living standards and reduces inequalities, hence "the economic model most conducive to economic growth also creates the best economic conditions (i.e., relatively modest inequalities) for democracy" (Balcerowicz 1995: 134f.). Since free market capitalism is supposed to have better growth performance than other models, economic liberalism is presented as the best strategy for political liberalism.

However, not all forms of marketization are viewed as equally conducive to democratic stability: radical and comprehensive reforms are superior to gradualist and less comprehensive strategies. This is made clear in the inverse formulation of the thesis which asserts that the lack of economic radicalism or more specifically the absence of governments' commitment impairs democracy and results in regression to authoritarianism (Aslund 1991: 19; Killick and Stevens 1991: 15). As Jeffrey Sachs and David Lipton (1990: 47f.) put it, "If the reform programs of the new democratic governments fail, the meager living conditions in Eastern Europe will fall further, which could in turn provoke serious social conflict and even a breakdown of the new democratic institutions." These authors proposed fast and decisive government action such as Poland's leap to the market economy in order to avoid the undesirable political outcome. In a similar vein, Yegor Gaidar, the acting Premier of Russia in 1992 in a speech delivered to the Congress of Peoples' Deputies said that if the economic reforms did not accelerate, but rather there would be further "criminal delays . . . then we will develop . . . according to African or Latin American patterns . . . [leading to] the chronic poverty and political instability, the populist politicians and dictatorships so common in Third World states" (quoted by Jeffries 1993: 482f.). Sachs and Lipton (1990) suggest the same: radical and comprehensive economic reforms to sidestep and neutralize the legacy of Communism.[1]

The Impossibility Theorem

As a polar opposite to the free market road to freedom thesis, the impossibility theorem challenges both the view that democratization of the polity goes hand in hand with the marketization of the economy and in its more specific formulations, the causal link stressed by the economic strategists of political freedom. Jon Elster, the leading advocate of this theorem, identified the optimal system as brought about by its essential ingredients of constitutional democracy, competitive markets, and a welfare state, but made "a systematic case for the conclusion" that "one cannot get from here, totalitarian communism, to there," the optimal system. "All regimes that are minimally satisfactory when evaluated in light of the three basic goals are unattainable," or, at least one cannot identify ex ante "a feasible path to a minimally satisfactory regime" (Elster 1993: 267). In line with this general argument David Ost pointed out that it is exactly economic liberalism, proposed as the free market road to freedom, which poses the major threat to democracy. "In this view, the danger to political liberalism comes from the reliance on economic liberalism" (Ost 1995: 178).[2]

But how does marketization undermine democracy? Just like the free market strategists of political freedom, their opponents assume that economic performance plays an important role in making democracies viable. However, their argument claims that radical marketization implies large losses for the majority of East Europeans "who become receptive to demagogues promising prosperity" and who will blame liberal democracy. Hence as a protest against economic hardship and the loss of the social guarantees of the past they will assist populist authoritarian leaders to come to power (Ost 1992: 49; similarly Hausner 1992: 124–28; Roland 1992: 1).

Radical economic reform, the solution for believers in the free market road to freedom, constitutes the major problem for Ost, and one of the problems for Elster.[3] In Ost's view "alternative economic policies, borrowing from populist and social democratic corporatist programs might be better able than neoliberalism to consolidate democracy in Eastern Europe" (Ost 1992: 48).

The Leninist Legacy Thesis

Just like the impossibility theorem the Leninist legacy thesis concludes that simultaneous economic and political reform under postcommunism is extremely difficult if not impossible. However, the reasoning in the latter case is entirely different. While the thesis considers marketization and political democratization as desirable and in principle mutually reconcilable, it also argues that in all likelihood both desired outcomes are simultaneously impaired by the "cultural, political, and economic 'inheritance' of forty years of Leninist rule": the Leninist legacy (Jowitt, 1992: 209).

What is the Leninist legacy, and how does it impair marketization and democratization? Different authors stress the reform-hampering impact of different elements of the past. Here is one example. Under communism, power was vested in a single party that prohibited opposition. In the absence of an established successor elite, one expects this legacy to undermine new institutions of power-sharing and perpetuate centralized structures of power that dominated Leninist regimes (Crawford and Lijphart 1997). But to the extent that centralized states remain in Eastern Europe, elites who control the state will continue to monopolize political and economic activity. Political participation will be weak and economic competition will be thwarted. Thus economic reforms will also fail if the old elites remain in power (Jowitt 1992: 208–15; Crawford and Lijphart 1997: 9–11). According to another version of the "legacist" view presented by Amitai Etzioni, psychological, sociological, and political "friction" is strong during most changes (Etzioni 1992: 28). However, the main source of friction slowing down or inhibiting the postcommunist transformation is the legacy of the past: personality traits and habits of working slowly without initiative and responsibility, featherbedding, using work time for other purposes, lack of management and entrepreneurial skills, the large share of untransferable capital assets, the shortage of proper infrastructure, labor immobility, and, last but not least, "a variety of social values, not easily compatible with capitalism" (Etzioni 1992: 10–19). Still a third version of the Leninist legacy thesis underlies Claus Offe's argument. He wrote that the nostalgia for the remarkable and attractive accomplishments of the past in terms of security and equality—that is, the positive components of the Leninist legacy—also may cast a shadow on the prospects of the transformation. "[S]izable portions of the population of postcommunist societies will be inclined to reason that 'we have given up much of the beneficial aspects of the old regime without having been able to redeem the promises of the new.' Needless to say, it is quite likely that this kind of evaluative perception may help to mobilize political forces of a reactionary, populist, authoritarian, and chauvinist kind, which in turn can jeopardize the accomplishments (. . .) thus reversing even the partial modernization that has actually occurred" (Offe 1993: 659f.).

As far as the major obstacles to the establishment of democratic market society are concerned, Jowitt also stresses that "Eastern Europe consists largely—not exclusively—of fragmented, mutually suspicious, societies with little religiocultural support for tolerant and individually self-reliant behavior" (Jowitt 1992: 224). There is only one way of overcoming these obstacles: to begin to build a modern citizenry with the help of the sporadic civic, secular, and individual forces in the region. However, these forces might turn out to be too weak against their opponents. Therefore the suggested way of getting around the Leninist legacy is to mobilize a "critical mass of civic effort—political, cultural, and economic—that can add its weight to civic forces in Eastern Europe" through Eastern Europe's adoption by Western Europe, similar to what West Germany attempted in East Germany (Jowitt 1992: 224).

The Communist Assets Thesis

The communist assets thesis is also "legacist" in the sense that it asserts that the legacy of the outgoing system will inevitably shape the new institutional pattern of postcommunist society. Some of its advocates such as David Stark and Lászlό Bruszt "look to the variation in how communism fell apart and how these partial ruins provide institutional building blocks for political, economic, and social reconstruction" (Stark and Bruszt 1998: 6). Hence unlike the Leninist legacy thesis the communist asset thesis emphasizes the positive impact of the inheritance.

Certain elements the outgoing system left behind can be useful, since they can become assets from the point of view of building the structures and institutions of the emerging new social formation. Various authors expect different elements of the Communist inheritance to become assets under postcommunism. David Stark favors the informal and interfirm networks and the Communist second economy, which "did not conform to officially prescribed hierarchical patterns" but "got the job done" of keeping afloat economic activity, under the old system. These properties did not collapse with the "formal structures of the socialist regime" (Stark 1996: 994f.). For Peter Murrell, even the formal structures of Communism may turn out to be valuable assets under postcommunism. When asking "Do existing institutions have any value?" Murrell's answer is positive. He argues that existing state institutions of the centrally planned economy should be used to exert control over the macroeconomic situation and over state enterprises "in the period before privatization and creation of market institutions can take place . . . Old inefficient institutions may be better than ones that are planned, but which do not yet exist" (Murrell 1992b: 49-51).[4] In a third political science application of the communist assets thesis Valerie Bunce showed how the postcommunist left in Hungary and Poland combined their past reform-Communist outlook with their recent capitalist ambitions and became assets for democratic stability. They are thus "less a threat to democracy than an investment in democracy" (Bunce 1997: 16).

For advocates of the communist assets thesis a major obstacle in the way of building a successful postcommunist market society is the destruction of Communist assets. This destruction, attributed to radical reforms, implies large and unnecessary socioeconomic losses of organizational efficiency, knowledge, innovation, and diversity (Murrell 1992b: 39; Burawoy 1996; Stark and Bruszt 1998). However, if appropriately used in the context of a path-dependent economic development strategy, these elements of the legacy "can become assets, resources, and the basis for credible commitments and co-ordinated actions in the postsocialist period" (Stark 1996: 994f.).

All in all, we face, an intricate pattern of four, mutually contradicting theses about the likely economic, social, and political dynamics of postcommunist market society. Following Hirschman, I have introduced them "in a sequence such that each successive thesis is in some respect the negation of the preceding one" (Hirschman 1992: 135). According to the free market road to freedom thesis, marketization is going to create an environment of economic growth and income equality which is favorable to political participation and liberal democracy. Advocates of one version of the impossibility theorem argue the opposite: economic liberalism is not the road to freedom, but the road to oppression and exclusion for labor and more broadly for the millions of people marginalized by the chosen strategy of economic transformation. In stark contradiction with the free market road to freedom thesis, this is a theory of impossible or self-destructing capitalism. The political systemic feature attributed to capitalism—political freedom—is undermined by another feature of the same systemic core, the relentless quest for economic freedom. Advocates of both the free market road to freedom thesis and of the impossibility theorem tend to infer politics from economics, and to accept that from the viewpoint of the future, the present—the compatibility or the conflict between market and democracy—matters more than the past. Specifically, they both agree that capitalist expansion influences postcommunist dynamics more than does the Communist legacy. But next to them, we have two theories focusing on the legacy. The Leninist legacy thesis demonstrates how the inheritance of Leninist rule impairs capitalism both in its economic and political dimensions. In this view it is not the capitalist expansion that is going to undermine democracy, the political manifestation of its own systemic identity, but it is rather the powerful remnants of the Communist society that will successfully resist the consolidation of the new system. This is a theory of the "specter of communism" haunting, and resisting, capitalism even after the Communist system collapsed. However, it is contradicted by the thesis of communist assets pointing out the importance of inherited routines, practices, organizational forms, and societal ties from the point of view of successful transformation. Finally, then, we end up with a theory of communism enhancing and facilitating capitalism. Both latter theories assert that, from the viewpoint of the future, it is the past that matters more than—or at least as much as—the present. To put it differently, in one way or the other, the Communist legacy has a stronger—or at least as strong—impact on postcommunist dynamics as the capitalist expansion does. In order to highlight the relation between the above theses it is helpful to present them schematically, in an ideology map.[5]

A closer look at the history of ideas reveals that the two pairs of rival accounts of the viability, and the identified sources of the strengths or weaknesses, of the postcommunist market society are not the conclusions of a new way of thinking developed specifically to explain these societies. Rather the schemata applied have their own history. The proof of this claim will be presented below by a brief summary of the theories collected in Hirschman's *Rival Views of Market Society*.

Table 11.1:
Dominance of Capitalist Expansion versus Influential Persistence of the Communist Legacy: Their Effects on Postcommunist Market Society

	Positive effects	*Negative effects*
Dominance of capitalist expansion	free market road to freedom thesis	impossibility theorem
Influential persistence of the Communist legacy	communist assets thesis	Leninist legacy thesis

Hirschman's "Tableau Idéologique"

What I rediscovered thus is the continuity of old debates about market society in the new context of capitalism's expansion at the end of the twentieth century. What took me by surprise was how well the structure of the discourse on capitalism under postcommunism fitted Hirschman's original *tableau idéologique*. Let us see below how the comparison of the new and old views of capitalism reveals a centuries-old lineage of intellectual kinship, sometimes of a peculiar nature.

Similar to recent architects of postcommunist market society, many observers of the early capitalist expansion—including Montesquieu, Sir James Steuart, William Robertson, Condorcet, Thomas Paine, David Hume, and Adam Smith—expected that the spread of commerce and industry would restrain the sovereign from taking arbitrary actions and from enjoying excessive power. In addition the spread of commerce and industry will give rise to human beings of a more "polished type"—a citizenry that by its manners, morals, and attitudes "will in turn greatly facilitate the smooth functioning of the market" (Hirschman 1992: 106–9). Thus by asserting that all good things go together: economic development brings about beneficial effects in both the political and social realms, the "doux-commerce thesis," as Hirschman named it, can be viewed as the archetype of the free market road to freedom thesis.

However, advocates of what Hirschman calls the "self-destruction thesis," challenged the doux-commerce thesis, since they adopted the view that capitalism "exhibits a pronounced proclivity to undermining the moral foundations on which any society, including its own, must rest" (Hirschman 1992: 110). As pointed out by Hirschman, while the thesis on capitalism's self-destruction forms the cornerstone of Marxian thought, it also found advocates among the conservatives responding to the expansion of market society in the 1730s, and among the romantic and conservative critics of the Industrial Revolution later in the early nineteenth century. For more recent formulations of this thesis Hirschman mentioned among others Karl Polányi, Joseph Schumpeter, and Fred Hirsch. Based on the above, I add to this list the contemporary advocates of the impossibility theorem and among them the social scientists who argue that economic liberalism poses a threat to political liberalism. Similar to their predecessors, a number of contemporary critics of capitalist expansion under postcommunism seem to have become deeply disappointed with the initial brutal consequences of marketization, and expressed their fears that all bad things would go together. In other words, the political outcome would be no less frustrating than the economic one.

In addition to the self-destruction thesis, however, Marx himself, as well as Schumpeter at the time of World War I, and more recently neomarxist analysts of the capitalist periphery came up with the rival view of the "feudal-shackles thesis," which demonstrates "how capitalism is coming to grief, not because of its own excessive energies, but because of powerful residues of precapitalist values and institutions" (Hirschman 1992: 135f.). The theory of precapitalist formations successfully resisting the expansion of market society can thus be interpreted as the direct predecessor of the "Leninist legacy" thesis. Finally, from Hirschman's journey through the history of ideas we learn that contrary to the "feudal-shackles thesis," sometimes it may be beneficial to have a precapitalist past with all its inherited values and institutions. The "feudal-blessings thesis," represented in Hirschman's collection by Louis Hartz, stresses something essentially similar to the "communist assets thesis": "a feudal background is a favourable factor for subsequent democratic capitalist development" (Hirschmann 1992: 136). According to Hartz, countries lacking a feudal past, such as the United States, are "deprived of what Europe has in abundance: social and ideological diversity" (Hirschmann 1992: 133). The argument that remnants of the past social formation can form assets for the new system is shared by path-dependentist evolutionists regardless of whether the preceding formation was feudalism or communism.

In order to visually highlight the structural similarity of the discourse of

Table 11.2:
Dominance of Market versus Influential Persistence of Precapitalist Forms: Their Effects on Market Society

	Positive effects	*Negative effects*
Dominance of market	doux-commerce thesis	self-destruction thesis
Influential persistence of precapitalist forms	feudal-blessings thesis	feudal-shackles thesis

Source: Hirschman 1992: 136.

market society across two (and more) distinct historical periods and a multitude of historical cases, let us finally recall Hirschman's tableau idéologique on the rival views of market society.

The similarity between the rival views of postcommunist market society and those of market society is quite surprising.[6] One might conclude that transitology has little original to contribute to our understanding of social change. At least in terms of theoretical agenda-setting, the "value-added" component of the postcommunism ideology map is modest, especially in the light of the original Hirschmannian tableau. However, we also should ask the question: what explains the continuity of the major views? One explanation could justify the recent reincarnation of rival views of market society by asserting that postcommunism is no more than the latest "great transformation" (Polányi 1946) to capitalism. Thus the continuity of its conceptualization may stem from the same systemic core beneath changing appearances in distant periods of capitalist expansion. But before accepting this explanation one might wonder how the advocates of the different types of views knew exactly what they would have to conceptualize at a time when the perceived result of the process—democratic market economy—did not yet exist (Dobry 1992: 30).[7] Furthermore, even if the prevailing systemic core of capitalism explains the enduring validity of one or another conceptualization, how could it account for the enduring applicability of any given view and its antithesis at the same time? As a last resort, one could still argue that the self-contradictory nature of the system under discussion justifies even a fundamental disagreement over its core attributes. However, this view would not take us far, and would simply be incorrect, since as I will show below, evoking contradicting interpretations is a feature not at all distinctive to capitalism.

Through a short excursion into a third realm of the history of social thought, I will try to put the rivalry of views in a new light. In a third ideology map I shall demonstrate that conflicting theories adding up to a structure similar to both of the above presented tables have also been advocated by observers whose ambition was to predict the dynamics of an entirely different system: socialism.[8]

Rival Views of Socialism

Just as it is a commonplace of Western political discourse to see capitalism as a high road to democracy, until about the time prior to World War I, orthodox socialists "claimed to be the only true democrats, the exclusive sellers of the genuine stuff, never to be confused with the bourgeois fake" (Schumpeter 1942: 235). Later in the century this and similar claims were repeatedly made by both the theorists and the political leaders of socialism, including Stalin, who in 1936 said, "We built a socialist society . . . in order that the human personality might feel really free" (quoted by Heilbroner 1990: 1100, with reference to John Strachey). Similar to the economic strategists of freedom in the postcommunism debate, socialist thinkers developed a theory of the economic road to democracy, which I call the collectivist road to true freedom thesis. While the thesis had many formulations, I refer to the one originating from Oskar Lange's and Fred M. Taylor's contribution to the debate on the practicability of a collectivist economy in the late 1930s.[9] As formulated by Benjamin E. Lippincott in his introduction to Lange's and Taylor's essays, "The essays show, in contradiction to popular thought, that there is nothing inherent in a socialist economy that requires an autocratic system of government, nor that would impair democracy. On the contrary, a socialist economy is far more in harmony with democracy than is a capitalist" (Lippincott 1964: 31). Let me briefly recall the argument. Two elements central to democracy are equality, which involves the removal of privilege: "of artificial inequalities that cannot be justified in terms of common welfare," and liberty. Collectivist economy characterized by the public ownership of the major factors of production, and by central planning, facilitates the realization of the objectives of equality and liberty more than the capitalist economy does. As far as equality is concerned, socialist collectivization eliminates the privilege that stems from wealth and private ownership, and is at the base of a capitalist society. Moreover, collectivist socialism performs better in terms of liberty. "With a more equal distribution of income free consumer's choice will be still freer. Where many under a capitalist economy must choose between a coat and a pair of shoes, under a socialist many could choose between a radio and a telephone" (Lippincott 1964: 32). It is interesting to see how those economic strategists of socialist democracy, just like the market reformers under postcommunism, argued that while radical reform—namely, radical collectivization—is the way to success, "partial," "half-hearted," "gradualist" attempts are self-defeating.[10] Lange teaches the same lesson about transformation: "Socialism is not an economic policy for the timid" (Lange and Taylor 1964: 125) as do Sachs, Aslund and others about the transition to capitalism.

As we know, Lange's and Taylor's theses were a response provoked by Ludwig von Mises's, Lionel Robbins's, and Friedrich Hayek's impossibility, or impracticability thesis, which is the second item in my ideology map on rival views of socialism.[11] From these authors von Mises advocated the view that, "Without economic calculation . . . there can be no economy. Hence, in a socialist state wherein the pursuit of economic calculation is impossible, there can be—in our sense of the term—no economy whatsoever" (Mises 1935: 105). While in the 1930s these thinkers questioned primarily the feasibility of the socialist and of the collectivist economy in general, they also elaborated on socialism's political consequences: the impossibility of democracy under socialism. This argument was then forcefully developed into an explanation about how collectivism results in fascist and communist totalitarianism in Hayek's 1944 "The Road to Serfdom." In the mid 1950s, Milton Friedman revisited the debate in a lecture series, and gave a new formulation to the argument: economic collectivism and freedom are incompatible, and a free collectivist society is impossible.[12] Let me show how Friedman's argument on collectivism's self-destruction as a democratic system is constructed. A collectivist economy, first of all, eliminates one central element of freedom, namely, freedom of economic arrangements, including the freedom of private property. "In the second place, economic freedom is also an indispensable means toward the achievement of political freedom" (Friedman 1962: 8). Why? Because a collectivist economy merges economic power with political authority thereby eliminating them as mutual checks on each other and facilitating the monopoly of power.

Up to this point the pattern of rival views of socialism compare well with the rival views of market society. I presented two conflicting theses, which essentially shared the perception of the strength of collectivism, resulting either in beneficial or in gloomy outcomes in terms of freedom and the quality of human life. But what about the other pair of theses evaluating the impact of the historical legacy on socialism? In this respect there is no perfect analogy. I did not find any influential theory arguing that socialism could not expand, since the powerful residues of capitalist values and institutions paralyzed it. Perhaps this is not by chance: it is well-known that Marx viewed capitalism as the precondition rather than an obstacle for socialism. Until Lenin, the socialist revolution was expected to occur first in the most developed capitalist countries. But even if we do not have a powerful "capitalist-shackles thesis," the feudal-shackles thesis is going to fit the ideology map of rival views of market society, and also of socialism. By constraining capitalist development, the residues of feudalism (and other precapitalist legacies) are indirectly the obstacles to socialism as well. Moreover, the "capitalist-shackles thesis" appears in the argument that after the socialist revolution the development of collectivist norms and the spirit of mutual help and cooperation is constrained by the "anachronistic survivals" of egoism, and other bourgeois or petty bourgeois values.

Finally, as pointed out above, Marxism provides us with an especially powerful formulation of the "possibilist" legacy thesis: by creating highly developed

Table 11.3:
Dominance of Collectivism versus Influential Persistence of Presocialist Forms: Their Effects on Socialist Society

	Positive effects	*Negative effects*
Dominance of collectivism	collectivist road to true freedom thesis	impossibility/impracticability thesis, (or road to serfdom thesis)
Influential persistence of capitalist forms	capitalist assets thesis	feudal-shackles thesis (or anachronistic survivals thesis)

"forces of production," and its own "gravedigger," the working class, capitalism facilitates and enables the formation of socialism. This way from the viewpoint of socialism, much of the capitalist legacy is an "asset."

All in all, I have collected a third set of rival views this time on socialism, yet these views add up to a logical structure similar to the previous ones.

What is the lesson we can draw? First and foremost, neither the specific historical, nor the specific systemic context of capitalist expansion alone can account for the prevalence of its similar but competing interpretations. Rather the latter is the standard way social scientists think about systems and systemic change in general. But what does this exactly mean?

Based on Joseph Schumpeter's concept of "visions" Robert Heilbroner offers a useful framework of interpretation (Heilbroner 1990; Schumpeter 1954). Consistent with Schumpeter's and Heilbroner's concept, I argue that the rival views of social systems—both of the market society and its postcommunist version and of socialism—are "visions," that is, "preanalytic cognitive acts" that precede "the scenarist's work as author or stage designer" (Heilbroner 1990: 1109). Schumpeter's assertion of the motivation and purpose of visions as "ideological" helps us to understand why fundamental visions are conflicting, why they survive the centuries, and why there is only a limited choice of them. As far as the origin of the conflicting visions is concerned, Heilbroner wrote, "Such general preconceptions cannot be proved or disproved—or worse, can all too readily be 'proved' or 'disproved' by appeal to historical example or introspec-

Table 11.4:
Rival Visions of History

	Positive effects	*Negative effects*
Future (or present) transcends past	Radical optimist theses • doux-commerce thesis • collectivist road to true freedom thesis • free market road to freedom thesis	Radical pessimist theses • self-destruction thesis • impossibility/ impracticability thesis (and road to serfdom thesis) • impossibility theorem
Past dominates future (and present)	Conservative optimist theses • feudal-blessings thesis • capitalist assets thesis • communist assets thesis	Conservative pessimist theses • feudal-shackles thesis • Leninist legacy thesis

tion. History or introspection will provide support for many such general assertions, but it will also yield evidence for the contrary kinds of generalizations. This is because the human psyche is itself full of contradictions, all aspects of which are mirrored in historical experience" (Heilbroner 1988: 197). As to the limited choice of social system visions, "[T]he most common typification of visions is between those that lead to 'conservative' and those that imply 'radical' expectations, broadly meaning those that see the future as dominated by the past, and those that see the future as transcending it" (Heilbroner 1990: 1112).

Coming back to our review of ideas, we have seen on the one hand the rivalry between radical and conservative preconceptions of history.[13] On the other hand, the review highlighted another useful dimension of classification: both radical and conservative visions can be "optimist" or "pessimist" depending upon the perceived quality of the past's effect on future, and vice versa. This way my schematic classification of rival views of social systems includes radical optimist, radical pessimist, conservative pessimist, and conservative optimist theses. To highlight the ideological kinship of the rival views of postcommunism with earlier preconceptions and to indicate their place in the family-tree of social thought along one dimension let me present a final map of rival visions of history.

As Heilbroner put it, "Both sides of this polarization of views can be amply illustrated and refuted by historical example, and both still wield vast influence in establishing our understanding of the world" (1990: 1112). This interpretation may account for the "visionary" and "ideological" origins of the transitology debate. However, this is not, what in my view is wrong with transitology. It is much more worrisome that social scientists tend to present their rival preanalytic cognitive orientations as "general theories" of postcommunist capitalism, and there is a disquieting lack of analytic efforts to identify the limits and conditions of the conflicting generalizations. In other words the analytic act of scientific inquiry as opposed to the generalized visions is underrepresented in transformation studies. There is only a small number of exceptions from the rule of exaggerated dominance of preconceptions, of the limited attention paid to evidence and details, and more generally, of the lost balance between the two equally important missions of social science: embracing complexity and having predictive power. This will be the subject of the next section.

Old and New Factors of the Disequilibrium between Embracing Complexity and Having Predictive Power

As a starting point one has to realize that there is one significant difference in the pattern of social science discourse on market society and on its postcommunist version. While Hirschman (1992: 106) pointed out that the ideas he presented in his tableau had constituted a rivalry without actual debate, the controversy about the postcommunist market society seems to be a debate without reconciliation.

In the latter case, the participants have frequently addressed and intrigued each others' views, but up till now there is no indication of an emerging reconsideration of ideas or search for new evidence. Instead, much of the discourse seems to have got stuck at the stage of rival archetypal visions.

What we have to understand, then, is what makes social scientists stick to sharply conflicting concepts either by not taking cognizance of their opponents or by not seeking reconciliation with them. The two versions of the conceptual trench-war may have partly common explanations. Let us examine first Hirschman's reasoning in the context of the original rivalry in order to see how far his arguments take us in understanding the discussed feature of the postcommunism debate.

Paying attention to diversity and complexity may facilitate reconciliation among the rival views. Rivals may accept that, "however incompatible the various theories might be, each might still have its 'hour of truth' and/or its 'country of truth' as it applies in a given country or group of countries during some stretch of time" (Hirschman 1992: 137). Embracing complexity in the postcommunism debate would, for instance, lead to the realization that while radical marketization may result in freedom in one group of countries, it may prove to be the road to serfdom in another, or that the Communist legacy resists capitalism in a given country while it is a lever of successful marketization in another. Why do advocates of most though not all rival views seem to dismiss such perspectives?

According to Hirschman older interpretations of market society developed in isolation essentially for three reasons: (1) the difficulty of perception of diversity and of dialectic processes; (2) the psychological temptation to predict "inevitable" outcomes, and (3) a self-confidence ideologies like to parade. In his view, for these features social science usually pays with a loss of the complex picture of society. I believe that all of the above factors are at work behind the in-built bias for irreconcilable rivalry evident in the discourse on postcommunism. In addition, I show below that two groups of specific conditions magnify the effect of these general factors: the first group includes the historically unique properties of the postcommunist transformation, while the second results from a number of new psychological and institutional features emerging in response to the mass-production of social science ideas. Hence in terms of flawed interpretation and simplistic view of reality, transitology has to pay an even higher price than did the older views.

The Difficulty of Perceiving Diversity and Dialectic Processes

By recognizing and defining the sources of the contradictory processes at work in society, the difficulty of accepting the existence of diverse and unpredictable outcomes can be tempered (Hirschman 1992: 139). The standard path of scientific inquiry that leads from the visions or preanalytic orientations to reliable interpretations and scenarios involves precisely the recognition and definition of the conditions that generate social processes. On this path, it is hard to avoid the examination of somebody's "conceptual scheme for its compatibility with other construals of reality" (Heilbroner 1990: 1112f.). If this comparison in turn happens, it may help to bridge the gap between competing interpretations. But to proceed this way requires two conditions to be met: interest in and empirical knowledge of the features making for contradictions and diversity. I think one reason why the gap between the rival views of postcommunism have not yet been bridged is that their advocates in a number of cases did not meet either of the two conditions.

Frequently, theorists made explicit that instead of diversity and variations they searched for generalizations based on the common systemic features of the postcommunist societies. Arguing that commonalties were more important than differences they conceptualized the likely dynamics of the market society's "systemic core" rather than its varied appearances; they predicted the fate of the entire region rather than that of the individual countries. A lack of interest in country-specificity and diversity were equally forcefully expressed by some representatives of the free market road to freedom thesis, the incompatibility theorem, and the Leninist legacy thesis.[14] Unlike them, advocates of the communist assets thesis repeatedly stressed their interest in diversity and variations.[15]

Clearly, most transitologists' bias for generalization may be fueled by an array of motivations from intellectual taste to professional position or political calculation. Nevertheless, I believe that ignorance about diversity is not always and not only a matter of deliberate choice. It can result from the lack of empirical data on the details of the subject. The existence of sketchy data is again explained by several factors. On one hand, a number of researchers are newcomers to the field and neither know the history of the countries under study, nor do they speak their language. Often they do not have the time or the funding to gather the required information. On the other hand, the rapid development of events, the actual lack of reliable data both on the past and the present state of affairs, and the unexpected outcome of regime change itself shocked even many "area specialists" and those "generalists" who were both interested in and well prepared to recognize both the common features and the diversity of the changes. One typical way of coping with the lack of solid empirical facts was to rely on the media as (sometimes the only) source of evidence. However, reliance on media coverage makes one wonder to what degree social science is capable of transcending daily news given its dependence on it.[16]

All in all, the above brief inventory of the intellectual arsenal of transitology reveals serious shortcomings. In the absence of interest in or evidence on the details, a number of transition theorists based their generalizations on the only tool available to them: their preanalytic cognitive orientations. The constitutive element of scientific inquiry was missing, the analytic act failed to follow, and the macrosocial prognoses and scenarios were directly inferred from visions, which happened to be mainly the reincarnations of centuries-old intellectual perspectives.

Thus first, a large part of transitology is an ironic proof of the timeless power of ideas and hence strongly supports John Maynard Keynes's belief that, "[T]he ideas of economists and political philosophers, both when they are right and when they are wrong, are more powerful than is commonly understood. Indeed the world is ruled by little else. Practical men, who believe themselves to be quite exempt from any intellectual influences, are usually the slaves of some defunct economists. Madmen in authority, who hear voices in the air, are distilling their frenzy from some academic scribbler of a few years back" (Keynes 1936/73: 383).

Second, the above interpretation of much of the postcommunism debate as a rivalry of visions and of generalized scenarios directly based on visions also helps us to understand why transitology continues to be a discourse without reconciliation. Unlike advocates of contradicting scholarly concepts, the believers in conflicting preconceptions are not forced to surrender to their rivals if their prognoses do not come true, because one vision cannot be superior to another one, and "the validity of the underlying vision cannot be inferred from the success of prognoses built on them" (Heilbroner 1990: 1112). For example, despite the fact that many democracies emerging in the postcommunist transformation process survived their first tough period of economic crisis and the ensuing radical austerity measures, it remains plausible to argue that reform radicalism precipitates political breakdown, or that the transformation is extremely difficult. However, in our world, where decisions of the international community of financiers and investors sometimes reflect the strong influence of rumors and fears rather than of reliable analyses, it may be irresponsible to stubbornly advocate negative visions even if the gloomy prophecies do not materialize. Doomsday forecasts may become self-fulfilling prophecies because nobody will invest or allocate loans in a country or a region suspected of never-ending economic and political chaos.

But even if the actors of international capital markets cannot be fooled by untested positive and negative general predictions, the lack of attention to falsification implies losses for social science. The major scholarly contribution of transitology could result from contrasting the real developments with the predicted scenarios. Even prediction failures may raise new questions for social science, because they may help to identify neglected explanatory variables. The next issue then is the problems associated with forecasting in social science and specifically in transitology.

The Obsession with Predicting the "Inevitable"

The wish to predict the future is the second item on Hirschman's list of factors responsible for the lack of communication and intellectual exchange among the older views of market society. As an explanation he mentions a psychological factor: social scientists had wanted "to impress the general public by proclaiming some inevitable outcome of current processes" (Hirschman 1992: 139). But for social analysis, there is a trade-off between embracing complexity and having predictive power. Neglecting the former in favor of the latter usually results in an increased chance for failed predictions. Up to this point Hirschman's argument fits the case of the postcommunism debate. Similar to their historical predecessors, advocates of rival views on postcommunism frequently made predictions that mostly failed. Given the above and many additional obstacles to reliable prognoses, it is neither surprising that most recent predictions have proved to be failures, nor is it difficult or intellectually challenging to find the reasons for the failures.[17]

However, there are two more interesting questions that arise in connection with the failed prophecies on the likely dynamics of postcommunist transformation. These are: (1) what can we learn from the prediction failures, and (2) what are the specific factors, in addition to the general ones observed by Hirschman, which make for the transitologists' obsession with future?

As to the first question I believe that there are three general messages to be taken seriously in social science: first, past is no fate; second, present is no fate either; and third, the market society has dramatically changed toward the end of the twentieth century.

The failure of universal prognoses stemming from the Leninist legacy thesis indicates that the past—even a communist one—does not predetermine the future. A number of East European countries have managed to cope with their Leninist legacy. Faced with this fact social science has to identify the specific conditions under which past legacies prevail and impair successful transformation. Or alternatively, we may ask what are the conditions under which legacies can be transcended, and can even become assets for postcommunist capitalism?

Present is not fate: this is clear from the failure of prophecies of serious disruptions of political stability and the breakdown of new democracies based on the assumption that economic frustration breeds political discontent. Faced with the fact that the unprecedented economic decline and social dislocation have not resulted in regionwide political breakdown under postcommunism, social science has to reconsider the earlier assumptions on the political impact of economic crises. It has to explore: in what way, other than precipitating systemic collapse, economic crises might affect the political dynamics of transforming societies.

Finally, the failure of some of the prognoses stemming from evolutionary, path-dependentist approaches underlying the communist assets thesis suggests that the choice of economic development paths is subject to international constraints. Development paths seem to be constrained at least as much by the arrangements of an integrated world economy, which the new Eastern capitalisms want to accommodate, and by the global actors, as by their past legacies (Bohle 1997). The latter seem to account for the individual risks and opportunities associated with the various East European governments' commitment to "going global" by becoming integrated.

With the second question I come back to the original topic of my inquiry: what explains the transitologists' rush to macrosocial prognoses even if the post-communist transformation has been "a bizarre time to engage in prediction" (Bunce 1993: 42)?[18]

My answer concludes that in addition to the general psychological temptation to predict, other specific and forceful incentives were also at work. I believe that paradoxically the failure to foresee the collapse of communism might have urged social science to predict the likely dynamics of—at least—the successor system and to "correct" the past failure by new "more adequate" prophecies. Also fueling self-criticism and doubts about the claim to predictive power, this failure might have substantially increased social scientists' interest in the future. John Kenneth Galbraith forcefully articulates the disappointment and the self-critical stance when writing that, "The greatest economic failure of our time, needless perhaps to say, was in not foreseeing the recent revolutionary changes in Central Europe and the Soviet Union" (quoted by Wojtyna 1992: 158).[19] Similar processes might have been in motion in the powerful international organizations, which, just like social scientists, did not foresee the changes.[20]

Beyond the motivation provided by the experience of the prediction failure, additional factors originating in the new psychological, political, and institutional environment specific to the mass-production of social science ideas toward the end of the twentieth century contributed to the eagerness to engage in making predictions. Specifically, in the last few decades social science underwent an extensive process of international integration and marketization. After the collapse of Communism influential factors pushed social scientists toward hurried prognoses, both on the supply and demand side of this market. Since Valerie Bunce succinctly described one possible supply side mechanism, I shall focus on the demand side below.[21]

On the demand side, an intensive need for all kinds of forecasts appeared: including economic, social, political, military, and geopolitical prognoses. Furthermore, there was no time to wait until empirical evidence had accumulated making reliable prognoses possible. Both old and new actors on the demand side stressed the significance of the time factor. At the same time that external public and private creditors worried about the future of their old loans and were eagerly looking for new allocations, they wanted information about the "area-risk" and "country-risk" to avoid earlier failures. International organizations; IMF, World Bank, EBRD, GATT, OECD, NATO, and last but not least the European Union, and the governments behind them expected new partners or members from the East. Thus they needed analysis about who these potential partners were in terms of their likely political, economic, and social developments; not only in the medium or long run, but in the short run as well. International investors searching for new investment opportunities became interested in the region because of the return on investment they expected. In addition, given the political, economic, and geopolitical interdependence in the region, in order to know for example Hungary's "country-risk," one had to be familiar with Russia's risks as well.

While this demand was primarily met by professional suppliers of predictions—economic and political research institutes, think-tanks, rating agencies, economic, political, and military advisors—in the early 1990s new developments changed the situation to some extent. First, the trust in these professional groups' ability to prognosticate was undermined as a consequence of their failure to foresee the collapse of Communism (and right after it, the deep and long "transformational recession" [Kornai 1994]). Second, because of the fuzziness of the empirical evidence, the professional prophets were in disarray themselves, and became more open than ever before to absorbing the available—more or less complex and careful—narratives and even visions. Third, the speed, scale, and complexity of changes justified and encouraged new nonprofessional or semiprofessional entrants to the market of predictions. Thereby East Europeanist (and, partly, the "generalist") social science arrived at an exceptional period of its existence during which its scenarios, evaluations, and prognoses were in great demand and could easily reach publicity. Also, for a limited time, and relative to earlier periods, private and public foundations, universities, government agencies, and international organizations channeled generous funding to the research area. Hence social scientists learned they could live on their analyses, forecasts, and recommendations, if they were competitive enough. Finally, the existing institutional framework of social science—the workshops, networks, scholarships, conferences, scholarly exchange programs, periodicals—were filled with new life, deepened by the exchanges, and by the intensified demand for forecasting the future. Often the showlike stage design and the media interest also strengthened the competitive rather than the cooperative dimension of international scholarly exchange forcing analysts to buttress their identity and to enhance their competitive advantage by original, provocative, and extremist predictions.

I do not mean that transitology with its accentuated prophetic orientation crept out of the bank-accounts and safe-deposits of various actors and institutions of global capitalism, only that social science, among many other motives, also felt the challenge of intensified practical interest in the future of the region well before it could be prepared for reliable prognoses. To highlight one peculiar aspect of the recent situation of social science by a somewhat absurd comparison, I just recall that Karl Marx was not urged to hasty speculations on the future of capitalism because his sponsor Engels worried about the return on its investments. Neither did Ludwig von Mises, Friedrich Hayek, or Oskar Lange have to argue about the feasibility and practicability of socialism in order to help forceful players to come to rapid decisions in the context of a forthcoming geopolitical reality or of the practical need for evaluating the "country risk" of the Soviet Union, or Nazi Germany. In our times, however, the political, financial, and institutional relationship between action and perception, power and social science imagination has become more intimate. Social scientists, perhaps more than ever, want to know reality in order to change it. In this respect it is telling that Douglass North, a social scientist who used to be among the last to be blamed with extreme practicist orientations, recently found it imperative to know more about the interaction between economy and politics. As member of a "Task Force on Economies in Transition" North wrote: "The interface between economics and politics is still in a primitive state in our theories, but its development is essential if we are to implement policies consistent with intentions" (North 1997: 17).

The Self-Confidence of Advisors and Utopists

Last, but not least, if social scientists are driven by the ambition to transform their ideas into policy their resistance to accepting the element of truth in alternative concepts is further magnified. In this respect both the unique historical challenge of prescribing concrete agendas for postcommunism, and new institutional features of the mass-production of social thought pushed many social scientists toward active participation in the process of transformation, and exaggerated the need for the self-confidence that ideologies generally like to parade. Two interrelated processes with essentially similar negative effects on scholarly quality have been put in motion: "advisorism" and the direct political involvement of social science.

As far as advisorism is concerned, it is striking how often recent economic, political, and sociological analyses of postcommunism end up with policy recommendations or prescriptions for action. A significant part of transitology seems to have given in to the temptation to advise the practitioners of transformation; top politicians and top policymakers, on "what is to be done." Clearly, on the largest scale this is characteristic of economists. But surprisingly, not just economics but sociology and political science as well appear to have elaborated a comprehensive set of economic conditions for democratic stabilization. As also demonstrated in the preceding sections, the list of policy suggestions includes adequate welfare provisions, less haste in economic transformation, various tactics of reform sequencing, engagement of labor unions and works councils in economic restructuring and privatization, employee ownership experiments, and neocorporatist strategies (Offe 1993; Walton and Seddon 1994; Dewatripont and Roland 1994; Roland 1992; Ost 1992, 1995). The latter conditions almost look like a social democratic counterpart to IMF-World Bank conditionality and they are in fact often in conformity with the views propagated by another circle of international organizations and sponsors of research: the International Labour Organisation, the United Nations, a number of agencies of the European Union, or the Friedrich Ebert Stiftung. It is not my aim here to point out that most advice occurred when legislative or executive efforts in the proposed direction had already been under way. Nor is it my intention to criticize the values underlying the advice. Rather my point is that reliable analysis is frequently substituted for or preceded by practical recommendations. Thus advisorism easily becomes a hindrance to open-minded, complex, and reliable conceptualization. In addition, an advisor, a social and economic "technician" more easily than a critical social scientist, may believe that his/her prescriptions are universal, and diversity and specificity do not really matter. This highlights one more factor of the difficulty of the perception of dialectic and diversity.[22]

Yet another consequence of social scientists' wish to translate views into policy, namely, their direct or indirect involvement in politics, further reduces their ability to capture complexity and produce reliable results. At one extreme social scientists become top politicians or top policymakers, yet continue to express social science views and macrosocial prognoses—under postcommunism this extreme sometimes became the norm. But even in less extreme cases, "To become policy, ideas must link up with politics—the mobilization of consent for policy" (Gourevitch 1989: 87). However, political competition entails mechanisms which may artificially increase the intellectual distance and distort the relationship between ideas. One such mechanism for example is the phenomenon that in order to mobilize political support, ideas often construct themselves as "utopias" and their alternatives as "pathologies." The latter are the merge-terms for all possible negative consequences if the utopia fails to materialize.[23]

In the framework of political competition between utopias and their pathologies, rival views risk to lose even the minimum of mutual respect and the chance for reconciliation. Social science suffers in both of the following ways: its capacity to capture complexity is fatally impaired, and a number of terms which originally served the conceptualization of a particular social phenomenon lose their empirical content and meaning. Instead they become mere catchwords of political discourse.[24]

Conclusions and Questions for Further Research

In my essay on the short history of social thought on East European transformations, I presented the structure of the discourse on the likely economic, social, and political dynamics under postcommunism. For mapping the discourse I chose four influential frequently asserted but mutually contradicting theses, which I called the free market road to freedom thesis, the impossibility theorem, the Leninist legacy thesis, and the communist assets thesis. The free market road to freedom thesis says that economic liberalism breeds political liberalism, while the impossibility theorem challenges this view arguing that capitalism and democracy are either mutually incompatible or in other versions, that economic liberalism is a threat to political liberalism. Next, the Leninist legacy thesis demonstrates how democracy and marketization are going to be undermined not by their mutual tensions and contradictions, but by the inheritance of Leninist rule; the powerful remnants of the Communist society. Finally, the communist assets thesis accepts that the legacy is important for the postcommunist society, but unlike the Leninist legacy thesis, asserts that its effect can be positive.

Examining the historical and theoretical roots of the four mutually contradicting theses, I found that they are not new but rather all have a long history. In addition, I discovered that while as a first step the debate on postcommunism can be traced back to the rival views of market society, neither the specific historical, nor the specific systemic context of capitalist expansion alone can account for the reincarnation of similar but competing interpretations. Rather the controversy and its pattern are a reflection of the manner social scientists think about systems and systemic change in general. Specifically, I argued that the rival views of market society strongly and directly reflect ideologies and visions: radical or conservative, optimist or pessimist preanalytic cognitive orientations.

The fact that these visions can both be confirmed and refuted by historical examples and have a vast influence on our understanding of the world is an explanation of the visionary and ideological manner in which many social scientists think about postcommunism. But what I believe is wrong with the transformation debate is not that many participants are "visionary" and "ideological." Rather what constitutes the problem is that much of the discourse seems to have got stuck at the stage of rival archetypal, preanalytic cognitive orientations, and the next step, the analytic act of scientific inquiry, often does not follow. I argue that this is mainly reflected in the fact that transitology exhibits a rivalry without reconciliation and fails to find a balance between two equally important missions of social science: the tasks of embracing complexity and of striving for predictive power.

Reconciliation between the rival views will be easier if attention is paid to the contradictions and diversity of reality. But many transitologists could not capture complexity because no less than their predecessors in social thought they were exposed to the fallacies and temptations characteristic to the production of ideas in general: in Hirschman's terms, the difficulty of perception of diversity and of dialectic processes; the psychological temptation to predict the "inevitable"; and the self-confidence ideologies like to parade. For these features, social science usually pays with failed predictions and an insufficiently complex picture of society.

However, I also believe that a number of transitologists failed to realize their potential because their scientific inquiry has been constrained by the absence of knowledge of local conditions and by a disinterest in empirical details and diversity. Hence, arguing that commonalties were more important than differences they preferred to conceptualize the likely dynamics of the "systemic core" rather than its varied appearances and the fate of the entire region rather than that of individual countries. The direct implication was that often the macrosocial prognoses and scenarios were directly inferred from visions which happened to be mainly the reincarnations of centuries-old intellectual perspectives. Thus follows the conclusion that the price transitology has had to pay in terms of failed predictions and an insufficiently complex picture of society is significantly higher than that paid by its predecessors. Visions are not falsifiable and cannot be declared as failures on the basis that their prognoses did not materialize. Consequently, too little debate about the prognoses and the predicted macrosocial scenarios takes place, even though unlike visions, predictions can be debated, since they reflect the efficiency (or in this case, more often than not, the inefficiency) of scientific inquiry.

Finally, I showed how the negative effects of the usual fallacies and temptations characteristic of the production of social thought in general were magnified by the influence of specific conditions: the historically unique properties of the postcommunist transformation and a number of new psychological and institutional features of the mass-production of social science ideas at the end of the twentieth century. Many transitologists acted as advisors, and their advisorism often resulted in substituting a cognitive with an activist attitude to society, and of mature and reliable analyses for practical recommendations. Other social scientists, driven by their wish to translate some of their ideas into policy, flirted with politics with a tendency of presenting their rivals' views as the pathologies of their own utopias. The dramatically increased demand for all types of hasty predictions, and the specific forms of institutionalization of social science in our times gave impetus to both of these tendencies, which in turn enhanced the bias for rivalry over reconciliation.

Consequently, transitology's contribution to our understanding of social change has been modest. At least in terms of theoretical agenda-setting, the "value-added" component of the postcommunist ideology map is quite insubstantial. Therefore, a pessimistic and ironic conclusion could claim that, while the emergence of the new systems has been unfolding at a rapid speed and on a large scale in the postcommunist East, their conceptualization has not gone far beyond the first step of routine exercises. At the end of the twentieth century history luckily surprised social scientists with a complex social laboratory that allows the undertaking of new intellectual experiments. So far, however, social scientists have been capable of little more than repeating their predecessors' visions, and teaching contradicting results.

A less ironic and more optimistic conclusion argues that the opportunities for improvement are abundant. If transitologists are willing to accept that even if none of their theories are universal, all may be relevant in different countries or different times, as Hirschman suggested, they will find opportunities to creatively combine the theses on the free market road to freedom, on the impossibility of democratic capitalism after communism, the Leninist legacy, and the communist assets, and probably a number of other approaches. This acceptance, however, implies that transformation studies will become less "elegant" than before and also more eclectic rather than reductionist.

Notes

I thank Lóránd Ambrus Lakatos, Valerie Bunce, Michel Dobry, Peter Katzenstein, Mihály Laki, Kamilla Lányi, Joan Nelson, Andreas Pickel, Jonas Pontusson, Phillippe Schmitter, and Sid Tarrow for their comments on various versions of this essay.

1. The Communist state bureaucracy which may ally with workers and managers in the declining economic sectors to help populist politicians to come to power (Sachs 1990: 21), or "the former party nomenclature" resisting the transition (Killick and Stevens 1991) are considered as a threatening Communist political legacy.

2. "Reliance on economic liberalism in the context of East European transformations according to this view includes establishing individual property rights, promoting market-based inequalities, supporting the evolution of a strong bourgeoisie, and limiting state intervention in the economy. Political liberalism, threatened by economic liberalism, however denotes: universal tolerance, the systemic guarantee of suffrage, freedom of speech and association, and of democratic political representation" (Ost 1995: 200).

3. In a framework similar to Elster's, John Walton and David Seddon predict that, "if government economic reform cannot be made compatible with adequate welfare provision to constitute the basis for a broadly acceptable, new moral economy (combining economic development with social justice) within the existing framework of the state, then the rule of law will all too easily be disregarded on a massive scale and popular protest against the cost of economic liberalization will all too easily be engulfed in the monstrous growth of ethnic violence and nationalism and break apart that framework from top to bottom" (Walton and Seddon 1994: 328).

4. In Burawoy's view the (reformed) party state, and the (reformed, and disciplined) public sector as a whole should be seen as an asset. "For the Russian 'reformers' the party-state was so morally and politically repugnant and its incumbents so corrupt and venal that the destruction of the state apparatus was worth any price. The Chinese 'reformers,' on the other hand, were prepared to go to any lengths to preserve the party state . . . at the present time the Chinese strategists can look back on a period of continuous growth, while Russia's reformers seem to have destroyed the economic capacity of their society in the process of saving it from the state" (Burawoy 1996: 1105).

5. In the context of the postcommunism ideology map Phillipe Schmitter asked about the history of individual social scientists' preference for one or another view, and about the direction and frequency of changes of views in the sense that for example somebody started as an advocate of the free market road to freedom thesis, but later became a believer in the Leninist legacy thesis. I believe that these questions are both interesting and important, but I cannot address them in the present essay.

6. Related to this observation Mihály Laki expressed the view that one should be careful with the suggestion of unrestricted similarity between the rival views of market society, and the rival views of its version under postcommunism. Because of the variation of their historical, philosophical, and contextual environments these apparently identical statements may express actually very different theoretical substances. I believe that this problem is relevant and should be explored by further research. However, I do not think that the similarity of the two collections of rival views is purely formal.

7. Apart from the fact that such an explanation would run counter to the extensive

literature both on the unique historical properties of postcommunist transformation and on the significant changes of capitalism over the past centuries, conceptualizing the postcommunist transformation mainly "by where it is heading" is not good social science methodology anyway (Bunce 1993: 36).

8. I shall present the rival views of socialism in a logical but not in a historical sequence.

9. For a thoughtful summary and evaluation of the debate, see Heilbroner (1990).

10. In this respect, the radical slogan known from the postcommunism debate, "You don't try to cross a chasm in two jumps" (quoted in Sachs 1990: 19), seems a late reincarnation of the manner Oskar Lange encouraged the socialist government to act rapidly and decisively. In a section of his essay called "On the Policy of Transition" Lange wrote "a socialist government really intent upon socialism has to decide to carry out its socialisation program at one stroke, or to give it up altogether. The very coming into power of such a government must cause a financial panic and economic collapse. Therefore, the socialist government must either guarantee the immunity of private property and private enterprise in order to enable the capitalist economy to function normally, in doing which it gives up its socialist aims, or it must go through resolutely with its socialisation program at maximum speed. Any hesitation, any vacillation and indecision would provoke the inevitable economic catastrophe" (Lange and Taylor 1964: 124f.).

11. Actually, Hayek accepted that a collectivist economy is theoretically possible but impracticable.

12. Friedman wrote "that there is an intimate connection between economics and politics, that only certain combinations of political and economic arrangements are possible, and that in particular, a society which is socialist cannot also be democratic, in the sense of guaranteeing individual freedom" (Friedman 1962: 8).

13. The role of radical and conservative visions during the postcommunist transformation was first raised by Murrell (1992c).

14. In their book called "Reform in Eastern Europe" five influential economists, Olivier Blanchard, Rudiger Dornbusch, Paul Krugman, Richard Layard, and Lawrence Summers—several of whom became advisors to one or another East European government later—point out in advance that, "Our goal is to identify and clarify the main issues and choices rather than to draw a detailed road map. We do not emphasize differences across Eastern European countries. . . . And while we occasionally refer to the Soviet Union, we make no attempt to deal with the specific political and economic aspects of reform in that country" (Blanchard et. al. 1991: xxii). Similarly, Jon Elster wrote, "Vital distinctions among the various countries are ignored. For some purposes it may be ridiculous to treat China and the Czech and Slovak Republic within the same framework. Yet I believe that all of these countries have some dilemmas in common, if we define them at a sufficiently high level of abstraction. To discuss exceptions and solutions, however, one would almost certainly have to use concepts of finer grain, and look at each individual country" (Elster 1993: 267). Or, as Ken Jowitt put it, "I have obviously, if not explicitly argued that the historical differences between countries and their current modes of transition from Leninism are not as important as the similarities" (Jowitt 1992: 219f.).

15. Ironically however, the evolutionary path-dependentists' susceptibility to the diversity of the cases did not always go hand in hand with their intellectual openness to the diversity of explanatory concepts, that is, to recognizing the element of truth in their

rival's argument. On the resulting conceptual problems and prediction failures see Bohle (2000).

16. This was wittingly put by Stephen Holmes: "In periods of dizzyingly rapid social change, exactly as in wartime, scholars and policy analysts are exceptionally dependent on journalists while journalists, in turn, rely intuitively on metaphors to knead and colour 'typical' anecdotes, making them chime with popular expectations and apprehensions" (Holmes 1996: 28).

17. However, I believe that most predictions failed because they were ideologically biased and were based on questionable theoretical premises, such as economic determinism, teleology, universalism, and globalism. See for a detailed analysis Greskovits 1998: chap. 1. To this list of reasons for the low survival rate of predictions, I want to add one more problem originally raised by Bunce: the improper choice of analogies. As put by Bunce, "When social scientists confront bewildering situations, they often turn to analogies in order to create a more coherent picture" (Bunce 1993: 39). Bunce argues that the more "bewildering" the given situation and the more "fuzzy" the available evidence, the greater is the chance for choosing the wrong analogy and for "misplacing stress." For the choice of the wrong analogy Bunce's main example is the application of the lessons of the Latin American democratization experience to Eastern Europe. While in general, I share Bunce's skepticism on the use of analogies in the context of postcommunism, I am more optimistic in the specific case of the Latin American democratization. I believe that this analogy provides useful points of reference and contrasts to our understanding of East European transformations provided that the right questions are asked and the analogy is not overused. I consider the passionate dispute between Bunce, and Schmitter and Karl on the appropriateness of analogies and on the tensions between "area-specific" and "generalist" approaches among the theoretically richest contributions to the transformation debate. (See Bunce 1993, 1995; Schmitter and Karl 1994.)

18. An alternative could have been to adopt a "wait and see" attitude by taking seriously that "the transitional period is quite unlike other types of social situations. It has its own logic; it requires very different assumptions and concepts than social scientists usually employ; and it is quite resistant to prediction" (Bunce and Csanádi 1992: 221).

19. Galbraith, like many other social scientists, had good reasons for self-criticism, because as late as 1984 he asserted, "That the Soviet economy has made great material progress in recent years . . . is evident both from the statistics . . . and from the general urban scene. . . . One sees it in the appearances of solid well-being of the people on the streets, the close to murderous traffic, the incredible exfoliation of apartment houses, and the general aspects of restaurants, theatres, and shops. . . . Partly, the Russian system succeeds because, in contrast with the Western industrial economies, it makes full use of its manpower" (quoted by Aslund 1991: 31).

20. "Even as late as 1979 the World Bank published a long and detailed study of Romania—the most Stalinist of the Eastern bloc. The Bank found, that from 1950 to 1975 the Romanian economy had grown faster than any other country in the world (9.8 percent per annum). The Bank attributed this startling performance to the fact that the government through its system of central planning, had control of all resources. The Bank forecast a rosy future for Romania—growing at 8.7 percent per capita to 1990. Nor was Romania an aberration. The Bank published in the same year of 1979 a most rosy history of, and prognostication for, Yugoslavia" (Walters 1992: 99f.).

21. On the supply side, the specialists in Eastern European politics, economics, and societies were joined by the students of southern European and Latin American economic reform and democratization, who, in the 1980s produced "a rich and seemingly exportable literature. . . . This was further aided by the considerable interest specialists in the above, 'southern' transitions had in the eastern European cases. To be credible theorists of democratisation, they needed to expand their focus to include the newest recruits to the democratisation process. Moreover, eastern Europe as a whole offered what could be termed an optimal research context. These regimes were similar in history, geographical location, and social structure, yet they varied in their methods of transition" (Bunce 1993: 37).

22. A straightforward formulation of such an attitude is Leszek Balcerowicz's opinion on the necessity of country-specific versus therapy-specific knowledge. He wrote, "Every country is specific in some respect, and the mere fact that a country is specific does not imply that there is any good specific strategy available to cure its basic economic ills. A Chinese and a Russian are different in some respects, but if they have tuberculosis, say, the best therapy available would be the same" (Balcerowicz 1995: 247f.).

23. "[U]topias and pathologies supply the raw material for political debates about the paradigms they express: one way of mobilizing support for a utopia is by suggesting that the only alternative is its pathology—even when the utopia is an unattainable ideal and the pathology an unrealistic threat" (Commisso et. al. 1992: 27, with reference to Robert Alford's work).

24. A far from complete list of social science terms suffering fatal decline of empirical content and specificity through their politicization in the transformation debate include *third way*, *shock therapy*, *market socialism*, *gradualism*, *neoliberalism* (Greskovits 1998).

Chapter 12

An Excursion to the Transitology Zoo: Comments on Béla Greskovits

Claus Offe

We all have known for a long time that capitalism is something that follows on precapitalist social and economic formations, as much as liberal democracy is something that follows on predemocratic regimes. But it took history until the tenth decade of the twentieth century to demonstrate that both the socioeconomic and the political features of democratic market societies can also originate from systems that thought of themselves, as well as were considered by others, as post-capitalist. What the social sciences are still in the process of coming to terms with is thus the unprecedented, as well as unanticipated and unsettling, "reversal" of history. Greskovits presents us with a somewhat idiosyncratic overview of the state of the art of understanding these shocking events. He promises to show that the same sorts of theories, or rather theoretical controversies, apply to the two transitions to democratic capitalism that occur, as it were, from two opposite directions, i.e., "regardless of whether the preceding formation was feudalism or communism."

A short metaphorical summary of the paper could be as follows. In the first part of the article, the author takes a tour to the transitology zoo. He visits four cages, all of them populated by animals that he intensely dislikes, although he keeps silent about which he dislikes most and for what reasons. In the second part, all these animals are addressed with admonitions and exhortations as to what they should do and how they must behave to become more likeable and to come closer to fulfilling what the author believes to be their missions on earth.

Is this an unfair characterization of what Greskovits is up to? Arguably it is. Isn't he right in being deeply dissatisfied with what social science transitologists have accomplished so far in terms of explanation and prediction? Living in and being a citizen of one of the postcommunist countries, isn't he also justified in being just fed up with being stared at like a fish (if not the proverbial fish soup) in an aquarium by people who pretend to know better what is happening to the local economy and society while not even knowing the language and the basics of the history of the object of their often rather recent curiosity? I am familiar (and more often than not sympathetic) with the angry responses that East Germans have to the nice and simple, largely meaningless, and often decidedly arrogant generalizations that West Germans have to offer on the causes of their plight and the appropriate remedies. Rather than being helped in meaningful ways, they feel they are made the victims of indiscreet curiosity, if not an outright breach of privacy. After all, it is "their" society that is at stake, and that should not be casually subsumed under a nonentity labeled "postcommunism." To understand it, you must have grown up with its specificities, complexities, and ambiguities.

But these understandable sentiments of indignation and anger do not justify, in my judgment, the veritable barrage of accusations that the author fires against the subdiscipline of postcommunist transitology. "Transitology has not brought novel ideas to the surface. . . . [it] is characterized by the exaggerated dominance of preconception, by the limited attention paid to evidence and details . . . there is no indication of an emerging consensus. . . . Social scientists [fail to take] cognizance of their opponents . . . [they are involved in a] conceptual trench-war . . . [they suffer from] the difficulty of perceiving diversity and dialectical processes . . . show a lack of interest in diversity [and a] bias for generalization. . . . A number of researchers are newcomers [who] neither know the history of the countries under study nor do they speak their language. . . . [The] intellectual arsenal of transitology reveals serious shortcomings . . . [they act] irresponsibl[y by] stubbornly advocat[ing] negative visions even if their gloomy prophecies do not materialize . . . [they wish] to impress the general public . . . [show] eagerness to engage in prognoses making and [willingly cater to] an intensive need for all kind of forecasts. . . . [Social scientists practice] resistance to accepting the element of truth in alternative concepts . . . many social scientists [are] pushed towards active participation in the process of transformation, [for which] adviserism and direct political involvement [they pay the price of] negative effects on scholarly quality. [All of which amounts to] a hindrance to open-minded, complex, and reliable conceptualization. [Instead,] they provide mere catchwords of political discourse." And so on.

Some of the heroic, aristocratic, and tragic attitude with which social science can be conducted resonates in these complaints. It reminds one of Max Weber's dictum: "Endlessly rolls the unfathomable river of events towards eternity." Yes, maybe; although even Weber believed in the possibility of bringing some conceptual order to the chaos of phenomena through the use of ideal types and conceptual distinction. But this is just one way to conduct social science, as well as just one view of social reality. And if our author believes it is the only legitimate one, it is necessary to demonstrate his claim with evidence and argument rather than by slandering practitioners of transition studies. Sure enough, we can always give up by concluding that social science is bound to live beyond its intellectual means and wait for the findings of future historians. But it sometimes happens, though not very often, that this truly reactionary stance is proved wrong by one or the other good and well-supported ideas that even social scientists come up with. Greskovits's litany cannot just be the result of anger and indignation of the kind I have alluded to. It is also not just an instance of the game of intellectuals accusing other intellectuals of being just intellectuals, with all their vanities, dishonesties, and tendencies to live beyond their means. In my reading of this lengthy diatribe that is driven by coarse psychological insinuation, Greskovits wants to promote a type of social science research characterized by heroic detachment from social and political realities, a tragic sense of its own incapability for practical matters, and an empiricist and historicist doubt of the possibility of reasonable judgment.

Had the author lived up to his own plea for "embracing complexity" and differentiated judgment, he might well have served his intended argument by pointing out differences as to who sins more and who less, instead of his condemnations of an entire field of social science research. He might also have taken cognizance of the fact that today, as early as some ten years after the end of Communism, nobody in the field would speak anymore in general terms about "postcommunism," but instead speaks of specific countries, phases of the transition process, policy areas, and institutional sectors. Similarly, nobody enjoying any recognition in the field would speak today just of "Leninist" legacies. Instead, s/he speaks of specific historical conditions, elites, mentalities, and cultural traditions that facilitate and constrain certain aspects of the development of specific countries. I cannot think of a single academic text to which, in fair judgment, all the accusations that Greskovits puts forward against the entire field of research even remotely apply. At least, he does not point to any single one example in his (highly selective) list of references that would support his point. Could it be that the charge of "mindless generalization" that, according to our author, applies to the field of transition studies is itself supported by fabricated evidence and is no more than empty rhetoric?

One of the many verdicts that Greskovits brings forward claims that "it is irresponsible to stubbornly advocate negative visions even if their gloomy prophecies do not materialize." Alas, there is no reference to anyone to whom this might apply. Of course not. But why should this be "irresponsible"? Because "forecasts may prove to be self-fulfilling." Sure enough, but they might also be self-disconfirming because they perform the useful function of warnings. For instance, Karl Marx might very well have been proved correct by history concerning his "doomsday forecasts" about the fate of capitalism—if only he had not published them and helped a powerful social and political movement come into being which operated on the basis of his theory.

Coming to the zoo itself, rather than the devastating judgment that the author has to pass on its animals, I am less impressed than the author with his rigid two-by-two logic that helps him to put the animals into cages. Borrowing generously from Albert Hirschman, Greskovits proposes in essence that social change can be driven by either historical legacies or present decisions, and that the subsequent outcome can either be of the nature intended and desired or otherwise. Fair enough. But it takes an Albert Hirschman and all the subtlety and erudition of an author like him to make compelling sense out of this schematic taxonomy. This is what Greskovits often fails to provide. For instance, he passes in silence over his predictable failure to provide any illustration for the "communist assets" thesis that he still needs to stick to his somewhat doctrinaire rectangular scheme. For whatever legacies of the state socialist past may have helped to assist in the process of economic or political transformation of state-socialist societies, nobody would be inclined to label them "communist." (Actually, the closest thing that comes to mind as fitting this cell of the schema is the following idea that a works council member of an East German plant mentioned to me in an interview: "I understand," he said, "that what is required of workers in the new 'Post-Fordist' capitalism of flexible specialization is the ability to adjust to unpredictable situations and to constantly improvise in the best interest of production going on smoothly and efficiently. Given the chaotic management of the labor process and procurement of supplies that was characteristic of state socialist production, we East German workers are particularly well trained in the art of working flexibly. Isn't that a valuable asset we have to offer?" If that training in flexibility is a "Communist legacy," so be it. Tragically for the person interviewed, this point of view is rarely appreciated by the new capitalist employers.)

Finally, there may be a point in comparing the three types of potential macro social change occurring in modern(izing) societies: the transition from feudalism to capitalism, from capitalism to socialism, and from communism to capitalism. Of course, one should make (and a complexity-aware author such as Greskovits should a fortiori be expected to make) the point that it is rather meaningless to dwell on the level of abstraction where the three "-isms" each appear in the singular, rather than as typological shorthand for a myriad of subspecies. But the distinction that is being missed, it appears to me, by the routine of processing all three transitions through the rigid machinery of the two-by-two logic is this: When people made the transition from "feudalism" to "capitalism," as well as when they attempted to make the transition from "capitalism" to "socialism," they were daringly sailing uncharted seas. They had a program, a "vehicle" of principles and demands, but could not have any certainty as to where they would eventually land. As Albert Hirschman has shown in *The Passions and the Interests* (1977), the early arguments for capitalism were very different from what were later seen as the actual accomplishments and essence of capitalism, namely, economic growth, efficiency, and prosperity. This is fundamentally different in the case of the transition from communism to capitalism. This transition is not a "revolution," but, as Habermas (1990) has argued, a project to "catch-up" with "the West." In contrast to the earlier transitions, people know very well and from empirical evidence where they want to go (namely, to "Europe"), but just don't know how to get there. So far, the evidence on the accomplishments of this journey is so mixed that all four of the trajectories that Greskovits juxtaposes in stereotyped simplicity do appear to find some support in some of the cases, at least for some of the time.

In conclusion, a word on "international constraints," which the author repeatedly refers to in a slightly irritating tone, perhaps because such "hostile externally imposed constraints" were the routine explanation offered by the proponents of the old regime for the slow economic progress of state socialism. Be this as it may, let me suggest that the term *constraint* is simply a misnomer if it comes to the role of external actors in the transition process from state socialism. I believe it is more accurate to speak of "externally contributed, though highly unevenly distributed, facilitating conditions and resources" that explain more of the progress made, and the progress that has failed to be made, in the dynamics of "catching up" than any of the alternative mechanisms on which Greskovits remains fixated.

Chapter 13

Commentary on Béla Greskovits, "The Path-Dependence of Transitology"

Valerie Bunce

In the brief span of one chapter, Béla Greskovits has managed to impose analytical order on the spirited and seemingly disparate debates surrounding postcommunist pathways; to demonstrate the historical resonance, if not repetition of these schools of thinking, despite the changing object of study (or postcommunism versus the rise of capitalism); and to explain why these positions, four in all, remain the durable template for understanding regime transitions, whenever they occur and in whatever direction. This is, in short, a rich and provocative discussion that marries philosophy of social science and contemporary political-economic debates, the historical analysis of socialism and capitalism, and the ongoing transition from the former to the latter.

I find his observations compelling. What I offer in this commentary is less a fundamental challenge to these arguments than some "decorative" points. Let me turn, first, to his explications of the four theorems. With respect to the free-market thesis, I would add three other considerations. One is the common observation that capitalism and democracy are based on similar underlying principles and are, therefore, compatible. For example, just as democracy rests on competition and rule of law, so capitalism rests on competition and secure property rights. Thus, they combine—and depend for their effectiveness—on uncertain outcomes and certain procedures. A second consideration is the argument that democracy makes a rapid transition to capitalism possible, despite short-term economic costs, because: (1) regime legitimacy promotes tolerance of unpopular policies and thereby lengthens political horizons, and; (2) democratic decision-making creates a larger band of shared responsibility. Finally, while it is true that many see a fast transition to capitalism as preferable in terms of both democracy and capitalism, it is also true that this introduces a "z" axis into the analysis. Speed, I would submit, is a third consideration, aside from what Greskovits refers to as a past versus a future orientation, positive versus negative predictions.

The impossibility theorem also contains some additional arguments. One asks us to draw the causal arrow in the other direction. Thus, rapid democratization, it has been suggested, can slow the transition to capitalism and compromise it in ways that deepen and prolong the economic recession. However, here I must bring in some empirical considerations. What we have seen over the course of the first decade of postsocialism is that the impossibility theorem has much less to recommend it than the free-market thesis. However, why that is the case—or why democratization and economic reform are so highly correlated, even when various controls are introduced into the analysis—is still quite debatable. My own sense is that one possibility in particular needs to be entertained. Fast democratization reflects a sizable public consensus that rejects state socialism and that embraces, as a result, its "other"—or democracy and capitalism. This is one reason why the outcome of the first competitive election predicts so well the subsequent course of democratization and economic reform. Large mandates for liberal parties, in short, have one advantage: they enable both democratization and a transition to capitalism. In this sense, mandate shapes both regime transitions rather than the assumption that movement in one arena shapes movement in another.

I have little to add, however, to his discussion of the Leninist legacy. Here, I merely observe that this line of thinking was more prominent early in the transitional experience than later. This is especially the case given the obvious point that about one-third of the region is securely in both the democratic and capitalist columns. Moreover, there are few surprises here, since most of us expected Slovenia, Poland, Hungary, the Czech Republic, and the Baltic states to be best positioned to pursue a liberal agenda. But some humility is in order. We did not expect consolidation of liberal orders in a mere decade, even under these optimal conditions.

The final category, Communist assets, reminds us of one important issue. If these revolutions did not kill people and if a successful transition from dictatorship to democracy, here as elsewhere, requires that the former authoritarians are neutralized, divided, or co-opted, then we can begin to see why the communist-assets thesis must be given some attention. This is especially the case where liberal mandates were large and Communist parties long populated by reformers.

Allow me to switch my concerns now to the puzzle Greskovits addresses in the final third of his paper: the entrenched analytical habits—if not lack of originality—of social scientists. Here, he makes a number of illuminating points. However, I would like to tack on several additional observations. One is the pronounced tendency of social scientists to treat the cases they know best as typical and, therefore, amenable to generalizations that speak beyond those specific cases. For example, is it accidental that Ken Jowitt, a specialist on Romania and someone with considerable intellectual capital invested in state socialism, would be the prime pusher of the Leninist legacy? More generally, the point is that each argument, to paraphrase A. O. Hirschman, has its hour and its place of truth.

A second influence is, simply, the constraints of time. It is hard to know very much about more than a few countries, especially when they have become in effect moving targets. In this sense, one can be nostalgic for the Brezhnev era—or the years of stagnation. If time is constraining, so are the concepts social scientists use. The fact is that most of our concepts are fuzzy. At the same time, one goal we have as social scientists is to streamline social reality to render it more tractable. But the costs of fuzzy concepts and analytical simplification are endless and unoriginal debates that are all too often exercises in parallel intellectual play. In this way, "visions" allow us to avoid both diversity and verification.

Let me conclude by addressing the pressure to predict—which Greskovits rightly emphasizes. Here, I would suggest that the drive to predict is especially influential in postcommunist studies for three reasons. First, this was precisely the scholarly culture of communist studies. Second, as we learned during the Communist era, the more deficient or ambiguous the data, the greater the interest in—and ease of—predicting the future as opposed to the laborious task of mapping the present. Finally, the grander the vision of elites and international advisors and the more this speaks to a "radiant" or "regressive" future, the more the propensity to outline future scenarios. Implied in all this is, of course, important parallels between how Communism was tracked and analyzed and how its successor has been tracked and analyzed.

Finally, it is true that failures of prediction often have the perverse consequences of encouraging further rounds of prediction—as opposed to questioning the enterprise of prediction itself. However, the best example of this may not be the collapse of Communism—which was predicted, after all, by both the extreme right in the West and by all those scholars who documented the growing and conjoined economic and political crises of the Communist world. Rather, the best example comes from international relations. No one predicted the end of the Cold War, but many scholars were quite willing to predict what followed. What happened, therefore, was an odd psychological dynamic—once burned, twice assertive. And the predictions of these specialists in international politics, it is interesting to note, fit quite well into the two-by-two table constructed by Béla Greskovits. Thus, there are optimists and pessimists, futurists and "pastists." International visions are no more original, it seems, than their domestic counterparts.

References

Agnew, J. 1994. "The Territorial Trap: The Geographical Assumptions of International Relations Theory." *Review of International Political Economy* 1 (1): 53–80.

Alexander, J. C. 1982. *Theoretical Logic in Sociology*, vol. 1. Berkeley, Calif.: University of California Press.

———. 1992. "Shaky Foundations." *Theory and Society* 21 (2): 203–17.

———. 1994. "Modern, Anti, Post and Neo: How Social Theories Have Tried to Understand the 'New World' of 'Our Time.'" *Zeitschrift für Soziologie* 23 (3): 165–97.

Almond, G. A. 1995. "The Record of Soviet Studies." In *Beyond Soviet Studies*, ed. D. Orlovsky. Baltimore: Johns Hopkins University Press, 193–97.

Alter, P. 1985. *Nationalismus*. Frankfurt/M: Suhrkamp.

Altvater, E. 1998. "Theoretical Deliberations on Time and Space in Postcommunist Transformation." *Regional Studies* 32 (7): 591–606.

Amato, G., and J. Batt (eds.). 1999. *Final Report of the Reflection Group on the Long-Term Implications of EU Enlargement: The Nature of the New Border*. European University Institute, Robert Schuman Centre of Advanced Studies, Florence.

Amsden, A., J. Kochanowicz, and L. Taylor. 1994. *The Market Meets Its Match: Restructuring the Economies of Eastern Europe*. Cambridge, Mass., and London: Harvard University Press.

Anderson, B. 1983. *Imagined Communities*. London: Verso.

Aniol, W., T. Byrne, and E. Iankova. 1997. "Poland: Return to Europe." In *Tamed Power: Germany and Europe*, ed. P. J. Katzenstein. Ithaca, N.Y.: Cornell University Press, 39–100.

Apostolou, A., and S. Safaev. 1997. "Is the Uzbek Model Working?" *Transitions* 4 (2): 98–101.

Armstrong, D. 1998. "Globalization and the Social State." *Review of International Studies* 24 (4): 461–78.

Armstrong, J. 1982. *Nations before Nationalism*. Chapel Hill, N.C.: University of North Carolina Press.

Arrow, K. J. 1975. "Gifts and Exchanges." In *Altruism, Morality and Economic Theory,* ed. E. S. Phelps. New York: Russell Sage Foundation, 13–28.

———. 1995. Foreword to *Privatization, Conversion and Enterprise Reform in Russia,* ed M. McFaul and T. Perlmutter. Boulder, Colo.: Westview, vii–viii.

Ash, T. G. 1993. *The Polish Revolution: Solidarity.* Oxford: Granta Books.

Aslund, A. 1991. "Principles of Privatisation." In *Systemic Change and Stabilisation in Eastern Europe,* ed. L. Csaba. Aldershot and Brookfield: Dartmouth, 17–31.

———. 1992. "Russia's Road from Communism." *Daedalus* 121 (2): 77–95.

———. 1995. *How Russia Became a Market Economy.* Washington, D.C.: Brookings.

———. 1996. "Reform vs. 'Rent-Seeking' in Russia's Economic Transformation." *Transition* 2 (2): 12–6.

———. 1999. "Why Has Russia's Economic Transformation Been So Arduous?" Paper Prepared for the Annual World Bank Conference on Development Economics, 28–30 April, Washington, D.C.

Aslund, A., P. Boone, and S. Johnson. 1996. "How to Stabilize: Lessons from Post-communist Countries." Brooking Papers on Economic Activity (1): 217–313.

Axelrod, R. 1988. *The Problem of Cooperation.* Fairfax, Va.: George Mason University Press.

Baer, H. L., and C. W. Gray. 1996. "Debt as a Control Device in Transitional Economies: The Experiences of Hungary and Poland." In *Corporate Governance in Central Europe and Russia. Vol. 1: Banks, Funds, and Foreign Investors,* ed. by R. Frydman, C. W. Gray and A. Rapaczynski. Budapest, London, and New York: CEU Press, 68–110.

Baglione, L. A., and C. Clark. 1997. "A Tale of Two Metallurgical Enterprises: Marketization and the Social Contract in Russian Industry." *Communist and Post-Communist Studies* 30 (2): 153–81.

Bagnasco, A. 1999. "Teoria del capitale sociale e '*political economy*' comparata." *Stato e Mercato* 57: 351–71.

Bailey, R. E. 1994. "A Voyage Around Economics." *Economic Journal* 104 (3): 660–77.

Balakrishnan, G. (ed.). 1996. *Mapping the Nation.* London: Verso.

Balcerowicz, L. 1995. *Socialism, Capitalism, Transformation.* London and Budapest: CEU Press.

Banfield, E. 1958. *The Moral Basis of a Backward Society.* Glencoe, Ill.: Free Press.

Bara, Z., and K. Szabó (eds.). 2000. *Gazdasági intézmények, országok, rendszerek. (Economic institutions, countries, systems).* Budapest: Aula Publ. Co.

Barber, W. 1995. "Chile con Chicago." *Journal of Economic Literature* 33 (4): 1941–49.

———. 1997. "Reconfigurations in American Academic Economics." *Daedalus* 126 (1): 87–103.

Barkey, K., and M. Hagen (eds.). 1997. *After Empire: Multi-ethnic Empires and Nation-building.* Boulder, Colo.: Westview.

Barnes, S. H., and J. Simon (eds.). 1998. *The Postcommunist Citizen.* Budapest: Erasmus Foundation.

Barro, R. 1997. *Determinants of Economic Growth: A Cross-country Empirical Study.* Cambridge, Mass., and London: MIT Press.

Bartlett, D. L. 1997. *The Political Economy of Dual Transitions: Market Reform and Democratization in Hungary.* Ann Arbor, Mich.: University of Michigan Press.

Baumol, W. J. 2000. "What Marshall Didn't Know: On the Twentieth Century's Contributions to Economics." *Quarterly Journal of Economics* 115 (1): 1–44.

Beattie, A. 2000. "Strains in Bank's Inclusive Model." *Financial Times*, 16 June.

Bekker, A. 1997. "Chubais's Financial Balancing Act." *Moskovskiye novosti*, 9-16 November.

Bence, G. and S. M. Lipset. 1994. "Anticipations of the Failure of Communism." *Theory and Society* 23 (2): 169–210.

Berdyaev, N. A. 1964. *The Origin of Russian Communism*. Ann Arbor, Mich.: University of Michigan Press.

Berend, I. 1986. "The Historical Evolution of Eastern Europe as a Region." *International Organization* 40 (2): 329–46.

———. 1999. *Central and Eastern Europe 1944-1993: Detour from the Periphery to the Periphery*. Cambridge: Cambridge University Press.

Berend, I., and G. Ranki. 1977. *East Central Europe in the 19th and 20th Centuries*. Budapest: Akademiai Kiad6.

Bhagwati, J. 1998. "The Capital Myth." *Foreign Affairs* 77 (3): 7–12.

———. 1999. "Growth Is not a Passive 'Trickle-down' Strategy." *Financial Times*, 27 September.

———. 2000. "Sustained Growth Central in Fight against Poverty." *Financial Times*, 22 June.

Bigsten, A., P. Collier et al. 1998. *Contract Flexibility and Conflict Resolution: Evidence from African Manufacturing*. Mimeo. Washington, D.C.: World Bank.

Birkland, T. 1997. *After Disaster: Agenda Setting, Public Policy, and Focusing Events*. Washington, D.C.: Georgetown University Press.

Blalock, H. M. 1984. *Basic Dilemmas in the Social Sciences*. Beverly Hills, Calif.: Sage.

Blanchard, O., M. Boycko, M. Dabrowski, R. Dornbusch, R. Layard and A. Shleifer. 1993. *Post-Communist Reform: Pain and Progress*. Cambridge, Mass., and London: MIT Press.

Blanchard, O., R. Dornbusch, P. Krugman, R. Layard and L. Summers. 1991. *Reform in Eastern Europe*. Cambridge, Mass., and London: MIT Press.

Blasi, J., M. Kroumova and D. Kruse. 1996. *Kremlin Capitalism: The Privatization of the Russian Economy*. Ithaca, N.Y.: Cornell University Press.

Blažek, J. 1997. "The Czech Republic on its Way Towards West European Structures." *European Spatial Research and Policy* 4 (1): 37–63.

Blažek, J., and S. Boeckhout. 2000. "Regional Policy in the Czech Republic and the EU Accession." In *Transition, Cohesion, and Regional Policy in Central and Eastern Europe*, ed. by J. Bachtler, R. Downes and G. Gorzelak. Aldershot: Ashgate.

Bohle, D. 1997. "Internationalisation and Institutional Fragmentation: The Case of the Polish Transport Industry." Paper Presented at the 4th Workshop on "Institution Building in the Transformation of Central and Eastern European Societies," 5–7 December, Budapest.

———. 2000. "Internationalisation: An Issue Neglected in the Path-Dependency Approach to Post-communist Transformation." In *Democratic and Capitalist Transitions in Eastern Europe: Lessons for the Social Sciences*, ed. by Michel Dobry. Dordrecht, Boston, and London: Kluwer, 235–61.

Boisot, M. 1994. *East-West Business Collaboration: The Challenge of Governance in*

Post-Socialist Enterprise. London: Routledge.

Boisot, M., and J. Child. 1988. "The Iron Law of Fiefs: Bureaucratic Failure and the Problem of Governance in the Chinese Economic Reform." *Administrative Science Quarterly* 33 (4): 507–27.

Bolle, F. 1998. "Rewarding Trust: An Experimental Study." *Theory and Decision* 45 (1): 85–100.

Bönker, F. 1994. "External Determinants of the Patterns and Outcomes of East European Transitions." *Emergo* 1 (1): 34–54.

———. 2002. *The Political Economy of Fiscal Reform in Eastern Europe: A Comparative Analysis of Hungary, Poland and the Czech Republic*. Cheltenham, UK and Northampton, Mass.: Elgar, forthcoming.

Böröcz, J. 2000. "The Fox and the Raven: The European Union and Hungary Renegotiate the Margins of 'Europe.'" *Comparative Studies in Society and History* 42 (4): 847–75.

Borowik, I. 1998. "Kirchlichkeit und private Religiosität in Polen." In *Religiöser Wandel in den postkommunistischen Ländern Ost- und Mitteleuropas*, ed. D. Pollack, I Borowik, and W. Jagodzinski. Würzburg: Ergon, 256–65.

Bresser Pereira, L. C. 1993. "Economic Reforms and Economic Growth: Efficiency and Politics in Latin America." In *Economic Reforms in New Democracies: A Social Democratic Approach*, ed. L. C. Pereira Bresser, J. M. Maravall, and A. Przeworski. Cambridge: Cambridge University Press, 15–76.

Breuilly, J. (ed.). 1992. *The State of Germany: The National Idea in the Making, Unmaking and Remaking of a Modern Nation-State*. London: Longman.

Brie, M. 1996. "The Constitutional Process in Eastern Europe: Preemptive and Reactive Institution Building." Paper Presented at the International Conference on Socio-Economics, 12–14 July, Geneva.

Brown, T. F. 1997. "Ideological Hegemony and Global Governance." *Journal of World-Systems Research* 3 (2): 250–58.

Brubaker, R. 1996. *Nationalism Reframed*. Cambridge: Cambridge University Press.

Brus, W., 1992. "From Revisionism to Pragmatism: Sketches to a Self-Portrait of a 'Reform Economist.'" In *Reform and Transformation in Eastern Europe: Soviet-type Economics on the Threshold of Change*, ed. J. M. Kovács and M. Tardos. London and New York: Routledge, 136–42.

Brus, W., and K. Laski. 1991. *From Marx to the Market: Socialism in Search of an Economic System*. Oxford: Clarendon Press.

Bruszt, L. 1992. "Transformative Politics: Social Costs and Social Peace in East Central Europe." *East European Politics and Societies* 6 (1): 55–72.

———. 1993. *Why on Earth Would Eastern Europeans Support Capitalism? Democracy, Capitalism and Public Opinion*. Mimeo. Budapest: Central European University.

Bruszt, L., and D. Stark. 1994. "Paths of Extrication and Possibilities of Transformation." In *Transition to Capitalism? The Communist Legacy in Eastern Europe*, ed. J. M. Kovács. New Brunswick and London: Transaction Publishers, 59–61.

Brym, R. J. 1996. "The Ethic of Self-Reliance and the Spirit of Capitalism in Russia." *International Sociology* 11 (4): 409–26.

Bunce, V. 1993. "Leaving Socialism: A 'Transition to Democracy'?" *Contention* 3 (1): 36–47.

———. 1995. "Should Transitologists Be Grounded?" *Slavic Review* 54 (1): 111–27.

———. 1997. "The Return of the Left and the Future of Democracy in Central and Eastern Europe." Paper Presented at the Fourth Workshop on "Institution Building in the Transformation of Central and Eastern European Societies," 5–7 December, Budapest.

Bunce, V., and M. Csanádi. 1992. "A Systematic Analysis of a Non-System: Post-Communism in Eastern Europe." In *Flying Blind: Emerging Democracies in East-Central Europe,* ed. Gy. Szoboszlai. Budapest: Hungarian Political Science Association, 204–26.

Bunge, M. 1996. *Finding Philosophy in Social Science.* New Haven, Conn.: Yale University Press.

———. 1997. "Mechanism and Explanation." *Philosophy of the Social Sciences* 27 (4): 410–65.

———. 1998. *Social Science under Debate*. Toronto: University of Toronto Press.

Burawoy, M. 1996. "The State and Economic Involution: Russia Through a China Lens." *World Development* 24 (6): 1105–17.

Burawoy, M., and K. Hendley. 1992. "Between Perestroika and Privatisation: Divided Strategies and Political Crisis in a Soviet Enterprise." *Soviet Studies* 44 (3): 371–402.

Burawoy, M., and P. Krotov. 1992. "The Soviet Transition from Socialism to Capitalism: Worker Control and Economic Bargaining in the Wood Industry." *American Sociological Review* 57 (1): 16–38.

———. 1993. "The Economic Basis of Russia's Political Crisis." *New Left Review* 198: 49–69.

Burki, J., and G. E. Perry. 1998. *Beyond the Washington Consensus: Institutions Matter.* Washington, D.C.: World Bank.

Calhoun, C. 1997. *Nationalism.* Minneapolis: University of Minnesota Press.

Camdessus, M. 1994. "Supporting Transition in Central and Eastern Europe: An Assessment and Lessons from the IMF's Five Years' Experience." Second Annual Francisco Fernández Ordóñez Address, 21 December, Madrid.

Campbell, J. 1993. "Institutional Theory and the Influence of Foreign Actors on Reform in Capitalist and Post-Socialist Societies." In *Institutional Frameworks of Market Economies,* ed. J. Hausner, B. Jessop, and K. Nielsen. Aldershot: Avebury, 45–67.

Caporaso, J. A. 1997. "Across the Great Divide: Integrating Comparative and International Politics." *International Studies Quarterly* 41 (4): 563–92.

Caprio, G., and P. Honohan. 1999. "Restoring Bank Stability: Beyond Supervised Capital Requirements." *Journal of Economic Pespectives* 13 (4): 43–64.

Carothers, T. 1999. *Aiding Democracy Abroad: The Learning Curve.* Washington, D.C.: The Carnegie Endowment.

Casanova, J. 1994. *Public Religions in the Modern World.* Chicago: University of Chicago Press.

———. 1998. "Ethno-linguistic and Religious Pluralism and Democratic Construction in Ukraine." In *Post-Soviet Political Order,* ed. B. R. Rubin and J. Snyder. London: Routledge, 81–103.

Cassel, D., and S. Rauhut. 1998. "Soziale Marktwirtschaft: eine wirtschaftspolitische Konzeption auf dem Prüfstand." In *50 Jahre Soziale Marktwirtschaft,* ed. D. Cassel. Stuttgart: Lucius und Lucius, 4–28.

Chase-Dunn, C. 1998. *Global Formation: Structures of the World Economy*. Lanham, Md.: Rowman & Littlefield.

Chavance, B. 1994. *The Transformation of the Communist System*. Boulder, Colo.: Westview.

Chavance, B., and E. Magnin. 1997. "Emergence of Path-dependent Mixed Economies in Central Europe." In *Beyond Market and Hierarchy: Interactive Government and Social Complexity*, ed. A. Ash and J. Hausner. Cheltenham: Elgar, 196–232.

Chilton, P. 1995. "Mechanics of Change: Social Movements, Transnational Coalitions, and the Transformation Processes in Eastern Europe." In *Bringing Transnational Relations Back. Non-state Actors, Domestic Structures and International Institutions*, ed. T. Risse-Kappen. Cambridge: Cambridge University Press.

Chirot, D. 1995. "National Liberations and Nationalist Nightmares: The Consequences of the End of Empires in the Twentieth Century." In *Markets, States, and Democracy: The Political Economy of Post-Communist Transformation*, ed. B. Crawford. Boulder, Colo.: Westview, 43–68.

Clague, C. 1993. "Rule Obedience, Organizational Loyalty, and Economic Development." *Journal of Institutional and Theoretical Economics* 149 (2): 393–414.

Clague, C., and G. C. Rausser. 1992. *The Emergence of Market Economies in Eastern Europe*. Cambridge: Blackwell.

Clarke, S. (ed.). 1996. *The Russian Enterprise in Transition: Case Studies*. Cheltenham: Elgar.

Clarke, S., and J. Holmes. 2000. *Poverty in Transition*. Final Report. Warwick.

Coase, R. 1998. "The New Institutional Economics." *American Economic Review* 88 (2): 72–74.

Codagnone, C. 1995. "New Entrepreneurs: Continuity or Change in Russian Economy and Society." In *Social Change and Modernization. Lessons from Eastern Europe*, ed. B. Grancelli. Berlin and New York: de Gruyter, 63–82.

Cohen, S. F. 1999. "Russian Studies without Russia." *Post-Soviet Affairs* 15 (1): 37-55.

Colander, D. 2000. "New Millennium Economics: How Did It Get This Way and What Way Is It?" *Journal of Economic Perspectives* 14 (1): 121–32.

Coleman, J. 1988. "Social Capital in the Creation of Human Capital." *American Journal of Sociology* 94: 95–121.

———. 1990. *Foundations of Social Theory*. Cambridge, Mass.: Belknap.

Coleman, J., and T. Fararo (eds.). 1992. *Rational Choice Theory. Advocacy and Critique*. London: Sage.

Comisso, E. 1998. "'Implicit' Development Strategies in Central East Europe and Cross-National Production Networks." Berkeley Roundtable on the International Economy, Working Paper 129.

Comisso, E., S. Dubb, and J. McTigue. 1992. "The Illusion of Populism in Latin America and East Central Europe." In *Flying Blind: Emerging Democracies in East-Central Europe*, ed. Gy. Szoboszlai. Budapest: Hungarian Political Science Association, 27–58.

Cortell, A. P., and S. Peterson. 1998. "Explaining Domestic Structural Change: Windows of Opportunity, Political Entrepreneurs, and Institutional Capacity." Paper Prepared for the Annual Convention of the American Political Science Association, 3–6 September, Boston.

Cottarelli, C., and G. Szapáry (eds.). 1998. *Moderate Inflation*. Washington, D.C. and Budapest: IMF and National Bank of Hungary.

Cox, C. et al. (eds.). 2000. "Russia's Road to Corruption. How the Clinton Administration Exported Government Instead of Free Enterprise and Failed the Russian People." Washington, D.C.: U.S. House of Representatives, 106th Cong., September.

Cox, R. 1991. "'Real Socialism' in Historical Perspective." *Socialist Register* 27.

———. 1993. "Creating Welfare States in Czechoslovakia and Hungary: Why Policymakers Borrow Ideas from the West." *Government and Policy* 11, 349–64.

Crawford, B. 1995. "Post-Communist Political Economy: A Framework for the Analysis of Reform." In *Markets, States and Democracy: The Political Economy of Post-Communist Transformation,* ed. B. Crawford. Boulder, Colo., San Francisco, and Oxford: Westview, 3–42.

———. 1998. "Mediating Globalization and Social Integration in Post-Communist Societies: A Comparison of Yugoslavia and Bulgaria." Paper Prepared for the Annual Convention of the American Political Science Association, 3–6 September, Boston.

———. (ed.). 1995. *Markets, States, and Democracy. The Political Economy of Post-Communist Transformation*. Boulder, Colo.: Westview.

Crawford, B., and A. Lijphart. 1995. "Explaining Political and Economic Change in Post-Communist Central and Eastern Europe: Old Legacies, New Institutions, Hegemonic Norms, and International Pressures." *Comparative Political Studies* 28 (2): 171–99.

———. 1997. "Old Legacies, New Institutions: Explaining Political and Economic Trajectories in Post-Communist Regimes." In *Liberalisation and Leninist Legacies: Comparative Perspectives on Democratic Transitions,* ed. B. Crawford and A. Lijphart. Research Series No. 96. Berkeley: University of California at Berkeley, 1–40.

Csaba, L. 1995. Privatisation and Distribution in Central and Eastern Europe: Theory from Evidence. Kopint-Datorg, Discussion Paper No. 32, Budapest.

———. 1996. "The Political Economy of the Reform Strategy: China and Eastern Europe Compared." *Communist Economies and Economic Transformation* 8 (1): 53–66.

———. 2001. "Convergence and Divergence in Transition and Integration." In *Zehn Jahre Wende in Osteuropa: Ergebnisse und Perspektiven ins 21te Jahrhundert,* ed. K. Maenicke. Frankfurt/M. et al.: Lang.

Curtiss, J. S. 1960. *Church and State in the Late Tsarist Empire*. New York: Columbia University Press.

Cyr, D. J. 1997 "Culture and Control: The Tale of East-West Joint Ventures." *Management International Review* 37: 127–45.

Dabrowski, M., S. Gomulka, and J. Rostowski. 2000. *Whence Reform? A Critique of the Stiglitz Perspective.* Mimeo. CASE, Warsaw.

Dann, O. 1993. *Nation und Nationalismus in Deutschland 1770-1990*. München: Beck.

Davies, N. 1982. *God's Playground: A History of Poland*. Oxford: Clarendon.

Dawisha, K. (ed.). 1997. *The International Dimension of Post-Communist Transitions in Russia and the New States of Eurasia*. Armonk, N.Y.: M.E. Sharpe.

Dawisha, K., and B. Parrot (eds.). 1997a. *Democratic Changes and Authoritarian Reactions in Russia, Ukraine, Belarus, and Moldavia*. Cambridge: Cambridge University Press.

——— (eds.). 1997b. *The Consolidation of Democracy in East-Central Europe*. Cambridge: Cambridge University Press.
de Long, B. J. 2000. "The Triumph of Monetarism?" *Journal of Economic Perspectives* 14, 1: 83–94.
De Vries, M. G. 1986. *The IMF in a Changing World 1945-1985*. Washington, D.C.: IMF.
Deacon, B., and M. Hulse. 1997. "The Making of Post-communist Social Policy: The Role of International Agencies." *Journal of Social Policy* 26 (1): 43–62.
Deacon, B., with M. Hulse and P. Stubbs. 1997. *Global Social Policy: International Organisations and the Future of Welfare*. New York: Sage.
Debreu, G. 1959. *Theory of Value*. New York: Wiley.
Deppe, R., and M. Tatur (eds.). 1996. *Ökonomische Transformation und gewerkschaftliche Politik. Umbruchsprozesse in Polen und Ungarn auf Branchenebene*. Münster: Westfälisches Dampfboot.
———. 1995. "Transformationssequenzen und Gewerkschaftskonstell-ationen in Polen und Ungarn." *Mitteilungen des Instituts für Sozialforschung* 6: 5–34.
Desai, R., and I. Goldberg. 2000. "Stakeholders, Governance, and the Russian Enterprise Dilemma." *Finance & Development* 37 (2): 14–18.
Dessler, D. 1989. "What's at Stake in the Agent-Structure Debate?" *International Organization* 43 (3): 441–73.
Deutsch, K. W. 1953. *Nationalism and Social Communication*. Cambridge, Mass.: MIT Press.
Dewatripont, M., and G. Roland. 1994. "Eastern Europe: Less Haste, More Speed." *European Economic Perspectives* (3): 1-3.
Diamond, L. 1994. "Toward Democratic Consolidation." *Journal of Democracy* 5 (3): 4–17.
———. 1996. "Is the Third Wave Over?" *Journal of Democracy* 7 (3): 20–37.
Diewald, M., and K.-U. Meyer (eds.). 1996. *Zwischenbilanz der Wiedervereinigung*. Opladen: Leske + Budrich.
Dilla, H. 1999. "Comrades and Investors: The Uncertain Transition in Cuba." In *Global Capitalism versus Democracy. Socialist Register 1999*, ed. L. Panitch and C. Leys. New York: Monthly Review Press.
DiMaggio, P., and W. Powell. 1991. "The Iron Cage Revisited: Institutional Isomorphism and Collective Rationality in Organizational Fields." In *The New Institutionalism in Organizational Analysis*, ed. W. Powell and P. DiMaggio. Chicago and London: University of Chicago Press, 63–82.
Dimitrov, M., W. Andreff, and L. Csaba (eds.). 1999. *Economies in Transition and the Varieties of Capitalism*. Sofia: Gorex Press.
Dinello-Evdokina, N. 1998. "Forms of Capital: The Case of Russian Bankers." *International Sociology* 13 (3): 291–310.
Dinkic, M. 1995. *Ekonomija destrukcije*. Beograd: VIN.
Dixit, A. 1996. *The Making of Economic Policy: A Transaction-Cost Politics Perspective*. Cambridge, Mass., and London: MIT Press.
Dmitrieva, O. 1997. "All Quiet on the Main Front." *Moskovskiye novosti*, 20–27 July.
Dobry, M. 1992. "Problems and Illusions in the Study of Transition to Democracy." Sisyphus. *Social Studies* 8 (2): 29–34.
Domanski, H. 1996. *Na progu konwergencji: Stratyfikacja spo'eczna w krajach Europy Srodkowo-Wschodniej*. Warsaw: Wydawn.

———. 1997. "Przyszoz naley do klasy zredniej: ale do 'nowej', nie do 'starej'." *Spoleczenstwo otwarte* 3: 7–12.

Dorf, M., and C. Sabel. 1998. "A Constitution of Democratic Experimentalism." *Columbia Law Review* 98 (2): 267–473.

Dornbusch, R. 2000. "Weg mit sämtlichen Subventionen." *Die Welt*, 21 August.

Dunlop, J. B. 1983. *The Faces of Contemporary Russian Nationalism*. Princeton, N.J.: Princeton University Press.

Dunn, D. J. (ed.). 1987. *Religion and Nationalism in Eastern Europe and the Soviet Union*. Boulder, Colo.: Rienner.

Easterly, W. 1996. "When Inflation Stabilisation Is Expansionary? Evidence from High Inflation." *Economic Policy* 22: 67–107.

Eatwell, J. 1996. "International Capital Liberalisation: The Impact on World Development." New School of Social Research, CEPA-Working Paper No. 1, New York.

Eatwell, J., and L. Taylor. 1999. "Towards an Effective Regulation of International Capital Markets." *Politics and Society* 27 (3): 279–86.

Eatwell, J., et al. 1995. *Transformation and Integration: Shaping the Future of Central and Eastern Europe*. Southampton: Institute for Policy Research.

Eatwell, J., M. Milgate, and P. Newmann (eds.). 1987. *The New Palgrave: A Dictionary of Economics*. 4 vols. Basingstoke and London: Macmillan.

Eberts, M. W. 1998. "The Roman Catholic Church and Democracy in Poland." *Europe-Asia Studies* 50 (5): 817–42.

EBRD. 1999. *Ten Years of Transition: Transition Report 1999*. London.

Economist. 1996. "The Backlash in Latin America." 30 November, 23–6.

Economist. 1999. "Converging Hopes." 13 February.

Eichengreen, B., and R. Kohl. 1998. "The External Sector, the State, and Development in Eastern Europe." Berkeley Roundtable on the International Economy, Working Paper 125.

Eisenstadt, S. 1987. *European Civilization in a Comparative Perspective: A Study in the Relations between Culture and Social Structure*. Oslo: Norwegian University Press.

———. 1992. "Center-Periphery Relationships in the Soviet Empire: Some Interpretive Observations." In *Thinking Theoretically About Soviet Nationalities: History and Comparison in the Study of the USSR*, ed. A. Motyl. New York: Columbia University Press, 205–23.

Eisenstadt, S., and S. Rokkan (eds.). 1973. *Building States and Nations*. Beverly Hills, Calif.: Sage.

Ekiert, G. 1996. *The State Against Society: Political Crises and Their Aftermath in East Central Europe*. Princeton, N.J.: Princeton University Press.

Elster, Jon. 1978. Logic and Society. New York:

Elster, J. 1993. "The Necessity and Impossibility of Simultaneous Economic and Political Reform." In *Constitutionalism and Democracy*, ed. D. Greenberg, S. N. Katz, M. B. Oliviero, and S. C. Wheatley. New York and Oxford: Oxford University Press, 267–74.

Elster, J., C. Offe, and U. Preuss, with Frank Bönker, Ulrike Götting, Friedbert W. Rüb. 1998. *Institutional Design in Post-communist Societies: Rebuilding the Ship at Sea*. Cambridge: Cambridge University Press.

Ericson, R. 1999. "The Post-Soviet Russian Economic System: An Industrial Feudalism?" SITE, Working Paper No. 140, Stockholm.

Etzioni, A. 1992. "A Socio-Economic Perspective on Friction." Paper presented at the Fourth Annual International Conference of the Society for the Advancement of Socio-Economics, 28 March, Irvine, Calif.

European Commission. 1997. "Agenda 2000: For a Wider and Stronger Union." *Bulletin of the European Union*, Supplement 5/97, Luxembourg: Official Publications of the European Communities.

European Community Studies Association (ed.). 1993. *The Legal, Economic and Administrative Adaptations of Central European Countries to the European Community*. Baden-Baden: Nomos Verlagsgesellschaft.

European Union. 1999. *Enlarging the EU: A Historical Opportunity*. Brussels.

Evangelista, M. 1999. *Unarmed Forces: The Transnational Movements to End the Cold War*. Ithaca, N.Y.: Cornell University Press.

Evans, P. B. 1995. *Embedded Autonomy: States and Industrial Transformation*. Princeton, N.J.: Princeton University Press.

Evans, P. B., and J. D. Stephens. 1988. "Development and the World Economy." In *Handbook of Sociology*, ed. N. Smelser. Newbury Park, London, and New Delhi: Sage, 739–73.

Evans, P. B, H. K. Jacobson, and R. D. Putnam (eds.). 1993. *Double-Edged Diplomacy*. Berkeley, Calif: University of California Press.

Evans, P., D. Rueschemeyer, and T. Skocpol (eds.). 1985. *Bringing the State Back In*. Cambridge: Cambridge University Press.

Eyal, G., I. Szelenyi, and E. R. Townsley. 1999. *Making Capitalism without Capitalists: Class Formation and Elite Struggles in Post-Communist Central Europe*. London: Verso.

Falke, A. 1994. "An Unwelcome Enlargement? The European Community and German Unification." In *German Unification: Process and Outcomes*, ed. M. D. Hancock and H. A. Welsh. Boulder, Colo: Westview, 163–95.

Fawn, R. 1995. "Central Europe Since the Revolutions of 1989: States, Economies, and Culture in a Time of Flux." In *Boundaries in Question: New Directions in International Relations*, ed. J. Macmillan and A. Linklater. London: Pinter, 69–87.

Fehr, E., and J. Gächter. 2000. "Fairness and Retaliation; the Economics of Reciprocity." *Journal of Economic Perspectives* 14: 159–81.

Fehr, E., and K. Schmidt. 1999. "A Theory of Fairness, Competition and Cooperation," *Quarterly Journal of Economics*: 817–68.

Feldstein, M. 1998. "Refocusing the IMF." *Foreign Affairs* 77 (2): 20–33.

Fischer, S. 1998. "Capital Account Liberalization and the Role of the IMF." *IMF Survey* 26 (19): 321–23.

———. 1999. "Reforming the International Financial System." *Economic Journal* 109, 6: 557–76.

Fischer, S., and R. Sahay. 2000. "The Transition Economies After Ten Years." IMF, Working Paper WP/00/30, Washington, D.C.

Fischer, S., R. Sahay, and C. A. Végh. 1996. "Stabilization and Growth in Transition Economies: The Early Experience." *Journal of Economic Perspectives* 10 (2): 45–66.

———. 1997. "How far is Eastern Europe from Brussels?" In *Quo vadis, Europe?*, ed. H. Siebert. Tübingen: Mohr Siebeck, 97–122.

Fish, M. S. 1998a. "The Determinants of Economic Reform in the Post-Communist World." *East European Politics and Societies* 12 (1): 31–78.

———. 1998b. "Democratization's Requisites. The Postcommunist Experience." *Post-Soviet Affairs* 14 (3): 212–47.

Fisher, W. F. 1997. "Doing Good? The Politics and Anti-politics of NGO Practices." *Annual Review of Anthropology* 26: 439.

Fleron, F. J., and E. P. Hoffmann (eds.). 1993. *Post-Communist Studies and Political Science*. Boulder, Colo: Westview.

Fligstein, N. 1996. "The Economic Sociology of the Transition from Socialism." *American Journal of Sociology* 101 (4): 1074–81.

Freeman, J. R. 1989. *Democracies and Markets: The Politics of Mixed Economies*. Ithaca, N.Y.: Cornell University Press.

Frey, B. S. 1997. *Not Just for Money. An Economic Theory of Personal Motivation.* Cheltenham and Brookfield: Elgar.

Friedland, R., and A. F. Robertson (eds.). 1990. *Beyond the Marketplace: Rethinking Models of Economy and Society*. Chicago: Aldine.

Friedman, J. (ed.). 1996. *The Rational Choice Controversy: Economic Models of Politics Reconsidered.* New Haven, Conn.: Yale University Press.

Friedman, M. 1962. *Capitalism and Freedom.* Chicago and London: University of Chicago Press.

Fries, S., M. Raiser, and N. Stern. 1999. "Stress Test for Reforms: Transition and East Asian 'Contagion.'" *Economics of Transition* 7 (2): 535–67.

Frydman, R., A. Rapaczynski, and J. S. Earle et al. 1993. *The Privatization Process in Central Europe*. Budapest, London, and New York: CEU Press.

Fukuyama, F. 1993. "The Modernizing Imperative: The USSR as an Ordinary Country." *The National Interest* 31: 10–18.

———. 1995. *Trust: The Social Virtues and the Creation of Prosperity.* New York: Free Press.

Funk, N., and M. Müller (eds.). 1993. *Gender Politics and Post-Communism.* New York: Routledge.

Furmann, D. 1998. "Religion und Politik im postkommunistischen Rußland." In *Religiöser Wandel in den postkommunistischen Ländern Ost-und Mitteleuropas,* ed. D. Pollack, I. Borowik and W. Jagodzinski. Würzburg: Ergon, 501–16.

Gaddy, C. 1998. *The Price of the Past: Russia's Struggle with the Legacy of a Militarized Economy*. Washington, D.C.: Brookings.

Gaddy, C., and B. W. Ickes. 1998. "Russia's Virtual Economy." *Foreign Affairs* 77 (5): 53–67.

Gaidar, Y. 2000. *Defeat and Victory*. Seattle: Washington University Press.

Garrett, G., and P. Lange. 1995. "Internationalization, Institutions, and Political Change." *International Organization* 49 (4): 627–55.

Gelb, A., and M. de Melo. 1997. "Transition to Date: A Comparative Overview." In *Lessons from the Economic Transition: Central and Eastern Europe in the 1990s,* ed. S. Zecchini. Dordrecht, Boston and London: Kluwer, 59–78.

Gella, A. 1989. *Development of Class Structure in Eastern Europe: Poland and Her Southern Neighbors*. Albany, N.Y.: State University of New York Press.

Gellner, E. 1983. *Nations and Nationalism*. Oxford: Blackwell.

———. 1991. "Nationalism in Eastern Europe." *New Left Review* 189: 127–34.

———. 1993. "Nationalism and the Development of European Societies." In *The Future of the Nation State in Europe,* ed. J. Iivonen. Aldershot: Elgar, 19–30.

———. 1994. *Conditions of Liberty: Civil Society and Its Rivals.* London: Hamish Hamilton.

Germani, L. S. 2000. "La dimensione internazionale delle mafie russo-euroasiatiche." Paper Presented to the Seminar, *La Russia dopo Eltsin. A dieci anni dalla scomparsa di Andrej Sacharov*, Trento, Centro Studi sulla Storia dell'Europa Orientale.

Gerschenkron, A. 1962. *Economic Backwardness in Historical Perspective.* Cambridge, Mass.: Harvard University Press.

Gibbon, P. 1993. "The World Bank and the New Politics of Aid." *European Journal of Development Research* 5 (1): 35–62.

Giesen, B. 1993. *Die Intellektuellen und die Nation: Eine deutsche Achsenzeit.* Frankfurt/M.: Suhrkamp.

Gill, S., and D. Law. 1988. *The Global Political Economy.* Baltimore and London: Johns Hopkins University Press.

Giszpenc, N., and L. Squire. 2000. "Global Development Network Helps Transform Economics in Transition Economies." *Transition* 11 (3/4): 16–18.

Glasman, M. 1994. "The Great Deformation: Polanyi, Poland and the Terrors of Spontaneity." In *The New Great Transformation?* ed. C. Bryant and E. Mockrzyki. London: Routledge, 191–217.

Goeckel, R. F. 1990. *The Lutheran Church and the East German State.* Ithaca, N.Y.: Cornell University Press.

Goetz, K. 2000. "European Integration and National Executives: A Cause in Search of an Effect?" *West European Politics* 23 (4): 211–31.

Gomulka, S. 1998. "Output: Causes of Decline and the Recovery." In *Emerging from Communism: Lessons from China, Russia and Eastern Europe,* Peter Boone, Stanislaw Gomulka, Richard Layard. Cambridge, Mass., and London: MIT Press, 13–41.

Gorbatova, L. 1995. "Formation of Connections between Finance and Industry in Russia: Basic Stages and Forms." *Communist Economies and Economic Transformation* 7 (1): 21–34.

Gould-Davies, N., and N. Woods. 1999. "Russia and the IMF." *International Affairs* 75 (1): 1–22.

Gourevitch, P. 1978. "The Second Image Reversed: International Sources of Domestic Politics." *International Organization* 32 (4): 881–912.

Gourevitch, P. A. 1989. "Keynesian Politics: The Political Sources of Economic Policy Choices." In *The Political Power of Economic Ideas: Keynesianism across Nations,* P. A. Hall. Princeton, N.J.: Princeton University Press, 87–106.

Gowan, P. 1995. "Neo-Liberal Theory and Practice for Eastern Europe." *New Left Review* 213: 3–60.

Grabher, G. 1994. "The Disembedded Regional Economy: The Transformation of East German Industrial Complexes into Western Enclaves." In *Globalization, Institutions and Regional Development in Europe,* ed. A. Amin and N. Thrift. Oxford: Oxford University Press, 177–95.

———. 1997. "Adaptation at the Cost of Adaptability? Restructuring the Eastern German Regional Economy." In *Restructuring Networks in Post-Socialism: Legacies, Linkages, and Localities,* ed. G. Grabher and D. Stark. Oxford and New York: Oxford University Press, 107–34.

———. (ed.). 1993. *The Embedded Firm: On the Socioeconomics of Industrial Networks.* London: Routledge.

Grabher, G., and D. Stark. 1997. "Organizing Diversity: Evolutionary Theory, Network Analysis, and Post-Socialism." In *Restructuring Networks in Post-Socialism: Legacies, Linkages, and Localities,* ed. G. Grabher and D. Stark. Oxford: Oxford University Press, 1–32.

———. (eds.). 1997. *Restructuring Networks in Post-Socialism: Legacies, Linkages, and Localities.* Oxford and New York: Oxford University Press.

Grancelli, B. 1995. "Il Management post-sovietico." *Sviluppo e Organizzazione* 149: 24–42.

———. 1996. "Theories of Transition: Is there any Room for Rational Choice Theory?" In *Building of Open Society and Perspectives of Sociology in East-Central Europe,* ed. P. Sztompka. London: Sage.

———. 1999. "Formare alla privatizzazione. I programmi Tacis per la formazione manageriale nell'ex-URSS: problemi e prospettive." *Sviluppo e Organizzazione* 179: 1–9.

Grandori, A., and G. Soda. 1995. "Inter-firm Networks: Antecedents, Mechanisms and Forms." *Organization Studies* 16 (2): 183–215.

Greeley, A. 1994. "A Religious Revival in Russia?" *The Journal for the Scientific Study of Religion* 33 (3): 253–73.

Greenaway, D., W. Morgan, and P. Wright. 1998. "Trade Reform, Adjustment and Growth: What Does the Evidence Tell Us?" *Economic Journal* 108 (5): 1547–61.

Greenfeld, L. 1993. *Nationalism: Five Roads to Modernity.* Cambridge, Mass.: Harvard University Press.

Gregory, P. R. 1999. *Ten Years of Transformation.* F.I.T., Discussion Paper No. 12/99, Frankfurt (O).

Greif, A. 1994. "Cultural Beliefs and the Organisation of Society: A Historical and Theoretical Reflection on Collectivist and Individualist Societies." *Journal of Political Economy* 102 (5): 912–50.

———. 1996. "Contracting, Enforcement, and Efficiency: Economics Beyond the Law." Paper Prepared for the Annual World Bank Conference on Development Economics.

Greif, A., and E. Kandel. 1994. "Contract Enforcement Institutions: Historical Perspective and Current Status in Russia." In *Economic Transition in Eastern Europe and Russia: Realities of Reform,* ed. E. P. Lazear. Stanford, Calif.: Hoover Institution Press, 291–321.

Greskovits, B. 1998. *The Political Economy of Protest and Patience: East European and Latin American Transformations Compared.* Budapest: CEU Press.

Grey, R. 1997. "The Impact of External Factors on the Future of Democracy in the FSU and Eastern Europe." In *Democratic Theory and Post-Communist Change,* ed. R. Grey. Upper Saddle River, N.J.: Prentice Hall.

Gros, D., and M. Suhrcke. 2000. "Ten Years After: What Is Special about Transition Countries?" HWWA, Discussion Paper No. 86, Hamburg.

Grosfeld, I. 1992. "Reform Economics and Western Economic Theory: Unexploited Opportunities." In *Reform and Transformation in Eastern Europe: Soviet-type Economics on the Treshold of Change,* eds. J. M. Kovács and M. Tardos. London and New York: Routledge, 62–79.

Habermas, J. 1990. *Die nachholende Revolution.* Frankfurt/M.: Suhrkamp.

Hada, M., and M. Voros (eds.). 1996. "Colonization or Partnership? Eastern Europe and Western Social Sciences" (*Replika,* Special Issue), Budapest.

Haerpfer, C., M. Raiser, and C. Wallace. 2000. *Trust and Civic Engagement in Transition: A Closer Look at the Evidence.* Mimeo. Vienna: IHS.

Haerpfer, C., M. Raiser, T. Nowotny, and C. Wallace. 2001. "Social Capitalism in Transition; A Preliminary Look at the Evidence." *Working Paper No. 61.*

Hahn, F. 1992. "The Relevance of General Equilibrium Theory for the Transformation of Centrally Planned Economics." *Prague Economic Papers* 1 (2): 99–108.

Hall, P. 1997. "The Role of Interests, Institutions, and Ideas in the Comparative Political Economy of the Industrialized Nations." In *Comparative Politics: Rationality, Culture, and Structure,* ed. M. I. Lichbach and A. Zuckerman. Cambridge: Cambridge University Press, 183–86.

Hamilton, W. (ed.). 1964. *The Transfer of Institutions.* Durham, N.C.: Duke University Press.

Hamp, M., et al. 1999. *Geography of Societal Transformation in the Czech Republic.* Charles University, Department of Social Geography and Regional Development, Prague.

Handleman, S. 1995. *Comrade Criminal: Russia's New Mafiya.* New Haven, Conn.: Yale University Press.

Hankiss, E. 1991. "The 'Second Society': Is There an Alternative Social Model Emerging in Contemporary Hungary?" In *Crisis and Reform in Eastern Europe,* ed. A. Arato and F. Feher. New Brunswick and London: Transaction.

Hanley, E., P. Mateju, K. Vlachová, and J. Kreci. 1996. "The Making of Post-Communist Elites in Eastern Europe." Academy of Sciences, Institute of Sociology, Working Paper No. 96/3, Prague.

Hann, C., and E. Dunn (eds.). 1996. *Civil Society. Challenging Western Models.* New York: Routledge.

Hanson, S. 1997a. "How Many Russias? Russia's Regions and Their Adjustment to Economic Change." *International Spectator* 32 (1): 39–52.

———. 1997b. *Time and Revolution: Marxism and the Design of Soviet Institutions.* Chapel Hill, N.C.: University of North Carolina Press.

———. 1997c. "Ideology, Uncertainty, and the Rise of Anti-system Parties in Postcommunist Russia." University of Strathclyde, Centre for the Study of Public Policy, *Studies in Public Policy,* no. 289, Glasgow.

Hardy, J. 1998. "Cathedrals in the Desert? Transnationals, Corporate Strategy and Locality in Wroclaw." *Regional Studies* 32 (7): 639–53.

Harriss, J., and P. de Renzio. 1997. "'Missing Link' or Analytically Missing? The Concept of Social Capital. An Introductory Bibliographic Essay." *Journal of International Development* 9 (7): 1–19.

Hart, O. 1993. *Firms, Contracts and Financial Structure*. Oxford: Clarendon Press.

Hartnell, H. 1997. "Subregional Coalescence in European Regional Integration." *Wisconsin Law Journal* 16 (1): 115–226.

Hausner, J. 1992. *Populist Threat in Transformation of Socialist Society*. Warsaw: Friedrich Ebert Foundation.

Havrylyshyn, O., and J. Odling-Smee. 2000. "Political Economy of Stalled Reforms." *Finance & Development* 37 (3): 7–10.

Hayek, F. A. 1988. *The Fatal Conceit: The Errors of Socialism*. Chicago: University of Chicago Press.

———. 1991. *The Road to Serfdom*. London and New York: Routledge.

———. 1989. *Order—with or without design?* London: Centre for Research into Communist Economies.

Hayri, A., and G. A. McDermott. 1998. "The Network Properties of Corporate Governance and Industrial Restructuring: A Post-Socialist Lesson" *Industrial and Corporate Change* 7 (1): 153–93.

Heilbroner, R. 1988. *Behind the Veil of Economics*. New York: W. W. Norton.

———. 1990. "Analysis and Vision in the History of Modern Economic Thought." *Journal of Economic Literature* 28 (3): 1097–114.

Hellman, J. 1998a. "Winners Take All: The Politics of Partial Reform in Postcommunist Transitions." *World Politics* 50 (2): 203–34.

———. 1998b. "Review of Elster et al. 1998" *East European Constitutional Review* 7 (3): 71–74.

Hellman, J. S., G. Jones, and D. Kaufmann. 2000. "Seize the State, Seize the Day. An Empirical Analysis of State Capture and Corruption in Transition." Paper for the Annual World Bank Conference on Development Economics.

Henderson, S. 1998. "Importing Civil Society: Western Funding and the Women's Movement in Russia." Prepared for Delivery at the 1998 APSA Annual Meeting, 3–6 September, Boston.

Hendley, K. 1998. "Struggling to Survive: A Case Study of Adjustment at a Russian Enterprise." *Europe-Asia Studies* 59 (1): 91–119.

Hermann, M. G. 1998. "One Field, Many Perspectives: Building the Foundations for Dialogue." *International Studies Quarterly* 42 (4): 605–24.

Hesse, J.-J. (ed.). 1993. *Administrative Transformation in Central and Eastern Europe: Towards Public Sector Reform in Post-Communist Societies*. Oxford: Blackwell.

Hetnai, A. 1999. "The Polish Catholic Church in Pre- and Post-1989 Poland: An Evaluation." *East European Quarterly* 32 (4): 503–29.

Hewett, E. A. 1988. *Reforming the Soviet Economy: Equality versus Efficiency*. Washington, D.C.: Brookings.

———. 1991. "Is Soviet Socialism Reformable?" In *The Soviet System in Crisis: A Reader of Western and Soviet Views*, ed. A. Dallin and G. W. Lapidus. Boulder, Colo.: Westview, 365–75.

Higley, J., J. Pakulski, and W. Wesolowski (eds.). 1998. *Postcommunist Elites and Democracy in Eastern Europe*. New York: St. Martin's.

Hirschman, A. O. 1977. *The Passions and the Interests. Political Arguments for Capitalism before its Triumph*. Princeton, N.J.: Princeton University Press.

———. 1981. "The Rise and Decline of Development Economics." In *Essays in*

Trespassing: Economics to Politics and Beyond, ed. A. O. Hirschman. Cambridge: Cambridge University Press, 1–24.

———. 1992. "Rival Views of Market Society." In *Rival Views of Market Society and other Recent Essays,* ed. A. O. Hirschman. Cambridge, Mass.: Harvard University Press, 105–41.

Hobden, S. 1999. "Theorising the International System: Perspectives from Historical Sociology." *Review of International Studies* 25 (2): 257–71.

Hodgson, G. 1998. "The Approach of Institutional Economics." *Journal of Economic Literature* 36 (1): 166–92.

Hollingsworth, R., and R. Boyer (eds.). 1997. *Contemporary Capitalism: The Embeddedness of Institutions*. Cambridge: Cambridge University Press.

Hollis, M., and S. Smith. 1991. "Beware of Gurus: Structure and Action in International Relations." *Review of International Studies* 17: 392–410.

Holmes, S. 1996. "Cultural Legacies or State Collapse? Probing the Postcommunist Dilemma." In *Postcommunism: Four Perspectives,* ed. M. Mandelbaum. New York: Council on Foreign Relations, 22–76.

Hopkins, T. K., and I. Wallerstein. 1996. *The Age of Transition. Trajectory of the World System, 1945-2025*. London: Zed Books.

Hough, J. F. 1997. *Democratization and Revolution in the USSR 1985-1991*. Washington, D.C.: Brookings.

Huber, P., and A. Wörgötter. 1998. "Observations on Russian Business Networks." *Post-Soviet Affairs* 14 (1): 81–91.

Humphrey, J., and H. Schmitz. 1996. "Trust and Economic Development." Institute of Development Studies, Discussion Paper No. 355, Brighton.

Hungarian Parliament. 1997. *The Hungarian Act CLV of 1997 on Consumer Protection.* Budapest: Bureau of Consumer Affairs.

Hutchinson, J., and A. Smith (eds.). 1995. *Nationalism. A Reader*. Oxford: Oxford University Press.

Iglesias, E. 2000. "Call for 'New Development Paradigm.'" United Nations, TAD/1907, 14 February.

Illner, M. 1994. "The Regional Aspect of Post-Communist Transformation in the Czech Republic." *Czech Sociological Review* 2 (1): 107–27.

———. 1997. "The Territorial Dimensions of Public Administration Reforms in East Central Europe." Institute of Sociology, Academy of Sciences of the Czech Republic, Working Paper 97/7, Prague.

IMF 1997. *Good Governance: The IMF's Role*. Washington, D.C.

———. 1999a. *World Economic Outlook: October*. Washington, D.C.

———. 1999b. "IMF Approach to Economic Stabilization: Does One Size Fit All?" *IMF-Survey* 28 (16): 257–60.

———. 1999c. *The Poverty and Growth Facility (PRGF), Operational Issues.* Washington, D.C.

———. 2000a. *World Economic Outlook: May*. Washington, D.C.

———. 2000b. *World Economic Outlook: October*. Washington, D.C.

———. 2001. *Streamlining Structural Conditionality*. Washington, D.C.

IMF et al. 1991. *The Economy of the USSR: Summary and Recommendations.* Washington, D.C.: World Bank.

Inotai, A. 1995. "From Association Agreements to Full Membership? The Dynamics of Relations between the Central and Eastern European Countries and the European Union." Hungarian Academy of Sciences, Institute for World Economics, Working Paper No. 52, Budapest.

Intriligator, M. 1997. "Round Table on Russia: A New Policy for Russia." *Economics of Transition* 5 (7): 225–27.

Jacobsen, J. K. 1996. "Are All Politics Domestic? Perspectives on the Integration of Comparative Politics and International Relations Theories." *Comparative Politics* 29 (1): 93–113.

Jacoby, W. 1999a. "Exemplars, Analogies, and Menus: Eastern Europe in Cross Regional Comparison." *Governance* 12 (4): 455–78.

———. 1999b. "Priest and Penitent: The European Union as a Force in the Domestic Politics of Eastern Europe." *East European Constitutional Review* 8 (1/2): 62–67.

———. 2000. *Imitation and Politics: Redesigning Modern Germany*. Ithaca, N.Y.: Cornell University Press.

———. 2001. "Tutors and Pupils: International Organizations, Central European Elites, and Western Models." *Governance* 14 (2), 169–200.

Jacoby, W., and P. Cernoch. 2001. "The EU's Pivotal Role in the Creation of Czech Regional Policy." In *Norms and Nannies: The Impact of International Organizations on Central and East European States,* ed. R. Linden. Lanham, Md.: Rowman & Littlefield.

Jancar-Webster, B. 1993. *Environmental Action in Eastern Europe*. Armonk, N.Y.: M. E. Sharpe.

Janos, A. C. 1991. "Social Science, Communism, and the Dynamics of Political Change." *World Politics* 44 (1): 81–112.

Jarosz, M. (ed.). 1994. *Spó3ki pracownicze*. Warszawa: PAN ISP.

Jeffries, I. 1993. *Socialist Economies and the Transition to the Market*. London and New York: Routledge.

Jerschina, J. 1990. "The Catholic Church, the Communist State, and the Polish People." In *Polish Paradoxes,* ed. S. Gomulka and A. Polonski . London: Routledge, 76–96.

Jessop, B. 1995. "Regional Economic Blocs, Cross-border Cooperation, and Local Economic Strategies in Postsocialism." *American Behavioral Scientist* 38 (6): 674–716.

Johnson, C., and E. B. Keehn. 1994. "A Disaster in the Making." *The National Interest* 36: 14–22.

Johnson, S., D. Kaufman, and A. Shleifer. 1997. *Politics and Entrepreneurship in Transition Economies*. William Davidson Institute, University of Michigan, Working Paper No. 57, Ann Arbor.

Johnson, S., J. McMillan, and C. Woodruff. 1998. *Trust or Torts? Contract Enforcement in Transition*. Mimeo. MIT and University of California at San Diego.

Joppke, C. 1995. *East German Dissidents and the Revolution of 1989*. New York: New York University Press.

Jordan, A. 1997. "Overcoming the 'Divide' between Comparative Politics and International Relations Approaches to the EC: What Role for 'Post-Decisional Politics'?" *West European Politics* 20 (4): 43–70.

Jowitt, K. 1992. "The Leninist Legacy." In *Eastern Europe in Revolution,* ed. I. Banac.

Ithaca, N.Y., and London: Cornell University Press, 207–24.
Käakkinnen, J. 1997. "Religiosity in Post-Soviet Russia." *Social Compass* 44 (4): 473.
Karl, T. L. 2000. "Economic Inequality and Democratic Instability." *Journal of Democracy* 10 (1): 449–56.
Katzenstein, P. J. 1997. *Mitteleuropa: Between Europe and Germany*. Providence, R.I.: Berghahn Books.
Katznelson, I. 1997. "Structure and Configuration in Comparative Politics." In *Comparative Politics: Rationality, Culture, and Structure,* ed. M. I. Lichbach and A. Zuckerman. Cambridge: Cambridge University Press, 81–112.
Keefer, P., and S. Knack. 1997. "Does Social Capital Have an Economic Payoff? A Cross-Country Investigation." *Quarterly Journal of Economics* 112 (4): 1252–88.
Keohane, R. O., and H. V. Milner (eds.). 1996. *Internationalization and Domestic Politics*. Cambridge: Cambridge University Press.
Keohane, R. O., J. S. Nye, and S. Hoffman. 1993. *After the Cold War: International Institutions and State Strategies in Europe, 1989-1991*. Cambridge, Mass.: Harvard University Press.
Keynes, J. M. 1973. *The General Theory of Employment, Interest, and Money. Collected Writings*. vol. 7. London and Basingstoke: Macmillan.
Khanna, V. R. 1991. "Privatization Is Top Priority in Eastern Europe, Says Sachs." *IMF Survey* 20 (11): 161, 170–73.
Kharkhordin, O. 1994. "The Corporate Ethic of Samostoyatelnost and the Spirit of Capitalism: Reflections on Market-building in Post-soviet Russia." *International Sociology* 9 (4): 405–29.
Khazanov, A. M. 1995. *After the USSR: Ethnicity, Nationalism, and Politics in the Commonwealth of Independent States*. Madison, Wis.: University of Wisconsin Press.
Killick, T., and G. Stevens. 1991. "Eastern Europe: Lessons on Economic Adjustment from the Third World." *International Affairs* 67 (4): 679–96.
Kirchgässner, G. 1994. *Bemerkungen zur Minimalmoral*. Mimeo. St. Gallen.
Kirkpatrick, J. J. 1981. *Dictatorships and Double Standards*. New York: Simon & Schuster.
Kiser, E. 1996. "The Revival of Narrative in Historical Sociology: What Can Rational Choice Theory Contribute?" *Politics and Society* 24 (3): 249–71.
Kitschelt, H., Z. Mansfeldova, R. Markowski, and G. Tóka. 1999. *Post-Communist Party Systems: Competition, Representation, and Inter-Party Cooperation*. Cambridge: Cambridge University Press.
Klaus, V. 1994. "So far, so Good." *The Economist*, 10 September, 33–5.
Koblinska, E., and A. Lawaty. 1994. *Religion und Kirche in der modernen Gesellschaft: Deutsche und polnische Erfahrungen*. Wiesbaden.
Köhn, J. 1998. "Thinking in Terms of System Hierarchies and Velocities: What Makes Development Sustainable?" *Ecological Economics* 26 (2): 173–87.
Kolodko, G. W. 1998. "Economic Neoliberalism Became Almost Irrelevant. . . ." *Transition* 9 (3): 1–6.
———. 1999. "Transition to a Market Economy and Sustained Growth: Implications for the Post-Washington Consensus." *Communist and Post-Communist Studies* 27: 233–61.
Kolodziej, E. A. 1997. "Order, Welfare and Legitimacy: A Systemic Explanation for the

Soviet Collapse and the End of the Cold War." *International Politics* 34 (2): 111–51.
Kornai, J. 1980. *Economics of Shortage*. Amsterdam: North-Holland.
———. 1990. *The Road to a Free Economy. Shifting from a Socialist System: The Example of Hungary*. New York and London: Norton.
———. 1992. *The Socialist System. The Political Economy of Communism*. Princeton, N.J.: Princeton University Press.
———. 1994. "Transformational Recession: The Main Causes." *Journal of Comparative Economics* 19 (1): 39–63.
———. 1996. "Paying the Bill for Goulash Communism: Hungarian Development and Macro-Stabilization in a Political Economy Perspective." *Social Research* 63 (4): 943–1040.
———. 1997. "Reform of the Welfare Sector in Post-communist Countries: A Normative Approach." In *Transforming Post-Communist Political Economies,* ed. J. M. Nelson, C. Tilly, and L. Walker. Washington, D.C.: National Academy Press, 272–98.
———. 2000. "Ten Years After 'The Road to a Free Economy': The Author's Self-Evaluation." Paper Prepared for the Annual World Bank Conference on Development Economics.
Kosta, J. 1997. "Die ökonomische Transformationsstrategie Tschechiens im Vergleich zur Slowakei, Ungarn und Polen." Wissenschaftszentrum Berlin für Sozialforschung, Discussion Paper FS II 97-602, Berlin.
Kotz, D., and F. Weir. 1997. *Revolution from Above: The Demise of the Soviet System*. London: Routledge.
Kozminski, A. 1993. *Catching Up? Organizational and Management Change in the Ex-Socialist Bloc*. New York: S.U.N.Y. Press.
Kregel, J., et al. 1992. *The Market Shock. An Agenda for the Economic and Social Reconstruction of Central and Eastern Europe*. Vienna: International Peace Institute.
Kriedte, P. 1997. "Katholizismus und verzögerte Nationsbildung in Polen." In *Säkularisierung, Entchristianisierung und Rechristianisierung im neuzeitlichen Europa,* ed. H. Lehmann. Göttingen: Vandenhoeck & Ruprecht, 249–74.
Krisch, H. 1999. "The Changing Politics of German National Identity." In *The Federal Republic of Germany at Fifty: The End of a Century of Turmoil,* ed. P. Merkl. Basingstoke and London: Macmillan, 33–42.
Krizan, P., J. Durian, and P. Krnác. 1995. "The Reform of the Structure, Management, and Financing of the Slovak Health Service from 1989 to 1993." *Sociológia* 27 (1/2): 105.
Krugman, P. 1995. *Development, Geography and Economic Theory*. Cambridge, Mass.: MIT Press.
———. 1999. "The Return of Depression Economics." *Foreign Affairs* 78 (1): 56–69.
Krzeminski, A. 1991. Polen im 20. *Jahrhundert*. München: Beck.
Kuczi, T., and C. Makó. 1997. "Towards Industrial Districts? Small-Firm Networking in Hungary." In *Restructuring Networks in Post-Socialism: Legacies, Linkages, and Localities,* ed. G. Grabher and D. Stark. Oxford and New York: Oxford University Press, 176–89.
Kummel, G. 1998. "Democratization in Eastern Europe: The Interaction of Internal and External Factors." *East European Quarterly* 32 (2): 243–68.

Kuznetzov, E. 1994. "Adjustment of Russian Defence-related Enterprises in 1992-94: Macroeconomic Implications." *Communist Economies and Economic Transformation* 6 (4): 473–513.

Kyvelidis, I. 2000. "Social Isomorphism in the Post-Socialist Transition." European Integration online Papers (EIoP) 4 (2) (http://eiop.or.at/eiop/texte/2000-002a.htm).

Lakatos, I. 1978. *The Methodology of Scientific Research Programmes*. Cambridge: Cambridge University Press.

Lane, C. 1978. *Christian Religion in the Soviet Union*. Albany, N.Y.: State University of New York Press.

Lange, O., and F. M. Taylor. 1964. *On the Economic Theory of Socialism*. New York, Toronto, and London: McGraw-Hill.

Lányi, K. 1997. "A globális konvergencia változatai: Washington és Maastricht, I-II." (Variants on convergence: the Washington consensus and the Maastricht treaty). *Külgazdaság* 41 (11): 5–29 and (12): 4–19.

Laski, K., and A. Bhaduri. 1997. "Lessons to Be Drawn from Main Mistakes in the Transition Strategy." In *Lessons from the Economic Transition: Central and Eastern Europe in the 1990s*, ed. S. Zecchini. Dordrecht, Boston, and London: Kluwer, 103–21.

Lavigne, M. 1995. *The Economics of Transition*. Basingstoke and London: Macmillan.

Layard, R., and J. Parker. 1996. *The Coming Russian Boom*. New York: The Free Press.

Lazear, E. P. 2000. "Economic Imperialism." *Quarterly Journal of Economics* 115 (1): 99–146.

Lebow, R. N., and T. Risse-Kappen (eds.). 1995. *International Relations and the End of the Cold War*. New York: Columbia University Press.

Lemoine, F. 1998. "Integrating Central and Eastern Europe in the European Trade and Production Network." Berkeley Roundtable on the International Economy, Working Paper 107.

Lepsius, R. M. 1991. *Demokratie und Demokratisierung in Deutschland*. Göttingen: Vandenhoeck & Ruprecht.

Levi, M. 1996. "Social and Unsocial Capital: A Review Essay of Robert Putnam's 'Making Democracy Work.'" *Politics and Society* 24 (1): 45–55.

———. 1997. "A Model, a Method, and a Map: Rational Choice in Comparative and Historical Analysis." In *Comparative Politics: Rationality, Culture, and Structure*, ed. M. I. Lichbach and A. S. Zuckerman. Cambridge: Cambridge University Press, 19–41.

Light, I., and S. Karageorgis. 1994. "The Ethnic Economy." In *The Handbook of Economic Sociology*, ed. N. Smelser and R. Swedberg. Princeton, N.J., and New York: Princeton University Press and Russell Sage Foundation, 647–71.

Linz, J. J., and A. Stepan. 1996. *Problems of Democratic Consolidation. Southern Europe, South America, and Post-Communist Europe*. Baltimore and London: Johns Hopkins University Press.

Lippincott, B. E. 1964. Introduction to *On the Economic Theory of Socialism*, ed. O. Lange and F. M. Taylor. New York, Toronto, and London: McGraw-Hill, 3–38.

Lipton, D., and J. D. Sachs. 1990. "Privatization in Eastern Europe: The Case of Poland." *Brookings Papers on Economic Activity* (2): 293–341.

———. 1992. "Prospects for Russia's Economic Reform." *Brookings Papers on Economic Activity* (2): 213–84.

Locke, R. 1995. *Remaking the Italian Economy*. Ithaca, N.Y.: Cornell University Press.
Luks, L. 1997. "Der 'Sonderweg' des polnischen Katholizismus." In *Säkularisierung, Entchristianisierung und Rechristianisierung im neuzeitlichen Europa,* ed. H. Lehmann. Göttingen: Vandenhoeck & Ruprecht, 234–48.
Madden, N. 1996. "In the Czech Republic, All Eyes are on TV Nova" *Transition* 2 (8): 14–15.
Majka, J. 1972. "Poland." In *Western Religion: A Country by Country Sociological Inquiry,* ed. H. Mol. The Hague: Mouton, 403–26.
Makarczyk, W. 1978. *Struktura spoeczna a warunki yciowe. Sprawozdanie z badan*. Warsaw: IFiS.
Malia, M. 1992. "Leninist Endgame." *Daedalus* 121 (1): 57–75.
Mann, M. 1986 and 1993. *The Sources of Social Power*. 2 vols. Cambridge: Cambridge University Press.
Manochin, P., M. Tucek et al. 1996. *Ceska spolecnost v transformaci: K promenam socialni struktury*. Prague.
Markovits, A., and S. Reich. 1997. *The German Predicament: Memory and Power in the New Europe*. Ithaca, N.Y.: Cornell University Press.
Markwick, R. D. 1996. "A Discipline in Transition? From Sovietology to 'Transitology.'" *The Journal of Post-Communist Studies and Transition Politics* 12 (3): 255–76.
Martin, D. 1978. *A General Theory of Secularization*. Oxford: Blackwell.
Matouschek, N., and A. J. Venables. 1998. *Evaluating Investment Projects in the Presence of Sectoral Linkages: Theory and Application to Transition Economies*. Mimeo. London, London School of Economics.
McAuley, A. 1997. "The Determinants of Russian Federal-Regional Fiscal Relations: Equity or Political Influence?" *Europe-Asia Studies* 49 (3): 431–44.
McDaniel, T. 1996. *The Agony of the Russian Idea*. Princeton, N.J.: Princeton University Press.
McMillan, J., and C. Woodruff. 1998a. *Interfirm Relationships and Informal Credit in Vietnam*. Mimeo. San Diego, Calif., Graduate School of International Relations and Pacific Studies, University of California.
———. 1998b. *Networks, Trust, and Search in Vietnam's Emerging Private Sector*. Mimeo. San Diego, Calif., Graduate School of International Relations and Pacific Studies, University of California.
Meltzer, A., and J. D. Sachs. 2000. "A Blueprint for IMF Reform." *The Wall Street Journal* Europe, 9 March.
Merkl, P. 1993. *German Unification in the European Context*. University Park, Pa.: Pennsylvania State University Press.
Meyer, J., and B. Rowan. 1991. "Institutionalized Organizations: Formal Structure as Myth and Ceremony." In *The New Institutionalism in Organizational Analysis,* ed. W. Powell and P. DiMaggio. Chicago and London: University of Chicago Press, 41–62.
Micewski, A. 1984. *Cardinal Wyszynski*. San Diego: Harcourt Brace.
Michel, P. 1991. *Politics and Religion in Eastern Europe*. Cambridge: Polity Press.
Michnik, A. 1993. *The Church and the Left*. Chicago: University of Chicago Press.
Michta, A. 1997. "Democratic Consolidation in Poland after 1989." In *Democratization and Authoritarianism in Postcommunist Societies,* ed. K. Dawisha and B. Parrot. Vol. 1 of *The Consolidation of Democracy in East-Central Europe*. Cambridge:

Cambridge University Press, 66–108.

Milgrom, P., D. North, and B. R. Weingast. 1990. "The Role of Institutions in the Revival of Trade: The Law Merchant, Private Judges, and the Champagne Fairs." *Economics and Politics* 2 (1): 1–23.

Millar, J. R. 1995. "Rethinking Soviet Economic Studies." In *Beyond Soviet Studies,* ed. D. Orlovsky. Washington, D.C.: Woodrow Wilson Center, 225–58.

Miller, W., S. White, and P. Heywood. 1998. *Values and Political Change in Postcommunist Europe*. Basingstoke and London: Macmillan.

Mises, L. von. 1935. "Economic Calculation in the Socialist Commonwealth." In *Collectivist Economic Planning,* ed. F. Hayek. London: Routledge and Sons, 87–130.

Moravcsik, A. 2000. "The Origins of Human Rights Regimes: Democratic Delegation in Postwar Europe." *International Organization* 54 (2): 217–52.

Morawska, E. 1995. "The Roman Church Unbound: Change of Face or Change of Context." In *Can Europe Work? Germany and the Reonstruction of Postcommunist Societies,* ed. S. Hanson and W. Spohn. Seattle: University of Washington Press, 47–75.

Mouzelis, N. 1993. "Evolutionary Democracy: Talcott Parsons and the Collapse of Eastern European Regimes." *Theory, Culture and Society* 10 (1): 145–52.

Müller, K. 1992. "Modernizing Eastern Europe. Theoretical Problems and Political Dilemmas." *European Journal of Sociology* 23 (1): 109–51.

———. 1995. "From Post-Communism to Post-Modernity? Economy and Society in the Eastern European Transformations." In *Social Change and Modernization: Lessons from Eastern Europe,* ed. B. Grancelli. Berlin and New York: de Gruyter, 265–93.

———. 1998a. "(Neo-)Totalitarianism, (Post-)Communist Studies and Social Science Theory." In *The Totalitarian Paradigm after the End of Communism: Towards Theoretical Reassessment,* ed. A. Siegel. Amsterdam and Atlanta: Rodopi.

———. (ed.). 1998b. *Postsozialistische Krisen.* Opladen: Leske + Budrich.

———. 1999. *The Political Economy of Pension Reform in Central-Eastern Europe.* Aldershot: Edward Elgar.

Murphy, C. N. 1999. "Inequality, Turmoil, and Democracy: Global Political-economic Visions at the End of the Twentieth Century." *New Political Economy* 4 (2): 289–305.

Murrell, P. 1992a. "Evolutionary and Radical Approaches to Economic Reform." *Economics of Planning* 25 (1): 79–95.

———. 1992b. "Evolution in Economics and in the Economic Reform of the Centrally Planned Economies." In *The Emergence of Market Economies in Eastern Europe,* ed. C. Clague and G. C. Rausser. Cambridge, Mass., and Oxford: Blackwell, 35–53.

———. 1992c. "Conservative Political Philosophy and the Strategy of Economic Transition." *East European Politics and Societies* 6 (1): 3–16.

———. 1995a. "Reform's Rhetoric-Realization Relationship: The Experience of Mongolia." In *The Evolutionary Transition to Capitalism,* ed. K. Poznanski. Boulder, Colo., San Francisco and Oxford: Westview, 79–96.

———. 1995b. "The Transition According to Cambridge, Mass." *Journal of Economic Literature* 33 (1): 164–78.

Mussa, M., and M. A. Savastano. 1999. "The IMF Approach to Economic Stabilization." IMF, Working Paper WP/99/104, Washington, D.C.

Mutti, A. 1998. *Capitale sociale e sviluppo: La fiducia come risorsa.* Bologna: Il Mulino.

Mygind, N. 1998. "The Internationalization of the Baltic Economies." Berkeley Roundtable on the International Economy, Working Paper 13.
Nagy, L. 1996. "La Transition Hongroise de 1990 à 1996." Chene-Bourg.
Naim, M. 2000. "Washington Consensus or Washington Confusion?" *Foreign Policy* 118: 86–103.
Narayan, D., and L. Pritchett. 1997. "Cents and Sociability: Household Income and Social Capital in Rural Tanzania." The World Bank, Policy Research Working Paper No. 1796, Washington, D.C.
Narojek, W. 1982. *Struktura spoeczna w dozwiadczeniu jednostki*. Warsaw.
Nellis, J. 1999. "Time to Rethink Privatization in Transition Economies?" IFC, Discussion Paper No. 38, Washington, D.C.
Nelson, R. 1995. "Recent Evolutionary Theorizing about Economic Change." *Journal of Economic Literature* 33 (1): 48–90.
Neumann, I. 1996. *Russia and the Idea of Europe*. London: Routledge.
Nogues, J., and S. Gulati. 1994. "Economic Policies and Performance under Alternative Trade Regimes: Latin America during the 1980s." *World Economy* 17 (3): 467–96.
North, D. C. 1981. *Structure and Change in Economic History*. New York: Norton.
———. 1990a. "Institutions and Their Consequences for Economic Performance." In *The Limits of Rationality,* ed. K. S. Cook and M. Levi. Chicago and London: University of Chicago Press, 383–401.
———. 1990b. *Institutions, Institutional Change and Economic Performance*. Cambridge: Cambridge University Press.
———. 1997. "Understanding Economic Change." In *Transforming Post-Communist Political Economies,* ed. J. M. Nelson, Ch. Tilly, and L. Walker. Washington D.C.: National Academy Press, 13–19.
North, D. C., and R. P. Thomas. 1973. *The Rise of the Western World: A New Economic History*. Cambridge: Cambridge University Press.
Nove, A. 1992. "Soviet Reforms and Western Neo-Classical Economics." In *Reform and Transformation in Eastern Europe: Soviet-type Economics on the Treshold of Change,* ed. J. M. Kovács and M. Tardos. London and New York: Routledge, 103–19.
Nunberg, B. (ed.). 1999. *The State after Communism: Administrative Transitions in Central and Eastern Europe*. Washington, D.C.: World Bank.
Nuti, D. M. 1990. "Internal and International Aspects of Monetary Disequilibrium in Poland." *European Economy* 43.
O'Donnell, G., and P. Schmitter (eds.). 1986. *Transitions from Authorian Rule*. Baltimore and London: Johns Hopkins University Press.
Ockenfels, A., and J. Weimann. 1999. "Types and Patterns: An Experimental East-West Comparison of Cooperation and Solidarity." *Journal of Public Economics* 71: 275–87.
OECD 2000. *Russian Federation: Economic Survey*. Paris.
OECD/DAC 2000. *Report on Development Co-operation*. Paris.
Offe, C. 1991. "Capitalism by Democratic Design? Democratic Theory Facing the Triple Transition in East Central Europe." *Social Research* 58 (4): 865–92.
———. 1993. "The Politics of Social Policy in East European Transitions: Antecedents, Agents and Agenda of Reform." *Social Research* 60 (4): 649–84.
———. 1997. "Cultural Aspects of Consolidation: A Note on the Peculiarities of

Postcommunist Transformations." *East European Constitutional Review* 6 (4).
———. 1999. "How Can We Trust Our Fellow Citizens?" In *Democracy and Trust,* ed. M. E. Warren. Cambridge: Cambridge University Press, 42–87.
Olsen, J. 1998. "Germany's PDS and Varieties of 'Post-Communist' Socialism." *Problems of Post-Communism* 45 (6): 42–52.
Olson, M. 1965. *The Logic of Collective Action.* Cambridge, Mass.: Harvard University Press.
OMAS Consortium. 1998. "Assessment of the European Union Phare Programme: Czech Republic Public Administration Reform." Report R/CZ/PAR/9701, 29 April.
Ost, D. 1992. "Labour and Societal Transition." *Problems of Communism* 41 (5/6): 48–51.
———. 1995. "Labour, Class, and Democracy: Shaping Political Antagonisms in Post-Communist Society." In *Markets, States, and Democracy. The Political Economy of Post-Communist Transformation,* ed. B. Crawford. Boulder, Colo., San Francisco, and Oxford: Westview, 177–203.
Ostrom, E. 1990. *Governing the Commons: The Evolution of Institutions for Collective Action.* Cambridge: Cambridge University Press.
Panitch, L. 1996. "Globalization and the State." In *Globalization: Critical Reflections. International Political Economy Yearbook,* ed. J. Mittleman. Vol. 9. Boulder, Colo.: Lynne Rienner.
Parsons, T. 1937. *The Structure of Social Action.* Glencoe, Ill.: The Free Press.
Pejovich, S. 1995. *Economic Analysis of Institutions and Systems.* Dordrecht, London, and Boston: Kluwer.
Petro, N. 1995. *The Rebirth of Russian Democracy: An Interpretation of Political Culture.* Cambridge, Mass.: Harvard University Press.
Pfaff, D. 1993. "Die Rezeption deutschen Rechts in Bulgarien." *Südosteuropa Mitteilungen* 33 (2): 125–28.
Phelps, E. 2000. "The Not So New Economy. Low Inflation, Low Unemployment. What Goes?" *The Wall Street Journal* Europe, 13 April.
Pickel, A. 1997a. "Neoliberalism, Gradualism, and Some Typical Ambiguities and Confusions in the Transformation Debate." *New Political Economy* 2 (2): 221–35.
———. 1997b. "Official Ideology: The Role of Neoliberal Reform Doctrines in Postcommunist Transformation." In *The Grand Experiment: Debating Shock Therapy, Transformation Theory, and the East German Experience,* A. Pickel and H. Wiesenthal. Boulder, Colo.: Westview, 212–28.
———. 1997c. "The Jump-Started Economy and the Ready-Made State: A Theoretical Reconsideration of the East German Case," *Comparative Political Studies* 30 (2) (April): 211–41.
———. 1998. "Is Cuba Different? Regime Stability, Social Change, and the Problem of Reform Strategy." *Communist and Post-Communist Studies* 1: 75–90.
Pickel, A., and H. Wiesenthal 1997. *The Grand Experiment: Debating Shock Therapy, Transition Theory, and the East German Experience.* Boulder, Colo.: Westview.
Piselli, F. 1999. "Capitale sociale: un concetto situazionale e dinamico." *Stato e Mercato* 57: 395–417.
Pistor, K., and A. Spicer. 1996. "Investment Funds in Mass Privatisation and Beyond: Evidence from the Czech Republic and Russia." HIID, Development Discussion Paper No. 565, Cambridge, Mass.

Platteau, J.-P. 1994a. "Behind the Market Stage Where Real Societies Exist—Part I: The Role of Public and Private Order Institutions." *Journal of Development Studies* 30 (3): 533–77.

———. 1994b. "Behind the Market Stage Where Real Societies Exist—Part II: Trust and Generalised Morality." *Journal of Development Studies* 30 (4): 754–817.

Poian-Srednicki, M. 1982. *Religious Change in Communist Poland: Secularization and Politics*. London.

Polányi, K. 1946. *Origins of Our Time: The Great Transformation*. London: Victor Gollancz Ltd.

Pollack, D. 1994. *Kirche in der Organisationsgesellschaft: Zum Wandel der gesellschaftlichen Lage der evangelischen Kirche in der DDR*. Stuttgart et al.: Kohlhammer.

Popper, K. 1943. *The Open Society and its Enemies*. Princeton, N.J.: Princeton University Press.

Portes, A. 1998. "Social Capital: Its Origins and Applications in Modern Sociology." *Annual Review of Sociology* 24: 1–24.

Portes, A., and P. Landolt. 1996. "The Downside of Social Capital." *American Prospect* 7 (26): 18–22.

Pospielovsky, D. 1984. *The Russian Church under the Soviet Regime 1917-1982*. Crestwood, N.Y.: St. Vladimir's Seminary Press.

Powell, W. W., and L. Smith-Doer. 1994. "Networks and Economic Life." In *Handbook of Economic Sociology,* ed. N. Smelser and R. Swedberg. Princeton, N.J., and New York: Princeton University Press and Russell Sage Foundation, 368–402.

Poznanski, K. Z. 1993. "An Interpretation of Communist Decay: The Role of Evolutionary Mechanisms." *Communist and Post-Communist Studies* 26 (1): 3–24.

———. (ed.). 1995. *The Evolutionary Transition to Capitalism*. Boulder, Colo., San Francisco, and Oxford: Westview.

———. 1996. *Poland's Protracted Transition: Institutional Change and Economic Growth 1970–1994*. Cambridge: Cambridge University Press.

———. 1998. "Comparative Transition Theory: Recession and Recovery in Post-Communist Economies." *Emergo* 5 (2): 36–52.

———. 1999. "Post-communist Transition as Institutional Disintegration: Explaining the Regional Economic Recession." *Acta Oeconomica* 50 (1/2): 1–36.

———. 2000. "The Morals of Transition: Decline of Public Interest and Runaway Reforms in Eastern Europe." In *Between Past and Future: The Revolutions of 1989 and Their Aftermath,* ed. Sorin Antohi and Vladimir Tismaneanu. London: CEU Press.

Pridham, G., E. Herring, and G. Sanford (eds.). 1997. *Building Democracy? The International Dimension of Democratisation in Eastern Europe*. London: Leicester University Press.

Prybyla, J. 1998. "Economics of Transition: A 'Survey' Article." *Europe-Asia Studies* 50 (2): 351–59.

Przeworski, A. 1991. *Democracy and the Market: Political and Economic Reforms in Eastern Europe and Latin America*. Cambridge: Cambridge University Press.

———. 1997. "The State in a Market Economy." In *Transforming Post-Communist Political Economies,* ed. J. M. Nelson, Ch. Tilly, and L. Walker. Washington, D.C.: National Academy Press, 411–31.

Przeworski, A. et al. 1995. *Sustainable Democracy*. Cambridge: Cambridge University Press.

Putnam, R. D. 1993. *Making Democracy Work: Civic Traditions in Modern Italy*. Princeton, N.J.: Princeton University Press.

Pyke, F. G. Becattini, and W. Sengenberger (eds.). 1990. *Industrial Districts and Inter-firm Cooperation in Italy*. Geneva: International Institute for Labour Studies.

Radice, H. 1999. "Taking Globalisation Seriously." In *Global Capitalism versus Democracy. Socialist Register 1999*, ed. L. Panitch and C. Leys. New York: Monthly Review Press.

Raiser, M. 1997. "Informal Institutions, Social Capital and Economic Transition: Reflections on a Neglected Dimension." EBRD, Working Paper No. 25, London.

Ramet, S. P. 1998. *Nihil Obstat: Religion, Politics, and Social Change in East-Central Europe and Russia*. Durham, N.C.: Duke University Press.

———. (ed.). 1991. *Religion and Nationalism in East European Politics*. Boulder, Colo.: Westview.

Rawls, A. W. 1992. "Can Rational Choice Be a Foundation for Social Theory?" *Theory and Society* 21 (2): 219–39.

Rawls, J. 1974. *A Theory of Justice*. Cambridge, Mass.: Harvard University Press.

Rendtorff, T. (ed.). 1993. *Protestantische Revolution?* Göttingen: Vandenhoeck & Ruprecht.

Review of International Political Economy. 1994. Editors Introduction. 1 (1).

Risse-Kappen, Thomas. 1995. *Bringing Transnational Relations Back in: Non-State Actors, Domestic Structures, and International Institutions*. Cambridge: Cambridge University Press.

Robinson, A. 1997. "US and EU Differ on Priorities on EBRD." *Financial Times*, 16 April.

Rodrik, D. 1996. "Understanding Economic Policy Reform." *Journal of Economic Literature* 34 (1): 9–41.

———. 1998. "Who Needs Capital-Account Convertibility?" In *Should the IMF Pursue Capital-Account Convertibility?*, ed. S. Fischer et al. Princeton, N.J.: Princeton University, Dept. of Economics, International Finance Section.

———. 2000a. "Development Strategies for the Next Century." Paper presented at the Conference on Developing Economies in the 21st Century, Institute for Developing Economies, Japan External Trade Organization, 26–27 January, Chiba, Japan.

———. 2000b. "Institutions for High-Quality Growth: What They Are and How to Acquire Them." NBER, Working Paper No. 7540, Cambridge, Mass.

Roland, G. 1992. "Issues in the Political Economy of Transition." Paper presented at the Conference "The Economic Consequences of the East," 22–23 March, Frankfurt/M.

Rona-Tas, A. 1998. "Path Dependence and Capital Theory: Sociology of the Post-Communist Economic Transformation." *East European Politics and Societies* 12 (1): 107–31.

Rose, R. 1993. Lesson-Drawing in Public policy: A Guide to Learning Across Time and Space. Chatham, NJ: Chatham House.

Rose, R., and C. Haerpfer. 1998. "Trends in Democracies and Markets: New Democracies Barometer 1991-1998." University of Strathclyde, Centre for the Study of Public Policy, Studies in Public Policy, No. 308, Glasgow.

Rose, R., W. Mishler, and C. Haerpfer. 1998. *Democracy and Its Alternatives: Understanding Postcommunist Societies*. Baltimore and London: Johns Hopkins University Press.

Rose, R., C. Haerpfer, and W. Mishler. 1997. "Getting Real: Social Capital in Post-Communist Societies." University of Strathclyde, Centre for the Study of Public Policy, Studies in Public Policy, No. 278, Glasgow.

Rosenau, J. N. 1997. *Along the Domestic-Foreign Frontier: Exploring Governance in a Turbulent World.* Cambridge: Cambridge University Press.

Rosenbaum, E. F., F. Bönker, and H.-J. Wagener (eds.). 2000. *Privatization, Corporate Governance and the Emergence of Markets*. Basingstoke and London: Macmillan.

Rudolph, R., and D. Good (eds.). 1992. *Nationalism and Empire: The Habsburg Empire and the Soviet Union.* New York: St. Martin's.

Rueschemeyer, D., E. Huber Stephens, and J. D. Stephens. 1992. *Capitalist Development and Democracy.* Chicago and London: University of Chicago Press.

Rutherford, M. 1994. *Institutions in Economics: The Old and the New Institutionalism.* Cambridge: Cambridge University Press.

Rutland, P. 1997. "The Antinomies of Privatisation in Eastern Europe." In *Restructuring Networks in Post-socialism. Legacies, Linkages and Localities,* ed. G. Grabher and D. Stark. Oxford: Oxford University Press, 265–83.

Sabel, C. F. 1992. "Studied Trust: Building New Forms of Co-operation in a Volatile Economy." In *Industrial Districts and Local Economic Regeneration,* ed. F. Pyke and W. Sengenberger. Geneva: International Institute for Labour Studies, 215–50.

Sachs, J. D. 1990. "Eastern Europe's Economies: What Is to Be Done?" *The Economist,* 13 January, 19–24.

———. 1994. *Poland's Jump to the Market Economy.* Cambridge, Mass.: MIT Press.

———. 2000. "Russia's Tumultuous Decade: An Insider Remembers." *Washington Monthly*, March.

Sachs, J. D., and D. Lipton. 1990. "Poland's Economic Reform." *Foreign Affairs* 69 (3): 47–65.

Sachs, J. D., and A. Warner. 1997. "Fundamental Sources of Long-run Growth." *American Economic Review* 87 (2): 184–88.

Sachs, J. D. and W. T. Woo. 1994. "Structural Factors in the Economic Reforms of China, Eastern Europe, and the Former Soviet Union." *Economic Policy* 18: 102–45.

Sakwa, R. 1996. *Russian Politics and Society.* London and New York: Routledge.

Samuels, W. 1995. "The Present State of Institutional Economics." *Cambridge Journal of Economics* 19 (4): 569–90.

Sartori, G. 1991. "Rethinking Democracy: Bad Polity and Bad Politics." *International Social Science Journal* 129: 437–50.

Savage, Robert. 1985. "Diffusion Research Traditions and the Spread of Policy Innovation in a Federal System," *Publius* 15 (4): 1–28.

Schiemann, J. 1998. "Myopic Bargains, Transitions to Democracy, and Democratic Consolidation: The Negotiated Origins of Hungary's Constitutional Court." Paper prepared for the Annual Convention of the Midwest Political Science Association, April.

Schmitter, P. 1990. "Sectors in Modern Capitalism: Modes of Governance and Variation in Performance." In *Labour Relations and Economic Performance,* ed. P. Brunetta and C. Dell'Aringa. Basingstoke and London: Macmillan, 3–39.

Schmitter, P. C., and T. L. Karl. 1994. "The Conceptual Travels of Transitologists and Consolidologists: How Far to the East Should they Attempt to Go?" *Slavic Review* 53 (1): 173–85.
Schöpflin, G. 1993. *Politics in Eastern Europe: 1945-1992*. Oxford: Blackwell.
———. 2000. *Nations, Identity, Power: The New Politics of Europe*. London: Hurst.
Schroeder, G. 1995. "Reflections on Economic Sovietology." *Post-Soviet Affairs* 11 (3): 197–234.
Schumpeter, J. A. 1954. *History of Economic Analysis*. New York: Oxford University Press.
———. 1992. *Capitalism, Socialism and Democracy*. London and New York: Routledge.
Sedaitis, J. B. 1997. "Network Dynamics of New Firm Formation: Developing Russian Commodity Markets." In *Restructuring Networks in Post-Socialism: Legacies, Linkages, and Localities,* ed. G. Grabher and D. Stark. Oxford and New York: Oxford University Press, 137–57.
Seifert, W. 1994. "East Germany and Eastern Europe Compared." University of Strathclyde, Centre for the Study of Public Policy, Studies in Public Policy, No. 233, Glasgow.
Selznick, P. 1953. *TVA and the Grass Roots: A Study in the Sociology of Formal Organization*. Berkeley, Calif.: University of California Press.
Sen, A. 1995. "Rationality and Social Choice." *American Economic Review* 85 (1): 1–24.
———. 1999. "The Possibility of Social Choice." *American Economic Review* 89 (3): 349–68.
Seton-Watson, H. 1977. *Nations and States*. Boulder, Colo.: Westview.
Shlapentokh, V. 1996. "Early Feudalism—The Best Parallel for Contemporary Russia." *Europe-Asia Studies* 48 (3): 393–411.
Shleifer, A. 1997. "Government in Transition." *European Economic Review* 41: 385–410.
Shleifer, A., M. Boycko, and R. Vishny. 1995. *Privatizing Russia*. Cambridge, Mass.: MIT Press.
Schleifer, A., and D. Treisman. 2000. *Without a Map. Political Tactics and Economic Reform in Russia*. Cambridge, Mass.: The MIT Press.
Shpak, V. 1997. "Three Acts of Intimidation." *Segodnya*, 16 June.
Shvetsova, O. 1998. "Assessing the Extent of the Endogeneity Problem in Institutional Selection: The Case of East European Election Laws." Washington University, Political Economy Working Paper, September.
Skilling, G. 1989. *Samizdat and an Independent Society in Central and Eastern Europe*. Basingstoke and London: Macmillan.
Skocpol, T. 1988. *States and Social Revolutions: A Comparative Analysis of France, China and Russia*. Cambridge: Cambridge University Press.
Slay, B. 1997. "The Search for Solutions in Enterprise Restructuring." *Transitions* 3 (1): 32–35.
———. 2000. "A Reply to Professor Stiglitz." *PlanEcon* 16 (7): 2–8.
Smiryagin, L. 1997. "Race of the Regions." *Rossiiskie vesti*, 20 May.
Smith, A. 1986. *The Ethnic Origins of Nations*. Oxford: Blackwell.
———. 1992. *National Identity*. Reno, Nev.: University of Nevada Press.
Smith, G. B. 1988. *Soviet Politics: Continuity and Contradiction*. New York: St. Martin's.
Smolar, A. 1996. "Civil Society after Communism: From Opposition to Atomization."

Journal of Democracy 4 (1): 24–38.

Sojka, M. 2000. "Ten Years of Transformation in the Czech Way: Transformation, Inequaility and Integration." In *Economic and Social Changes in Czech Society after 1989: An Alternative View,* ed. L. Mlcoch, P. Machonin, and M. Sojka. Prague: Karolinum Press.

Solinger, Dorothy 1991. "Urban Reform and Relational Contracting in Post-Mao China: An Interpretation of the Transition from Plan to Market." In *Reform and Reaction in Post-Mao China: The Road to Tiananmen,* ed. R. Baum. New York: Routledge.

Solnick, S. 1996. *Center-periphery Bargaining in Russia.* National Council for Soviet and East European Research, Report.

———. 1998. *Stealing the State: Control and Collapse in Soviet Institutions.* Cambridge, Mass.: Harvard University Press.

Solomon, S. G. (ed.). 1993. *Beyond Sovietology.* New York: M. E. Sharpe.

Solow, R. 1956. "A Contribution to the Theory of Economic Growth." *Quarterly Journal of Economics* 70 (1): 65–94.

———. 2000. "Towards a Macroeconomics of the Medium Run." *Journal of Economic Perspectives* 14 (1): 151–58.

Soros, G. 1998. *The Crisis of Global Capitalism: Open Society Endangered.* New York: Public Affairs.

Spohn, W. 1991. "Religion and Working-Class Formation in Imperial Germany 1871–1914." *Politics and Society* 19 (1): 109–32.

———. 1995. "United Germany as the Renewed Center in Europe: Continuity and Change of the German Question." In *Can Europe Work? Germany and the Reconstruction of Postcommunist Societies,* ed. S. Hanson and W. Spohn. Seattle: University of Washington Press, 79–128.

———. 1996. "Protestantism, Secularization, and Politics in 19th Century Germany." In *Render Unto Caesar: The Religious Sphere in World Politics,* ed. S. P. Ramet. Washington, D.C.: American University Press.

———. 1997. "Religion and Modernization in Comparative Perspective: David Martin's Theory of Secularization Reconsidered." In *Differenz und Integration: Die Zukunft moderner Gesellschaften,* ed. K.-S. Rehberg. Opladen: Westdeutscher Verlag, 455–59.

———. 1998. "Religion und Nationalismus: Osteuropa im westeuropäischen Vergleich." In *Religiöser Wandel in den postkommunistischen Ländern Ost-und Mitteleuropas,* ed. D. Pollack, I. Borowik, and W. Jagodzinski. Würzburg: Ergon, 87–120.

Srinivasan, T. N. 1999. "Variety of Routes to Development Already Known." *Financial Times,* 28 September.

Stallings, B. 1992. "International Influence on Economic Policy: Debt, Stabilization and Structural Reform." In *The Politics of Economic Adjustment: International Constraints, Distributive Conflicts, and the State,* ed. S. Haggard and R. Kaufman. Princeton, N.J.: Princeton University Press, 41–88.

Stallings, B., and W. Peres. 2000. *Growth, Unemployment and Equity: The Impact of Economic Reforms in Latin America and the Caribbean.* Washington, D.C.: Brookings.

Staniszkis, J. 1984. *Poland's Self-limiting Revolution.* Princeton, N.J.: Princeton University Press.

———. 1991a. "Dilemmata der Demokratie in Osteuropa." In *Demokratischer Umbruch in Osteuropa,* ed. R. Deppe, Helmut Dubiel, and Ulrich Rödel. Frankfurt/M.: Suhrkamp, 326–47.

———. 1991b. *The Dynamics of Breakthrough in Eastern Europe.* The Polish Experience. Berkeley, Calif.: University of California Press.

———. 1994/95. "The Politics of Post-Communist Institutionalization in Historical Perspective." University of Michigan, Advanced Study Center, Working Paper No. 1, Ann Arbor, Mich.

———. 1995. "In Search of a Paradigm of Transformation." In *After Communism: A Multidisciplinary Approach to Radical Social Change,* ed. E. Wnuk-Lipinski. Warsaw: Institute of Political Studies, Polish Academy of Sciences, 19–56.

———. 1995/96. "Polityka postkomunistycznej instytucjonalizacji w perspektywie historycznej." *Studia Polityczne* 4: 39–60 and 5: 99–116.

Stark, D. 1990. "Privatization in Hungary: From Plan to Market or from Plan to Clan." *East European Politics and Societies* 4 (3). Reprinted in: D. Stark and L. Bruszt. 1998. *Postsocialist Pathways: Transforming Politics and Property in East Central Europe.* Cambridge: Cambridge University Press, 51–79.

———. 1996. "Recombinant Property in East European Capitalism." *American Journal of Sociology* 101 (4): 993–1027.

Stark, D., and L. Bruszt. 1998. *Postsocialist Pathways: Transforming Politics and Property in East Central Europe.* Cambridge: Cambridge University Press.

Stewart, F. 1997. "Williamson and the Washington Consensus Revisited." In *Economic and Social Development into the XXI Century,* ed. L. Emmerij. Washington, D.C.: IADB.

Stiglitz, J. E. 1994. *Wither Socialism?* Cambridge, Mass.: MIT Press.

———. 1998a. "More Instruments and Broader Goals: Moving Towards the Post-Washington Consensus." WIDER Annual Lecture No. 2, Helsinki: World Institute for Development Economics Research.

———. 1998b. "The Private Uses of Public Interest: Incentives and Institutions." *Journal of Economic Perspectives* 12 (2): 3–22.

———. 1999. "Whither Reform? Ten Years of the Transition." Paper presented at the Annual Bank Conference on Development Economics, 28–29 April.

Stokes, G. 1989. "The Social Origins of Eastern European Politics." In *The Origins of Backwardness in Eastern Europe,* ed. Daniel Chirot. Berkeley, Calif.: University of California Press, 210–51.

Stölting, E. 1990. *Eine Weltmacht zerbricht: Nationalitäten und Religionen in der UdSSR.* Frankfurt/M.: Eichborn.

Stoner-Weiss, K. 1997. *Local Heroes. The Political Economy of Russian Regional Governance.* Princeton, N.J.: Princeton University Press.

———. 1999. "Central Weakness and Provincial Autonomy: Observations on the Devolution Process in Russia." *Post-Soviet Affairs* 15 (1): 87–106.

Strange, S. 1994. *States and Markets.* London: Pinter.

Strange, S. 1998. "Globaloney? Review Essay." *Review of International Political Economy* 5 (4): 704–20.

Streeck, W. 1997. "Beneficial Constraints: On the Economic Limits of Rational Voluntarism." In *Contemporary Capitalism: The Embeddedness of Institutions,* ed. J. R. Hollingsworth and R. Boyer. Cambridge: Cambridge University Press, 179–219.

Suganami, H. 1989. *The Domestic Analogy and World Order Proposals*. Cambridge: Cambridge University Press.

Swatos, W. H. (ed.). 1994. *Politics and Religion in Central and Eastern Europe*. Westport, Conn.: Praeger.

Szacki, J. 1996. *Liberalism after Communism*. Budapest: CEU Press.

Szczerbiak, A. 1998. "Electoral Politics in Poland: The Parliamentary Elections of 1997." *Journal of Communist Studies and Transition Politics* 14 (3): 58–83.

Szelenyi, I., and S. Szelenyi. 1995. "Wstep: Zaoenia teoretyczne i metodologia." In *Elity w Polsce, w Rosji i na Wegrzech: Wymiana czy reprodukcja?* ed. I. Szelenyi, D. Treiman, and E. Wnuk-Lipiñski. Warsaw, 7–34.

Sztompka, P. 1993. "Civilizational Incompetence: The Trap of Post-Communist Societies." *Zeitschrift für Soziologie* 22 (2): 85–95.

———. 1994. "Teorie zmian spoecznych a dozwiadczenia polskiej transformacji." *Studia socjologiczne* 1.

Tanzi, V. 1997. "The Changing Role of the State in the Economy: A Historical Perspective." IMF, Working Paper No. 97/114, Washington, D.C.

Tarkowska, E., and J. Tarkowski. 1990. "'Amoralny familizm' czyli o dezintegracji spoecznej w Polsce lat osiemdziesi1tych." In *Grupy i wiêzi spoeczne w systemie monocentrycznym*, ed. E. Wnuk-Lipiñski. Warsaw.

Task Force on Economies in Transition. 1997. "Research Priorities for the Post-Communist Economies." In *Transforming Post-Communist Political Economies*, ed. J. M. Nelson, C. Tilly, and L. Walker. Washington, D.C.: National Academy Press, 473–90.

Tatham, A. 1997. "European Community Law Harmonization in Hungary." *Maastricht Journal of European and Comparative Law* 4 (3): 249–83.

Tatur, M. 1989. *Solidarnosc als Modernisierungsbewegung. Sozialstruktur und Konflikt in Polen.* Frankfurt/M. and New York: Campus.

———. 1991. "Zur Dialektik der 'civil society' in Polen." In *Demokratischer Umbruch in Osteuropa,* ed. R. Deppe, H. Dubiel, and U. Rödel. Frankfurt/M.: Suhrkamp, 234–55.

———. 1995. "Interessen und Norm. Politischer Kapitalismus und die Transformation des Staates in Polen und Ungarn." In *Transformation sozialistischer Gesellschaften: Am Ende des Anfangs,* ed. H. Wollmann, H. Wiesenthal, and F. Bönker. Opladen: Westdeutscher Verlag, 93–116.

Thompson, M. G., J. France, R. Levacic, and J. Mitchell (eds.). 1991. *Market, Hierarchies and Networks: The Coordination of Social Life*. London: Sage.

Thornhill, J. 2000. "Russia's Unique Economic Crisis May Have Led to 1998 Crisis." *Financial Times*, 22 February.

Thornton, J., and N. Mikheeva. 1996. "The Strategies of Foreign and Foreign-assisted Firms in the Russian Far East: Alternatives to Missing Infrastructure." *Comparative Economic Studies* 38 (4): 85–119.

Tilly, C. (ed.). 1975. *The Formation of National States in Western Europe*. Princeton, N.J.: Princeton University Press.

———. 1990. *Coercion, Capital and European States, AD 990-1990*. Oxford: Blackwell.

———. 1992. *Coercion, Capital, and European States, Ad 990-1992*. London: Blackwell.

———. 1997. "Democracy, Social Change, and Economies in Transition." In *Transforming Post-Communist Political Economies,* ed. J. M. Nelson, Ch. Tilly, and L. Walker. Washington, D.C.: National Academy Press, 403–11.

———. 2001. "Mechanisms in Political Processes." *Annual Review of Political Science* 4: 21–41.

Tiryakian, E. 1995. "Modernization in a Millenarian Decade. Lessons for and from Eastern Europe." In *Social Change and Modernization. Lessons from Eastern Europe,* ed. B. Grancelli. Berlin and New York: de Gruyter, 249–64.

Tismaneanu, V. 1998. *Fantasies of Salvation: Democracy, Nationalism, and Myth in Post-Communist Europe*. Princeton, N.J.: Princeton University Press.

Treisman, D. 1999. *After the Deluge: The Politics of Regional Crisis in Post-Soviet Russia.* Ann Arbor, Mich.: University of Michigan Press.

Trigilia, C. 1999. "Capitale sociale e sviluppo locale." *Stato e Mercato* 57: 419–39.

True, J. 1999. "Expanding Markets and Marketing Gender: The Integration of the Post-socialist Czech Republic." *Review of International Political Economy* 6 (3): 330–59.

———. 2000. "Gendering Post-socialist Transitions." In *Gender and Global Restructuring,* ed. M. Marchand and A. Sisson Runyan. New York and London: Routledge.

UN/ECLAC. 2000. *The Equity Gap: A Second Assessment*. Santiago: ECLAC.

Vachudová, M. 2001. "The Influence of International Factors on the Czech Republic." In *The Impact of International Factors on Democratic Consolidation in Eastern Europe,* ed. A. Pravda and J. Zielonka. Florence: EUI Press.

van Brabant, J. M. 1998. *The Political Economy of Transition: Coming to Grips with History and Methodology*. London and New York: Routledge.

Verdery, K. 1996. *What Was Socialism and What Comes Next?* Princeton, N.J.: Princeton University Press.

Verny, A. 1998. "Rechtsangleichung und EU-Integration: Die Reformen in den assoziierten Ländern Mittel- und Osteuropas." In *Im Osten was Neues: Aspekte der EU-Osterweiterung,* ed. Hans-Jürgen Wagener and Heiko Fritz. Bonn: Dietz Verlag, 265–82.

Vogel, S. 1996. *Freer Markets, More Rules: Regulatory Reform in Advanced Industrial Countries*. Ithaca, N.Y.: Cornell University Press.

Von Zon, H. 1998. "The Mismanaged Integration of Zaporizhzhya with the World Economy: Implications for Regional Development in Peripheral Regions." *Regional Studies* 32 (7): 607–21.

Vybomá, O. 1994. "The Reform of the Czech Health Care System." CERGE-EI, Working Paper 64, Prague.

Wade, R. 1996. "Globalization and Its Limits: Reports of the Death of the National Economy are Greatly Exaggerated." In *National Diversity and Global Capitalism,* ed. S. Berger and R. Dore. Ithaca, N.Y.: Cornell University Press, 60–88.

———. 2001. "Showdown at the World Bank." *New Left Review* (II) 7: 124–37.

Waelbroeck, J. 1998. "Half a Century of Development Economics." *World Bank Economic Review* 12 (2): 323–52.

Walicki, A. 1990. "The Three Traditions in Polish Patriotism." In *Polish Paradoxes,* ed. S. Gomulka and A. Polonsky. London: Routledge, 21–39.

———. 1995. *Marxism and the Leap to the Kingdom of Freedom*. Stanford, Calif.: Stanford University Press.

Walker, Jack. 1969. "The Diffusion of Innovations Among the American States," American Political Science Review 63(3): 880-899.

Wallerstein, I., et al. 1996. *Open the Social Sciences. Report of the Gulbekian Commission on the Restructuring of the Social Sciences*. Stanford, Calif.: Stanford University Press.

Walters, A. 1992. "The Transition to a Market Economy." In *The Emergence of Market Economies in Eastern Europe,* ed. C. Clague and G. C. Rausser. Cambridge, Mass., and Oxford: Blackwell, 99–108.

Walton, J., and D. Seddon. 1994. *Free Markets & Food Riots. The Politics of Global Adjustment*. Oxford and Cambridge: Blackwell.

Waltz, K. 1979. *Theory of International Politics*. New York: McGraw-Hill.

Waschkuhn, A. (ed.). 1999. *Politische Soziologie Ostdeutschlands*. München: Oldenbourg.

Waterbury, J. 1999. "The Long Gestation and Brief Triumph of Import-Substituting Industrialization." *World Development* 27 (2): 323–41.

Wedel, J. 1997. "Cliques and Clans and Aid to Russia." *Transitions* 4 (2): 66–71.

———. 1998. *Collision and Collusion: The Strange Case of Western Aid to Eastern Europe*. New York: St. Martin's.

Weiss, L. 1998. *The Myth of the Powerless State*. Ithaca, N.Y.: Cornell University Press.

Wendt, A. 1987. "The Agent-Structure Problem in International Relations Theory." *International Organization* 41 (3): 335–70.

White, S., B. Miller, A. Grodeland, and S. Oates. 1998. "Religion and Political Action in Postcommunist Europe." University of Strathclyde, Centre for the Study of Public Policy, Studies in Public Policy, No. 307, Glasgow.

White, S., I. McAllister, and O. Krishtanovskaya. 1994. "Religion and Politics in Postcommunist Russia." *Religion, State and Society* 22 (1): 73–87.

Whitley, R. 1999. *Divergent Capitalisms; The Social Structuring and Change of Business Systems*. Oxford: Oxford University Press.

Whitley, R., and P. Kristensen (eds.). 1995. *The Changing European Firm*. London: Routledge.

Williamson, J. 1990. "What Washington Means by Policy Reform." In *Latin American Adjustment: How Much Has Happened?* ed. J. Williamson. Washington, D.C.: Institute for International Economics, 7–20.

———. 1994. "In Search of a Manual for Technopols." In *The Political Economy of Policy Reform,* ed. J. Williamson. Washington, D.C.: Institute of International Economics, 9–29.

———. 1997. "The Washington Consensus Revisited." In *Economic and Social Development into the XXI Century,* ed. L. Emmerij. Washington, D.C.: IABD.

———. 2000. "What Should the Bank Think About the Washington Consensus?" *World Bank Research Observer* 15 (2): 251–64.

Williamson, O. E. 1985. *The Economic Institutions of Capitalism*. New York: The Free Press.

Wnuk-Lipiñski, E. (ed.). 1985. "Nierownoœci spoeczne - poczucie wiezi - wiara w siebie." IFiS Warsaw, Research Report.

Wojtyna, A. 1992. "In Search of a New Economic Role for the State in the Post-Socialist Countries." In *Mixed Economies in Europe,* ed. W. Blaas and J. Foster. Aldershot and Brookfield: Elgar, 158–77.

Wolfensohn, J. D. 1999. *A Proposal for a Comprehensive Development Framework.* Mimeo. Washington, D.C.: World Bank.

Wolfensohn, J. D., and S. Fischer. 2000. "The Comprehensive Development Framework (CDF) and Poverty Reduction Strategy Papers (PRSP)." Joint Note. Washington, D.C.: IMF.

Wood, B. 1968. "Area Studies." In *International Encyclopedia of the Social Sciences* 1, ed. David L. Sills. New York: Macmillan, 401–7.

Woolcock, M. 1998. "Social Capital and Economic Development: Toward a Theoretical Synthesis and Policy Framework." *Theory and Society* 27 (2): 151–208.

World Bank. 1996. *From Plan to Market. World Development Report 1996.* Oxford and New York: Oxford University Press.

———. 1997. *The State in a Changing World. World Development Report 1997.* Oxford and New York: Oxford University Press.

———. 2000. *Attacking Poverty. World Development Report 2000/1.* Oxford and New York: Oxford University Press.

Wyplosz, C. 1999. "Ten Years of Transition: Macroeconomic Lessons." World Bank, Policy Research Working Paper No. 2288, Washington, D.C.

Young, A. 1998. "Growth without Scale Effects." *Journal of Political Economy* 106 (1): 41–63.

Zak, P. J., and S. Knack. 1999. *Trust and Growth.* Mimeo. IRIS, University of Maryland.

Zapf, W. 1996. "Zwei Geschwindigkeiten in Ost- und Westdeutschland." In *Zwischenbilanz der Wiedervereinigung,* ed. M. Diewald and K. U. Mayer. Opladen: Leske + Budrich, 317–28.

———. (ed.). 1971. *Theorien des sozialen Wandels.* Köln: Kiepenheuer & Witsch.

Zey, M. 1998. *Rational Choice Theory and Organizational Theory: A Critique.* Thousand Oaks, Calif.: Sage.

Zey, M. (ed.). 1992. *Decision Making: Alternatives to Rational Choice Models.* Newbury Park, Calif.: Sage.

Ziebe, J. 1992. "Die Reform des Bankensystems und das neue Bankengesetz in der CSFR." *Recht der Internationalen Wirtschaft* 38 (9): 723–28.

Zucker, L. G. 1986. "Production of Trust: Institutional Sources of Economic Structure, 1840-1920." *Research in Organisational Behaviour* 8: 53–111.

Index

About the Contributors

Frank Bönker is lecturer at the Department of Economics at European University Viadrina, Frankfurt (Oder). He is coauthor of *Institutional Design in Post-communist Societies: Rebuilding the Ship at Sea* (1998) and coeditor of *Transformation sozialistischer Gesellschaften: Am Ende des Anfangs* (1995) and *Privatization, Corporate Governance and the Emergence of Markets* (2000).

Valerie Bunce is professor in the Department of Government at Cornell University. Her latest book is *Subversive Institutions: The Design and the Destruction of Socialism and the State* (1999).

László Csaba is senior economist at Kopint-Datorg Economic Research, professor at the College of Foreign Trade in Budapest, and president of the European Association for Comparative Economic Studies. Among his various publications on transformation issues are *The Capitalist Revolution in Eastern Europe: A Contribution to the Economic Theory of System Change* (1995) and *Privatization, Liberalization and Destruction: Recreating the Market in Central and Eastern Europe* (edited, 1994)

Bruno Grancelli teaches sociology at the University of Trento in Italy. His publications include *Soviet Management and Labour Relations* (1988), *Privatization and Entrepreneurship in Post-Socialist Countries: Economy, Law, and Society* (edited, 1992), and *Social Change and Modernization: Lessons from Eastern Europe* (edited, 1995).

Béla Greskovits teaches political science at the Central European University in Budapest. His book, *The Political Economy of Protest and Patience: East European and Latin American Transformations Compared,* was published in 1998.

Wade Jacoby is associate professor of political science at Brigham Young University and author of *Imitation and Politics: Redesigning Modern Germany* (2000).

Klaus Müller is visiting professor at the Institute for Eastern European Studies, Free University, Berlin. He is author of *Totalitarismus, Modernisierung und Transformation* (forthcoming) and editor of *Postsozialistische Krisen* (1998).

Claus Offe, professor of political sociology at Humboldt University, Berlin, is one of the world's leading political theorists. Most of his papers on the East European transitions are collected in *Varieties of Transition: The East European and East German Experience* (1996). He is also coauthor of *Institutional Design in Post-communist Societies: Rebuilding the Ship at Sea* (1998).

Andreas Pickel is associate professor of political science at Trent University, Ontario. His latest book (with Helmuth Wiesenthal) is *The Grand Experiment: Debating Shock Therapy, Transition Theory, and the East German Experience* (1997).

Kazimierz Z. Poznanski is professor of international studies at the Jackson School, University of Washington, Seattle. He is one of the leading representatives of an evolutionary approach to transformation. He is author of *Poland's Protracted Transition: Institutional Change and Economic Growth, 1970–1994* (1997) and editor of *The Evolutionary Transition to Capitalism* (1995).

Martin Raiser is a senior economist at the Office of Chief Economist at the European Bank for Reconstruction and Development, London. In addition to various articles, he is author of *Soft-Budget Constraints and the Fate of Economic Reforms in Transition Economies and Developing Countries* (1997).

Peter Rutland is a professor of government at Wesleyan University in Middletown, Connecticut. From 1995–1997 he was assistant director of research at the Open Media Research Institute in Prague, and in spring 2000 he was a Fulbright professor at the European University in St. Petersburg. His most recent publication is the edited volume *Business and the State in Contemporary Russia* (Westview, 2001).

Willfried Spohn is professor of sociology at University of Pennsylvania, Philadelphia, and at Free University of Berlin. Author of numerous essays, he is also coeditor of *Can Europe Work? The New Germany and the Reconstruction of Postcommunist Societies* (1995) and *Deutschland und die Polen* (forthcoming).

Melanie Tatur is professor at J. W. Goethe University, Frankfurt am Main, and has written several books on "political capitalism" and trade unions in Hungary, Poland, and Russia.

Jacqui True is currently assistant professor of political science at the University of Michigan, East Lansing, and starting in the fall of 2002 will be in the Political Science Department at the University of Auckland, New Zealand. Her work on international political economy, postcommunist transformation, and gender has been published in *Review of International Political Economy*.